Monterre
St George
Georg
la Rue Rigaud Malineau
Langlade
Pion Musset Pramdamon
Marliere
Villebout
Parlac
Pu Seguin
le Cros
le Laur
Bouzy
Vignem
St Philippe
les Sagues
St Jean
Vernon Minge
Aiguilhe
Montagne
les Sall
St Genes Gardegau
de Castillon
Rabelot le Masson Pine
Les gues Maine Flaugeagu
Beney Bouscamber Tourtirac Beauch
Touron
St Hippolite
St Etienne
Faure de Lusse
Cous
Rocher
Colombe
Casten
Barbey
le Bois
Bourg des
les Pompes Parau
la Balle
les Paillasses Faignes Viremont
Peyrou Guinotte
Menichotte
Mauperier
le Parc
Tauzinat
la Forest
St Pey Beausejour St Magne
les Mor Thevenot la Chapoutaire
Armens
Mazouet
Bonete Gorry Maizieres Expert
Peyrouquet Chaboties
Rivierre Jeanblanc German
Gerbau Pillebois CHATILLON
Joliet Perrin Mare tine
arthe Somverd Solinard la Fenichette la Baisse le Roux Bordieu
Ventre Daudet Pareau la Plaine la Burthe
Verguille Malromey Caffol Rouzet le Port le Pas de Rauzan
Gueiraux Terrasse Cazeau la More Pillard le Passager Mars
les Jannot Coulet la Grave Monberol Marcou
les Guillemins Mauvilla Brandey Naudet Pas de Jeanbard Pique Segue
Maubés Coustaud la Condamine Mauvillat Piquero les Jeanjean le G Houstau Talaret Roque
ourdins St Terre Civrac la Barthe Souchet Villemartin
nadas la Chapelle Bicot Conteline Verneuil la Faugere la Coste la G Borie
G Pierre Marsandon le Barry la Garouss
Guillen du Port les Graves Lembege Mouliets Gravi
Peche la Defuite Peyrat Verneuil la Flamen Fourchou
gueyrau Gamage Escouachon R Romendol R Ramounet
Villepreux Roquette Moulton R Martin
Broward Denois la Rivierre
Ste Florence

THE WINES OF
Saint-Émilion and Pomerol

THE WINES OF
Saint-Émilion and Pomerol

Jeffrey Benson & Alastair Mackenzie

SOTHEBY PUBLICATIONS
in association with
THE WINE APPRECIATION GUILD

© Jeffrey Benson & Alastair Mackenzie
First published 1983 for
Sotheby Publications by
Philip Wilson Publishers Ltd,
Russell Chambers, Covent Garden,
London WC2E 8AA

Available to the USA book trade from
Sotheby Publications,
81 Adams Drive, Totowa, New Jersey 07512

Exclusive distribution to the Wine Trade
in the USA:
THE WINE APPRECIATION GUILD
1377 Ninth Avenue, San Francisco,
California 94122
(415) 566-3532

ISBN 0 85667 169 X

Designed by Mary Osborne
Printed in Great Britain by BAS Printers Ltd,
Wallop, Hampshire and bound by
Mackays of Chatham Ltd

Contents

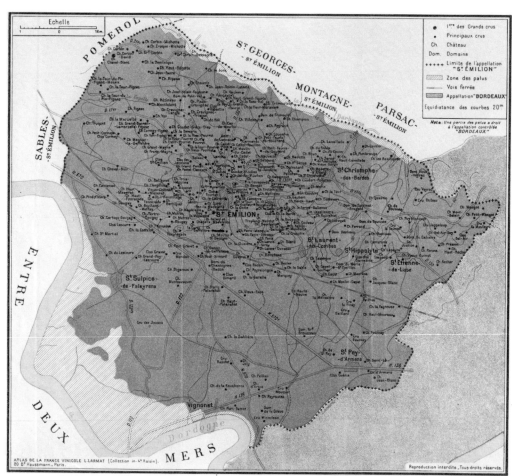

Saint-Émilion and the other communes entitled to the appellation. It should be noted that Sables-St-Émilion is now a part of the commune of Saint-Émilion.

Contents continued

Foreword

Those who visit the marvellous little stone-built town of Saint-Émilion might come away thinking of it as a shrine to the best of all produce of the soil. It is hard to think otherwise of an ancient settlement, half delved in the ground, half built on it out of gritty golden blocks from its quarries, dedicated entirely to the cultivation and enjoyment of the vine. The formal trellised rows, even in the heart of the houses, the luxurious leafage, frail tendrils and heavy fruit are all the decoration the plain stone buildings require. The pagan in me sees an organic form even in the curl of the road up the narrow defile into the cluster of steep streets around the town's most famous feature, its great monolithic cave-church.

To those who have never visited them, Saint-Émilion and its neighbour, Pomerol, still represent all the comforts that stout, smooth, strong red wine can provide. They give us the accessible red Bordeaux, the warm one – never so toughly tannic and astringent as fine Médocs—reaching sweet maturity sooner, but often holding on to the fullness of its flavour for two decades or more. And it is available. There is masses of it. The immediate Saint-Émilion and Pomerol area alone produces as much red wine as the whole of the Côte d'Or of Burgundy. With its 'satellite' neighbours, the total is approximately five million cases a year (or one quarter of all red Bordeaux).

Strangely, up until now, this great well of honest pleasure has not had a full description and catalogue devoted to it. There are more than 2,000 separate Châteaux, or wine-making entities, in the region of which only the best-known hundred or so are regularly chronicled in wine literature. The task is certainly a daunting one, but Jeffrey Benson and Alastair Mackenzie have been astonishingly thorough.

You may picture them in your mind's eye, *tastevins* in hand, tottering gleefully from one Château to another, day after day, month after month. But writing wine books is not that simple. It takes great patience and persistence to compile this sort of detailed information. They have done a unique, extremely painstaking job. They have set on record the vast range and variety of the region, provided faces for what were merely names on lists, and attempted to account for the role played by this variety of grape and soil, weather and climate and, most of all, man.

If you buy claret regularly, are looking for value, and want to add method and substance to your searches, you need this book. I certainly do.

HUGH JOHNSON, 28th March 1983

Preface

Saint-Émilion and Pomerol, situated some 30 kilometres east of Bordeaux, are two of the oldest vineyard areas in the Gironde. Yet they have only become well-known throughout the world for the quality of their wines comparatively recently; most books about Bordeaux wines devote much more space to the Médoc. In fact the best and most comprehensive book in English on the subject, *The Wines of Bordeaux*, by Edmund Penning-Rowsell, has one hundred and forty-five pages on the Médoc, twenty-six on Saint-Émilion and twenty on Pomerol. There are, of course, very good reasons for this, but it is an indication that these two areas, which together produce more wine than the Médoc (much of it very fine), are still somewhat neglected and perhaps less appreciated than they deserve to be. They still tend to be overshadowed for many by the great Médocs which have been famous for so much longer.

We feel that the wines of Saint-Émilion and Pomerol, although different in style, are truly comparable in quality to wines of the Médoc at all levels. Therefore we have tried in this book to give as thorough an account as we can of the two areas, the associated districts of Lalande de Pomerol and the communes which are entitled to add 'Saint-Émilion' to their own names. We also describe, with the help of the camera's eye, the geography, soil and climate, the grape varieties and their combination, the methods of viticulture and vinification, the individual properties and, of course, the taste and smell of the wines themselves (as far as the printed word can convey this!).

In the course of preparing this work we have naturally read many books and articles, but most of the information it contains has been derived from actual visits to the properties and many hundreds of conversations, telephone calls and much correspondence with proprietors, oenologists, *Maîtres de Chai* (cellar-masters) and *Chefs de Culture* (vineyard-managers). We have received invaluable assistance from very many people in both areas and from organisations like the Union des Producteurs and the other Co-operatives at Puisseguin and Lussac-St Émilion, the Syndicat de Saint-Émilion and the CIVB. We are most grateful to them for all that they have done for us.

We owe a particular debt of gratitude to the following: Professor Engalbert of the University of Bordeaux, Department of Geography and Regional Studies, who is preparing a book on the soil of the area and the history of the emergence of Saint-Émilion and Pomerol as fine-wine-producing areas, for the generous assistance and advice that he has given us; Thierry Manoncourt, the proprietor of Château Figeac, Jean-Claude Berrouet, the oenologist of the firm of J-P Moueix and Pascal Delbeck, the *Régisseur* (manager) of Château Ausone.

JEFFREY BENSON and ALASTAIR MACKENZIE, 1982

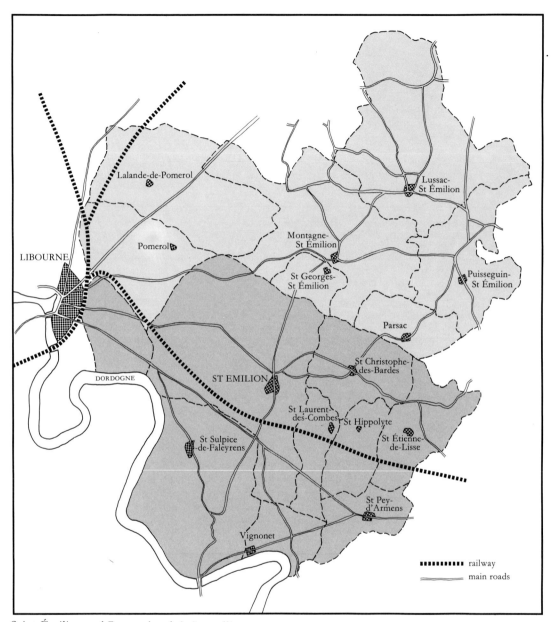

Lalande-de-Pomerol

Lussac-
St Émilion

LIBOURNE

Pomerol

Montagne-
St Émilion

St Georges-
St Émilion

Puisseguin-
St Émilion

Parsac

St Christophe-
des-Bardes

DORDOGNE

ST EMILION

St Laurent-
des-Combes

St Hippolyte

St Étienne-
de-Lisse

St Sulpice-
de-Faleyrens

St Pey-
d'Armens

Vignonet

▪▪▪▪▪▪▪ railway
——— main roads

Saint-Émilion and Pomerol and their satellites.

The Area of Saint-Émilion and Pomerol

The vineyard areas of Saint-Émilion and Pomerol which, together with Fronsac, make up the Libournais vignoble, have more charm and individuality than their distinguished rivals in the Médoc, some 45 kilometres away to the east and slightly north.

The Médoc is generally flat, low-lying country, intensively planted with vines; but the feature that dominates our area is the steep limestone escarpment of Saint-Émilion with the beautiful medieval town itself at the end of a re-entrant valley overlooking the Dordogne. This escarpment has numerous indentations and gullies known as 'combes', which probably accounts for the ancient name of Saint-Émilion – Ascombas or Accumbitum – a word of Celtic origin. The town is surrounded by vines – for the area is even more intensively planted than the Médoc; some on the plateau alongside the town, others on the slopes leading down from the heights. There are even some vines inside the little town itself, including the single hectare that makes up the vineyard of Château le Couvent, Grand Cru Classé. To the north-east of the Saint-Émilion plateau, where the five communes are entitled to attach Saint-Émilion to their names, the land rises again in a series of hills, the highest of which is over 300 feet above sea-level. The landscape is less dominated by the vines here and generally has a more rural appearance.

The average height above sea-level of the area of Saint-Émilion is about 230 feet as compared to the mere 55 feet of the Médoc.

About 3 miles to the north-east of the town, Saint-Émilion meets the plateau of Pomerol which slopes gently down from its highest point, about 120 feet, near Vieux-Château-Certan, to the outskirts of the old town of Libourne which, before the days of motor transport and the railway, was the port from which the wines of Saint-Émilion, Pomerol and Fronsac were shipped. There is virtually nothing but vines to be seen here, for most of the properties are small and modest and almost every square metre is devoted to wine-growing. The only exceptions are the low-lying marshy areas near the streams, the Barbanne and Taillas, in which vine-growing is prohibited, and some wooded parkland at Château de Sales in the extreme north-west. On the other side of the Barbanne is the commune of Lalande de Pomerol and this includes Néac which had its own appellation until 1954. As with the outlying areas of Saint-Émilion, this is much more mixed, agricultural land in marked contrast to the neat, highly-regimented vine-gardens of Pomerol, and the whole area has a more rustic character.

The biggest town in the area is Libourne. Once a flourishing port and headquarters of the Saint-Émilion, Pomerol and Fronsac wine-trade, it was founded by Roger de Leybourn (from whom it takes its name), the Seneschal of Guyenne, on the orders of the future king Edward I in 1268. In 1289 Edward I granted a charter establishing its limits and according it the rights of a commune. Today it is no longer a busy port, but it is a thriving market-town with a variety of shops, an interesting museum and a number of hotels and restaurants of which perhaps the Hotel Loubat is known best. The famous firm of M J-P Moueix has its offices on the old quayside and other important firms still based there are those of Beylot and Danglade.

The only other town is Saint-Émilion itself. It has a positively fairy-tale quality about it with its remarkable situation and beautiful, ancient buildings. It takes its name from the hermit-monk Aemilianus who, according to legend, and with several miracles to his credit, came to the area in the eighth century. Some versions say that he was on a pilgrimage to St James at Santiago de Compostella but in France such pilgrimages did not start until the beginning of the ninth century. He is said to have hollowed-out a cell in the hillside and a chapel where he lived and prayed. This was the origin of the famous monolithic church, according to the story. He gathered a small community of disciples around him, living in caves, and this was the first village of Saint-Émilion. This is legend rather than fact, and some authorities claim that there was a flourishing community here long before the Saint made his appearance. Whatever the truth may be, he gave his name to the town.

Saint-Émilion is remarkably unspoilt and there is a feeling of history about every street in the town. Perhaps the most impressive of the many interesting and beautiful reminders of the past is the unique church carved out of the solid rock, probably started in the eighth or ninth century and gradually enlarged over the next few hundred years. This, together with the Hermitage and its spring (said to have been miraculously created by the Saint), the catacombs and the thirteenth-century Chapel of the Trinity was part of a monastery dedicated to Saint-Émilion by the Benedictines. Then there is the large and imposing Collegiate church (fifteenth and sixteenth century) with its beautiful cloisters, the Abbot's house, the Chapter's Chapel and the Deanery. All these are part of the monastery of Saint Augustine.

Other main features include the ancient defensive walls dating from the twelfth century with two of the original six gateways surviving, the King's and Watchman's towers and the bell-tower of the church (twelfth and fifteenth century) which rises out of the town-square next to a restaurant. Also of interest are the ruins of the Cardinal's palace, the monasteries of the Dominican and Franciscan friars (the Cloisters and Convent des Cordeliers), the Gothic house and the cave of the Girondins.

The calcareous rock upon which the town is built is soft enough to be readily excavated. Over the centuries much of it was dug out of the hillsides to be used as building material for Saint-Émilion itself and Libourne. Some owners of the surrounding vineyards mature their wines in the caves thus created. Three of the largest and most spectacular are those of Château Beau-Séjour (Bécot), Clos Fourtet and Château Villemaurine. Not all the growers choose to do this because the temperature in the deeper cellars is so low that the wine matures very slowly indeed. Alain Querre of Château Monbousquet told us that some years ago he was offered the hire of a vast area of deep chalk cellars under the town, for the price of an ox. He rushed home to tell his father, Daniel Querre, the good news. 'What is the temperature of the cellar?' he was asked. It was about 8°–10°C. His father pointed out that their wines would take three times as long to mature at that temperature as in their present cellaring conditions. Monsieur Querre went on to say that many growers keep just a token amount of wine there because 'it looks nice'.

Some of these cellars, which were excavated in the fourteenth century, are beneath the Cloisters of the Cordeliers, and are used for making and maturing sparkling wines made by the champagne method. Since 1892 the Société les Cordeliers have been making red, white and rosé sparkling wines here; the best-known is the *Blanc de Blancs, Cuvée St Jean*, made from Ugni Blanc, Muscadel and Sémillon grapes grown in Entre-deux-Mers.

Besides its beauty, its historical interest and its wines, Saint-Émilion is also famous for its macaroons. They are based on a recipe of the Ursuline sisters dating from 1620. There are five major producers, each selling several thousand boxes per year: only one claims to have the genuine original recipe. Production by all the manufacturers is controlled, as Saint-Émilion macaroons must be eaten within five days of baking.

Saint-Émilion attracts more than twenty thousand visitors each year, yet it has largely avoided the temptations and dangers of commercialisation, and in the European Heritage Year of 1975 – coincidentally a great vintage for its wines – it won the Gold Medal of the Council of Europe.

History

The area of Saint-Émilion, at least that part which lies near the town, has claims to be considered the oldest wine area of the Gironde. The vine furrows cut in the rock that can still be seen at Châteaux Belair, Beau-Séjour (Bécot) and Soutard, among others, are clear evidence that the Romans grew vines there in the third and fourth centuries AD and it is virtually certain that the other areas of Saint-Émilion and Pomerol were also vineyards at this time. When Valerius Probus became Emperor of Rome in 276 he rescinded the edict issued by Domitian some one hundred and eighty years earlier which had ordered that all vineyards outside Italy should be pulled up and no new ones planted. We also know that he ordered the clearing of the forest of Cumbris to graft new imported vine varieties on to the root-stock 'vitis biturica' which already grew there wild. Whether or not the area 'Lucianicus', where the fourth-century poet and pro-consul Ausonius had his villas and vineyards, occupied the site of the present Château Ausone, there is plenty of archaeological evidence of Roman civilisation and viticulture in these parts in the three-hundred years up to the beginning of the fifth century when the invading Visigoths devastated the region. There was further destruction with the Moorish invasion in the eighth century, from which Château Villemaurine is said to take its name.

Nothing more is known of the viticultural activities of the region until 1152 when the marriage of Eleanor of Acquitaine to Henry II of England made this part of France an English possession.

In 1199 King John granted a charter of privileges to the town of 'Semelione', granting it the rights of a commune and the right to elect their own magistrates. A similar charter was granted to Libourne in 1270.

In 1289 a charter issued by Edward I laid down the famous 'Jurisdiction' of Saint-Émilion and strictly established the viticultural district of Saint-Émilion as the are immediately around the town and the eight neighbouring parishes: St Martin-de-Mazerat (later to be absorbed into Saint-Émilion itself). St Christophe-des-Bardes, St Laurent-des-Combes, St Hippolyte, St Étienne-de-Lisse (also called St Estèphe), St Pey-d'Armens, St Sulpice-de-Faleyrens and St Brice-de-Vignonet.

This was confirmed by Royal Letters Patent granted by Edward I in 1289 and by Edward III in 1341. These limits are almost exactly the same as those of the present Appellation.

In 1312 we know that the citizens of Saint-Émilion, after some troubles a few years earlier, only won back the right to elect their own mayor and receive various other privileges by promising to deliver 50 tonneaux (1 tonneau = 900 litres) of 'vin clair, pur et bon' to the English King before Easter.

The area suffered badly from the ravages of The Hundred Years War leading up to the final defeat of the English at the Battle of Castillon in 1453. Saint-Émilion and Libourne changed hands many times in the thirteenth and fourteenth centuries. The last time they were occupied by the English was in 1452 when John Talbot, Earl of Shrewsbury, landed in the Médoc and Saint-Émilion, Libourne and Castillon along with Bordeaux and the other towns welcomed the invaders. Charles VII's army defeated Talbot in the Battle of Castillon the following year and captured Castillon, Saint-Émilion and Libourne before entering Bordeaux unopposed.

A deed of 1460 shows that the weekly markets and the fairs held on various Saints' days had to be discontinued for much of the duration of the Wars and a charter dated April 22nd, 1469, of Louis XI, records that the population of Saint-Émilion, formerly two-thousand souls of all estates, had fallen to a mere two hundred.

Saint-Émilion and Pomerol also suffered in the civil wars of the sixteenth century. On a number of occasions between 1562 and 1580 the town of Saint-Émilion and the surrounding countryside including, no doubt, the vineyards, were pillaged and laid waste by both Protestant 'invaders' and Catholic 'allies'.

During the latter part of the sixteenth century, the main export market of the Gironde changed. The Netherlands replaced England as the leading trading nation in Bordeaux wine and their preference was for cheap white wines; this preference was reflected in the big increase in white wine production in the area overall, although Saint-Émilion and the Médoc seem to have continued to produce mainly red.

Although Louis XIV is alleged to have visited Libourne in 1650 and compared the wine of Saint-Émilion to 'nectar of the gods', one must remember that he was only twelve years old at the time. No doubt some wine from the area was exported in this period, for about the same time one Henry Thompson, an English wine-merchant in Bordeaux, is recorded as buying wine from Saint-Émilion. But it is not until well into the eighteenth century that the Libournais wines (Saint-Émilion, Pomerol and Canon Fronsac) began to establish a wider reputation for quality.

The first area to gain a name for quality wines in the 1740's was Canon Fronsac. The decade 1760 to 1770 saw the emergence of the high limestone plateau and the true Côtes (slopes) areas of Saint-Émilion and at about the same time the names of Graves de Figeac and Pomerol became known. Pomerol was equally well-known for its white 'Graves' wine at this time and remained so until about 1830. Libourne also supplied its 'vin de palus', from vineyards on the low-lying marshy lands near the river with clayey-alluvial soil, at a good price to the navy and the colonies until the time of the Crimean War.

Thus by the mid-1780's, on the eve of the Revolution, the three privileged sectors of the Libournais had all begun to establish a reputation. Canon Fronsac was still the leader, then the Haut Saint-Émilion, with Pomerol (including the Graves de Figeac) falling behind a little. The prices were sometimes as much as three times those of 'ordinary' wines, the reds being more expesnive than the whites.

After the upheavals of the Revolution with much of the wine going to the armies, there was a brief period of prosperity during 1795 to 1802 until the economic crisis caused by Napoleon's wars and the blockade. Trade was better again during 'La Belle Époque' (1814 to 1822) and by now Haut Saint-Emilion had taken over from Canon Fronsac as the most highly-regarded Libournais area with Pomerol and Figeac still in third place.

The thirty years from 1822 were a bad time for the Libournais wine-makers. They were still more or less ignored by the Bordeaux trade and though they continued to export wine from the port of Libourne to Brittany, Northern France and The Netherlands, prices were low and remained so until the 1850's.

The next twenty-five years brought a dramatic increase in the reputation of the Haut Saint-Émilion wines, while Pomerol and Figeac became more widely known leaving Fronsac in comparative obscurity. There were two main reasons for this. In the first place, the *oidium* disaster (a blight of powdery mildew) drastically reduced production and raised prices all over the Gironde, but Saint-Émilion and Pomerol were affected rather less and rather later than the Graves and Médoc; consequently the Bordeaux trade began to buy these wines for export. Secondly, the development of the railways led to direct trade between Libourne and Paris and Belgium.

The export of Saint-Émilion and Pomerol wines grew steadily in the 1860's and 1870's, encouraged by the Anglo-French Commercial Treaty in 1860, and other treaties with Belgium and Prussia which reduced duties. Another factor in the increase was the development of the German market after the Franco-Prussian War of 1870. This expansion encouraged the planting of new vineyards but the *phylloxera* devastation put a brake on this, combined with the demise of the short-lived Free-Trade Movement. In the aftermath of *phylloxera*, new agricultural and viticultural techniques were developed with the use of fertilizers and the necessary grafting on to American root-stocks. The increased production and commercial success of their neighbours encouraged local non-wine-growing landowners to join in and plant vines. In about 1900 people started planting haphazardly over the plain of the Dordogne, south of Saint-Émilion, where previously there had been general agriculture. Earlier, before the Revolution, it had been forbidden to plant vines in these areas where cereal crops could be grown because of the danger of famine. This is why in the early days, Saint-Émilion wines were produced from difficult, inclining surfaces, with poor soil. This area of the plain, covering the commune of St Sulpice-de-Faleyrens, Vignonet and St Pey-d'Armens, had been less than a quarter planted with vines before *phylloxera*.

Saint-Émilion and Pomerol further increased their production and prestige (relative to the Médoc and Graves) as a result of the *phylloxera* crisis of the 1870's and 1880's for they were somewhat less seriously affected, although Saint-Émilion was one of the first areas to suffer. This growing reputation was reflected in a number of successes in international exhibitions. Château Cheval Blanc won a bronze medal (still shown on its label) at the International Exhibition in London in 1862 when Château la Dominique also won a prize. In 1867 at the International Exhibition in Paris, thirty-seven properties from the Côtes and plateau combined to form a collective exhibit, showing various vintages from 1834 to 1864, which won a gold medal. At the same venue in 1889, sixty Saint-Émilion properties collectively won the Grand Prix. Meanwhile Château Pétrus had won a gold medal at the Paris Exhibition of 1878.

In 1865 prices of the leading four Saint-Émilions were about on par with the Médoc fifth growths. By 1890 they, together with Pétrus, were commanding the same price as second growths.

Both the twenty-five years before the First World War and, apart from a short post-war boom, the Inter-War Period, were difficult times for the Bordeaux wine-trade generally with prices very low, even for the finest wines. The 1914 War naturally had a disastrous effect on the national economy and extreme protectionist measures abroad kept foreign markets to a minimum just at the time when plantation of vines reached a maximum. This resulted in a continuing crisis through the 1920's and 30's, exacerbated by the loss of the important German market and the effect of the world slump. In the late 20's and the 30's, Château owners were losing money and merchants were doing no better. The finest vintages of top Médocs and Graves were ludicrously cheap so that it was difficult for Saint-Émilion and Pomerol to increase their comparatively new-found prestige further.

After the Second World War, trade prospered. Growers began to do well in the 1950's and prices, especially of the leading growths, began to rise. Château Cheval Blanc and Pétrus, from being about half the price of the Médoc first growths in 1945, had almost caught them up by the mid-fifties; and now, since the price explosion of the early 1970's, Pétrus is often the most expensive claret of all.

The prices of other leading properties such as Château Figeac and Vieux-Château-Certan are usually about on par with Médoc second growths and sometimes higher.

The popularity of the wines of Saint-Émilion and Pomerol continues to grow, perhaps partly because they have a more immediate appeal than those from the Médoc and Graves. Since the Second World War they have completed the last stage of their journey towards world wide acceptance as worthy rivals and comparable first cousins to the great wines of the Médoc and Graves, and not just poor relations.

Local Gastronomy

Compared with the other fine wine areas of France such as Alsace, Burgundy and the Loire and Rhône valleys, all of which are well-served with restaurants sporting one, two or three rosettes in Michelin's *Guide*, Bordeaux is something of a gastronomic backwater.

One reason that has been suggested for this comparative dearth of fine restaurants is that in the Bordeaux area, with its many impressive Châteaux, much more entertaining of visitors and business colleagues goes on at home, whereas in other areas they would be taken to a restaurant.

At all events there are only three restaurants near Bordeaux which boast two Michelin rosettes. The first is 'Le Saint-James' in Bouliac, 7 kilometres from Bordeaux, run by Jean Marie Amat, who made such a success of two restaurants of the same name in Bordeaux before opening this one in 1980. Then there is 'La Reserve' in Pessac, managed by Mme Flourens, and 'Auberge Saint-Jean' at St Jean de Blaignac, much the closest to our area, being just a few kilometres south of Vignonet, on the south bank of the Dordogne, whose chef/proprietor, Jean-Paul Mâle, provides the recipe given here.

Other Bordeaux restaurants of some quality include: 'Le Bistrôt de Bordeaux'; 'Le Chapon Fin'; 'Restaurant Christian Clement'; 'Chez Clavel'; 'Dubern'; 'Restaurant Le Loup'; 'Le Marais'; 'Chez Philippe'; 'Le Perigord St Jean'; 'Le Rouzic'; 'Le Tupina'; 'Le Vieux Bordeaux'.

Outside Bordeaux there is the 'Restaurant Claude Darroze' at Langon, and 'Auberge du Pont-Bernet' at Le Pain-Médoc.

The main local restaurants of the area of Saint-Émilion and Pomerol are the 'Restaurant l'Étrier' and the 'Restaurant Loubat' in Libourne; and in Saint-Émilion itself the 'Hostelrie de la Plaisance', on the roof of the monolithic church and alongside the bell-tower, 'Auberge de la Commanderie', where both the authors enjoyed comfortable hospitality on their working visits, 'Chez Germaine' and 'Logis de la Cadène'.

Specialities of the Bordeaux region include lampreys cooked in Bordeaux red wine, entrecôte Bordelaise, foie gras and confits de Landes. Sea-food, from the Arcachon basin, includes oysters, lobster, red mullet, bass, turbot, bream, shrimps and large prawns. There is also a small amount of caviar from the Gironde sturgeon, and lamb from Pauillac with a slightly salty flavour obtained from the lambs grazing on the salt marshes. The nearby Dordogne area provides fresh truffles.

Other local specialities are escargots Bordelaises, oeuf brouille aux truffes (scrambled eggs with truffles), crêpes Bordelaises (a species of large mushroom) and, especially associated with Libourne, 'Success' – a kind of layered gâteau. We must not forget, of course, the macaroons of Saint-Émilion.

As we have said, the outstanding restaurant of the area we are writing about is the 'Auberge Saint-Jean' at St Jean de Blaignac and we are most grateful to Jean-Paul Mâle for the following recipe for his Oyster and Caviar Gâteau with Mousseline Sauce:

Oyster and Caviar Gâteau (served hot)
Mousseline Sauce

Ingredients 500g *Fillet of sole*
300g *Half-cooked foie gras*
100g *Bread-crumbs*
100g *Fish sauce (velouté)*
100g *Parish mushrooms*
600g *Double-cream*
4 *Large cloves of garlic, steamed*
8 *Large shallots, steamed*
60 *No. 1 grade oysters*
100g *Caviar*
10g *Salt*
5g *Pepper*
3g *Paprika*
1 *Soup-spoon of cognac*
Parsley, chervil
100g *Cream*
500g *Butter*
100g *Glaze of sole*

Preparation
of Gâteau

Strain: sole, foie gras, bread-crumbs, fish velouté, steamed garlic, steamed shallots, parsley, chervil, cognac, salt, pepper, paprika, double-cream.
Pour into a bowl, add finely-chopped mushrooms, caviar and raw, drained oysters.
Place in two enamelled moulds: 25cm L, 8cm W, 7cm H.
Cooking time: 60 mins, at 180°C in a bain-marie. Keep hot until served.

Preparation
of Sauce

Reduce the glaze of sole and cream to half in shallow frying pan, add 4 drops of white vinegar, thicken with butter pommade made from the 500 g of butter.
Let down if necessary with a little cooked seaweed juice.
Check for salt, ground pepper.

To Serve

Place a slice of oyster gâteau on a bed of mousseline sauce and decorate with a few sprigs of chervil. Serves 20.

Monsieur J. P. Mâle in his restaurant, 'L'Auberge Saint-Jean', with a selection of desserts.

The Making of the Wine

Soil

It is generally agreed that the nature of the soil and sub-soil, together with drainage, is one of the most important determining elements in the character and quality of wine.

In the early Tertiary age the whole of the Gironde was part of a vast area known as the Aquitaine basin which was covered by the Aquitanian sea. As the sea receded, it left huge amounts of sediments of different kinds.

There are five more or less distinct layers of soil which date from the Tertiary age.

The highest and first to emerge as land as opposed to sea-bed is a layer of 'starfish' limestone of marine origin with abundant fossil remains. It is this that forms the plateau on which the town of Saint-Émilion is built and out of which the quarries and cellars have been excavated. The thickness of these layers varies from 30 to 80 metres above sea-level and towards the base there is a stratum which is rich in oyster fossils, especially just to the south-west of the town.

The second level is composed of white or yellowish clay with lumps of limestone. It varies in thickness from 1 to 4 metres and is lacustrine (formed from lakes) in origin, containing no fossils. Naturally this bed of clay retains the water which filters down through the limestone and emerges again in the form of springs. There is a series of such springs which feed little streams, all at a height of about 50 metres above sea-level; this indicates that the clay-bed is roughly horizontal. As the plateau extends eastwards over St Christophe, St Laurent and St Hippolyte, the soil changes to a chalkier white limestone known as Castillon limestone.

The third level is called molasse de fronsadais and is another lacustrine deposit, consisting of coarser sand containing mica and flinty limestone. Some of these layers are cohesive and even form blocks of sandstone; others are sandy clay. The colour of the sandier parts is ash-grey. This layer forms the middle and lower parts of the slopes of the Saint-Émilion hillsides. It is often covered with outcrops of stones from the hilltops and reconstituted soil formed from the decomposition of 'starfish' limestone or from its own decomposition. Its overall make-up is very varied and complex as, apart from the flint and lime, it contains clay, iron salts, and some potassium, sodium, magnesium and other salts.

The fourth level, comprising the bottom of the slopes, is another layer of molasse, also of lacustrine origin, with rather more clay than the former and containing an unusual kind of sand. It, too, has a very varied and complex mineral composition.

At the foot of the north-western slopes there is a terrace of more ancient deposits, 30 to 40 metres above sea-level, which scarcely exists in the Dordogne valley but is much more fully-developed here in the valley of the Isle. It is this terrace which produces the wines of the best part of Pomerol and of Châteaux Cheval Blanc and Figeac. The gravel and sand of this terrace date from the end of the Tertiary age.

There is no equivalent of this terrace on the south side of Saint-Émilion because it has been eroded by the flooding of the Dordogne in ancient times. Furthermore the chemical and geological differences between the sand and gravel deposits of the valley of the Isle and those of the Dordogne are caused by the different sources (the jurassic plateau of Millevaches and the central granitic plateau), and their different courses. These two factors are chiefly responsible for the difference in quality and character between the wines of Cheval Blanc, Figeac and the best Pomerols on the one hand and those of Vignonet and St Sulpice on the other.

The next two terraces of the plain, 30 to 20 metres and 20 to 10 metres, consist of more alluvial deposits (clay, sand and gravel) which are not subject to modern flooding by the Dordogne. The land is very fertile but does not give such good wine as the older and higher soils.

The 30 to 20 metre level is a belt of about 400 metres of alluvial sandy soil mainly formed from soil that has come down from the slopes but there is no sharply-defined boundary between it and the 20 to 10 metres level.

The lowest level, below 10 metres, consists of more recent alluvial soil. It is extremely fertile but contains very little of the limestone and molasse of Saint-Émilion and the wines it produces, although quite commercial, lack the quality of those grown on the older soils.

This information is based on the researches of Professor Blayac, formerly Professor of Geology at the University of Montpelier; Robert Villepigue, agricultural engineer, former proprietor of Château Cadet-Piola and President and Founder of the Cave Co-operative of Saint-Émilion; and his son, André Villepigue, also an agricultural engineer.

The soil of the Médoc and the northern part of Graves, where many of the finest red Bordeaux wines come from, consists mainly of deep gravel banks which drain well and retain the heat of the sun. In the north in St Estèphe there is more clay in the soil and the southern part of Graves is sandier. The height above sea level of the finest vineyards in these areas is appreciably lower than those of Saint-Émilion and Pomerol.

The area which we are considering has a number of different soils and various combinations of them. It is likely that the predominantly limestone and clay-limestone soils will produce one kind of wine, the gravel soils another and the clay soils and sandy soils others again. And then there are the mixtures of soils.

A feature of the area generally is the iron to be found in the sub-soil at a depth of about 50 to 80 centimetres. When ploughing is deeper than usual, as at the time of replanting, it can be brought to the surface and forms lumps. It is found in many parts of Pomerol, at Cheval Blanc and Figeac, and also in other parts of Saint-Émilion and is said to impart a particular flavour to the wine.

Another consideration is that in certain years one type of soil will be favoured whereas others will be less successful, and *vice versa*. For instance, in wet years gravel soils do better because the water drains through whereas in drought years clay soils benefit because the clay, being non-porous, retains the moisture. Certain grape varieties too are suited by certain soils. It is no coincidence that at Château Pétrus where the soil is almost entirely clay, virtually 100% Merlot is grown, while at Vieux-Château-Certan, Merlot is planted in the clay part of the vineyard and the Cabernets in the gravel part.

There has long been a misconception that there are only two kinds of Saint-

Émilion wines: the 'Côtes' and the 'Graves'. If one reads Cocks et Feret, *Bordeaux et Ses Vins*, one certainly gets the impression that all wines which are not 'Côtes' are 'Graves'. Others, like the writer of an article in a German wine publication in February 1982, suggested that all those that are not 'Côtes' are 'plaine'.

In fact there are five main areas:

1   The raised limestone plateau on which the town stands; its continuation through St Christophe, St Laurent and St Hippolyte (a slightly different, chalkier limestone), and the slopes at the edges of the plateau.

2   A plateau to the north-west of Saint-Émilion extending about 1 kilometre from the Pomerol border and running from the railway-line in the south to the Barbanne in the north. It consists of ancient Aeolian (wind-blown) sand on a mixed sand and molasse[1] sub-soil.

3   A very small parcel of land, some 60 hectares only, of very fine-quality gravel is found close to the border with Pomerol. This is the true 'Graves'.

4   An area of gentle slope covered by ancient sand between the edge of the west and north-west limestone 'Côtes' and the sandy plateau and between the northern 'Côtes' and the Barbanne; the sub-soil is sand and lower molasse.

5   The large area roughly south of the railway-lines, some 1,000 hectares of vineyard, incorporating the southern part of Saint-Émilion itself, the village of St Sulpice, Vignonet and St Pey-d'Armens, and parts of St Hippolyte and St Étienne. This is the plain. It is largely sandy with some gravel and some richer soil (limon[2]). The soil gets richer and less suitable for wine-making as it gets nearer to the river Dordogne.

The higher part of the Pomerol plateau has gravel similar to that of area 3 above with some sand and clay. As the land slopes gently down to the west and south there tends to be more gravel and sand and less clay and in the extreme north-west and west the soil is markedly sandier.

The following tables have been prepared with the help of Professor Engalbert of the University at Bordeaux, Department of Geography and Regional Studies, who is preparing a book on the soil of the area and the history of the emergence of Saint-Émilion and Pomerol as fine-wine-producing areas.

Of course we are aware that areas and types of soil and sub-soil are not generally arranged in consistently straight lines or regular patterns and, despite attempts to indicate when one property lies partly in one area and partly in another, we present it as a guide rather than an absolute and definitive pronouncement.

---

[1] A mixture of soft limestones, sandstones, marls and clays, washed down from the Massif Central.
[2] A loam closely related to wind-blown loess. It is a finely-grained deposit consisting of wind-blown material subsequently re-sorted by water.

SAINT-ÉMILION

AREA	TOPOGRAPHY	SOIL	SUB-SOIL
St Martin plateau	Plateau 80 to 85 m	Sandy – clay Clay – sand Clay – limestone	Limestone

Properties include: $\frac{3}{4}$ of Ch. Belair, $\frac{1}{2}$ of Magdelaine, $\frac{1}{4}$ of Ausone, Clos Fourtet, $\frac{1}{2}$ of Berliquet, $\frac{3}{4}$ of Canon, $\frac{1}{2}$ Beau-séjour (Bécot).

Plateau east of Saint-Émilion	Plateau 80 to 105 m	Clay – sand Clay – limestone	Limestone

Properties include: Chx Trottevieille, la Clotte, la Serre, Sansonnet, Troplong-Mondot, Soutard.

St Laurent St Christophe plateau	Plateau 80 to 105 m	Clay – limestone Red soil Sandy limon	Limestone

Properties include: Chx Haut-Sarpe, Gaubert, Laroque, Bellisle-Mondotte.

Southern Côtes (from Daugay to St Laurent Grand Côte and Pied de Côte)		Sand–clay–limestone Clay–limestone	Molasse

Properties include: Chx Daugay, l'Arrosée, Fonplégade, $\frac{1}{2}$ of Magdelaine, $\frac{1}{4}$ of Belair, $\frac{3}{4}$ of Ausone, la Gaffelière, Pavie, Larcis-Ducasse, Bellefont-Belciers.

Northern Côtes (from Mazerat to St Christophe 'Petites Côtes')		Clay – sand Clay – limestone	Molasse

Properties include: Chx $\frac{1}{2}$ of Berliquet, $\frac{1}{2}$ l'Angélus, $\frac{1}{4}$ Canon, Beau-séjour (Duffau-Lagarrosse), $\frac{1}{2}$ Beau-séjour (Bécot), Grand-Mayne, Grand Pontet, Franc-Pourret, Chatelet, $\frac{1}{2}$ of Fonroque, Badette, du Cauze, Fombrauge.

Sand-covered slope north-west and north of Saint-Émilion	Slope covered with sand	Sand (ancient)	Sand and lower Molasse

Properties include: Chx $\frac{1}{2}$ Angélus, Laroze, Yon-Figeac, la Gomerie, la Grâce Dieu, $\frac{1}{2}$ Fonroque, Cap de Mourlin, Baleau, Larmande, Peynaud, Dassault.

AREA	TOPOGRAPHY	SOIL	SUB-SOIL
North-western area along Pomerol border (*Excluding* Cheval Blanc and Figeac)	Sandy slopes and gentle incline	Sand, and a little gravel near cheval Blanc and Figeac	Sand and molasse

Properties include: Chx la Tour-Figeac ($\frac{1}{5}$ gravel), la Tour-du-Pin-Figeac ($\frac{1}{5}$ gravel), Dominique ($\frac{1}{3}$ gravel), Croque-Michotte ($\frac{1}{4}$ gravel), Corbin, Jean Faure, Ripeau.

AREA	TOPOGRAPHY	SOIL	SUB-SOIL
Cheval Blanc and Figeac	High alluvial terrace 36 to 40 m	$\frac{2}{3}$ very fine gravel $\frac{1}{3}$ ancient sand	The same gravel Sand and molasse

Properties include : Chx Cheval Blanc and Figeac.

AREA	TOPOGRAPHY	SOIL	SUB-SOIL
Area south of railway 'plain' (incorporating the southern part of Saint-Émilion, St Sulpice, Vignonet and St Pey-d'Armens and parts of St Hippolyte and St Étienne	Low terrace 6 to 15 m	Sandy gravel Sand and limon	Gravel and sand

Properties include: Chx Monbousquet, Lescours, Bigaroux, Martinet, Cruzeau, Quinault, Canon-la Gaffelière, Petit Gravet, Simard, la Garelle.

AREA	TOPOGRAPHY	SOIL	SUB-SOIL
Lussac-Saint-Émilion	Slopes Plateau	Clay–limestone Limestone	Molasse Limestone

Properties include: Chx Lyonnat, Lucas, Lussac

AREA	TOPOGRAPHY	SOIL	SUB-SOIL
Puisseguin-Saint-Émilion	Slopes Plateau	Clay – limestone Limestone	Molasse Limestone

Properties include: Ch. des Laurets.

AREA	TOPOGRAPHY	SOIL	SUB-SOIL
Montagne-Saint-Émilion	Slopes Plateau	Clay – limestone Limestone	Molasse Limestone

Properties include: Ch. des Tours.

AREA	TOPOGRAPHY	SOIL	SUB-SOIL
St Georges-Saint-Émilion	Slopes Plateau	Clay – limestone Limestone	Molasse Limestone

Properties include: Ch. St Georges.

AREA	TOPOGRAPHY	SOIL	SUB-SOIL
High part of Pomerol plateau	High alluvial terrace 38 to 40 m	Small or medium-sized gravel with some clay	Gravel with some clay

Properties include: Ch. Beauregard, la Conseillante, l'Évangile, Petit-Village, la Fleur-Pétrus, Gazin, Clinet, Trotanoy.

Exception			
Ch. Pétrus	40 m	Clay–sand (Some gravel in the part that used to be Gazin)	Clay
West, north-west and south part of Pomerol	Middle terrace 20 to 36 m	Gravel and sand a little clay	Gravel and sand a little clay

Properties include: Ch. la Grave-Trigant-de-Boisset, Rouget, Moulinet, Nenin (more gravel than others in the southern part), la Pointe, Marzy, Plince, Taillefer, du Tailhas.

Extreme north-west and west	Lower terrace 10 to 15 m	Sandier gravel than middle terrace	Sandier gravel than middle terrace

Properties include: Ch. de Sales, Mazeyres.

Lalande de Pomerol	Middle and lower terrace 15 to 25 m	Gravel and sand	Gravel and sand

Properties include: Chx. Belair, Musset, Bourseau.

Lalande de Pomerol (Néac)	Middle and lower terrace 20 m	Pomerol-type gravel	Gravel and molasse

Properties include: Ch. Tournefeuille, Belles-Graves, Moulin-à-Vent.

Climate

The area of the Gironde is blessed with a climate that is particularly favourable for wine-growing. It is a maritime climate with a latitude far enough south to give it plenty of warmth and sunshine while avoiding extremes of temperature because of its proximity to the modifying influence of the sea and rivers. It is protected from the easterly and north-easterly winds by the Massif Central and, to a lesser extent, from the westerlies, by the forest of the Landes.

The vineyard areas of Saint-Émilion and Pomerol are some 50 kilometres inland from those of the Médoc, and climate is therefore slightly less maritime and more continental; this means that the winters are a little colder and the summers a little warmer. The sea and rivers as we have remarked, have a moderating effect on climate; the humidity in the air reduces heat in the summer and inhibits freezing in the winter. There is also likely to be greater precipitation (mostly rainfall) in coastal regions. The following charts and graphs show, for comparison, the average maximum and minimum temperatures for the years 1968 to 1979 and the average precipitation figures, month by month, for the years 1964 to 1980, recorded at the meteorological stations at Lesparre in the Médoc and Vignonet, one of the communes entitled to the appellation Saint-Émilion. These are the only periods for which we have comparable data from the two stations. They confirm that the Médoc, stabilised by the Atlantic ocean and the Gironde estuary, has rather milder winters and more temperate summers than Saint-Émilion and Pomerol, and greater monthly precipitation for most of the year.

It is evident that the Médoc has appreciably greater precipitation in the crucial months of August and September and even more so in October, November, December and January. These differences may seem inconsiderable but, together with those in elevation, soil, drainage and the proportion of grape varieties, they may play a significant part in forming the style and character of the wines of the two areas.

One of the most important differences is that in anti-cyclonic conditions in the more hilly country near Saint-Émilion, a phenomenon called *cold-air drainage* occurs as a result of heat-loss by radiation at night, especially when the skies are clear. Very cold air forms on higher ground and drains down the slopes settling on the first flattish area it comes to. This explains the much worse frost danger that this area faces and especially that plateau which includes the vineyards of Châteaux Cheval Blanc and Figeac, their neighbours in the north-west of Saint-Émilion and many of the top Pomerols. It is this plateau that suffered the worst frost damage of recent years, in February 1956, when the temperature reached −24°C and so many vines were killed. The vineyards on the slopes and the higher ground were not nearly as severely affected.

TEMPERATURE 1968–1979

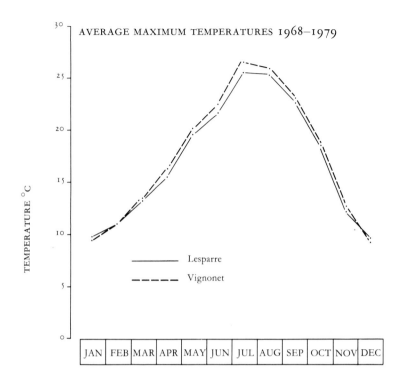

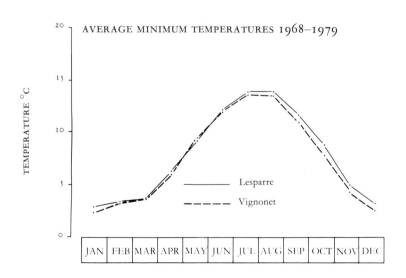

TEMPERATURE 1968–1979

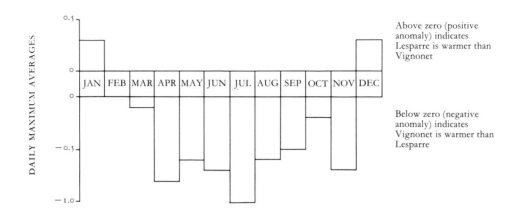

DAILY MAXIMUM AVERAGES

Above zero (positive anomaly) indicates Lesparre is warmer than Vignonet

Below zero (negative anomaly) indicates Vignonet is warmer than Lesparre

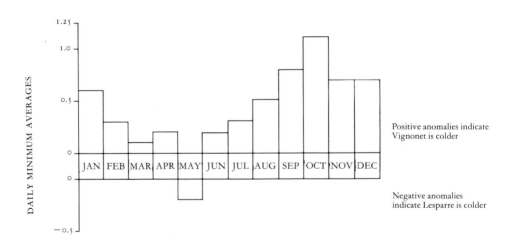

DAILY MINIMUM AVERAGES

Positive anomalies indicate Vignonet is colder

Negative anomalies indicate Lesparre is colder

PRECIPITATION 1964–1980

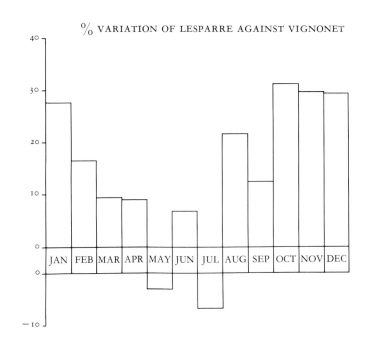

% VARIATION OF LESPARRE AGAINST VIGNONET

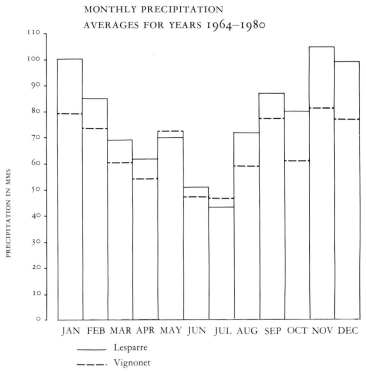

MONTHLY PRECIPITATION
AVERAGES FOR YEARS 1964–1980

——— Lesparre

– – –. Vignonet

Grape Varieties

The wines of Saint-Émilion and Pomerol are somewhat different in style and character from those of the Médoc, Graves and other areas of Bordeaux. One of the main reasons for this is that although the same grapes are used as in the Médoc and Graves – namely Cabernet Sauvignon, Cabernet Franc (Bouchet), Merlot and Malbec (Pressac) – the proportions are significantly different. A typical Médoc or Graves vineyard might consist of the following:

    Cabernet Sauvignon 55%
    Bouchet 20%
    Merlot 20%
    Pressac 5%

whereas a Saint-Émilion might consist of:

    Merlot 70%
    Bouchet 30%

or

    Merlot 60%
    Bouchet 30%
    Cabernet Sauvignon 10%

and Pomerol is the same with perhaps 5 to 10% Pressac. Interesting exceptions include Château le Couvent, the tiny Grand Cru Classé vineyard actually inside the town of Saint-Émilion, which has 100% Merlot; Château Pétrus, the most famous of Pomerols (95% Merlot, 5% Bouchet), and the two great properties of north-west Saint-Émilion which have a preponderance of gravel in their soil, Château Cheval Blanc (33% Merlot, 66% Bouchet, 1% Pressac) and Château Figeac (30% Merlot, 35% Bouchet, 35% Cabernet Sauvignon).

It is clear that in areas covered by the Appellations Contrôlés Saint-Émilion and Pomerol, the Merlot is the most important grape. It plays the same role that the Cabernet Sauvignon does in the Médoc and Graves. There are differences of soil between the various parts of Saint-Émilion and Pomerol (and, of course, within each individual part), and hundreds of years of trial and error have helped to determine the mixture of grape varieties currently used by each area and property. The first edition of Cocks et Feret (1850), the register of Bordeaux Châteaux, says that the grapes traditionally used in this area are Merlot, the two Cabernets and Malbec; also, very rarely, Chalosse Noire and Teinturier.

Principal Grape Varieties of Saint-Émilion and Pomerol

The Merlot
The secondary grape of the Médoc, but very much the first grape of Saint-Émilion and Pomerol, it ripens earlier than the Cabernet Sauvignon; the berries are larger and looser in the bunch. It is quite a big producer of softer, fleshier wines which tend to mature early. It is, however, more liable to rot in wet weather and more vulnerable to red spider.

Cabernet Franc (Bouchet)
A close relative of the Cabernet Sauvignon; it produces rather softer, spicier and less deep-coloured wines. The grapes are a little larger than the Cabernet Sauvignon

and less tightly packed in the bunch. It ripens earlier but is not quite so resistant to disease.

Cabernet Sauvignon
A hard-skinned, small-cropping grape, late-ripening and resistant to disease. The berries are small and tightly packed in the bunch. In conditions best suited to it, it produces deep, tannic, slow-developing, very complex wine.

It is interesting to note that in the three most famous properties in these areas (Cheval Blanc, Ausone and Pétrus) no Cabernet Sauvignon is used, whereas Figeac, a neighbour of Cheval Blanc and which makes wine almost as distinguished as these three, has one of the highest percentages of this grape in the entire district (35%).

Malbec (Pressac)
A large-cropping, early-ripening grape which produces rather soft wine, like the Merlot, but with less distinction. It is somewhat liable to *coulure*. It is easily the least-used of the four. Comparatively few properties in Saint-Émilion still grow it, though it is still fairly common in Pomerol and M Nicholas of Château la Conseillante certainly believes that the 10% Malbec is essential to the character of his wine.

The Merlot has long been the main grape variety of this part of the Gironde vignoble and the terrible frost of 1956 which ravaged so many of the Pomerol vineyards (as well as lower-lying properties of Saint-Émilion) led to an increase in the Merlot proportion in that area as there was a tendency to replace all vine varieties with Merlot. Occasionally the established order is challenged. Some thirteen years later there was a move to increase the proportions of Cabernet Sauvignon when the Institut National des Appellations d'Origine ordered extensive planting of that variety between 1970 and 1975. The venture did not prove a success as this variety does not ripen very well in the mainly colder soil of this area. The order was subsequently rescinded and the young vines replaced with Merlot.

Viticulture

The main difference between viticultural procedure in Saint-Émilion and Pomerol and the other red-wine producing areas of the Gironde is the method of training and pruning the vine. In the Médoc and elsewhere, the guyot double method is generally used, where two widely-spaced branches with two or three buds on each are tied to three wires running along the rows of vines. The vines are 1 metre apart with a little more between rows. In Saint-Émilion and Pomerol and their satellites, the guyot simple is traditional – one branch with seven to ten buds. The guyot mixte, which has a second short branch with another two buds, is also used and one can often see two full fruit-bearing branches. The mixte is used occasionally as a sort of insurance policy against the possibility of the main branch not producing the desired amount of fruit. The double is used to try to obtain the maximum possible fruit from the vine within the limits of the appellation. This may well militate against quality and the wiser growers will only use the double on very old and strong vine-stocks. The vines are 1.2 metres apart and there are 1.5 metres between the rows, which now tend to be rather further apart owing to the requirements of mechanisation. The traditional distance was 1.33 metres, as can be seen in Old Roman vine-furrows still visible at Châteaux Bélair, Beauséjour and Soutard.

The 1850 edition of Cocks et Feret says that a kind of *goblet* method of pruning is used with one, two or three branches. The vines are individually supported by stakes and the use of wire is unknown. All the cultivation is done with the spade. The 1868 version mentions the use of the plough in cultivation, the adoption of the guyot system of pruning and the use of wires.

The following account of the vineyard year is based on the yearly cycle of work at Châteaux Ausone and Belair.

Work in the vineyards goes on throughout the year and will start in October, after the vintage, with men spreading organic manure to replace nutritious elements in the soil used up by the previous season's growth. In November, the men carry out the first ploughing to build up the soil over the base of the vine to protect it against frost; this also buries the manure and provides a drainage trench between the rows for the winter. The women collect the clips which are used to hold the two parallel middle vines together in the period of maximum growth. The men then start the most important part of the viticultural process – the pruning – which is essentially the vigorous cutting out of all unwanted growth so that the plant's energies may be channelled entirely into the production of good-quality grapes and not dissipated and wasted in luxuriant foliage and long shoots. It also slows down the ageing process of the vine, thus prolonging its potential for quality and long-term quantity production.

As with the selection of grape varieties, the method of training has evolved through years of trial and error to become established as being the most suitable for this particular area. This vital operation is continued through December, January and February, the time when the vine is dormant, before the sap has begun to rise, so that the vine will not 'bleed' when it is cut. It is arduous, demanding work, often done in the most unpleasant weather conditions. Some, however, advocate later pruning ending in April or even May as a protection against spring frosts.

In December and January the women will take out all the cut branches and use them at home for cooking or burn them in bonfires or mobile braziers. In February they tie the future fruit-bearing branch along the bottom wire with reeds. In March the men's task is to replace any loose or damaged stakes with new ones (made of acacia wood) and change any defective wires while the women place the wires under the vine before vegetation starts. April sees the men planting the young vines which will have been purchased already grafted on to American root-stocks (in this case, at Ausone and Bélair, where the soil is mainly limestone with a little clay, graft 41b which is a crossing of Berlandieri, the Texan vine, and Chasselas). The next ploughing takes place, also, to uncover the base of the vines, aerate the soil, destroy weeds and create a dry, loose bed of soil before the growing period. There is also harrowing with a small harrow about 1 metre wide and 1.20 metres long to get rid of surface weeds and level the earth. Immediately after the ploughing the women scrape away any earth left clinging to the vine-stocks with a special kind of rake. There is further harrowing in May and the women eliminate any suckers, shoots or branches which might use up nutrition beneficial to the grapes, with an implement called a 'guinette'. In June there is a further ploughing to bank-up the earth against the vine-stocks again.

After the soil has been banked-up and hardened, it is loosened and flattened again by a 'griffe', a set of scratchers with teeth which penetrate 10 centimetres into the soil and also remove some weeds. The women train the vegetation straight and arrange it to receive the maximum sunshine and increase aeration to avoid diseases caused by the presence of humidity in bunched vegetation; again they tie young shoots to the wires. The Bouchet grows straight and is comparatively easy to train; the Merlot breaks easily, unless one is very careful, and grows less straight. There is also a further thinning of unwanted vegetation immediately after the flowering. This thinning disposes of young shoots on which mildew may develop rapidly.

About the middle of July, the fourth ploughing takes place uncovering the base of the vines again and levelling the earth; there is further harrowing to combat the weeds. Meanwhile, the women again train and thin the vine. In August harrowing continues and is repeated at intervals until the vintage. The women again clear the earth from the vine-stocks and thinning the vines also continues until the vintage.

The vintage itself usually occurs in the second half of September or early October, a week or so earlier in Saint-Émilion and Pomerol than in the Médoc. It is very arduous work done by hand except in the few properties that use a vintaging-machine; only three of the leading estates, Château la Gaffelière, Premier Grand Cru Classé Saint-Émilion and Châteaux de Sales and Gazin, in Pomerol, were using them for part of their crop in 1981. As the notes on individual Saint-Émilion and Pomerol properties indicate, a number are using these machines for the first time for the 1982 vintage, including several of the best-known.

This is a stage which may well see dramatic large-scale changes in the next few years and many people feel that, in ten years time, vintaging-machines will be the rule rather than the exception in Saint-Émilion and Pomerol. The duration of the picking depends on the size of the vineyards and the number of pickers. At Château Ausone it took eighty-five pickers thirteen hours to pick the 7 hectares of vines in 1981. Larger estates may take up to ten days. Nowadays weather-forecasting is more accurate and there are ways of assessing the sugar-content of the grapes: for example, with a refractometer, in which light passing through a drop of juice held between two prisms bends at a different angle according to its sugar-content and the percentage of sugar can be read off on a scale. So the decision to start picking, clearly a critical one, can be made with comparative certainty. In the old days a good deal of luck, as well as judgement, was involved.

Enemies of the vine
Apart from the natural meteorological hazards of winter and spring frosts, summer hail, excessive heat or insufficient sunshine and too much or too little rain, there are a number of diseases and parasites which constantly threaten a vineyard.

First there are the *physiological diseases*:

Chlorose – when the leaves turn yellow, then white, vegetation thins and finally the vine dies – is caused by lack of chlorophyl due to excess chalk in the soil. This is a particular danger in the Côtes and plateau Saint-Émilion properties with their predominantly limestone soil. It is effectively countered by the use of Berlandieri,

THE WINES OF SAINT-ÉMILION AND POMEROL

which is calcium-resistant, as part of the grafted vines making up the root-stock; but is aggravated by humidity and sudden fall in temperature. It also prevents the vine from assimilating iron. Ferrous-sulphate fertiliser helps to counterbalance this.

Coulure and *millerandage* are related diseases: in one, the flowers drop or contract and fail to fertilise or pollinate, in the other the grapes ripen unevenly and fail to form properly. They can be caused by too much rain or excessive heat at flowering-time.

Next come the *cryptogamic diseases*:

1   *Peronospera* or downy mildew (which caused such havoc in the Gironde when it first struck in the 1880's) thrives on humidity and heat. It stains the leaves and prevents the grapes from ripening.

2   *Oidium* or powdery mildew was the first of the three great scourges of the Gironde in the nineteenth century when it arrived in the 1850's. Like the former it is a fungus and survives the winter, not in dead branches and leaves as *Peronospera*, but in the buds of dormant shoots. It, too, stains the leaves, fruit and shoots and the stains are later replaced by holes.

3   *Botrytis Cinerea*, *pourriture gris* or grey rot. This fungus thrives in humid weather when the temperature is about 77°F. It is the same that produces such miraculous results with white grapes in Sauternes, Germany and Tokay in Hungary, but it is fatal to red grapes, destroying the colour cells; the grapes shrivel and wither with grey powder forming on the skins.

4   *Black rot* occurs at temperatures of about 70°F in humid weather. Black spots appear on the leaves, and the fruit shrivels up.

5   *Anthracnose* forms spots on leaves and grapes, grey at first then brown. Later the spots dry and holes appear in the leaves and grapes which later shrivel up. This is liable to occur in humid weather.

Then there are the *parasites*:

Phylloxera Vastatrix is a species of louse that has a very complicated life-cycle and in one of its many stages it lives underground and attacks vine-roots, eventually killing the plant. A native of the United States of America, it was accidentally brought over to the continent in the middle of the nineteenth century and devastated the Gironde area in the 1870's and 1880's. The only completely effective remedy was to graft every single European vine-stock (*vitis vinifera*) on to one of the native American vine-roots (*vitis riparia, vitis rupestris* and *vitis Berlandieri*), or on to a crossing of two of them. This huge task was duly carried out and now most *vitis vinifera* vines throughout the world are grafted on to American roots except in a few areas where particularly sandy soil or some other unusual condition discourages *phylloxera*. There is another stage which attacks the vine leaves, but fortunately most *vitis vinifera* species are immune to this.

Other parasites include the larvae of various moths (*cochylis, eudemis* and *pyralis*), and two or three species of beetles and *red spider* but these are now effectively controlled by using modern insecticides and acaricides which are applied with the frequent sulphur and copper-sulphate sprayings, which from late April are carried out regularly to combat *Oidium, Peronospera* and the other potential threats. At Ausone spraying will take place every eight to ten days right through until shortly

24

before the vintage. Meticulous general vineyard care and hygiene, of course, helps to minimise the danger.

Finally, there is a virus disease, *Court Noue* or Fanleaf. It is spread in the soil by a species of thread-like worms, or nematodes, *Xiphinema Index*, and is one of the chief contributors to '*degenerescence infectieuse*' which, together with *chlorose* and *pourriture grise*, Pascal Delbeck, *Régisseur* of Château Ausone, regards as the most serious enemies of his vines. One of the first indications of the conditions is that the distance between the nodes (the potential buds) is shorter. Later the leaves will turn yellow. Up-rooting affected vines and disinfecting or fumigating the soil to kill the nematodes before replanting is the only effective treatment. It seems probable that the degeneration of the soil which prevents it from resisting the virus carried by the nematodes is mainly caused by not allowing the soil to lie fallow long enough before replanting in order to regenerate itself naturally.

Planting

The rules of Appellation d'Origine Contrôlée are drawn up by the Institut National des Appellations d'Origine des Vins et Eaux-de-Vie (INAO). They insist on a limited number of vines to be planted per hectare. In Saint-Émilion it is 5,500 to 6,000, and in Pomerol the same. Likewise there is a basic maximum yield per hectare. This is called the 'rendement de base'; it may be adjusted up or down each year on the recommendation of the syndicate of growers of each 'appellation' if confirmed by the INAO. This adjusted figure is known as the 'rendement annuel'. The decree, published in October 1974, says that an increase in the 'rendement de base' shall be made 'only in an exceptional year when quality and quantity coincide'. It must be said, however, that such an increase was immediately granted for 1974, admittedly a large harvest, but hardly one that many would claim as exceptional in quality.

In addition a further upward percentage of that yield may be granted in the same way as the former. For all Bordeaux appellations this figure, known as the 'plafond limite de classement' (PLC) is 20% above the annual one, whether it has been adjusted up or down or not.

Before December 1st, a grower whose crop has exceeded the annual figure may apply to have his entire crop, unless it exceeds the PLC, granted the appellation. He must agree that any such excess will be delivered for distillation or the production of vinegar or unfermented grape-juice, or he will lose the right of appellation for any of his production. Such an application will involve a chemical analysis and testing by a committee who may turn down his entire crop. This kind of stringent testing had already been the practice in Saint-Émilion before 1974.

The permitted basic maximum yields for our areas are as follows:

42 hectolitres per hectare

Saint-Émilion Premiers Grands Crus Classés
Saint-Émilion Grands Crus Classés
Saint-Émilion Grands Crus
Saint-Émilion
Lussac-St Émilion

Montagne-St Émilion
Puisseguin-St Émilion
St Georges-St Émilion

40 hectolitres per hectare
Pomerol
Lalande de Pomerol (now incorporating Néac)

Naturally the actual yield varies very considerably from year to year. In 1977 there was a small, poor crop and many properties produced between 5 and 10 hectolitres per hectare. In 1979, a very big and good quality harvest, around 50 was a normal yield.

Vinification

When the grapes arrive at the first year '*chai*' they are usually de-stalked nowadays and crushed in a machine called an '*egrappoir-fouloir*'. The crushing must be fairly gentle so as not to squash the pips which contain unpleasant-tasting bitter oils. Before that, it is important that damaged, diseased or mouldy grapes should be rejected as they might impart an off-taste to the wine. The stalks contain a great deal of tannin and the purpose of the de-stalking is to avoid an excess of this in the '*must*' (unfermented grape juice), but it is by no means universal. Some of the smaller properties still do not de-stalk at all. Others vary their practice according to the year. The J-P Moueix properties, for examples, will de-stalk all their grapes in a good year like 1975. When there has been an abundance of sun and no more than the desired amount of rain, the wine will naturally have plenty of extract and a firm structure. When there has been much less sun and rather too much rain (as in 1977), the wine will benefit from some extra tannin and they will de-stalk only 80% of the grapes. At Château Soutard, the Comte de Ligneris never de-stalks his grapes completely: in 1975 he de-stalked 80% – the same as the Moueix properties in 1977 – while in 1977 he de-stalked only 20%. On the other hand, M Bécot of Château Beau-Séjour (Bécot), who is advised by the renowned oenologist Professor Peynaud, says that it is always preferable to ensure the presence of 'good' tannins through a long maceration of de-stalked grapes than to have the 'bad' tannins gained through allowing an excess of stalk to accompany the fermentation and '*cuvaison*'. The 'bad' tannins will impart a bitter, 'grassy' and coarse flavour to the wine, he claims.

The resultant *must*, consisting of juice, skins and pips and, as we have seen, sometimes a proportion of stalks, is pumped to the fermenting vats which may be made of wood, stainless-steel or cement, lined with glass, fibre-glass or tiles. They may be open, but most are sealed nowadays.

It is at this stage, the beginning of the fermentation, that in some years sugar may be added to the *must* in order to increase the alcohol content of the finished wine. This is only permitted by the Minister of Agriculture after application by the INAO, but permission has been granted with great regularity over the last twenty years. The process is called 'Chaptalisation', after the French Scientist, Jean-André Chaptal (1756–1832). It is only allowed when the potential alcohol content of the *must* is up to the minimum strength permitted for its appellation. Not more than 3 kilograms of sugar per hectolitre of *must* may be added, nor more than 200 kilos per hectare of vineyard under production.

Sulphur-dioxide (30 to 40 milograms per litre) may be added to the *must* before fermentation to kill off the wild Apiculata and Pichia yeasts and allow the wine yeasts, Saccharomyces, to work on the sugar to produce ethyl alcohol and carbon-dioxide.

Temperature is vitally important for the start of fermentation and throughout its duration. It will have to be between 20° and 30°C to start and in cold weather the *cuvier* may have to be heated. Once the yeasts have started working on the sugar the fermenting *must* will generate extra heat and great care has to be taken to ensure that the temperature does not rise above 30°C. Many would regard the ideal temperature for the fermentation as being somewhere between 25° and 28°C.

There are many methods of controlling the temperature in the vats. The first is known as '*remontage*' which, in its simplest form, involves pumping the wine from the bottom of the vat up through a pipe outside it and back to the top. Besides cooling the *must* this also ensures maceration because it covers and helps to break up the 'cap' of skins, pips and, in some cases, stalks which, once fermentation has started, will be forced up to the top of the *must*. The gradually increasing alcohol in the *must* draws the colour pigments out of the grape skins and into the *must*. Most of the tannin in the eventual wine come from the skins.

The *must* may be pumped through cooling radiators or through a tank of cold water before being returned to the vat; cold-water pipes may be run through the vat or water may be sprayed on the outside of the vat and left to evaporate. Some fermentation vats are out of doors (as at Château Matras). The most modern stainless-steel vats can be thermostatically controlled.

The fermentation period usually lasts from ten to fourteen days but it may be as short as four or five days or sometimes as long as three weeks. A vat control-chart logs the progress of the fermentation. The specific gravity of the *must* is plotted daily, recording the drop in sugar content as the yeasts convert it into alcohol. The temperature is likewise recorded on the chart.

When the alcoholic fermentation is completed, the wine may remain on the skins for a further period of maceration so that the total time of the wine's contact with the skins may vary from ten days to as long as four weeks in some of the more traditional properties. Maceration is shorter today than it was thirty years ago.

At the end of the maceration period, or *cuvaison*, the free-run wine, 'vin de goutte', is run off into casks or another vat while the remaining mass of skins, pips and sometimes stalks (known as '*marc*') is removed to a press, either a hydraulic vertical press or a more modern horizontal one. At this stage the *marc* will contain a considerable quantity of liquid and the wine which results from this pressing, known as the 'vin de presse', may be of good quality, though it will naturally be rather strong in the more astringent tannins. A proportion of it used always to be added to the free-run wine, but now that modern methods of re-pumping during the fermentation have become so effective in extracting the 'noble' tannins, this is done less often nowadays.

Press at Château Figeac.

After this pressing, the dry *marc* of pips and skins will be wetted, refermented and distilled to produce *'eau-de-vie-de-marc'*, not by growers but by specialist spirit-makers; the lees, too, are distilled. The growers are bound by Law to hand over a certain amount of this distillate each year to the government. Some of the dried pips and skins may also be used as fertilizer.

After the alcoholic fermentation – often actually overlapping it, sometimes several months after – comes the malolactic fermentation. This is caused by lactic-acid bacteria and the effect is that each molecule of malic acid affected is split and one molecule of the much weaker lactic acid and one molecule of carbon-dioxide are created. It is a necessary stage in the wine's development and the earlier it takes place the better – or at least the more convenient. Nowadays this can generally be induced by warming the *must*.

There is considerable variation from property to property in the next stage after the pressing. In most of the leading properties, the wine is run off into oak casks. In some of the wealthiest, as at Châteaux Pétrus, Ausone and Cheval Blanc, these 'barriques' are new each year. This is a very costly operation and most cannot afford it. Some buy a proportion of new casks each year and use older ones for the rest of the vintage, rotating the wines at each racking. Others use no new casks. Some growers, including M de Lambert of Château de Sales in Pomerol, have told us that they actually prefer to use new casks because of the sometimes almost exaggeratedly 'oaky' character that they can impart to the young wine, though this does fade as the wine matures. Others again will use no new casks in years that are particularly light in extract.

There are two kinds of Bordelaise cask: 'type Château' and 'type transport'. The latter are made of appreciably thicker wood and we were told at Château Petit-Village that they are becoming more popular because their sturdiness ensures a better re-sale price. A barrique holds 225 litres so that four barriques amount to 1 tonneau of 900 litres.

Some estates, such as Château Haut Rocher in St Étienne-de-Lisse, use no casks at all and the wine spends all its maturation time before bottling in cement vats. The fact that it is matured in a container made of non-porous material will reduce the evaporation inevitable in wine that is stored in wood; but it will necessarily slow down the development of the wine and there is a general feeling that it will lack the character of that which is matured in wood. Monsieur de Monteuil, who makes the wine at Château Haut Rocher and was trained at the School of Oenology and Viticulture at Beaune, told us that he thought that only wines of the very greatest potential justified the expense of oak-casking and that while he was proud of the quality of his own wines he did not think that they would be improved by being matured in cask. Nor is this view unknown in loftier echelons. Monsieur Bécot of Château Beau-Séjour (Bécot), Premier Grand Cru Classé Saint-Émilion, also told us that he allows his wine to complete its entire maturation period in cement in poorer years.

It would be interesting to conduct a controlled experiment by maturing part of the vintage of one property, after *assemblage*, in vats and part in casks; only thus is it possible to reach anything like a definitive judgement. This is the method employed by the Comte de Malet Roquefort at Château la Gaffelière to try to determine the effects, if any, of using a vintaging-machine. That part of the 1981 crop which has harvested by machine is being vinified and matured separately from the rest of the crop picked by hand. To revert to the expense of new oak-casking, M Thienpoint at Vieux-Château-Certan told us (in 1980) that a new cask cost him 1,000 francs; he could sell it after two years for 350 francs and after three years for 200 francs.

Some properties will keep the wine in vats for as much as three months after it has been run off the skins, before racking it into casks. This is the process of transferring wine to a fresh cask. By this time the malolactic fermentation will probably have taken place. Others will have run the wine into casks as soon as the *cuvaison* and the pressing are completed and the malolactic fermentation may take place in cask. Some, as at Châteaux Beauséjour (Duffau-Lagarrosse) and Soutard, put part of the vintage into new oak, part into used casks and part into vats or tanks. After *assemblage* the wine will be circulated, by means of the various rackings, through each of these three containers.

This does not mean that the *assemblage*, that all-important blending of the different grape varieties, always takes place at the same time. Here again, as with almost every stage of the vinification process, practice differs widely from Château to Château. At Château Cheval Blanc the wines from the different *cépages* are blended immediately after fermentation and before the wine is put into cask. Many of the leading estates, including Château Pétrus, the other J-P Moueix pro-perties and Château Figeac, assemble their wines after the first racking; some, like Beauséjour (Duffau-Lagarrosse), after the second. Châteaux Canon, la Gaffelière and Matras, on the other hand, do not put the different varieties together until the September of the year following the vintage – after the third racking. Again each individual property may vary its time of assembling from year to year according to the character of the vintage.

Very unusually, Jean Brun filters the wine at all the properties where he is *Maître de Chai*, at the beginning of its maturation, thereby reducing by half the number of rackings required.

During the first ten months or so of the wine's time in cask it is necessary to top it up once or twice a week to counter evaporation. The casks lie with the bung, often made of glass, fairly loose and at the top during this time. There are usually three or four rackings in the first year and in the second year when the casks lie with the bung, now tight, at an angle of 45° to reduce ullage, there are three more. During this second year, before the wine is bottled, at between sixteen months and two and a half years, the wine is fined, usually with whites of eggs. This process removes any unwanted particles of matter suspended in the wine which have not been deposited in the various rackings. In very tannic vintages there may be another fining and indeed one leading grower told us another light fining was by no means unusual, though rarely publicised.

Before the bottling and after the fining, many properties assemble the wines again, returning them to the large vats. This *égalisage* is not, of course, a blending of grape varieties: that has already been done. It levels out any minor difference of character between casks and is more convenient for bottling. A number of properties give the wine a light filtration before it is bottled.

Bottling at the Château is now almost universal among the leading properties and is compulsory for Saint-Émilion Premiers Grands Crus Classés and Grands Crus Classés, but some properties still sell their generic wines in cask; Grands Crus must be Château-, or French-bottled. A recent innovation is the mobile bottling-plant and an ever-increasing number of properties, including Château Canon and Clos Fourtet, among the more famous, use this facility. It is an extremely efficient piece of equipment, carried on a lorry and driven around to the various properties. More and more find that it is convenient for an operation which lasts for only a certain number of hours in a year, and whose timing does not have to be exact, and prefer it to keeping, renovating, cleaning and maintaining their own equipment.

The general practice is to bottle the wines of Saint-Émilion and Pomerol rather earlier than those of the Médoc and Graves but, here again, individual practice varies widely.

The Wines

The wines of Saint-Émilion and Pomerol are distinctively different in style and character from those of the Médoc and the Graves. As we have seen there are a number of reasons for this including climate, soil, elevation, drainage and the proportion of grape varieties used.

As a general rule Saint-Emilions and Pomerols are rounder and richer wines than Médocs and Graves. They have sometimes been called the 'Burgundies' of Bordeaux. But these generalisations can be misleading. Many people suppose that all Saint-Émilion and Pomerols mature far more quickly and have a much shorter life than Médocs. We have found that the finest wines of the limestone plateau and

Côtes of Saint-Émilion are slow developers and particularly long lasters and for all their eventual perfumed elegance they can be quite austere and almost steely in youth.

The gravel, sand and sand-gravel wines below the slopes tend to form their character rather more quickly and are easier to enjoy at an earlier age. This is true even at the highest level, as with Cheval Blanc, but the wines nevertheless often last very well. Indeed we have come across comparatively few Saint-Émilions or Pomerols of the 1966 vintage which were, in our opinion, really ready to drink, and this includes some of the southernmost properties of the plain of Saint-Émilion where one would expect to find the quickest-developing wines. The two finest gravel wines, Cheval Blanc and Figeac, can be very long-lived.

Pomerols, like the gravel and sand Saint-Émilions, show their character rather earlier than Médocs, but the best ones, with their great extract and intensity of flavour, can be very long-lived as may be judged from the tasting notes at the end of the book.

Many people find that the wines of the Médoc, in which the Cabernet Sauvignon is often the dominating grape, have a bouquet and flavour reminiscent of blackcurrant or cedar wood. The great wines, of course, have delicacy and complexity far beyond this. The predominantly Merlot wines in our areas produce different effects of smell and taste. On the limestone and clayey soil of the slopes and plateau of Saint-Émilion the wines are rather lighter in colour than the best gravel wines like Cheval Blanc and Figeac or the Pomerols. They have a distinctly flowery bouquet, often reminding people of pinks or violets with suggestions of raspberries or strawberries. We have said that they are slow maturers but they are less obviously tannic and astringent in youth and young middle-age than Médocs. As they mature they develop a mellow, almost sweet but elegant and perfumed fruitiness with a long flavour and a somewhat burgundian strawberry character in the middle of the taste.

Jean-Claude Berrouet, the oenologist of the firm of J-P Moueix, who makes some of the finest wines of the area, told us that the colour of these wines tends more to vermilion when the limestone predominates and purple where there is more clay. He also feels that mainly limestone wines have particularly attractive earthy nuances in the bouquet.

The two famous properties to the north-west of Saint-Émilion near the Pomerol border, Châteaux Cheval Blanc and Figeac, which have a preponderance of fine gravel soil, make deeper-coloured wines. They are big, rich and full of character with great vinosity and extract and an almost creamy or velvety texture. They begin to form their character somewhat earlier than the limestone wines and those of the Médoc and Graves, but are capable of very long life in good vintages. By any standard these are very fine wines with great intensity of flavour, and it would be hard to say that any red wine was 'better' than an outstanding vintage of Cheval Blanc such as 1921 or 1947.

The neighbours of these two properties, which have a small amount of fine gravel, make wines of good quality somewhat similar in character but less intense in flavour and not quite so fine.

The sand-covered slope just below the limestone slopes to the north-west and north produces some very fine wines like *Châteaux Cap de Mourlin* and *Dassault*, both

31

Grands Crus Classés, similar in style and longevity to those on the limestone slopes themselves.

In the area south of the railway the wines with gravel in the soil are of good quality and last well like Château Monbousquet, and the ones on sandier soil are lighter and mature more quickly.

The communes entitled to hyphenate their names with Saint-Émilion produce wines similar to those of the slopes and plateau of Saint-Émilion but generally of a somewhat lesser quality. Exceptions include Châteaux Lyonnat (Lussac-St Émilion), Roudier (Montagne-St Émilion) and St Georges (St Georges-St Émilion) which make very fine wine.

The wines of Pomerol are very deep in colour and, like Cheval Blanc and Figeac, their attractive qualities of bouquet and flavour become apparent earlier than is the case with most other fine clarets. The bouquet is very rich and perfumed, with suggestions of plums, truffles and brown sugar, as opposed to the subtler, violet and strawberries aroma of most Saint-Émilions. The taste is very rich and full; often almost sweet and reminiscent of dark chocolate. Opinions seem to be divided about the character of these wines. Some authorities, including Alexis Lichine, describe them as combining something of the Médoc (especially St Estèphes and Pauillacs) with the fullness and aroma of St Émilion. Others, like Edmund Penning-Rowsell, find them similar to St Émilion only more so, although Mr Penning-Rowsell says that he, too, has sometimes mistaken them for Pauillacs in a blind tasting.

When such distinguished critics disagree there can be no 'right' answer. Most would agree, however, that the best wines, from the high and middle terraces of gravel-clay or gravel, sand and clay, have great intensity of flavour, a velvety richness and fullness and often an almost overwhelming perfume. The supreme example is also something of an exception, Château Pétrus, which is generally accepted as the finest Pomerol, has soil which is almost entirely clay with some sand and a little gravel in the area that used to be part of Château Gazin. Again, unusually, the wine is made from almost 100% Merlot grapes.

Despite the fact that these wines often start to reveal their charm comparatively early, the best ones are capable of very long life. We have certainly tasted wines in perfect condition at more than fifty years of age. Château Pétrus 1964 has still not opened out fully yet (in 1982), although M Berrouet, whose first Pétrus vintage it was, says that with hindsight he would have made that wine somewhat differently, so that it would have been rather less hard and slow in developing.

He says, however, that Pomerol wines generally are less apparently tannic in structure than most red Bordeaux wines. Pomerols, like Saint-Émilions, tend to be a little higher in alcohol than Médocs and perhaps this helps to preserve them for longer than one might expect.

The wines of the extreme north-west and west, on much sandier soil, are comparatively lighter and less long-lived, though Château de Sales is an exception. Those of Lalande-de-Pomerol, beyond the Barbanne, now including Néac, which used to have its own appellation, resemble the lesser Pomerols although some properties, especially those with predominantly gravel or gravel-molasse soil and sub-soil, make finer and longer-lasting wines.

We have tried to give our own impression of what the wines of Saint-Émilion and Pomerol taste like but we realise that this is a very difficult and highly subjective exercise. Different people inevitably smell and taste different things in the same wine: or rather the smell and taste of the wine suggests different analogies to them. Let us give three examples:

1   Jean-Claud Berrouet, the J-P Moueix oenologist, on the smell of Pomerol: 'powerful, warming bouquet in which the perfumes of truffles, blackcurrants, strawberries, fresh cream and grilled almonds blend harmoniously'.

2   M Bécot, proprietor of Château Beau-Séjour (Bécot), on the smell of the limestone Saint-Émilions: 'One to four years – blackcurrants, strawberries, mulberries, prunes, cherries, peaches, grenadines, figs. Two to five years – violets, mignonettes, roses. Five to thirty years – vanilla, liquorice, pepper, cinnamon, cloves, tobacco, coffee, nutmeg, caramel, cacao, grilled bread, nuts, grilled almonds. Thirty to fifty years – dead leaves, truffles, mushrooms'.

3   Ted Hale MW, chief buyer of Harveys, on the smell of limestone Saint-Émilions: 'raw sausage meat'. Cheval Blanc and Figeac: 'chewed white string imposed on raw sausage meat'. Pomerol: 'similar to Saint-Émilion but intenser flavour, probably due to the greater incidence of frost on the plateau – the great pruner in the sky!'

Most writers and authorities on claret take the view that the wines of the Médoc are somewhat more aristocratic or more intellectually stimulating than the wines of Saint-Émilion and Pomerol. They claim for the former more finesse and subtler nuances of flavour.

We feel that while a mature Château Lafite of a fine year will be a subtler and more delicate wine than a Pétrus, a Cheval Blanc or an Ausone of comparable vintage and maturity, it will also be subtler and more delicate than a Latour or a Mouton. This is not to say that it is a better wine than any of the other four; merely that it is different.

Of course, as with most generalisations, there is some truth in the traditional view, but we feel that in the past perhaps insufficient justice has been done to the longevity and the complexity of the finest Pomerols and Saint-Émilions. Always with wine it is ultimately a matter of personal taste; but the wise (or lucky) man or woman will surely find room in the cellar for these wines alongside their peers from the Médoc and the Graves.

Saint-Émilion, a general view.

A typical cobbled street in Saint-Émilion.

The Porte Cadet, Saint-Émilion.

SAINT-ÉMILION

Appellations and Classification

In 1199 a royal charter of King John of England proclaimed the right of Saint-Émilion to the status of a commune. Then in 1289 another, this time issued by King Edward I laid down the limits of the area entitled to that name. These included not only the commune of Saint-Émilion itself, but also the neighbouring villages of St Martin-de-Mazerat, St Christophe-des-Bardes, St Hippolyte, St Laurent-des-Combes, St Étienne-de-Lisse, St Pey-d'Armens, St Sulpice-de-Faleyrens, Vignonet and part of the territory of Libourne, which were to be under its jurisdiction. As we have seen, this was confirmed by Edward I and Edward III, and the Syndicat Viticole et Agricole de Saint-Émilion proudly proclaims that these boundaries have also been confirmed by four Kings of France: Charles VIII, François I, Louis XIII and Louis XIV. It also states that they remain unchanged today, which is more or less true.

Disputes arose from time to time between the inhabitants of the old Saint-Émilion district and those of the surrounding areas about the right to use the words 'Saint-Émilion' in the name of their wines, but for the first three-quarters of the nineteenth century nobody was much concerned about whether wines were called 'Saint-Émilion' or 'near Saint-Émilion'. However, as competition and production began to grow and wine became harder to sell, attitudes changed. In the 1890's the Syndicat Viticole et Agricole de Saint-Émilion was formed, which claimed the right of *Appellation d'Origine* to the commune of Saint-Émilion alone. Not long afterwards, the other communes included in the ancient jurisdiction of Saint-Émilion granted by the English kings, formed their own 'Syndicat de la Jurisdiction de Saint-Émilion' in order to defend their right to the appellation which the young 'Syndicat de Saint-Émilion' was contesting. Also a legal wrangle between the two grew up in which a judgement was made in 1908 granting the communes of the jurisdiction the right of a syndicat and the use of the appellation for their syndicat. Later, in 1914, an agreement was reached and the two syndicats joined forces and continued to protect their appellation against a third group to the north consisting of Montagne, Puisseguin, St Georges, Parsac and Lussac.

The lack of clarity with regard to official denomination or appellation in the nineteenth century is indicated by some observations in the early editions of Cocks et Feret. The 1850 edition says that under the denomination of the wine of Saint-Émilion one should include that of the communes of Saint-Émilion, St Martin-de-Mazerat, St Christophe-des-Bardes, St Laurent-des-Combes, St Sulpice-de-Faleyrens, Pomerol, Néac, St Georges, Montagne. After these it adds Lussac, Puisseguin, St Magne and Castillon.

The 1868 edition uses the term 'Saint-Émilionais' for the first time and recalls the confirmation in 1289 by Edward I of Saint Émilion's rights of jurisdiction over its neighbouring villages, but does not include St Pey-d'Armens, St Sulpice-de-

Faleyrens or Vignonet. It mentions St Sulpice later, however, and says that it produces two entirely different wines from different soils – good wines called *Sables-Saint-Émilion* of which there are only three properties, Châteaux Lescours, Monbousquet and le Castelot. It also mentions the very poor quality wines of the Palus.

The 1874 edition includes St Pey-d'Armens in the 'Saint-Émilionais' along with Libourne, Pomerol, Néac, St George, Montagne, Puisseguin, Parsac, Monbadon, St Cibard, St Philippe-d'Aiguille, Gordegan, St Gene's and Ste Colombe, while the 1897 edition also includes Ste Terre.

Two laws, in 1919 and 1927, called the 'Lois Capus' after Jean Capus (Deputy and Senator for the Gironde and Minister of Agriculture), who was instrumental in getting them passed, sought to ensure that appellations were confined to areas suitable for producing quality wines and that those wines were made by methods traditional to the area concerned. This paved the way for the setting-up in 1935 of a Comité National d'Origine to adminster a strict system of 'appellation contrôlée' and eventually to the formation of the Institut National d'Origine des Vins et Eaux-de-Vie. As a direct result of this, the decree of November 14th, 1936, established a clear ruling. This confirmed the right of the areas mentioned above to call their wines 'Saint-Émilion' and also entitled five villages to the north and east to attach the words to their own names: Montagne-St Émilion, St Georges-de-Montagne-St Émilion (often abbreviated to St Georges-St Émilion), Lussac-St Émilion, Parsac-St Émilion and Puisseguin-St Émilion. Since then and by the decree of December 5th, 1972, St Georges and Parsac have been merged with Montagne and so have ceased to exist as wine areas in their own right, although sixteen growers have been allowed to retain the St Georges appellations for their wines. Another area, previously having its own appellation, was Sables-St Émilion. As its name implies, this is a sandy low-lying piece of land, between Libourne and the Dordogne. It has now, by the decree of December 24th, 1973, been incorporated in the commune of Saint-Émilion itself for appellation purposes.

No wines from Saint-Émilion were included in the 1855 classification of the red wines of the Gironde. Indeed, Château Haut-Brion was the only property outside the Médoc to be listed. It is said that Château Ausone would have been included if its production had not been so small (12 to 15 tonneaux).

The first edition of Cocks et Feret, *Bordeaux et ses Vins* (1850), lists 37 first growths and 21 seconds, after the list of 'Le coutre de Beaudais in 1811' and adds another six or seven which go under the name of 'Sables-St Emilion'. The third edition of Francks, *Traité sur les Vignes du Médoc*, mentions Saint-Émilion and lists 42 first growths including Ausone, Beau-Séjour, Belair and Canon and 17 seconds including Cheval Blanc and Figeac which seems to confirm the greater reputation of the Côtes and plateau Saint-Émilion wines at this time.

In the 1868 edition of Cocks et Feret, the first growths have increased to 44 (including Cheval Blanc and Figeac) and two St Christophe properties, Laborde and de Sarpes. The seconds have gone up to 43. Of their selection in this edition the authors say that they have consulted a large number of local proprietors and *négociants* and, although they do not claim that it is an official document, it is the result of long and conscientious research. In the 1881 edition the authors add an intermediate class between the first and second growths.

In the 1886 edition each class again increases and in the 1897 the first growths reach 58, the intermediates 11 and the seconds 50. There are 8 firsts of the so-called 'Graves de Saint-Émilion' and 21 seconds. By the 1922 edition, the firsts are up to 79, the intermediates to 25 and the seconds to 160; and in the 1929 edition the firsts are 110 and the intermediates (now called second-firsts) and the seconds similarly enlarged.

Apart from the Cocks et Feret 'ratings', the only official list that appeared over the next ninety years was that produced by the Ministry of National Economy during the Second World War when it attempted to fix the price of all goods, including wine. Almost all the wines of Saint-Émilion were graded according to price and, presumably, quality. After the War, things got rather out of hand with virtually every property claiming the status of first, secondary-first or second growth. In 1948 the President of the Syndicat asked the Institut National d'Origine to declare these self-conferred 'appellations' illegal until a fully-authorised system of appellation contrôlée could be established. This was done and by the decree of October 7th, 1954, Saint-Émilion had its first fully-established classification. The four appellations were as follows:

Saint-Émilion Premier Grand Cru Classé
Saint-Émilion Grand Cru Classé
Saint-Émilion Grand Cru (an annual classification, granted for 1 vintage only)
Saint-Émilion

It should be noted that this classification applies only to those wines admitted to the Appellation Contrôlée Saint-Émilion which is confined to the above-mentioned eight communes within the ancient boundaries of Saint-Émilion and confirmed by the 1936 decree. It is not designed to be a fixed classification, but to be revised every ten years.

The first official list was published in July, 1955, and revised in August, 1958. By the decree of October 18th, 1958, a distinction was made within the Premier Grand Cru Classé category. It was divided into two parts: A and B. A included only the two estates, Châteaux Ausone and Cheval Blanc, while B consisted of the remaining ten. On November 7th, 1969, there was a further revision and eight Grands Crus were elevated to Grands Crus Classés. There were no demotions, although apparently one of the Premiers Grands Crus Classés came very close to relegation and received an official warning. The next revision of the classification is due to take place in 1983.

Since 1954, in order to qualify for the appellation, all Saint-Émilion wines must undergo tastings. These are set up by a commission of the Syndicat Viticole et Agricole de Saint-Émilion which is responsible to the INAO. The first, usually in the January following the vintage, is obligatory for all wines of the area from Premier Grand Cru Classé downwards to decide whether they are deserving of the minimum appellation 'Saint-Émilion A C'. The second tasting is the one in which the Grands Crus for that particular year are selected. Samples are collected from each property by a Government inspector and a *négociant* and the tasting is conducted by a series of three-man juries, each consisting of a *négociant*, a grower and a *courtier* or broker.

They may accept, adjourn or reject the samples. If they adjourn a sample, it is then passed to another jury whose decision will be final. There is no appeal against rejection which means that the wine can only be sold as Saint-Émilion AC.

The results of the June tasting held in 1971 of the large and good-quality 1970 vintage showed that of 244 wines put forward for Grand Cru status, 192 were accepted and 52 were adjourned. Of these, 42 were approved by a second jury and awarded Grand Cru status while the remaining 10 had to be content with the rank of Saint-Émilion AC.

A Grand Cru must have earned its status for at least ten years consecutively before it can apply for promotion to Grand Cru Classé.

The top three categories must all have their wine bottled at the property. There are a number of exceptions where the wine is bottled at one of the owner's other properties: for instance, Grandes Murailles, where there is no *chai*. Only Saint-Émilion AC wines may be sold in bulk.

There is a committee, consisting of twenty-six owners of Grand Cru Classé properties, which represents the Grands Crus Classés and aims to maintain quality control. There is also a Syndicat of Premiers Grands Crus Classés properties whose President is Jean-Paul Valette of Château Pavie.

A possible problem which may affect the two lower categories of the classification is that the latest EEC wine-laws will require the classification of vineyards rather than wines. As we have seen, the Grands Crus are decided each year by a tasting of their wines, so the next few years may see a change in the system which has been in operation for the last twenty-eight years. If this change comes about, it will pose a problem for growers who sell wines under different 'sous marques' (or second wines), which may, under the existing rules, qualify for Grand Cru status.

Many growers register a 'sous marque' or brand-name either for their second wine (often made from young vines) or for a part of their main crop which is sold exclusively to a particular country or organisation under an exclusive brand-name.

This can be confusing, as a single property may produce wine under several different labels, although the wines may be identical. Many reference books, including Cocks et Feret, do not distinguish between 'sous marqués' and actual properties.

There are one thousand and thirty-two growers within the jurisdiction of Saint-Émilion and the total area of their vines amounts to 5,104 hectares. The size of the individual properties is as follows:

Owners of more than 25 hectares: 21
Owners of 12 to 25 hectares: 80
Owners of 6 to 12 hectares: 201
Owners of 3 to 6 hectares: 225
Owners of 1 to 3 hectares: 272
Owners of less than 1 hectare: 235

Two-hundred and ninety of these owners, whose vines cover 991 hectares, have their wine made by the Co-operative, the 'Union des Producteurs'. Mostly they are the owners of the smaller properties, but seven of them are in the 12 to 25 hectares category.

Street-scene, Saint-Émilion.

The cellar where the monk Aemilianus is said to have lived.

The harvest figures indicated in hectolitres from 1950 have been as follows; the figures for 1970 to 1980 also show how the total was divided between the different appellations.

Year	Total	Saint-Émilion	Saint-Émilion + Saint-Emilion Grand Cru	Saint-Émilion Grand Cru	Saint-Émilion Grand Cru Classé	Saint-Émilion Premier Grand Cru Classé
1950	203,006					
1951	120,827					
1952	129,992					
1953	213,447					
1954	124,400					
1955	187,221					
1956	20,444					
1957	47,365					
1958	103,477					
1959	97,700					
1960	138,900					
1961	74,608					
1962	221,936					
1963	81,554					
1964	234,553					
1965	143,716					
1966	147,146					
1967	193,863					
1968	74,544					
1969	113,801					
1970	293,344		243,931		39,431	9,982
1971	161,901		135,882		21,076	4,943
1972	187,828		159,967		22,696	5,165
1973	306,047		258,461		37,959	9,627
1974	270,117		225,204		35,949	8,964
1975	193,324		161,904		25,318	6,102
1976	245,883		209,438		28,425	8,020
1977	113,397	64,518		31,317	14,204	3,458
1978	213,251	112,636		67,841	26,118	6,656
1979	287,885	149,775		92,916	35,942	9,352
1980	187,051	87,458		67,759	24,317	7,517
1981	201,151	—		—	—	—
1982	290,091	—		—	—	—

In an average year, the Premiers Grands Crus Classés will produce 3% of Saint-Émilion wine, Grands Crus Classés 12%, Grands Crus 32% and Saint-Émilion AC 52%. The satellites will make together, under their different appellations, about 60% of the amount produced within the jurisdiction of Saint-Émilion, from their 3,200 hectares.

The breakdown of vineyard areas in each commune within the jurisdiction is as follows:

Libourne: 120,00 hectares
Vignonet: 330,22 hectares
St Sulpice-de-Faleyrens: 744,31 hectares
St Pey-d'Armens: 389,61 hectares

St Laurent-des-Combes: 242,21 hectares
St Étienne-de-Lisse: 405,15 hectares
St Hippolyte: 268,49 hectares
St Christophe-des-Bardes: 584,89 hectares
Saint-Émilion: 2,020,00 hectares

Classification List of Saint-Émilion (in alphabetical order)

Premiers Grands Crus Classés

A Château Ausone
   Château Cheval Blanc
B Château Beauséjour (Duffau-
     Lagarrosse)
   Château Beau-Séjour (Bécot)
   Château Belair
   Château Canon
   Clos Fourtet
   Château Figeac
   Château la Gaffelière
   Château Magdelaine
   Château Pavie
   Château Trottevieille

Grands Crus Classés

Château l'Angélus
Château l'Arrosée
Château Baleau*
Château Balestard-la-Tonnelle
Château Bellevue
Château Bergat
Château Cadet-Bon
Château Cadet-Piola
Château Canon-la-Gaffelière
Château Cap de Mourlin (Jacques Cap
   de Mourlin)
Château Capdemourlin (Jean Cap-
   demourlin)
Château Chapelle-Madeleine***
Château Chauvin
Château Corbin (Giraud)
Château Corbin-Michotte
Château Coutet
Couvent des Jacobins*
Château Croque-Michotte
Château Curé-Bon

Château Dassault*
Château Faurie-de-Souchard
Château Fonplégade
Château Fonroque
Château Franc-Mayne
Château Grand-Barrail-Lamarzelle-
   Figeac
Château Grand-Corbin-Despagne
Château Grand-Corbin
Château Grand-Mayne
Château Grand-Pontet
Château Grandes-Murailles
Château Guadet-St Julien
Château Haut Corbin*
Château Haut Sarpe*
Château Jean-Faure
Clos-des-Jacobins
Clos la Madeleine
Clos Saint-Martin
Château la Carte**
Château la Clotte
Château la Clusière
Château la Couspaude
Château la Dominique
Château Laniote*
Château Larcis-Ducasse
Château Lamarzelle
Château Larmande
Château Laroze
Château la Serre
Château la Tour-du-Pin-Figeac
   (Guiraud)
Château la Tour-du-Pin-Figeac
   (Moueix)
Château la Tour-Figeac
Château le Chatelet
Château le Couvent
Château le Prieuré

Château Matras*
Château Mauvezin
Château Moulin-du-Cadet
Clos l'Oratoire*
Château Pavie-Decesse
Château Pavie-Macquin
Château Pavillon-Cadet
Château Petit-Faurie-de-Souchard
Château Petit-Faurie-de-Soutard
Château Ripeau

Château St-Georges-Côte-Pavie
Château Sansonnet
Château Soutard
Château Tertre Daugay*
Château Trimoulet
Château les Trois-Moulins**
Château Troplong-Mondot
Château Villemaurine
Château Yon-Figeac

* These properties were added when the list was revised in November 1969.
** These properties were amalgamated with Château Beau-Séjour (Bécot) after 1978 vintage and no longer exist in their own right.
*** This property was amalgamated with Château Ausone in 1970.

Decree of November 14th, 1936

Article 1 (Modified (i) April 30th, 1974)
Only those red wines which conform with the conditions stated hereunder and are harvested on the land of the following communes have the right to use the Appellation Contrôlée St Émilion: Saint-Émilion, St Christophe-des-Bardes, St Laurent-des-Combes, St Hippolyte, St Etienne-de-Lisse, St Pey-d'Armens, Vignonet, St Sulpice-de-Faleyrens and Libourne, excepting that land which by virtue of the type of soil or its situation is not suitable for the production of wine under this appellation.

The boundaries of this production area shall be entered on the surveyor's plans of the communes in question by experts appointed by the Managing Committee of the National Institute for Appellation of Origin of Wines and Spirits and, after approval by the National Institute for Appellation of Origin, the plans thus prepared will be registered with the Town Hall of the communes in question.

(Completed D. October 7th, 1954, Article 1)

Only those red wines with the right to use the Appellation Contrôlée Saint-Émilion in the areas which have received official approval of classification by the National Institute of Appellation of Origin have the right to use the Appellations Contrôlées Saint-Émilion Premiers Grands Crus Classés, Saint-Émilion Grands Crus Classés.

The Institute will review this classification every ten years. Only those red wines who may use the Appellation Contrôlée Saint-Émilion have the right to use the Appellation Contrôlée Saint-Émilion Grand Cru.

Article 2
Only those wines made from vines of the following stock shall have the right to the Appellation Contrôlées Saint-Émilion, to the exclusion of all others; Cabernet, Bouchet, Malbec or Pressac, Merlot.

(Completed D. December 26th, 1960, Article 1)

As from the harvest of 1961, any producer of appellation contrôlée wine defined by this decree who owns plots of land containing hybrids within his property located in the area described may not claim the right to use this appellation.

Article 3
Those wines having the right to use the Appellation Contrôlée Saint-Émilion shall only be made from *must* containing 187 grammes of natural sugar per litre before any additions, and with a minimum alcoholic content of 11° after fermentation. (In 1979 this was changed to 10.0°, and the grammes of natural sugar per litre to 162.)

Article 4 (Modified February 8th, 1948)
Base-yield is fixed at 42 hectolitres per hectare of vines in production. [These provisions were completed by Decrees Nos 74.872 of October 19th, 74.958 modified of November 20th and 75.842 of September 8th.]
– classification ceiling: 20%.
– increase percentage established in Article 6 of the above main decree; 60% of annual yield for 'appellation Bordeaux'.
The young vines may only be counted in the surface-area planted, from and including the fourth year's leafing.

Article 5
Within a period of one year, proposals aimed at regulating the pruning of vines producing Appellation Contrôlée Saint-Émilion wines shall be submitted to the National Committee of Appellation of Origin by the Syndicat Viticole et Agricole de Saint-Émilion.
Pruning at 15th February, 1947:

Guyot simple	Pressac	
	Merlot	} 9 eyes max
	Cabernet Sauvignon	
	Bouchet	10 eyes max
Guyot double	Cabernet Sauvignon	
(2 branches)	Pressac	} 7 eyes max
	Merlot	
Density	Not less than 5,500 vines per hectare	

Article 6
The grapes are harvested at full maturity. Harvests showing more than 20% damaged or diseased grapes shall be screened and removed.

Vinification shall be carried out in accordance with local practice. All oenological practices allowed under current law are permitted.
(Completed D. October 7th, 1954, Article 3, then modification replaced D. May 11th, 1966, Article 1.)

Wines under Appellations Contrôlées Saint-Émilion Premiers Grands Crus Classés, Saint-Émilion Grands Crus Classés and Saint-Émilion may not be sold on the market without a certificate issued by the National Institute for Appellation of Origin of Wines and Spirits on advice of the Syndicat for these appellations. This committee will study whether the wine meets the requirement of current regulations and, in particular, of this decree. Its reasoned opinion will be passed to the interested party and to the indirect taxation authority.

An internal regulation approved by the National Institute for Appellation of Origin shall determine the procedure to be followed in issuing the certificate. (These provisions were completed by decree No. 74.871 on October 19th.)

Wines having the right to use the Appellations Contrôlées Saint-Émilion Premiers Grands Crus Classés; Saint-Émilion Grands Crus Classés, and Saint-Émilion Grand Cru may not be sold for consumption until July 1st of the year following the year of harvest.

Article 7
Those wines which, under the terms of this decree have the right to use the Appellation Contrôlée Saint-Émilion may not be declared after the harvest, offered to the public, despatched, put on sale or sold unless in the harvest declaration, in advertisements, on brochures, labels or any forms of container, the above-mentioned appellation of origin is accompanied by the words Appellation Contrôlée in very clear form.

Article 8
The use of any indication or any sign which may lead the purchaser to believe that a wine has the right to use the Appellation Contrôlée Saint-Émilion when it does not conform with all conditions required in this decree shall be prosecuted under the general laws relating to fraud and to the protection of appellation or origin. (L. August 1st, 1905, Articles 1 and 2: May 6th, 1919, Article 8; d. August 1st, 1905, Article 1 and 2; L. May 6th, 1919, Article 8; D. August 1921, Article 13), without prejudice to any kind of fiscal sanctions which may be applicable.

Union des Producteurs

This famous Co-operative was found in 1933 when many of the comparatively new properties of the plain were ill-equipped and had no cellars or satisfactory maturing space. Their products were sometimes of low quality and poorly stored and it was to help such people and to ensure that the lesser wines did not prejudice the reputation of Saint-Émilion that the Caves Co-operative was started by Robert Villepigue. Most of its early members were plain growers. Their wine was vinified by a highly-qualified oenologist, stored in healthy conditions and systematically and efficiently marketed. As a gesture of goodwill, several of the most famous properties, among them Ausone and Figeac, contributed a small part of their harvest to the newly-formed Co-operative for its first vintage. It has nearly five-hundred member-growers who together own some 1,150 hectares of vineyards of which 523.53 are under vine producing generic Saint-Émilion wines and 322.49

hectares are under vine producing Grand Cru Saint-Émilion wines. The members sell their grapes to the Co-operative which then takes over total responsibility for the making of the wine and marketing it.

They have a permanent technical advisor, M Peres, who works for them all year helping and advising the members in all aspects of viticulture. At vintage time, he assesses the grapes brought in by the members. They are never paid for the grapes they have just handed over. Payments are made quarterly and are based on the original quality assessment and always in arrears: that is, not until the wine made from the original grapes has been sold. All overheads are also deducted from the price.

There are currently (1981) five members whose properties have Grand Cru status: Châteaux Haute Nauve, Lamartre, Grangey, Destieux Berger and Berliquet. Grands Crus are, of course, determined by tasting each year. Château Berliquet hopes to acquire the status of Grand Cru Classé in 1982/3. All wines entitled to that appellation must be bottled at the Château and Château Berliquet already has its wines made and bottled at the Château by employees of the Co-operative.

There are three other wines which are entitled to Grand Cru status. All are made from the grapes of a number of good properties which are too small to operate independently. They are *Royal Saint-Émilion* (about 600 tonneaux a year) which is made entirely from properties in the plain area around St Sulpice-de-Faleyrens, and *Côtes Rocheuses* (about 1,200 tonneaux a year) from properties in the Côtes area. These two have been in production for some thirty years. The third is a new venture, started in 1978, *Haut Quercus*. It is the only Union wine, apart from Château Berliquet, which is aged in oak casks (new in 1978). Some thirty thousand numbered bottles (25 tonneaux) are made each year and the painter Michel Pourteyron, who designed the label for the 1979 vintage will do a new one for each year.

Of the remaining wine, that which is assessed as up to standard is sold as A C *Saint-Émilion*, always showing the vintage on the label. A certain amount is sold under brand-names or as 'buyer's own brands', exclusive to particular hoteliers, restaurateurs or companies.

Wine not up to this standard is sold, according to quality, as *A C Bordeaux Supérieur*, *A C Bordeaux* or *Vin de Table*.

The Co-operative is formidably well-equipped to handle a vast amount of wine annually – some 5,500 tonneaux. There are 1,100 tanks for fermentation and maturation; some cement, some stainless-steel, with an average capacity of 250 hectolitres.

The fermentation, which may take up to three weeks, is controlled at an average of 27 to 28°C and cooled if necessary by huge refrigeration units. Then there are two pressings. There is a first fining (with white-of-egg) after the malolactic fermentation and then a light second fining (with Kieselguhr) before bottling, and a final filtration through EK sheets. The Grand Cru wines are, of course, vinified separately.

In 1981 they installed a new sterile bottling-plant which can turn out six-thousand bottles an hour.

In 1980 they sold three million bottles and they have up to three million bottles at any one time maturing in their cellars. They also keep some five-thousand bottles of older vintages going back to 1943. They have a shop in the centre of the town for direct sales. Thirty-five percent of their output is sold to *négociants* in Bordeaux and the balance sold by their own salesmen throughout France.

The Co-operative is a non-profit-making organisation and once a member has signed the contract for twenty years he cannot sell his grapes to anyone else. It has a high reputation for efficiency and for the quality and integrity of its wines.

A list of growers belonging to the Union des Producteurs de Saint-Émilion may be found at the end of this book on p. 255.

Jurade of Saint-Émilion

The Jurade of Saint-Émilion dates from the time when England, through Henry II's marriage to Eleanor of Acquitaine, owned the whole of Western France. Their son Richard, 'Coeur de Lion', first granted Saint-Émilion its privileges, franchises and free customs and appointed individual Jurats to govern the province.

The oldest known document relating to the Jurade is the Charter of Falaise, issued on July 8th, 1199, by King John 'Lackland' at his castle at Falaise in Normandy. This royal charter was a reward for the citizens of Saint-Émilion for their faithful support for the English crown. It confirmed the privileges granted by his brother and predecessor on the throne of England and Acquitaine, and officially established the Jurade as a body of men of property, elected and charged by their fellow-citizens to administer the interests of the commune, in the widest sense of the word, and look after its commercial interests, which were based almost exclusively on the wine.

In 1312 Edward II increased the powers of the Jurade and defined its territorial jurisdiction, including the election of their council, magistrates and Premier Jurat to rule the legal, financial, productive and cultural life of Saint-Émilion. The only powers that they were not granted were the right to impose the death penalty and to mint money.

In return for these privileges, the English crown required regular consignments of wine from the commune, contained in casks branded with the seal of the Jurade, the town's coat-of-arms.

The duties and responsibilities of the Jurade in these times included the care of the infirm, the administration of the hospital, the imposition of taxes on the nobility and the clergy and, of course, control of the wine-trade. Their first concern was to ensure the quality of the wine. In accordance with their customs and privileges they held the brand-mark with the town's coat-of-arms, already mentioned; they officially proclaimed the '*bon des vendages*' – that is, the vintage. At racking-time they inspected the quality of the wine, visited the cellars and *chais* and inspected the casks. They ordered any wine not up to the required standard to be destroyed by fire, and dealt strictly with corruption and fraud. They also issued certificates without which no wine could be moved.

Its political and administrative powers ceased with the French Revolution in 1789, but in 1948 the Jurade was reconstituted largely thanks to the dedication and

The Jurade of Saint-Émilion.

energy of Jean Capdemourlin, who became the Premier Jurat, and Daniel Querre. Of course it no longer has its old civic powers but it takes very seriously its ancient duty of maintaining the quality of the wines of Saint-Émilion.

The council of the Jurade sits once a year in spring to conduct a blind tasting of the Premiers Grands Crus Classés and the Grands Crus Classés. It also re-enacts several of the ancient rituals including the 'ban des vendages'.

In 1979 a British Chapter of the Jurade was founded by Peter Shamash, its present Chancellor, who is one of only three men, other than vineyard owners in Saint-Émilion, who have been elected to the Grand Council of the Jurade; he is also a Chevalier de l'Ordre du Merité Agricole. Apparently, the Jurade has lost all records of British members who have been intronised over the years and Peter Shamash is anxious to hear from any such who may not know about the British Chapter. His address is No. 243, Kenton Lane, Harrow, Middlesex.

The following is a translation of the oath solemnly sworn by all Jurats before the mayor of Saint-Émilion, and his confirmation of their office:

mayor: Gentlemen, do you swear to defend faithfully the reputation of this town and its vineyards? To give it priority over your personal interests? To serve it in word and deed?

Jurats: WE DO SWEAR

mayor :	Do you swear to protect the honourable traditions of your fathers? To practise and preach respect for a man's word? To act jointly and through friendship? To commune in true faith and in respect for the wine of St Emilion? To join your efforts for the perpetuation of its glory?
Jurats :	WE DO SWEAR
mayor :	Gentlemen jurats, I confirm you in your office to defend and act to the glory of the wine of Saint-Émilion; to ensure proper observation of customs which ensure its excellence; to proclaim the vintage; to teach the skills which must be given to the vines and cellars; to carry the word, to praise and magnify the virtues of the wine of Saint-Émilion; to combat all those who by deceit or fraud may try to vilify it; to welcome as friends all those who love it and work for its prestige.

Saint-Émilion Premiers Grands Crus Classés

Château Ausone

One of the oldest properties of the area, it takes its name from the fourth-century poet, Ausonius. Tradition tells us that he had a villa here and that the Château is built on its site.

Since 1800 the property has been in the hands of one family, owned successively by Jean Cantenat, Pierre Cantenat, Mme Lafargue, Eduoard Dubois-Challon, Jean Dubois-Challon and Mme Cécile Vauthier (brother and sister). The present proprietors are Mme Jean Dubois-Challon (widow of the former) and her nephew, Alain Vauthier, who administers the estate. Madame Dubois-Challon also owns Château Belair and Château Latour de Parc. In 1970 the 0.2 hectares of the former Grand Cru Classé, Château Chappelle-Madelèine, was absorbed into the Ausone vineyard.

In the nineteenth and early twentieth centuries, Ausone probably had the highest reputation of all Saint-Émilion wines and in the 1955 Classification it was accorded, with Château Cheval Blanc, a special place of honour among the Premiers Grands Crus Classés. Since the twenties, however, its wine has not been quite so highly regarded, though there has been some improvement in the sixties and early seventies.

A new team has recently taken over the making of the wine. Pascal Delbeck became '*Régisseur*' in 1975 and M Lanau *Maître de Chai* in 1978. They have also had the benefit of advice from Jean-Claude Berrouet, the distinguished oenologist, who makes the wine of Château Pétrus and all the other J-P Moueix properties. The 1976, 1978 and 1979 wines promise to be of great distinction.

There are 8 hectares of which 7.16 hectares are under vine (50% Merlot, 50% Bouchet). Six.57 are old vines and 0.59 young vines; they produce on average 20 to 25 tonneaux at about 25 hectolitres per hectare. The oldest vines are

Château Ausone. Entrance to the cellars.

eighty years old, with an average age of forty-five years. The vineyard has near-perfect east and south-east exposure and is very steep in some parts, where a horse (currently a white one), has to be used for ploughing: 'Le Cheval Blanc de Château Ausone'! The soil is exclusively clay and limestone. After picking, which takes three to four days, the grapes go through a *fouloir-égrappoir* to be de-stalked and crushed. Fermentation, in 50-hectolitre oak vats, lasts from seven to ten days and is controlled at 28 to 29°C by refrigeration. The skins remain in contact with the *must* for fifteen to twenty-two days before pressing. Since 1981, the malolactic fermentation takes place in large, stainless-steel vats which are then covered. It occurs from fifteen days to two months after the alcoholic fermentation. The wine is then matured for eighteen months to two years in new oak casks in the ancient cellars cut into the side of the limestone hill where the temperature never varies more than a degree or two from 10°C. During the maturation period, the wine will be 'assembled' and racked six to eight times before being fined and bottled. It is then sold to *négociants* in Libourne and Bordeaux for world-wide distribution.

A second wine is produced under the name of *Château Chappelle-Madeleine*.

Château Beau-Séjour Bécot

This ancient vineyard, at the top of the plateau immediately west of Saint-Émilion, has been planted with vines since the Gallo-Roman era of the third century and, as at Belair, Soutard and elsewhere, one can still see the vine-furrows dug out of the rock in those days. In the last two-hundred and fifty years there have been a number of changes of name, and in the extent of the vineyard area.

In 1722 the property was called St Martin, presumably after the nearby church, like Château Canon, and was owned by M de Fères. In 1761 Jacques Armediède

Carles de Figeac was the proprietor. From 1775 to 1823 it was the property of Armand de Carles-Trajet and had changed its name to St Martin-Beau-Séjour. In 1823 it was purchased by M Troquart who, after extending it to 17 hectares, sold it in 1847 to his cousin, Pierre-Paulin Ducarpé. Then in 1869, the latter divided the estate and the appellation – by now simply Beau-Séjour – between his two children.

This part now, in 1869, called Beau-Séjour Ducarpé and comprising 8 hectares of vines, remained in the hands of Léopold Ducarpé, who built the Château, and his successors until 1924 when M Fagouet took it over as Beauséjour Fagouet. He was an eccentric doctor who used, in place of conventional floors in the Château, sand which had to be raked before the guests arrived. Since 1969 the present owner, M Bécot, who moved into the Château in 1971, has been in charge of the wine-making and again the name has changed to Beau-Séjour Bécot, to distinguish it from its neighbour, Beauséjour Duffau-Lagarrosse. The latest change in extent is a considerable one and rather controversial in its implications. In 1979 M Bécot, whose family has owned Château la Carte since 1931 (4.5 hectares in extent), bought Château les Trois Moulins (5 hectares). Both of these neighbouring vineyards were Grands Crus Classés, but Beau-Séjour Bécot, like the other Beauséjour, is a Premier Grand Cru Classé. From 1979 M Bécot and his sons have been making all the wine together as Château Beau-Séjour Bécot. There are no longer any such properties as Château la Carte or Château les Trois Moulins and M Bécot is claiming the entire estate, now comprising 18.5 hectares as a Premier Grand Cru Classé. This has not met with unqualified approval from the other Premiers Grands Crus Classés proprietors and it remains to be seen whether M Bécot's claim will be upheld.

Château Beau-Séjour Bécot.

The soil is clay-limestone and clay-sand with a sub-soil three parts limestone (star-fish) and one part limestone (shell-fish). There are 14.6256 hectares of vines (70% Merlot, 15% Bouchet, 15% Cabernet Sauvignon) which produce some 70 tonneaux at about 40 hectolitres per hectare. The oldest vines are ninety years old and the average age is thirty-five years.

In addition to the *cuvier* and *chai* which, together with the reception room, were built in 1975, there are 2 hectares of cellars dating back to the Middle Ages, which extend under the vineyard and the adjoining cemetery, and are used for slowly maturing previous vintages in bottle. There are 180,000 bottles stored here. The oldest vintage is 1823.

The entire process of vinification is that recommended by the renowned oenologist, Dr Emile Peynaud, Professor of Oenology at the University of Bordeaux. The grapes are completely de-stalked and the juice is then run into stainless-steel tanks and fermented for four to six days with the temperature controlled by water circulation at 28 to 32°C. The skins remain in contact with the *must* for maceration which lasts from 15 to 30 days before pressing. For the malolactic fermentation, the stainless-steel tanks are kept at a regulated temperature of 18 to 20°C. The wine is then run off into oak casks, some of them new, some of them once-used, to be matured, assembled (after about a year), racked and fined, before being bottled from eighteen months to two years after the vintage. In poorer years the wine may do all its maturation in cement tanks. Since 1980 M Bécot has produced a second wine from young vines, *Château la Carte*.

In 1982 M Bécot signed a contract giving the exclusive agency for his wines to the house of De Luze to apply retrospectively from the 1975 vintage onwards.

Château Beauséjour Héritiers Duffau-Lagarrosse

The history of this property up to the mid-nineteenth century is shared with the other Château Beau-Séjour. When in 1869 the estate and the appellation, by now simply Beau-Séjour, were divided between the two Ducarpé children, this part,

Château Beauséjour Duffau-Lagarrosse.

which included the family home, became the property of M Ducarpé's daughter, who was married to Dr Calixte Duffau-Lagarrosse, who practised in Saint-Émilion. It subsequently passed to the children and then to two of the grandchildren of Mme Duffau-Lagarrosse. It has now been made into a company in which all the shares are held by direct descendants of Pierre Paulin Ducarpé: his great-grandson, Pierre Duffau-Lagarrosse, who is in his eighties, and the children of his great-granddaughter, Mme Redaud, now deceased. Jean-Michel Ferrandez is the *Régisseur*.

There are 7 hectares of which 6.5845 hectares are under vine (55% Merlot, 20% Bouchet, 25% Cabernet Sauvignon) which usually produce 20 to 25 tonneaux at 36 to 42 hectolitres per hectare. The oldest vines are about fifty years old and average age is between ten and twenty years.

The grapes are usually completely de-stalked and lightly crushed. Fermentation, in vats, some of which are cement and some stainless-steel, is longer than most – two to three weeks – and the skins may stay in contact with the *must* for up to five weeks (longer than any property in Saint-Émilion or Pomerol), before being pressed in a hand-operated hydraulic press. The wine is run off into oak casks, of which one-third are new each year, and into cement *cuvées*.

During its maturation period of two to three years, the wine is racked from wood to cement and *vice versa*. It is assembled in the February or March following the vintage. There are six or seven rackings, one fining and sometimes a light filtration before bottling.

Sixty per cent of the wine is exported, mainly to The United States of America, Belgium, Switzerland and the Netherlands.

The wine is traditional in style; tannic in youth and very long-lasting.

Château Belair

One of the oldest properties, Château Belair, like its neighbour, Château Ausone, is said to have been part of the estate of the Roman poet Ausonius in the fourth century. Roman vine-furrows can still be seen cut in the rock of the vineyard, with a gap between rows of 1.30 metres, which is still the standard distance, although recent demands of mechanisation have made 1.50m preferable.

We know that in the fourteenth century the property was owned by Sir Robert Knolles, the English Governor of Guyenne, and then handed down through his family who remained after the end of English rule, the name changing to Canolle. The family lost the property briefly at the time of the Revolution but regained it in 1793 through François-Antoine-Joseph de Canolle de Lescours. Subsequent owners were his widow and her children, the Baron de Marignan who married a de Canolle daughter and, in 1893, his widow. In 1916 Jean Dubois-Challon acquired the property and his widow, Mme Dubois-Challon, now owns it and is also part-owner of Château Ausone.

Belair has always been among the most renowned of Saint-Émilions and the 1868 edition of Cocks et Feret places it at the top of the list and confirms this. It was one of the very few growths of the area to have an international reputation before the First World War, winning honours at exhibitions in London, Paris, Antwerp, St Louis and Brussels between 1862 and 1910. It continues to make very good wine, similar to

Château Belair.

Ausone, but is perhaps rather lighter and a little harder – that is, slower to mature.

There are 13 hectares, of which 11.4 hectares are under vine (45% Merlot, 50% Bouchet, 5% Cabernet Sauvignon) which produce an average of 36 tonneaux at about 25 hectolitres per hectare. As with Ausone, there are many very old vines and regular replanting is necessary. The oldest vines are eighty years old and the average age is forty to forty-five years. The two vineyards are worked together and have the same *Régisseur* and *Maître de Chai*.

The wine has for many years been made in the cellars of Ausone but since 1976 they have been using their own deep chalk cellars once again. The methods are exactly the same except that for each vintage a third of the casks for maturation are new, a third have been used for one vintage, of Ausone, and a third are three to five years old. Ausone uses new casks each year. A second wine, made from young vines, is made and sold under the name *Château Roc Blanquant*.

Château Canon

This famous estate with its walled vineyard lies immediately to the south-west of the town, on the limestone plateau just above Ausone and behind the old church of St Martin. Immediately below the estate are the caves where the Girondins hid at the time of the Revolution.

Until 1857 it was called 'Le Domaine de St Martin' after the church and its name was then changed to Canon in memory of a former proprietor. In fact M Kanon had founded the estate in the eighteenth century before selling it in 1770 to Raymond Fontemoing, a leading wine-merchant in Libourne at the time. His grandson, Jules Howyne de Tranchère, sold the property in 1857 to the Comte de Bonneval from whom it passed in 1883 to M Domecq-Cazaux. Monsieur Guignard acquired it in 1891 and in 1919 it passed into the hands of the Fournier family, the present owners.

Eric Fournier has been the director since 1972, when he took over from his grandmother, Mme A. Fournier, who still takes a lively interest in the wine-making. Paul Cazenave has been *Maître de Chai* since 1967 (he is also *Maître de Chai* at Château Haut-Sarpe) and M Geremie *Chef de Culture* since 1979. Monsieur Fournier told us that in the eighteenth century Canon had a vineyard of 14 hectares and that its wines were exported by merchants in Libourne to the Low Countries, Flanders and Brittany. Since the nineteenth century Canon has consistently been among the best properties of the area.

There are 20 hectares of which 16.9761 hectares are under vine (53% Merlot, 40% Bouchet, 4.7% Cabernet Sauvignon and 2.3% Pressac) which produce on average 70 tonneaux at around 35 hectolitres per hectare. The oldest vines are sixty years old. The grapes are completely de-stalked before being lightly crushed in an Amos *fouloir*. The *must* is fermented in oak vats, of which eleven new ones were installed in 1980, at a cost of 22,000 francs each. Fermentation lasts from four to six days and the skins are left in contact for ten to fifteen days before the pressing in vertical hydraulic presses. The temperature is regulated by refrigeration. After the malolactic fermentation the wine is run off, two-thirds into new oak casks and one-third into once-used casks. Thereafter it is matured, racked (six times), assembled (usually in the September following the vintage) and fined once, during the second year, before being bottled after about twenty-two months. The wine is bottled by contract with a mobile bottling plant.

The family also owns Château Broustet in Barsac and Mme Fournier, grandmother of Eric Fournier, told us that she remembers the 1900 vintage at Broustet when seventy women picked the 14 hectares grape by grape, and woe betide anyone who had a drop of juice at the bottom of her basket as that would mean she had picked a grape insufficiently shrivelled by *pourriture noble*!

Château Canon.

Château Cheval Blanc

The most famous of all the Saint-Émilion estates is almost in Pomerol. It is at the extreme north-western tip of Saint-Émilion and its vineyards actually border on those of Châteaux la Conseillante and l'Évangile.

Although this property was still a part of the Figeac estate until 1832 and, until the end of the century, was perhaps less widely-known than its neighbour and several of the top Côtes Saint-Émilion Châteaux, it has certainly established itself as the finest of the Saint-Émilions over the last sixty years or so.

The building and 16 hectares of the Figeac estate were detached and sold off to M Ducasse in 1832 and he decided to plant a vineyard and build a *chai*. The wine was called *Vin de Figeac* until 1854 when his son-in-law M Fourcaud-Laussac decided upon the name 'Cheval Blanc' taken appropriately from the name of a meadow on the estate; it is said to be derived from an ancient post-house which once stood there, where King Henri IV (Henry of Navarre) stopped to change his horses which were always white. The Inn was called Cheval Blanc in honour of these horses.

The buildings are about three-hundred years old but the neat, cream-coloured house was largely re-built in about 1890. The Fourcaud-Laussac family has owned Cheval Blanc since 1852, when M Fourcaud-Laussac married the daughter of the previous owner, M Ducasse. The descendants of the Fourcaud-Laussac family are the present owners and Jacques Hebrard has been manager and co-proprietor since 1970. He is also President of the Syndicat Viticole et Agricole de Saint-Émilion. His wife is the last member of the Fourcaud-Laussac family. Monsieur Hebrard and his wife are the first proprietors to live in the Château. Their predecessor lived in Libourne, next to the *chai* where wine was bottled until 1973.

As at Figeac, and unlike the other properties of what has so often been called 'Graves' Saint-Émilion, gravel really does predominate here over sandy soil – there are 25 hectares of gravel – but there is a complex mixture. There are heavy soils on clay, light soils on a combination of gravel and clay, and stony soils on sandstone with traces of iron. Doubtless this helps to account for the rich, almost voluptuous character of the wine in good years.

Monsieur Gaston Vaissière has been *Maître de Chai* for forty years and Guy Haurut *Chef de Culture* for sixteen years.

The estate comprises 42 hectares of which there are 35.11 hectares of vines (33% Merlot, 66% Bouchet, 1% Pressac) producing an average of 110 tonneaux at around 32 hectolitres per hectare. Naturally, the yield varies widely according to the year. In 1979 it was 46 hectolitres per hectare, in 1977 it was a mere 7 hectolitres. The oldest vines are seventy-five years old and the average age is thirty-seven years.

The grapes are completely de-stalked and crushed. Fermentation lasts a mere three to four days in cement vats with the temperature controlled by refrigeration. The skins remain in contact with the *must* for eighteen to twenty-four days before pressing, and after the malolactic fermentation the wine is run off into new oak casks (380 in 1978, 540 in 1979 and 320 in 1980). This is an expensive business as the price of a new cask has risen from 170 francs in 1971 to 1,200 francs in 1980. Occasionally, in light years, two-year-old casks may be used. The wine is then matured, assembled, racked and fined in the usual way, before being bottled after

Rear view of Château Cheval Blanc.

Picking the grapes at Château Cheval Blanc.

about two years. In 1980 the wine was sold to Bordeaux *négociants* at 60,000 francs a tonneau.

The rather small vat-house dates from 1964. In 1973 a new *chai* and reception area were added and the bottling has been done there since 1974. Previously the wine had been bottled in Libourne. This was the last of the Premiers Grands Crus Classés Châteaux to sell a part of its wine in casks. The practice was discontinued in 1969.

Like its neighbours in the rather flat area of Graves Saint-Émilion and Pomerol, Cheval Blanc was devastated by the terrible frost of February 1956, when the temperature fell to $-24°C$. Many vines were killed – though some which were thought to have died subsequently recovered – and a single cask of wine was made in that year.

The wine seems to combine the best qualities of the Côtes Saint-Émilions with the depth and intensity of flavour of the neighbouring Pomerols. Alexis Lichine has described the wine as 'one-third Pomerol, one-third Graves and one-third Saint-Émilion'. It reaches 12 to 12.5% alcohol on average but the 1976 vintage was 13.6%. Monsieur Hebrard rates the 1975 as the best vintage of the decade and the 1947 best of all the post-war vintages.

The wine is sold through five leading houses: J-P Moueix, Calvet, Delor, Cruse and Horeau-Beylot. The main markets outside France are Great Britain, Belgium, Scandinavia, The Netherlands, The United States of America and Japan.

Château Figeac

This property has, after its neighbour, Château Cheval Blanc, the greatest reputation of the group of Saint-Émilion growths near the Pomerol border. There was a Roman villa and vineyard here in the fourth century and later a medieval Château which belonged in 1450 to the Decazes family. The Château was burned down by the Huguenots in 1590 and re-built in the Renaissance style five years later. In 1654 Marie Decazes de Figeac married François de Carles whose family held the property until 1835 and also owned Château Beau-Séjour for some time. In 1780 the central part of the house was demolished and re-built with a courtyard in the style of the late eighteenth century. In 1832 Château Cheval Blanc had become an independent property (though not yet under that name), but Figeac was still a big estate and included all thirteen of the neighbouring vineyards which still have Figeac as part of their name.

In the middle of the nineteenth century the property changed hands a number of times and various parcels of land were sold off. In 1868 M Loyer was the proprietor and some years later M Lavene, the son of the former owner of the other Figeac property, bought the main estate. The next two owners were M Fournier (no relation to the Fourniers of Château Canon) and M de Chèvrement who was married to an English lady, Elizabeth Drake.

In 1875 another piece of the estate was sold to M Corbière who sold half of it to M Marrais. Monsieur Corbière's plot was called La Tour-Figeac and M Marrais' La Tour-du-Pin-Figeac; the latter has since been divided again. In 1892 M de Chèvrement bequeathed it to his daughter and her husband M André Villepigue

Château Figeac.

and later it passed to Antoine Manoncourt and his wife, a daughter of the Villepigue family. Since 1947 their son, Thierry Manoncourt and his wife have lived in the Château, which had been left empty for some fifty years before that. The estate was run from Paris and the house used only as a holiday home. It is a large three-storey mansion, somewhat Georgian in appearance, mostly built as we have seen in 1780, though some parts of the Renaissance building remain. It has two wings, a gravel courtyard and is set in a park; an avenue of fine trees leads up to it. This majestic setting is in marked contrast to the average Saint-Émilion property.

In the eighteenth century, the estate was much larger than the present 52 hectares and included the whole of what is now Château Cheval Blanc. In the mid-nineteenth century, when both began to gain an international reputation, Figeac was the more highly regarded. Towards the end of the century there were several changes of ownership and for a time the reputation of the wine declined somewhat. However, there were some outstanding inter-war vintages and over the last thirty-three years, in which M Manoncourt has been personally involved with the making of the wine, Figeac has been generally accepted as one of the greatest of the Saint-Émilions. He has held the office of Premier Jurat in the Jurade of Saint-Émilion for over fifteen years. Monsieur Clément Brochard has been *Maître de Chai* since 1953.

There are 52 hectares of which 33.9143 (3 hectares of young vines) are under vine planted with 30% Merlot, 35% Bouchet and 35% Cabernet Sauvignon – an unusually high proportion – though, as M Manoncourt emphasises, Merlot being a rather bigger producer than the other two, the approximate percentages in the finished wine are 40 : 32 : 28. The oldest vines are about eighty years old and there is regular grubbing up of old vines and planting of young ones – about half a hectare a year. They produce 120 to 150 tonneaux on average at around 28 hectolitres per hectare. Monsieur Manoncourt sows grass between the rows of his wines and uses the minimum possible treatment against pests and disease. In the terrible frost of February, 1956, 11 hectares of vines were killed and only one and a half casks of wine were made that year.

The soil here is unusually gravelly, with volcanic quartz pebbles. Monsieur Manoncourt explains that Figeac is the southern extreme of a kind of ridge of concentrated gravel soil, three little hills of which are on his estate, and two on that of Cheval Blanc. The ridge continues running roughly north through Vieux-Château-Certan in Pomerol and Pétrus where, however, the top-soil is almost entirely clay. The difference between Figeac and its neighbours (other than Cheval Blanc), M Manoncourt claims, is that whereas his soil is two-thirds gravel to one of sand, the proportion of sand in theirs is considerably higher than that of gravel. The sub-soil is flinty with traces of iron, similar to the sub-soil in many parts of Pomerol.

The thick siliceous layer of this 'Graves' plateau was mainly brought down from the Massif Central by the Isle, the small river that separates Fronsac from Saint-Émilion and Pomerol. In those days, the confluence of the Isle and the Dordogne, now at Libourne, was at Figeac.

The grapes are completely de-stalked and crushed and the *must* is transferred by a very slow traditional Italian-made pump to the fermenting vats, ten of which are oak (one-hundred years old) and ten stainless-steel. These were installed in 1972 in a very modern and well-equipped first and second year *chai* and were among the first in the area. At the same time a very impressive underground storage cellar was added. There are 500 casks in the *chai* and the oldest vintage in the bottle cellar is 1893. All the wine has been château-bottled since 1960.

Fermentation lasts from five to fifteen days during which time the skins remain in the *must*. Pressing follows in two old vertical hydraulic presses made in about 1900. Then after the malolactic fermentation, which usually occurs towards the end of the main fermentation, or a few days later, the wine is run off into oak casks at least 80% of which are new each year. The wine is assembled in the December, January or February following the vintage and matured for eighteen months to two years before being bottled after the usual rackings and fining. The wine is sold by brokers in Bordeaux to merchants and usually costs rather less than second growth Médocs and about the same as Châteaux Vieux-Château-Certan, la Conseillante and l'Évangile in Pomerol. A second wine, *Château de Grangeneuve*, is made from the young vines.

The wine is very fine and rich, in some ways comparable to Cheval Blanc in that it has some of the character of Pomerol as well as Saint-Émilion. The high proportion of Cabernet Sauvignon, however (35% as against none in Cheval Blanc), gives it more firmness and backbone. It is certainly much closer to its famous neighbour in quality than the difference in price would suggest.

Clos Fourtet

This property lies just at the north-eastern edge of the town and its main gateway opens almost into the Place de l'Église. It has perhaps the most spectacular underground cellars in the area. They extend over 12 hectares, right under the town

Clos Fourtet.

on three levels. The lowest is unused and contains an underground lake, the middle one is used for the cultivation of mushrooms and the top one for the maturation of the wines in bottle. Some years ago 600 bottles of the 1967 vintage were stolen by intruders who managed to find a way into the cellars through a pot-hole.

Monsieur Leperche owned the estate in the 1890's and thereafter it belonged to Pierre Ginestet for many years before he sold it just after the last War to François Lurton. It now belongs to his children and is therefore a family company consisting of André (who is the director), Lucien, Dominique and Simone. Lucien also owns Châteaux Brane Cantenac and Durfort-Vivens (Médoc), Bouscaut (Graves) and Climens (Barsac); André owns Châteaux la Louvière, Clos du Roy (Graves), Bonnet (Entre-deux-Mers); Dominique owns Châteaux Reynier and Martouret (Entre-deux-Mers). Dominique's son, Pierre, lives at Clos Fourtet with his wife and administers the property. It had a considerable reputation in the nineteenth century and has always been one of the leading Saint-Émilion wines, though it has perhaps not quite lived up to its reputation since the last War. From the early 1970's there have been various improvements made in the *cuvier* and the policy is now to make wines which mature rather earlier. The 1978 and 1979 vintages are very promising.

There are 19 hectares of which 14.4537 are under vine, 1 hectare being replanted at present (55% Merlot, 23% Bouchet, 22% Cabernet Sauvignon). Production varies from 21 tonneaux (in 1977 – a very sparse year) to 45 in 1975, 1976 and 1978 right up to 75 in 1979. In favourable conditions the average yield is about 38 hectolitres per hectare. The oldest vines are eighty years old and the average age is thirty years. A replanting programme was started in the late 1970's.

The grapes are completely de-stalked and crushed in a *fouloir-égrappoir*. Fermentation, in epoxy-lined stainless-steel vats, replacing the old oak ones, takes from seven to fourteen days, before pressing in a vertical hydraulic press which has been in use since 1900. The temperature is controlled by cold-water circulation. The skins are left in contact with the *must* for fourteen days and after four weeks the wine is run off into casks, one-third new, one-third two years old and one-third four years old. In light years however, like 1977 and 1980, no new casks are used. It is then matured, assembled (five months after fermentation), racked and fined, before being bottled by a mobile bottling plant about two years after the vintage.

Château la Gaffelière

This ancient estate takes its name from a leper colony (gaffet) which once occupied the site and has been the property of the family of the present owner, Comte Léo de Malet Roquefort, for several centuries. The Comte, who succeeded to the estate on the death of his father in 1958, told us that his is the most ancient family still living in the area. Parts of the attractive Château, which lies on the D.122 road, just to the south of the town below Ausone, Bélair and Magdelaine, date back to the thirteenth century. It was restored in the nineteenth century while the wings were re-built in the seventeenth and eighteenth centuries. There are beautiful gardens in which one of the features is a Lebanese cedar over three-hundred years old.

In 1906, the family purchased the neighbouring estate of Château Naudes and the property became known as la Gaffelière-Naudes. In 1955, the Naudes estate was sold and in 1964 the suffix was dropped from the title. The Comte is a 'Marquillier' (Warden) of the Jurade de Saint-Émilion and has also owned Châteaux Tertre-Daugay (Grand Cru Classé) and de Roquefort (Grand Cru) since 1978 and 1965 respectively.

With its south-facing slopes and typical limestone and clay soil of the Côtes, Château la Gaffelière has consistently produced wine of fine quality. Lucien Julien has been *Régisseur* since 1944 and Jean Marie Galer has been *Maître de Chai* since 1978.

The estate comprises 25 hectares, 17.46 under vine (65% Merlot, 25% Bouchet, 10% Cabernet Sauvignon, although there are plans to replace the latter with more Bouchet). These produce some 90 tonneaux at about 35 hectolitres per hectare. The

Château la Gaffelière.

oldest vines are seventy years old with an average age of thirty-five years. A vintaging-machine was used for the first time on part of the 1981 vintage and the wine made from this part of the vineyard is being vinified separately.

The grapes are completely de-stalked and crushed and the fermentation takes place in twelve stainless-steel vats installed in 1974. This lasts from fifteen to twenty days with the temperature regulated between 26 and 29°C and the skins remain in contact with the *must* for twelve days before pressing. After the malolactic fermentation, the wine is transferred to oak casks, one-third new each year, for maturation. There are 450 casks in the *chai*. There are the usual rackings and one fining before bottling after two years, but in light years (as in 1973) only three eggs per cask are used in the fining instead of the usual four and in years of very exceptional extract (as in 1961), there may be two finings. The bottling has only been done at the Château since 1965. A second wine, *Moulin du Biguey*, is produced from the young vines.

Château Magdelaine

This estate was for well over two-hundred years the property of the Chatonnet family. Monsieur M G Jullien, a notary in Saint-Émilion and son-in-law of the late Jean Chatonnet, was the proprietor in the late nineteenth and early twentieth centuries and his son, M J Jullien succeeded him. Average production was about 20 tonneaux and from about 1933 the wine was sold exclusively through the firms of Eschenauer in Bordeaux and Beylot in Libourne.

Château Magdelaine.

In 1952 the well-known firm of Jean-Pierre Moueix bought the property and much of the 10.5 hectare vineyard was replanted. The house has not been lived-in since then. It is admirably sited, west–south-west of the town, close to Ausone and Bélair, with rather more than half of its 10.0656 hectares of vines on the limestone plateau and the rest on the limestone and clay 'Côtes'.

Michel Gillet has been *Régisseur* since 1977 and Jean Veysierre *Maître de Chai* since 1967. The distinguished oenologist, Jean-Claude Berrouet, is responsible for the wine-making and all of these three work on all the J-P Moueix properties.

Eighty per cent of the vines are Merlot and 20% Bouchet. The oldest vines are eighty years old and the average age thirty-seven years. Production is 45 to 50 tonneaux at about 40 hectolitres per hectare. The grapes at Magdelaine are among the last to be picked of the eleven J-P Moueix properties in Saint-Émilion and Pomerol. Only Pétrus is picked later. They are usually de-stalked, though in years when the wine would otherwise be too light, 20% of the stalks may be left on.

Fermentation, which is water-cooled in cement tanks, takes four to six days and the skins remain in the *must* for two to three weeks (varying according to the year) before pressing. The wine is then run off into casks, a third of which are new and two-thirds of which are two years old – products of the company's own Cooperage. After two months the wine is racked again and assembled. Thereafter it is racked every three months and fined once, before being bottled after twenty to twenty-two months. Hitherto, the wine was bottled in Libourne, but from the 1979 vintage it has been bottled at the Château.

Since the early sixties the property has been making very fine wine with great character, finesse and depth which develops and lasts very well in bottle. The United States of America, Belgium and Great Britain are among the leading foreign markets.

Château Pavie

This is the largest of the Premiers Grands Crus Classés of Saint-Émilion, some 41 hectares, and covers most of the hill of Pavie. Like nearby Ausone, it was a Roman vineyard in the fourth century. In the late nineteenth century and up to about 1920 it was owned by Ferdinand Bouffard of Bordeaux who maintained the already considerable reputation of the wine. Monsieur Porte then acquired the property and it was purchased in 1943 by the Valette family, the present owners. Jean Paul Valette has been the Director since May 1st, 1967, and is also the President of the Syndicate of Premiers Grands Crus Classés. Gabrile Establet has been *Chef de Culture* since 1965 and Pierre Rabeau *Maître de Chai* since 1967. The Valette family also own the Grands Crus Classés Châteaux Pavie-Décesse and la Clusière.

Between the Wars the quality of the wine seemed to fall off a little but in the last thirty years or so it has made very fine wine.

There are 41 hectares of which 35 including 2 hectares of young vines are under vine, 8 on the limestone plateau at the top of the hill, 22 on the south-facing limestone rock of the hillside and 7 at the bottom where the soil is more gravelly. The *cépages* are 55% Merlot, 25% Bouchet, 20% Cabernet Sauvignon and average production is some 130 tonneaux at about 32 hectolitres per hectare. The oldest vines are one hundred and nine years old and the average age is thirty-seven years.

Château Pavie.

There is about 1 hectare of very old vines which give only about 15 hectolitres but of very fine-quality wine. Monsieur Valette has devised a sixty-year replanting scheme, with the aim of achieving and maintaining an average vine age of thirty years.

The grapes are completely de-stalked by an Amos *égrappoir* before being lightly crushed. The *must* is run off into epoxy-lined cement vats for fermentation which lasts for eight to ten days and the skins are left in for a further ten days. Pressing then takes place in a new horizontal electrically-programmed press of Spanish make. After the malolactic fermentation, the wine is run off into casks, one-third of which are new each year. Thereafter, it is racked, fined and matured in the usual way before being bottled, usually after about twenty-two months. All the wine has been Château-bottled since 1969. The large cellars cover 3,000 square metres and hold 1,100 casks in which the wine is matured. They are of Roman origin, quarries dug out of the rock below the vineyard, and in some places one can actually see the roots of the vines 8 metres above one's head. Over the centuries, rainwater caused a gradual erosion of the limestone rock and in 1974, a very wet year, part of the roof fell in and many casks of the 1973 vintage were destroyed.

The wine of another Valette property, the neighbouring Château la Clusière, is also made and matured here.

Château Trottevieille

This old property is said to take its name from an old serving-woman who worked at an inn which once stood on this site and who was famous for the speed with which she brought the customers their food and drink. The name means 'the old lady who rushes about'.

It is unique among the Premiers Grands Crus Classés in two ways. First it is on its own, away from the others, on high land about 1 kilometre to the east of the town; and its top-soil is rather different – redder – with seams of fine pebbles. Secondly it is the only one of the Premiers Grands Crus Classés to be owned by a big firm based outside the Libourne region. It was purchased in 1950 by the house of Borie-Manoux from the heirs of Jean Gibaud who had owned it since the eighteenth century. Since the death of Marcel Borie, the estate has been managed by his son-in-law, Emile Casteja, now assisted by his own son, Philippe. The firm also owns and manages a number of other well-known properties including Châteaux Bergat (Saint-Émilion Grand Cru Classé), Batailley, Beausite and Haut Bages Monpelou in the Médoc and Domaine de l'Eglise in Pomerol.

Jean Brun has been *Maître de Chai* here since 1939. He also holds this office at Châteaux Croque-Michot, Grandes Murailles, Bergat and several others.

There are 10 hectares of which 7.4395 are under vine (60% Merlot, 30% Bouchet, 10% Cabernet Sauvignon) producing 40 to 45 tonneaux at about 40 hectolitres per hectare, and some of the vines are over one-hundred years old.

The grapes are 60 to 80% de-stalked by a Coq *fouloir-égrappoir* and crushed. The *must* is fermented in cement vats for about fifteen days, the skins remaining in contact for all that time. They are then pressed in a forty-year-old Coq vertical hydraulic press. The temperature is regulated at 25 to 32°C by water-circulation. After the malolactic fermentation the wine is racked off into new or once-used

Château Trottevieille.

casks, but it is first filtered, a most unusual procedure, thereby reducing the number of rackings necessary by about half. Thereafter the wine is assembled, racked twice or three times only and fined in the usual way before being bottled after two years and distributed by the house of Borie-Manoux in Bordeaux.

The wine of Trottevieille has been among the most highly-regarded Saint-Émilions since the area acquired an international reputation in the nineteenth century, but we feel that in recent years it has been rather light-weight in style.

The main markets outside France are The United States of America, Belgium, Great Britain and The Netherlands.

Saint-Émilion Grands Crus Classés

Château l'Angélus

This is the property of the de Boüard Frères and in 1909, M de Boüard's father inherited Château Mazerat from his aunt. It was one of several properties in the neighbourhood including Châteaux Jean Dumaine and d'Argay.

In 1924 the Gurchy family sold the whole area known as l'Angélus to the du Boüard family who grouped all these properties together. All the other names except Château Mazerat disappeared and the rest of the property then became known as Château l'Angélus. In the 1940's the vineyard area of Château Mazerat was amalgamated with Château l'Angélus. Monsieur de Boüard's mother lived in the very attractive Château (Mazerat) until her death in 1981. Monsieur de Boüard manages the property with the assistance of his son who is an oenologist and is responsible for the vinification. There is a *chai* and cellar, but no house.

The property covers 27 hectares of which 24.3551 are under vine planted with 40% Merlot and 60% Bouchet. Since the former produces more juice, the resulting wine generally reflects an equal proportion of the two types. The yield is approximately 40 hectolitres per hectare and production varies between 130 and 150 tonneaux per annum.

The de Boüard family still use traditional methods of viticulture although they feel that mechanisation must come. The wine is fermented in concrete vats and has been matured in new oak casks since 1980. Prior to that time the wine was matured in the concrete vats and no casks were used. The cellars are very large and modern and can hold up to 4 to 5 harvests. The major modernisation programme started in 1963 is now in its final stages.

The soil on this site on the southern slopes of Saint-Émilion is clay, limestone and sand, with the same aspect as Châteaux Ausone and la Gaffelière. The land on which Angélus stands is part of the former hamlet, now simply an area, known as Mazerat.

Château l'Arrosée

Madame Rodhain became the owner of this attractive property in 1979. It is now a company, GFA du Château l'Arrosée, and it is managed by her son, François Rodhain. It has been in the family since 1910.

Nine of the 16 hectares, situated on the southern face of the Saint-Émilion slopes, are planted with vines of Merlot (45%), Cabernet Sauvignon (40%) and Bouchet (15%) on a varied soil of predominately chalk. They produce approximately 35 hectolitres per hectare. A second wine is produced and sold to the Co-operative.

Monsieur Oizeau has been *Maître de Chai* since 1971. The methods of vinification are traditional. Château l'Arrosée wines are bottled on the premises, using the equipment and facilities of the Château.

In the nineteenth century the property belonged to Pierre Magne, a Minister of Napoleon III. It was inherited by his daughter, the Marquise Riverseaux de Rouvray whose husband was Ambassador to Vienna. It is said that in 1867 to 68 the Emperor Napoléon III came to the area and, having heard of Château l'Arrosée, stayed the night at the property when obliged to break his journey.

Château Balestard-la-Tonnelle

This ancient property takes its name from Balestard, a Canon of the Chapter of Saint-Émilion, and la Tonnelle from a very old tower which still stands in the vineyard. It used to be a look-out tower at an intersection of the road from Haut-Sarpe to Saint-Émilion and is now a reception and tasting-room. The fifteenth-century poet, François Villon (1421–1485), wrote a poem which is printed on the wine-label about 'this divine nectar which bears the name of Balestard'.

Its present owner, Jacques Capdemourlin, also owns Châteaux Capdemourlin and Roudier, the original family property in Montagne. The family have been in the area for five centuries. Monsieur Capdemourlin's grandfather bought the property in the 1920 from M A du Courrech de Raquine who purchased it from Bertauts Couture.

The soil is clay and limestone on this 11.5 hectare estate (65% Merlot, 20% Bouchet, 12% Cabernet Sauvignon, 3% Pressac). The oldest vines are seventy-eight years old and the average age is about thirty years. They produce some 49 tonneaux at an average of 42 hectolitres per hectare. A programme of replanting was started three years ago. This property has a reputation for producing consistently fine wine.

The grapes are completely de-stalked and fermentation lasts for about fifteen days with the temperature controlled by *remontage*. Pressing takes place in a hydraulic press and after the malolactic fermentation, which takes place in cement vats, the wine is run off into oak casks, some new, some up to five years old. It is racked several times before and after the *assemblage* in the spring following the vintage, fined once with egg-whites and bottled after about two years. The chief markets outside France are Belgium, Switzerland, The Netherlands and West Germany.

Château Bellevue

This Château, originally called 'Fief de Bellevue', shares the ancient history of the oldest Saint-Émilion properties whose vineyards were hewn out of the rocks at the same time as Ausone, and Soutard. Its more recent history is also colourful as at the time of the Revolution it was the refuge for Girondin leader Gaston Lacaze who was finally returned to Paris and guillotined.

The Lacaze family and their descendants were the owners from 1642 until 1938 and today the property operates as the Société Civile du Château Bellevue. The owners who inherited it from M Horeau were the three Horeau sisters; L Horeau, Mme de Lavaux and Mme de Coninck, until the wife of René de Coninck died recently. The property is now managed by M René and his son Jean de Coninck who also own Château Pavillon Figeac.

The 10 hectare property, high over the Dordogne valley, includes varied lands of which 4.7125 hectares are under vine planted with 70% Merlot, 15% Bouchet and 15% Cabernet Sauvignon. The annual production is approximately 300 tonneaux with an average yield of approximately 40 hectolitres per hectare.

Monsieur de Coninck has an open mind about the effect of mechanical harvesting on the wine; he feels sure that it will be used extensively in the area in the near future. He has purchased a machine but it is not yet in full use.

The vinification methods at Bellevue are typical of the region. The grapes are completely de-stalked and the wine is fermented in cement vats and matured in oak casks. As in neighbouring Ausone, the casks are stored in ancient rock-hewn cellars where it slowly matures.

Bellevue operates a mobile bottling unit which it hires out to other properties – and also uses it for its own wines.

Château Bergat

This Château on the plateau just to the east of the town, has been in the Bertin family for three generations. Most recently it was owned by Colonel J-A Bertin and for many years operated by Heritiers Borie-Manoux, with Emile Casteja as Manager. Today it is owned by Colonel Bertin's daughter, Mme Clause Bertin, and managed by Philippe Casteja, son of Emile.

There are 3.0646 hectares of vineyards, planted with 50% Merlot, 25% Bouchet and 25% Cabernet Sauvignon. The property produces an average of 12 to 15 tonneaux per annum.

The *Maître de Chai* is Jean Brun, who started work in the cellars at Château Trottevieille, another Borie-Manoux property, in 1939, at the age of 16 years.

The method of production is the same as at Château Trottevieille.

In one corner of the vineyard beside the road from Ausone to Trottevieille, covering about 1 hectare, an area has been identified at the foot of the cliffs which was a pre-historic Magdelenian site. In what appear to be recesses at the base of the rock, hearths have been uncovered and fire-sites which may be of the Upper-Paleolithic period.

Château Cadet-Bon

This Château situated just north of the town of Saint-Émilion on one of the highest slopes is owner-operated by M F Gratadour, who manages and markets the production of his wine himself. The estate was originally owned by Justin Bon and passed through various hands to the Gratadour family.

The vineyard, dominated by its old and picturesque mill dating back to 1744, can easily be seen from the Palais du Cardinal. The property covers 4 hectares of which 2.5 are under vine planted with 65% Merlot and 35% Bouchet. The yield from this vineyard varies between 5 to 25 tonneaux, but the average production is approximately 16 tonneaux per annum. Viticulture is still very traditional. Monsieur Gratadour is anxious not to introduce mechanised harvesting.

Monsieur Couvert, the *Maître de Chai* and manager of the vineyards, is in charge of the vinification processes which are generally traditional and the bottling which is carried out using Cadet-Bon's own equipment and resources.

Château Cadet-Piola

This is one of the oldest walled properties of the region set upon a hill with a lovely view of Saint-Émilion. The vines grow on a thin layer of arable soil over a sub-soil on deep rock in which medieval cellars were hollowed out and today house wines both in bottle and cask.

In the late nineteenth century, M Piola, the then owner of Le Cadet, is said to have brought in and planted vines imported from Romanée Conti. He was renowned for his means of fighting *phylloxera* 'by judicious use of the sulphur of carbon and by the grafting of the fine plants of the country with resistant American roots' (Cocks et Ferret 1883). Ownership passed to Robert Villepigue in the first part of this century; he was President and founder of the Cave Cooperative of Saint-Émilion and published an important paper on the soil of the area.

Today Cadet-Piola is owned by Maurice Jabiol and his son Alain manages this, his other Grand Cru Classé property Faurie-de-Souchard and Domaine de Pasquetter. Monsieur Guillou has been the *Maître de Chai* for thirty-five years.

The vines cover 7 hectares and with a yield of 30 hectolitres per hectare they produce approximately 35,000 bottles per annum. The vineyard is planted with 51% Merlot, 28% Cabernet Sauvignon, 18% Bouchet and 3% Pressac.

The viticulture and vinification are generally traditional.

Château Canon-la Gaffelière

This is one of the oldest Châteaux of the region and is situated on the main road entering Saint-Émilion at the bottom of the south-facing slopes.

Its reputation reached its current high level approximately one hundred and fifty years ago when it was owned by Boitard de la Poterie, and called 'Canon-Boitard'.

It was later owned by the Peyraud family who in turn sold it to the present owner, Le Comte de Neippièere, in 1971. The current management has instigated major modifications in recent years. The wine is matured in oak casks, fermentation carried out in stainless-steel vats and bottling is done at the Château using its own equipment. The manager, Michel Boutet, also manages Châteaux la Tour-Figeac and l'Oratoire, both also Grands Crus Classés, and Château Peyreau where he lives. He also has his own vineyard, Château Haut-Plantey, Saint-Émilion Grand Cru.

Canon-la Gaffelière covers 19.05 hectares of vineyard and is planted with 60% Merlot, 32% Bouchet and 8% Cabernet Sauvignon which produce 100 tonneaux per annum at an average of 50 hectolitres per hectare. There is also a plot covering 4.16 hectares of Grand Cru, producing wine under the name of *Château la Mondotte*.

Château Cap de Mourlin (Jacques Cap de Mourlin)
Château Capdemourlin (Jean Capdemourlin)

This attractive estate which lies on the northern slopes of Saint-Émilion has been in the hands of the Capdemourlin family for more than five hundred years and the family name has replaced its old name of Artugon. There are, in fact, two separate vineyards; one of 9.40 hectares and the other, 9.3914. The present owners are Mme Madeleine, the widow of Jean Capdemourlin, and her nephew, Jacques Cap de Mourlin. The two properties are worked and harvested separately but by the same small team and the wines are vinified separately although the proportion of the grape varieties and the methods of vinification are the same. The labels are identical except for the Christian names; one is labelled Jean Capdemourlin, the other, Jacques Cap de Mourlin. Both properties produce a second wine: *Jean Château Mayne d'Artugon* and *Jacques la Rose Faurie*. The late Jean Capdemourlin was President of the Syndicat Viticole de Saint-Émilion and the Federation des Grands Vins de Bordeaux and was instrumental – with Daniel Querre, late owner of Château Monbusquet – in reconstituting the Jurade de Saint-Émilion in 1948; he was Premier Jurat of the revised Jurade. The *Maître de Chai* is Bernard Oizeau, who also makes the wine of several other properties.

There are 19 hectares planted with two-thirds Merlot and one third Bouchet producing some 75 tonneaux at about 40 hectolitres per hectare. The oldest vines are forty-five years old.

The grapes are completely de-stalked and fermentation takes place in cement vats and lasts about two weeks. The skins remain in the *must* for this period and the temperature is controlled by *remontage*. Pressing takes place in a horizontal cylindrical press and after the malolactic fermentation, the wine is run partly into new, partly into used oak casks to be matured, racked, assembled and fined in the usual way before being bottled from eighteen to twenty-seven months after the vintage.

Château la Carte

This land lies on the famous west plateau of Saint-Émilion approximately 300 metres from the Collégiale and 200 metres from the old church of St Martin-de-Mazerat. Vines have been grown on the site since Roman times.

The property, which was 4.5 hectares in extent, has belonged to the Bécot family since 1931. It now no longer exists as a separate entity. Monsieur Bécot also owns Château Beau-Séjour and la Carte is operated as part of this property. In 1971 M Bécot moved from Château la Carte to live at his new property, Beau-Séjour. His parents still live at Château la Carte. The label of Château la Carte can now only be found on vintages up to 1978, as from that date it became absorbed into the Beau-Séjour vinification process.

Château Chapelle-Madeleine

This tiny property, a mere 0.2 of a hectare in its later days, is mentioned in the 1908 edition of Cocks et Feret as being owned by Belair which was then itself under separate ownership from Ausone. Its production is given as 5 tonneaux. The 1949 edition tells us that in 1916 M Dubois-Challon, the owner of Ausone, acquired both Belair and Chapelle-Madeleine and the three have been under the same ownership ever since. This edition lists Belair and Chapelle-Madeleine as a single property producing 40 tonneaux. In the 1969 edition (updated to January 1st, 1974), it is listed as a separate property producing 30 tonneaux. However, we have been told by Pascal Delbeck, the *Régisseur* of Ausone and Belair, that since 1970 the property has not existed as a separate entity and that the 0.2 hectares have been absorbed into Ausone. Before this absorption the wine, which was of very good quality, was sold almost exclusively to Belgium.

Château le Châtelet

This property on the northern Côtes near the Château Beau-Séjour has been owned by the Berjal family for nearly a century. Today it belongs to M Pierre Berjal who also manages the property.

The estate comprises 6 hectares, of which 4.5 hectares are under vine planted with one-third Merlot, one-third Cabernet Sauvignon and one-third Bouchet. With traditional cultivation methods the yield is approximately 42 hectolitres per hectare, thus giving production of 252 hectolitres per annum. Monsieur Berjal can see the introduction of vintaging-machines in the not-too-distant future.

Standard vinification processes produce a wine which is bottled at Châtelet by their own staff.

Monsieur Berjal also owns Château la Tour-de-Segur in Lussac, Clos St Valery Grand Cru Saint-Émilion and Domaine Chante l'Alouette, Saint-Émilion A C. He manages Domaine des Menuts Grand Cru Saint-Émilion and Château Bon Pasteur Saint-Émilion A C.

Château Chauvin

This modern property is on the Saint-Émilion/Pomerol border to the south and east of Château Ripeau, and is owned by Henri Ondet. There are 12.9 hectares of which 10.9512 are under vine planted with 60% Merlot, 30% Bouchet and 10% Cabernet Sauvignon. The average age of the vines is thirty-five years and they produce some 60 tonneaux of wine.

The grapes are completely de-stalked and the skins remain in the *must* for up to three weeks during fermentation which takes place in cement vats. The pressing is done with a horizontal press and the wine is then run off into two-year-old casks and assembled, racked and fined in the usual way, before being bottled after two years. The 1981 price was 35 to 40 francs per bottle and the chief market outside France is Belgium.

Clos-des-Jacobins

This beautiful ivy-covered Château, situated on the slopes and on the main road to Cheval Blanc, is a single-storey building. It was bought by M Cordier in 1964 and is now operated as Cordier S A. The General Manager, M Carmagnac, has been with the company since 1975. Previous owners have been M Régnier-Vauthier and Emile Vauthier.

The property covers 8 hectares of which 7.14 are under vine planted on very varied soils, comprising 55% Bouchet and 45% Merlot. This produces approximately 40 tonneaux per annum with an average yield of 45 hectolitres per hectare.

Popular history tells us that a revolutionary group was involved in the origins of this Château, but today all the methods of cultivation and vinification are firmly traditional. Fermentation takes place in tanks and the wine is then matured in casks. Bottling is performed on the premises with its own equipment.

Château la Clotte

This property incorporates the former Clos Bergat-Bosson-Pigasse, which has belonged to it since 1904. It was bought in 1913 by Sylvain Chailleau and M G Chailleau is the present owner.

It is immediately to the south-east of the town and former owners, the Marquis de Grailly and Adolphe Pigasse were so jealous of these growths that they built a wall which still surrounds the entire vineyard area. This property is well-sited, sheltered from the north winds by the ramparts, the ruins of Saint-Émilion and the rocks of Château la Clotte and Château Bergat. The soil is clay and chalk on a sub-soil of sand and clay.

The vineyard covers 5 hectares (85% Merlot, 15% Bouchet) producing about 15 tonneaux at around 40 hectolitres per hectare. The oldest vines are eighty years old and the average age is forty-three years.

The firm of J-P Moueix takes three-quarters of the crop. It does all the work in the vineyard and makes the wine. All the details of vinification are the same as at Château Magdelaine except that no new casks are used, only those between two and four years old. Monsieur Chailleau takes the remaining quarter of the crop.

Château la Clusière

This little property is an enclave in the vineyard area of Château Pavie. It was owned in the nineteenth century by Amédée Thibeaud and then his daughter, Alix Fauré. The Valette family then purchased it in 1953, ten years after they had bought Pavie itself.

It comprises 4 hectares of which 2.68 are under vine on a south-east facing slope of the hill of Pavie with typical Côtes limestone soil. The vineyard is worked with that of Château Pavie and all the various stages of making the wine are carried out in its cellars and in the same way, but the composition of the vineyard is strikingly different – 80% Merlot, and 10% each of Bouchet and Cabernet Sauvignon, as against 55%, 25%, 20% respectively at Pavie.

The oldest vines are sixty years old and the average age is about twenty years. Some 13 to 15 tonneaux of wine is made at about 35 hectolitres per hectare. The very high Merlot content and the comparative youthfulness of the vines combine to make the wine rather lighter and quicker-developing than that of Pavie.

Château Corbin

The Corbin estate, lying on the Saint-Émilion/Pomerol border, was the central part of a large fiefdom which once belonged to the Black Prince, and it has one of the oldest vineyards in Saint-Émilion. In the grounds there are the remains of a feudal Château (fourteenth century). The Château itself is a large, imposing, ivy-covered building set back from the road in its own drive-way. The owners do not live here.

The Château was previously owned by Paul Chaperan. The present owners are members of the Giraud family and the property is operated by the Société Civile des Domaines Giraud. This family also owns other properties operated in the same way: one in Saint-Émilion – Grand Corbin; and two in Pomerol – Château Certan-Giraud and Clos du Roy.

Château Corbin today comprises 13.50 hectares of which 11.6365 are under vine, planted with two-thirds Merlot and one-third Bouchet. The latter is vinified separately since it is gathered later but the wine produced reflects the same percentages as the grape varieties. Average production per annum is around 100 tonneaux.

Traditional means of cultivation are used. The vinification processes are also standard and reinforced concrete vats are used. Wine is also produced under the names of *Château Latour Corbin* and *Château Corbin-Vieille-Tour*.

Château Corbin-Michotte

Jean-Noël Boidron, on behalf of the GFA de Domaine de Calon, adminsters this property as well as the two Châteaux Calon, one of 22.09 hectares in Montagne-St Emilion and one of 5.5 hectares in St Georges. The family of his maternal grandfather, M Naud, have owned the two Châteaux Calon since 1755. He has been in charge of the vinification of these two properties since 1955 and has managed the estate since 1973. He bought Château Corbin-Michotte in 1959. Monsieur Boidron is a qualified oenologist, as is his wife.

There are 7 hectares of which 6.4654 hectares are under vine (60% Merlot, 30% Bouchet, 10% Cabernet Sauvignon); 1 hectare consists of very old vines, up to 100 years and 3 hectares contain vines between five and twenty-five years. They produce some 20 tonneaux at an average yield of 36 hectolitres per hectare.

The vineyard work is traditional with no pesticides used. The *chai* was thoroughly modernised in 1980. The grapes are completely de-stalked and then crushed and the *must* is fermented in stainless-steel vats. The skins remain in the *must* for three weeks before pressing. The wine is matured, partly in casks, a third of which are new each year, and partly in vats. It is bottled, after the usual rackings, assembled and fined about two years after the vintage.

Château Côte Baleau

This is one of the oldest growths in the commune of Saint-Émilion and the castle-like Château was built two-hundred years ago. It stands in 20 hectares on the clayey-limestone hillsides to the west of the Saint-Émilion Coteaux.

It is owned and operated by the Société Civile des Grandes Murailles (which incorporates the Héritiers Malen) and is run as a single unit with the Château Grands Murailles and the Clos St-Martin, under manager Jean Brun.

The three properties together comprise 26 hectares of which 23 are planted with 70% Merlot, 15% Bouchet and 15% Cabernet Sauvignon. There are still some very old vines on these properties – up to ninety years old and, due to replanting, there are

THE WINES OF SAINT-ÉMILION AND POMEROL

some of only one year. The average age, however, is thirty years. They yield 42 hectolitres per hectare. Average production would thus be 966 hectolitres. The vines are cultivated using traditional methods. Up to one-third of the grapes may be de-stalked and fermentation in cement vats lasts fifteen days, with the skins remaining in contact for a period of eighteen days. Malolactic fermentation takes place immediately after the alcoholic fermentation and egg-white is used for fining. Monsieur Brun told us that the wine is stored in oak casks, renewed every four years in rotation and bottled after two years; but when we visited the *chai* in March, 1982, both the 1981 and 1980 vintages were still in cement vats and there was no sign of any casks. Very unusually the wine is filtered before maturation, thereby reducing the number of rackings by half.

The wine is generally sold through the wholesale system and for export. Retail sales go direct to individual clients. Main export markets are the Benelux countries, The United States of America and Switzerland. When there is a second wine, this is marketed under the name of *Château des Roches Blanches, Saint-Émilion*.

Château la Couspaude

This property is about 400 metres east–south-east of the town of Saint-Émilion, on the clay and limestone plateau between Château Villemaurine and Sansonnet. The owner is Mme E Aubert and the property is administered by the Société d'Exploitation des Vignobles Aubert, whose directors are her children. She also owns Château St Hubert, a Grand Cru in St Pey-d'Armens and Domaine-Roudier in Montagne-St Émilion which are also administered by the Société. The Société owns Domaine de Musset in Lalande de Pomerol. Madame Aubert's grandfather, who was the owner of the neighbouring Château Sansonnet at the time, bought Château la Couspaude in 1900. The origins and meaning of the name is unknown.

There are 7.01 hectares of vines (one-third each of Merlot, Bouchet and Cabernet Sauvignon) which produce some 30 tonneaux at about 42 hectolitres per hectare.

After fermentation and pressing, the wine is matured in oak casks, some of which are new each year, and racked, assembled and fined in the usual way, before being bottled.

Château Coutet

This well-kept property is situated close to the bell-tower overlooking the picturesque Dordogne valley and the Château is built in the style of the famous eighteenth-century architect, Victor Louis. This pleasant setting lies in 13 hectares of land, including the top and south-west slopes of the Côtes.

In the nineteenth century it was owned by Alphonse David, then David-Beaulieu and thereafter by successive generations of the family. It is now owned by the Société Civile Immobilière du Château Coutet and the manager and *Maître de Chai* is Jean David-Beaulieu.

The vineyard covers 11 hectares of which 9.9680 are planted with vines (40% Merlot, 10% Pressac, 40% Bouchet and 10% Cabernet Sauvignon). Production may vary from anything between 20 to 40 tonneaux per annum but an average yield would be 30 hectolitres per hectare.

Traditional viticulture methods are used at Coutet and the vinification process is also traditional. The wine is bottled on the premises by Coutet staff, using their own equipment.

Château le Couvent

This tiny property takes its name from an ancient convent, on whose site it is, and it lies actually within the walls of the town of Saint-Émilion itself – the only one to do so. The Convent was the Couvent des Ursulines, whence is said to have originated the recipe for the famous macaroons, and the site is at the foot of the bell-tower and the Château du Roi.

It was acquired by M Moucheboeuf, a well-known estate-agent in Libourne, in 1979, and before that M Galhaud had been the proprietor for many years after purchasing it from Ferdinand le Perche.

The property is very run-down at the moment (1982), but in October, 1981, the Company Marne et Champagne, a big Champagne house in Epernay, bought it and no doubt changes are imminent. They also own Château Pontet Claugure, Grand Cru. There is just 1 hectare of which 0.3737 is under vine planted unusually with 100% Merlot. The oldest vines are one hundred years old and there is a high average age of about sixty years. Underneath the vineyard the cellars also extend for 1 hectare.

The grapes are 50% de-stalked by a *fouloir-égrappoir* and then fermentation lasts about three weeks, during which time the skins are left in contact with the *must*. Temperature is controlled by *remontage*. After the malolactic fermentation, the wine is run off into new oak casks before bottling after two years. Most of the wine is sold to private customers.

Couvent des Jacobins

This property was built in the thirteenth century, right in the heart of Saint-Émilion. It was a gift to the Jacobin Dominican friars (Frères Prêcheurs Jacobins), confirmed later in 1389 by the Duke of Lancaster, Lieutenant-General of Guyenne and son of the King of England, Henry III.

The vines were cultivated within the ramparts and when the friars ceased cultivation in the eighteenth century, this was taken over by various families. The present owners, the Joinaud-Borde family, have operated the estate since 1902.

The vineyards cover 9.5 hectares, separate from the house, of which 7.9330 are under vine planted with two-thirds Merlot and one-third Bouchet. Average production is approximately 35 to 40 tonneaux per annum. Madame Joinaud-Borde, who is involved in the management of the Château, indicated that viticulture on the property is still highly traditional and she would not want to see any mechanisation of harvesting. Vinification methods are also traditional and the wine is stored in oak casks which are gradually renewed over a period of six years. Couvent des Jacobins uses its own equipment and resources for bottling the wine. A second wine is sold under the name of *Château Beau Mayne*, Grand Cru. This second wine represents approximately 20 to 25% of the total production which is planted on 1.666 hectares.

Château Croque-Michotte

This attractive property, set back slightly from the main road to Pomerol, just north–north-west of Cheval Blanc and close to the Pomerol border, is owned by Mme Hélène Rigal-Geoffrion. She inherited it from her father, Samuel Geoffrion, who bought it in 1890. Jean Brun, who is also *Maître de Chai* of Châteaux Trottevieille and Grandes Murailles, has made the wine here since 1950. The soil is mainly sand with some gravel.

There are 15 hectares of which 13.6715 are under vine planted with 80% Merlot and 20% Bouchet and produce around 60 tonneaux at an average of 40 hectolitres per hectare. The oldest vines are about eighty years old. The grapes are 80% de-stalked by a 'Coq' *fouloir-égrappoir* and the fermentation takes 15 to 18 days. The skins are left in contact for all of that time. Fermentation temperature of 25° to 32°C is regulated by the circulation of water. Malolactic fermentation takes place between the end of the main fermentation and *assemblage* and the wine is then matured in new, two-year-old or four-year-old casks, racked, fined and bottled two years after the vintage in the usual way. The wines have a reputation for quality and consistency.

Château Curé-bon

This Château stands in an excellent position on the La Madeleine plateau between the Ausone and Belair estates and Château Canon. The vineyards were planted at the beginning of the last century by Curé Bon. It is known, though, that there were vines on this site as far back as Roman times.

The property has belonged to the Landé family for a great many generations and there is documentary proof reaching back to 1320. When Curé Bon bequeathed it to his nephew, Camille Lapelletrie, in order to distinguish this Château from others bearing the name 'La Madeleine', the latter had the touching thought of adding his uncle's name to the title: Curé Bon la Madeleine.

Today the property is managed by Maurice Landé who is also the owner. His son, Bertrand, is responsible for the commercial side of the operation.

The estate consists of 6 hectares of which 4.47 are under vine planted with 80% Merlot, 20% Bouchet and produce approximately 23 tonneaux per annum at 4 tonneaux per hectare.

Viticulture is still traditional and harvesting is done by hand using Spanish workers who arrive every year for this specific purpose. The maturation takes place entirely in oak casks and the cellars for storage are carved out of the rocks. The *Maître de Chai*, M Cassin, has been with the Landé operation since 1947, and he also oversees the complete bottling process which is carried out by Curé-Bon staff with their own equipment.

Château Dassault

This attractive estate lies just over 1 kilometre to the north-east of Saint-Émilion below Château Haut-Sarpe. It is owned by Marcel Dassault, the aircraft manufacturer and industrialist and in 1955 changed its name from Château Couperie, formerly owned by M Renaud, to that of its new owner. The vineyard and the wine-making is looked after by André Vergriette, a Jurat of Saint-Émilion who acts as director.

The property comprises 34 hectares of which 21.0353 is Grand Cru Classé and 4.4990 generic Saint-Émilion. The vineyards are planted with two-thirds Merlot and one-third Bouchet/Cabernet Sauvignon, which produce an average of 90 to 100 tonneaux per annum. The oldest vines are about 40 years old.

The grapes are fermented with strict temperature control for four to seven days, the skins remaining in the *must* for one to three weeks. Pressing takes place in an electronically-programmed Marzola horizontal press. The wine remains in the stainless-steel 135 hectolitre vats for two to four weeks and after the malolactic fermentation it is run off into new oak casks to be matured, assembled (in the February or March after the vintage), racked and fined in the usual way, before bottling after eighteen months to two and a half years.

Château la Dominique

At the end of the nineteenth century this Château belonged to M H Greloud who sold it to the de Bailliencourt family. Then in 1969 it was purchased by the present owner, Clément Fayat. It is said that it was given its name by a very wealthy gentleman who purchased the Château on his return from the Island of Dominica where he had made his fortune.

The property, which borders on Château Cheval Blanc, is operated entirely by M Musset, who manages the 15.5141 hectares of vine planted in the total property of 21 hectares. The soil is mainly sand with some gravel. The vine-stock of two-thirds Merlot and one-third Cabernet Sauvignon and Bouchet produces approximately 100 tonneaux in good years with a yield which is, on average, 45 to 50 hectolitres per hectare. There is also a plot of 0.7350 of a hectare which produces generic Saint-Émilion.

The soil on Château la Dominique is black sand on the surface with 1 hectare of gravel, over a clayey base with iron pan. The old traditional methods of viticulture are used. In the cellars the fermentation takes place in stainless-steel vats and the wine is stored in oak casks of which one-third are new each year, until bottling takes place approximately two years after the harvest. Contract bottlers are called in to bottle the wine on the premises and M Musset also has the regular service and advice of an oenologist in all phases of his production.

Château Faurie-de-Souchard

This Château used to be part of the Petit-Faurie-de-Souchard estate and for many years belonged to the Souchard family who were active in local and national affairs. In the seventeenth century a member of the Souchard family was an advocate at the Bordeaux Parliament and a Jurat and Mayor of Saint-Émilion.

The estate once included areas of land at Faurie and Aigrières but when it was split up in 1933, the best slopes were happily retained in the vineyards of Faurie de Souchard. The boundaries of this property are curiously irregular since they follow a famous line of springs.

The Jabiol family has owned this Château since it split from the larger estate and it is run today by Alain, although still owned by his father, Maurice. The *Maître de*

Chai is M Guillou who has held this position for thirty-five years.

The vineyards today cover 10 hectares of the total area of 11 and they produce approximately 35 to 40 tonneaux per annum at 30 hectolitres per hectare. The vine stock is 65% Merlot, 26.5% Bouchet and 8.5% Cabernet Sauvignon.

Viticulture is traditional and classic Saint-Émilion methods are completed by Château-bottling using their own equipment and resources. The wine is stored in a net-work of underground cellars.

The Jabiol family also owns Châteaux Cadet-Piola and Domaine de Pasquette.

Château Fonplégade

This very attractive property set on a hill lies about 1 kilometre to the south-west of Saint-Émilion, opposite the Co-operative and overlooked on three sides by the vineyards of Château Magdelaine. It gets its name from the several natural springs (*fonts*) to be found there and since 1953 it has been the property of A Moueix et Fils.

Previous owners include M P Beylot, M A Sabatier, M le Duc de Morny and the Comtesse de Galard, Paul Boisard, his widow and Mlle Rochefort. The Château was built in 1848. Monsieur Armand Moueix is responsible for the care of the vineyard and the making of the wine.

The property covers 20.5 hectares of which 17.175 hectares are under vine planted with two-thirds Merlot, one-third Bouchet which produce about 60 tonneaux. The oldest vines are sixty years old, the average age being thirty years. The soil is silicon, chalk and clay.

The grapes are completely de-stalked and then fermentation lasts eight to ten days and takes place in cement vats using a special method peculiar to the A Moueix et Fils properties in this area (Châteaux Fonplégade, la Tour-du-Pin-Figeac, Touzinat l'Hermitage and Clos la Fleur Figeac in Saint-Émilion; Château Taillefer, Clos Beauregard and Clos Toulifaut in Pomerol), with the single exception of Château Moulinet in Pomerol. This is the Blachère or Ducellier Isman system. In this process the fermentation is carried out in a closed container and the resulting pressure increase, due to CO_2 produced in the fermentation, pushes the *must* up through a column and subsequently allows it to percolate the whole surface of the cap. A valve system that allows pressure equalisation ensures that the cycle is repeated as long as fermentation produces the CO_2. The system is often completed with a refrigerating container placed in the *remontage* column. It makes for a relatively quick fermentation and ensures a good washing of the 'cap' of the grape skins, thus guaranteeing a well-coloured wine with plenty of tannin, and saving the labour involved in manual *remontage*.

The wine is controlled at 25° to 30°C by refrigeration and the skins remain in contact with the *must* for ten to fifteen days. After two months in the vat the wine is run off into casks: one-third new, one-third two years old and one-third three years old. The wine is assembled in the February or March following the vintage and matured, racked, fined and bottled after eighteen months to two years.

The monolithic church at Saint-Émilion.

Château Fonroque

This well-maintained, secluded property lies immediately north-west of the town surrounded by palm trees. It was originally owned by the Malet Roquefort family, of la Gaffelière. Then it passed to Hubert Chantonnet and in 1952 to Elie Laporte who also owned Château Beauséjour in Montagne-St Émilion. Since then proprietors have included Jean Moueix and later his widow. The present owners are G F A du Château Fonroque.

There are 19 hectares of which 16.8944 are under vine planted with 70% Merlot, 30% Bouchet producing some 85 tonneaux at around 40 hectolitres per hectare. The oldest vines are fifty-five years and the average age is thirty-six years.

The vineyard management and the making and selling of the wine is done by the firm of J-P Moueix and all the details of vinification, etc, are the same as at Château Magdelaine except that no new casks are used.

Château Franc-Mayne

This property, about 1½ kilometres west–north-west of Saint-Émilion and just south of the D.17, consists of 6.1470 hectares of well-kept vines (75% Merlot, 25% Cabernet Sauvignon and Bouchet) and produces some 30 tonneaux on average. Monsieur Theillassoubre is the owner and Jean Brun, manager of a number of Saint-Émilion properties, was in charge of the wine-making until December 1981 when he resigned.

In the nineteenth century it was a split property divided between M G des Cordes and M Chevalon.

Château Grand-Barrail-Lamarzelle-Figeac

This property, set back from the main road to Libourne, stands besides Château la Marzelle and is owned and operated by the same Association. M Carrère is the manager. The word 'barrail' means a plot of land planted with vines – and this is a large one. The soil is mainly sand and clay with 2 hectares of gravel.

The Grand-Barrail covers 36 hectares, 34.71 planted with 60% Merlot, 20% each of Cabernet Sauvignon and Bouchet. The yield is 40 hectolitres per hectare and the average production is approximately 110 tonneaux.

Methods of cultivation and vinification are mainly traditional but M Carrère has introduced the use of a vintaging-machine, which is used on both Carrère properties. Bottling is carried out on the property, using the equipment and resources of the Château itself.

The motto of this property is 'Qui me goûte, m'aime et ne veut que moi' which means 'Whosoever tastes me, loves me and wants no other'.

Château Grand-Corbin

This impressive Château with a large modern *chai*, is situated on the boundary between the communes of Saint-Émilion and Pomerol, on land which used to be part of the famous estate which belonged to the Black Prince. There are remains to be seen here which date back to the fourteenth century.

In the nineteenth century the property was owned by Domecq-Cazeaux and today the property is owned and operated by the Société Civile des Domaines Giraud, which also owns Châteaux Corbin, and Certan Giraud, which is in Pomerol.

The properties are managed by Alain Giraud, together with his father, Philippe, and uncle, Emmanuel Giraud.

This property comprises 12.60 hectares of which 11.6926 are planted with two-thirds Merlot and one-third Bouchet. Average production is 75 tonneaux per annum.

The cultivation is traditional: the *must* is fermented in cement vats and the wine is bottled on the premises using the equipment of Château Corbin.

Château Grand-Corbin-Despagne

This property has belonged to the Despagne family for several generations and is owned and operated today by Les Consorts Despagne. The present members of the Despagne family who manage the estate and the production of the wine are M Guy and Gérard Despagne and their mother. Monsieur Gérard Despagne also owns Château Maison-Blanche in Montagne.

The property covers 30 hectares of which 24.6372 are under vine planted with 60% Merlot, 25% Bouchet, 10% Pressac and 5% Cabernet Sauvignon and is located close to the best Pomerol growths. Some vines are, in fact, very old, as they were quite unexpectedly resuscitated after the frosts of 1956, whilst others are relatively young. The average yield is in the region of 35 to 40 hectolitres per hectare and they produce 130 tonneaux per annum.

Cultivation methods are traditional and the vinification processes are also standard for this region, with fermentation taking place in cement vats and the wine being bottled after two years.

Château Grand Mayne

Admirably sited on a hill off the main road, about $\frac{3}{4}$ kilometre west–north-west of the town, the *cuvier* and *chai* of this property date from 1767 while the well-maintained Château itself is older still. In 1928, the neighbouring property of Château Beau-Mazerat was incorporated into the estate.

At the beginning of this century the property was owned by Termes-Dubroca and the present owner is Jean-Pierre Nony, and René Venat has been *Maître de Chai* since 1977. The soil is clay-chalk and sandy-gravel with sandstone sub-soil.

There are 22 hectares, 15.9469 of which are planted with vines (50% Merlot, 40% Bouchet and 10% Cabernet Sauvignon) producing an average yield of 85 tonneaux, at about 40 hectolitres per hectare. The oldest vines are fifty-five years old and the average age is about twenty-five years.

The de-stalking is sometimes complete and sometimes only partial. Fermentation lasts about a week and the skins remain in contact for some thirty days in stainless-steel vats. The grapes are pressed in a horizontal press. The wine is then run off into casks, some new, some up to seven years old, where it is matured, racked (usually six times), assembled, about six months before bottling and fined once. In some years a second wine is produced from young vines and sold under the name *Château Beau-Mazerat* or *Château Cassevert*.

Château Grandes Murailles

This old vineyard which has belonged to the same family for many centuries is today part of the company Société Civile des Grandes Murailles which incorporates the Heritiers Malen and operates the vineyards of three properties.

It stands on a rocky platform situated at the heart of Saint-Émilion and above some ancient quarries.

Together with Clos St-Martin, this property covers 19.81 hectares which are worked as part of the company which operates from Château Côte Baleau. For details concerning the viticulture, vinification and management, headed by Jean Brun, see the description for Château Côte Baleau.

Château Grand-Pontet

This estate is well-sited some $\frac{1}{2}$ kilometre west of the Collegiate Church in Saint-Émilion by the side of the road to Libourne.

For many years in the early part of the century it was owned by M G Combrouze, Mayor of Saint-Émilion and deputy of the Gironde, and more recently by the firm of Barton and Guestier. In May 1980 it was acquired by M Bécot, proprietor of Château Beau-Séjour (Bécot), who, as we have seen, has already added the former Châteaux la Carte and les Trois Moulins to his estate.

The property comprises 14.5 hectares of vines (75% Merlot, 25% Bouchet and Cabernet Sauvignon) and there are some very old vines which escaped the frosts of 1956. It produces some 50 to 60 tonneaux on average.

Château Guadet-St Julien

This small property, immediately north of the town of Saint-Émilion on the road to Montagne, has belonged to the family of the present owner, Robert Lignac, for many years.

It was originally purchased from a deputy of the Gironde and was called le Domaine de St Julien. Robert Lignac makes the wine himself in his cellars behind his house in the Rue Guadet in the town.

There are 5.5 hectares of which 4.62 are under vine planted with 75% Merlot and 25% Bouchet. The average age of the vine is twenty-two years. They produce about 20 tonneaux at 35 hectolitres per hectare.

After being completely de-stalked, the grapes are fermented for fifteen to twenty-one days in plastic-lined cement vats and pressed in a 'Coq' press. Then the wine is run off into casks, some of which are new, some up to six years old, where it is assembled, racked, fined and bottled after two years. Seventy five per cent of the wine is sold direct, 25% through the trade. The main foreign markets are Belgium, The Netherlands, Germany and Canada.

Production from 1975 to 1979 has been as follows:

1975 – 15 tonneaux	1978 – 12 tonneaux
1976 – 25 tonneaux	1979 – 20 tonneaux
1977 – 4 tonneaux	

Château Haut Corbin

Château Haut Corbin is situated in the north-western part of the Saint-Émilion commune, 800 metres from Pomerol, at the foot of the area of great classified growths. The property covers 8 hectares, of which 4.29 are planted with two-thirds Merlot and one-third Cabernet Sauvignon stock. The vines are on average twenty years old and give an average yield per hectare of 45 hectolitres with production of 20 tonneaux per annum.

Edouard Guinaudie is the owner of this property and also owns Château le Jurat in Saint-Émilion. He has already introduced the use of a vintaging-machine.

About two-thirds of the vintage is de-stalked and the skins remain in contact with the *must* for approximately twenty-one days. Fermentation lasts about fifteen days and the wine then remains in the reinforced concrete vats for approximately one week after fermentation. After the pneumatic pressing the malolactic fermentation takes place as soon as possible. There is one fining with egg-white and two rackings before and two after *assemblage*. The wine is stored in casks which may be from two to ten years old and bottling takes place approximately two years after the vintage. A second wine is made and this is marketed under the name of *Vin d'Edouard*.

The wines of Château Haut Corbin are sold to many European countries and to The United States of America, both to the trade and direct to clients.

Château Haut-Sarpe

This Château, one of the most handsome buildings in the area, was built at the beginning of the eighteenth century by the architect Léon Droyn who based his design on Château le Trianon at Versailles. It is situated splendidly at the top of a hill about 500 metres from the town of Saint-Émilion overlooking Château Dassault. Part of the estate is in the commune of Saint-Émilion and part in St Christophe-des-Bardes.

Previous owners include Comte Jacques Amadée de Carles, Lieutenant-General of the King's armies in the mid-nineteenth century, and Comte du Foussat de Bogeron. The present proprietor is Joseph Janoueix and the family also owns Châteaux Haut Badette, le Castelot and Vieux-Sarpe in Saint-Émilion and Châteaux la Croix, la Croix St Georges, la Croix Toulifaut and Clos des Litanies in Pomerol. The Janoueix family are also important *négociants* in Libourne. Paul Chabrerie has been *Chef de Culture* since 1971 and Paul Cazenave *Maître de Chai* since 1964. The latter holds the same post also at Châteaux Canon and le Grace Dieu. Monsieur Janoueix bought the property in 1934 for £300.00. It was raised to the status of Grand Cru Classé in 1969.

Other features of the estate are a charming 'mini village' of old peasant dwellings, where the one hundred and twenty vintagers are housed each year, and an ancient windmill.

The estate comprises 15 hectares, 10.5793 of them under vine (60% Merlot, 30% Bouchet and 10% Cabernet Sauvignon) which produces an average of 56 tonneaux at approximately 45 hectolitres per hectare.

The oldest vines are fifty years old and the average age is about thirty-five years. The root stocks are 101.24 and Riparia Gloire.

The grapes are de-stalked, crushed and fermentation takes place in wood and enamelled cement vats over a period of approximately eighteen days, with the temperature controlled at 28°C.

After three to four weeks in the vats after pressing in a hydraulic press, the wine is run off into oak casks, a quarter of which are renewed each year. The wine is racked eight times, twice before *assemblage* in March and six times after, before being fined and bottled after two years. The cellars are beautifully decorated with murals depicting the various stages of vintaging. A considerable part of the production of the Château is exported to England, Belgium, Australia, The United States of America and Hong Kong.

Château Jean Faure

This is one of the north-western Saint-Émilion properties, just to the north-east of Château Ripeau. The proprietor, on behalf of the GFA Jean Faure, is Michel Amart who also owns Château Montaiguillon in Montagne-St Émilion. Only since he took it over in 1976 have the wines of Château Jean Faure regained their own identity as for many years previously the vineyard had been attached to the neighbouring Château Ripeau. Previous owners include M Peynaud and Mme Vve Marcel Loubat.

The property has 20 hectares of which 16.43 hectares are planted under vine (30% Merlot, 60% Bouchet, 10% Pressac). The average age of the vines is twenty-five years; they produce some 60 to 80 tonneaux per annum.

The grapes are completely de-stalked and the fermentation, in stainless-steel vats, lasts about eight days with the skins remaining in the *must* for two to three weeks. Pressing takes place in a hydraulic press. The wine is run off into casks, some new, some up to five years old. There it is matured, assembled, racked and fined in the usual way, before being bottled after about eighteen months. The price in 1981 was about 40 francs per bottle and the chief market outside France is Belgium. The property has a reputation for making consistently good wine.

Château Laniote

The beautiful old vicarage building and the old cellars of Château Laniote are located in the heart of the commune of Saint-Émilion, 900 metres from the bell-tower. The Heritiers Freymond Roujat, descendants of the Roujat family, still own the historic thirteenth-century Saint-Émilion Chapel of the Trinity and the Holy Grotto (where Saint Émilion lived in the eighth century), which are located within the property.

Standing beside Château Fonroque, the vineyards of Laniote cover 5 hectares of which 4.5302 are under vine and the vines range from one to eighty years old with a majority (80%) Merlot and 15% Bouchet and 5% Cabernet Sauvignon. Production is approximately 40 tonneaux per annum.

Methods of cultivation are traditional but the introduction of vintaging-machines is foreseen in the not-too-distant future. Vinification is also traditional. Twenty per cent of the harvest is de-stalked and whilst fermentation in cement vats lasts fifteen days, the skins remain in contact with the *must* for eighteen days. The oak storage casks are renewed in rotation over a four-year period. The wine is bottled on the premises after about two years by a mobile bottling plant.

The *Régisseur* is Jean Brun who is involved in the management of Château Trottevieille and several other important properties of the area.

Château Larcis-Ducasse

This well-kept Château set beneath Château Pavie straddles the border of St Laurent-des-Combes and Saint-Émilion itself. At the beginning of this century the property was owned by M Raba and its current owner, Mme Hélène Gratiot has maintained its status of Grand Cru Classé Saint-Émilion. D-P Dubois is the manager and has held this position for two years.

The property covers 13 hectares of which 9.6 are planted with vines (70% Merlot, 20% Bouchet and 10% Cabernet Sauvignon). Average yield is in the region of 35 hectolitres per hectare and average production is 40 tonneaux per annum.

The wine is fermented in concrete vats and a hydraulic press is used. The period of fermentation and length of each process varies each year according to the characteristics of the grapes harvested. Egg-white is used for fining and the wine is stored in oak casks which are renewed over a period of four years. The wine is bottled between eighteen and thirty months after the harvest.

Château Larmande

This Château is one of the oldest in the northern Côtes area and has been in the hands of the Méneret-Capdemourlin family since the beginning of this century. The date carved in the wall above the cellar door indicates that wine was being produced on this site in 1640.

The current owner, M J F Méneret-Capdemourlin took over possession in 1977 and is still able to benefit from the advice and experience of the eminent oenologist, Professor Peynaud, who has been advising Larmande since 1955. The Professor also works with Châteaux Margaux, Lafite and a number of other properties throughout the Gironde.

By 1984 the total area of 16 hectares will be planted with vines, and current production from 13.0714 hectares is in the region of 60 tonneaux, with an average yield of 32 hectolitres per hectare. Vine-stocks are 50% Merlot, 35% Bouchet and 15% Cabernet Sauvignon and the average age of the vines is thirty-five years. There is also a plot of land covering 3.5326 hectares which produces Grand Cru wine.

Traditional cultivation methods are used and there is no mechanisation of the vintage. Vinification equipment is very modern and includes stainless-steel tanks, although the wine is matured in casks. Larmande carries out its own bottling on the premises and in years when there is a second wine, this is sold as *Château des Templiers*.

Château Laroze

This estate, with its very attractive, towered Château, lies at the foot of a hill about 1 kilometre north-west of Saint-Émilion. It is owned by the Héritiers Meslin-Gurchy (Société Civile du Château Laroze), whose director is M G Meslin. Monsieur Duporge has been *Régisseur* since 1980 and M Dornais the *Maître de Chai* since 1978.

There are 30 hectares of which 24.0607 are under vine (50% Merlot, 40% Bouchet, 10% Cabernet Sauvignon) and the average age is about twenty years. Production is around 110 tonneaux at about 35 hectolitres per hectare. The soil is sandy with iron in the sub-soil.

After partial de-stalking, the grapes are placed in cement vats for fermentation. Pressing takes place in a hydraulic press. After the malolactic fermentation, the wine is racked off into casks of which a certain number are new each year, and assembled (in February or March following the vintage), racked and fined in the usual way, before being bottled after eighteen months to two years. Outside France, the main markets are Belgium, The Netherlands, Switzerland and Great Britain.

Clos la Madeleine

Hubert Pistouley owns this property which stands on the Coteau beside la Magdelaine and Belair. He also owns Château Magnan la Gaffelière, Grand Cru.

The property covers 2 hectares which are completely planted with 50% Merlot and 50% Bouchet and Cabernet Sauvignon. There are also another 2 hectares of generic Saint-Émilion. Production is in the region of 10 tonneaux per annum and traditional cultivation and vinification methods are practised. The bottling of Clos la Madeleine is carried out on the premises by a sub-contractor.

Château Matras

The name of this estate, which is very well-sited on the southern slopes of Saint-Émilion below Château Canon and adjacent to Châteaux l'Angélus and Tertre Daugay, is derived from the old French word for a cross-bolt, also used to describe a soldier armed with a cross-bow. There is a story that the estate was founded by a soldier of the Hundred Years War who decided to settle there and that he planted the first vines. More recent owners have been M Bourricaud (1874), M R Chaperon (1883), M A R Chaperon (1893), the Comte de Carles (1949) and, since 1962, the present proprietor, the agricultural engineer and oenologist, Jean Bernard-Lefèbvre, who also farms the vineyards and makes the wine at Château Haut Cadet, Grand Cru Saint-Émilion and owns Château Bourseau in Lalande de Pomerol. The official proprietor is the G F A Matras. Since 1976 the estate has been operated by Bernard Lefèbvre's son-in-law and daughter, Francis and Veronique Gaboriaud.

The vineyard lies in a little hollow in the side of the hill which helps to protect it from north and east winds and the soil is silico-limestone, with clay-limestone in some parts, mixed with sandstone grit. There are about 16.5 hectares of vines planted with one-third each of Merlot, Bouchet and Cabernet Sauvignon, producing about 40 tonneaux at around 35 to 45 hectolitres per hectare. The oldest vines are sixty years old and the average age is about nineteen years, with a great deal of replanting currently in progress. Nine .2264 hectares produce the Grand Cru Classé Château Matras; 5.2725 hectares of young vines produce the Grand Cru Château Jean Voisin (not to be confused with the property of the same name some 2 miles north of Saint-Émilion).

The grapes are completely de-stalked and for about fifteen days fermentation takes place in epoxy-lined stainless-steel tanks, located out of doors. Two of the five tanks have two tiers with a top section of 160 hectolitres and bottom 70 hectolitres capacity. There are also two tanks of the same material indoors. The skins are kept in contact with the *must* throughout fermentation and, unusually, after the malolactic fermentation, the wine is matured for a full year in these large tanks, being racked four times. It is then assembled and put into new oak casks to complete its second year of maturation, being racked twice more, this time into older casks, before being fined and bottled. The current vintage wine is sold at approximately 20 to 25 francs per bottle (1980).

Château Mauvezin

The Château Mauvezin was never the principal dwelling of the Mauvezin family, so the house on the property was only of manor-house status. The land was the important factor and, in true Bordeaux fashion, any house which has vines grown in adjoining land is automatically accorded the title of Château.

In 1968 Pierre Cassat, father of the present owner, bought the property from Bertin-Morel. Olivier Cassat now owns and manages this and the Domaine de Peyrelongue Grand Cru Saint-Émilion.

The 3.71 hectares currently planted with vines is undergoing vigorous evolution. Some of the vine-stock is eighty years old or more and, as a result of replanting programmes, some is very new indeed. The present balance of 60% Merlot and 40% Bouchet will be altered in the replanting, with the object of achieving a more equal percentage of the two vine types. The aim is to plant very much more of the total 4.5 hectares which comprises the whole property. With the introduction of young vines, the current production of very concentrated wine at 25 hectolitres per hectare giving 12 to 15 tonneaux per annum will be increased to nearer 35 to 40 hectolitres per hectare.

The property stands on the plateau to the north-east of Saint-Émilion near to Châteaux Soutard, Balestard-la-Tonnelle and Haut-Sarpe. The soil is very hard limestone and clayey limestone and traditional cultivation processes are followed by a first fermentation in tanks. The wine is stored in casks, some of which are new each year, and bottled by Mauvezin personnel on the property.

Château Moulin du Cadet

This property, its house unlived-in and in a poor state of repair, is on the limestone plateau about ¼km due north of the town. It was owned by Xavier Duperrieu in the middle of the nineteenth century and from 1887 to 1924 by his nephew, Lucien Brissaud-Rideau. His son-in-law, Albert Fagouet, succeeded him and the present proprietors are the Société Civile du Château Moulin de Cadet.

The property covers 5 hectares of which 3.6705 are under vine planted with 90% Merlot and 10% Bouchet, producing some 22 tonneaux at around 40 hectolitres per hectare. The oldest vines are eighty years old and the average age of the plants is thirty-four years.

The vineyard management and the making of the wine is done by the firm of J-P Moueix, and all the details of the vinification are the same as at Château Magdelaine, except that no new casks are used.

Clos de l'Oratoire

This property and its vineyards just to the south and east of Château Dassault are owned and operated by the Société Civile du Château Peyreau. It is managed by Michel Boutet and the *Maître de Chai*, M Obre, has been here for ten years. There is no house.

The vineyards cover an area of 7.9550 hectares which give an annual production of 40 tonneaux at a yield of 39 hectolitres per hectare. Vine-stock is composed of 65% Merlot and 35% Bouchet and there is close liaison with the operation of Château Peyreau where the wine is actually vinified.

Cultivation in the vineyards is traditional and vinification processes are self-contained. Clos de l'Oratoire-bottling, however, is carried out using the facilities of Château Peyreau but maintained as a completely separate operation.

Monsieur Boutet also manages the vineyards of Châteaux Canon-la Gaffelière, Vieux-Pourret, la Tour-Figeac and Peyreau. He also owns Château Haut Plantey.

Château Pavie-Decesse

This attractive Château and estate lies on the upper slopes of the hill of Pavie with superb views. Recent owners were M R Marzelle until 1967 and M Bleynie until 1970. In the latter year it was purchased by the Valette family who already owned the neighbouring Chateaux Pavie and la Clusière.

Jean Paul Valette of Pavie is the director and the three properties have the same *Chef de Culture* and *Maître de Chai*.

There are 8.5 hectares of which 7.9873 are under vine planted with 60% Merlot, 25% Bouchet and 15% Cabernet Sauvignon with production averaging 36 tonneaux per annum at about 38 hectolitres per hectare. There are some one-hundred-year-old vines and the average age of the plants is around thirty years.

The methods of vinification are virtually the same as at Pavie but there is a fully automatic electronically programmed Spanish Lorza press and there are some stainless-steel fermentation vats (the first to be installed in Saint-Émilion) and some Eprite cement ones. The temperature of the stainless-steel vats is electrically controlled.

The wine is rather less rich and fine than that of Pavie but maintains a good standard of quality.

Château Pavie-Macquin

Antoine Corre inherited this property from his father in 1977. He is now the owner and manager.

M Jouinaud is the *Maître de Chai* and he oversees a traditional vinification process.

The property, on the southern Côtes, contains 9.2 hectares planted with vines out of a total of 30 hectares.

The vineyard is planted with 80% Merlot with the rest made up of 10% Bouchet and 10% Cabernet Sauvignon.

Château Pavillon-Cadet

This Château stands on the Colline des Cadets and on the slopes surrounding the hill. It has belonged to the Gratadour family and their descendants since the beginning of the century and is managed today by Mme Anne Llammas, née Le Morvan, who inherited the property from her parents. It operates under the name of the Société Civile Pavillon Cadet.

The soil on this site is very clayey and there are 3 hectares of which 1.5 are under vine. The annual production is about 15 to 20 tonneaux, with a yield of approximately 40 hectolitres per hectare. Vine-stock is 50% Merlot and 50% Bouchet, and the wine reflects the same traditional vinification process. The wine is stored in oak casks and the first bottling usually takes place within two years of harvest and the contract bottler performs this service for Pavillon-Cadet on the property.

Madame Llammas also owns the Château Rio Tailhas, Saint-Émilion where there is 0.5 of a hectare of vines.

Château Petit-Faurie-de-Soutard

This property, which lies to the north and east of Château Soutard used, at one time, to be owned by its larger neighbour. It is well-sited and extends over soils on the limestone plateau, down the Côtes and into sandy soil at the foot of the slope.

Madame Aberlen, the previous owner, transferred the property to her daughter, Mme François Cap de Mourlin but it is, in fact, operated today by the Société Civile des Vignobles Aberlen. Since the beginning of 1977 the property has been managed by Mme Cap de Mourlin's husband, Jacques Cap de Mourlin. She is a scientist and prefers to leave Petit-Faurie-de-Soutard in his hands as he already has experience as owner/manager of Châteaux Cap de Mourlin, Balestard-la-Tonnelle and Roudier.

The property covers 7.8 hectares of which 7.0734 are under vine planted with 60% Merlot, 30% Bouchet and 10% Cabernet Sauvignon, which produce between 20 to 25 tonneaux per annum with a yield of 35 hectolitres per hectare. There is a regular system of replanting to ensure a good balance of vine maturity.

The *Maître de Chai*, Bernard Oizeau, manages a mainly traditional cellar and the Château carries out its own bottling.

With regard to cultivation and harvesting, M Cap de Mourlin does not use vintaging-machines at Petit-Faurie-de-Soutard at present, but feels that they must come in the not-too-distant future.

Château le Prieuré

It is said that at one time the Franciscan friars made sparkling wine from vines grown on this site; it used to be part of the Clos des Cordeliers which no longer exists as a property. There is, however, still a small vineyard growing grapes which are made into white sparkling wine (méthode champenoise) in a *chai* by the side of the cloisters.

Today, Château le Prieuré belongs to Baronne Madeleine Guichard whose family purchased it in 1880. It is run by M Rouchier, the *Régisseur* and the wines are marketed by Olivier Guichard.

Of the 6.5 hectares belonging to le Prieuré, 4.8078 are planted with vines which are 75% Merlot and 25% Bouchet. Nearly all the vines are very old, except for half a hectare of new plants, and 16 tonneaux production per annum represents a yield of 30 hectolitres per hectare. Cultivation methods are traditional and, indeed, the uneven levels of the ground would make the use of mechanisation difficult.

Le Prieuré wine is bottled on the property by a mobile bottling unit. Baronne Guichard, the current owner, is also proprietor of Château Siaurac, Lalande de Pomerol and Château-Vraye-Croix-de-Gay, Pomerol. The methods of vinification are the same as those used at Château Siaurac.

Château Ripeau

Monsieur and Mme Michel Janoueix de Wilde have owned this property, about 1 kilometre south-east of Château Cheval Blanc, since 1976 having bought it from M Gunsbourg. The attractive Château is set well back from the road down a long drive-way and its main reception-room has an attractive ceiling. Monsieur de Wilde has a large collection of old artifacts and books.

There are 20 hectares of which 14.5841 are under vine planted with one-third each of Merlot, Bouchet and Cabernet Sauvignon, with an average age of eighteen years and producing some 55 tonneaux per annum. The soil is predominantly sand on a sand and molasse sub-soil.

The grapes are usually completely de-stalked and fermentation, in cement vats, lasts for seven to eleven days. The pressing takes place in a horizontal Vaslin press and the wine is run off into cement vats where it is assembled, racked, fined and bottled, after two years.

The main markets outside France are Belgium, Switzerland and The United States of America.

Château St Georges-Côte-Pavie

The Masson family has owned this property for one hundred years and it was inherited by the present owner, Jacques Masson, in 1980.

The property is located opposite Château Ausone and beside Châteaux la Gaffelière and Pavie on the south–south-west facing slopes. Vines have been cultivated here for many centuries and in the course of planting, Roman remains, such as mosaics, have been found.

Today there are 5.7 hectares of which 5.42 are under vine. Planted on clay soil comprising 50% Bouchet and 50% Merlot. Some vines are extremely old and others less than fifteen years old.

'Racotage' (the replacement of some plants in between old ones), takes place every year and the replanting of a whole area of $\frac{1}{3}$ of a hectare, every three or four years. Production averages 20 tonneaux per annum at 35 hectolitres per hectare.

The new Maître de Chai is M Laure who has been learning his trade for seven years and was appointed successor to M Cassin at the beginning of 1982.

Viticulture methods are very traditional and the must is fermented in stainless-steel vats and the wine stored in casks until it is two years old. Bottling is done on the premises, either by Château staff or, if requested, by the wholesale purchaser.

It is said that the name St Georges has its origin in the period when Acquitaine was occupied by the English and that the final 's' was only added to the English spelling 'George' about two generations ago.

Clos St-Martin

This property stands beside the old church of the same name on one of the highest points of Saint-Émilion. It is surrounded by two of the Premiers Grands Crus Classés and has a stony sub-soil containing potassium nitrate.

The Clos St-Martin is owned and operated by the Société Civile des Grandes-Murailles which also manages the Château Grandes Murailles and the Château Côte Baleau. The Maître de Chai and Régisseur of the properties is Jean Brun.

Together with Grandes Murailles, this property covers 6 hectares and all details of viticulture and vinification will be found under the heading Côte Baleau where the wine is also made.

Château Sansonnet

This property, just outside the town of Saint-Émilion, on the plateau and backing on to Château Trottevieille, has belonged to the Robin family since 1882 and it is owned and managed to day by Francis Robin who also owns Châteaux Doumayne (Saint-Émilion) and Busquet (Lussac), Clos Vieux Taillefer (Pomerol) and Château Gontet Robin (Puisseguin).

There is no house and the chai is in a rather poor state of repair. The estate covers 7 hectares of which 4.80 are under vine (50% Merlot, 30% Bouchet, 15% Cabernet Sauvignon and 5% Pressac) which produce between 350 and 500 hectolitres per annum at a yield of 30 to 45 per hectare.

The wine is fermented in cement vats and then transferred for maturation in oak casks to Château Doumayne and bottled after the usual rackings, assemblage and fining. The wines from all M Robin's properties, except Château Busquet, are fermented at Château Sansonnet and matured at Château Doumayne. There are also 1.81 hectares of vines producing Saint-Émilion A C wine under the label *Domaine de la Salle*.

Château la Serre

This small property with its ivy-covered house and imposing cedar trees is a neighbour of Châteaux Ausone and Pavie, situated outside the La Porte Brunet, one of the gates leading into the city of Saint-Émilion. Indeed, it was part of the Pavie estate until some fifty years ago when it assumed its own identity. Some time between the Wars, M Ducolon purchased the estate and later Château la Pointe in Pomerol. In 1949 both properties, now rather run-down, were sold to Paul Delahoutre who did much to improve standards and conditions. Since 1956 his son-in-law, Bernard d'Arfeuille, has run both as well as Châteaux Tourmalin and Pey-la-Brie in the Côtes de Fronsac. The *Maître de Chai*, Louis David, makes the wine at Château la Pointe as well.

Four.446 hectares of the 7 are under vine (80% Merlot, 20% Bouchet) which produce 30 to 35 tonneaux. The average age of the vines is about twenty-five years. The soil and sub-soil are very similar to those of its neighbour, Ausone.

After complete de-stalking, pressing, and about fifteen days fermentation in cement vats, the wine is transferred to oak casks (some new, some up to seven years old), for *assemblage* (November, December), racking and fining. The wine is bottled after eighteen to twenty months. The main markets outside France are Belgium and Great Britain.

Château Soutard

The vineyards of Château Soutard lie on the limestone plateau and slopes less than a kilometre to the north-west of Saint-Émilion. This is another ancient estate and, as at Bélair, Roman vine-furrows can still be seen cut out of the rock with the traditional distance of 1.3 metres between rows. The property is owned by the des Ligneris family and the Comte and Comtesse live in the Château which was built in 1740 by M Lavau who sold it in 1780 to the Berthomieu family. It has been passed down, through the female line, to the present owners. Formerly it was part of a larger estate which was divided in 1851.

There are 23 hectares of vines (70% Merlot, 25% Bouchet and 5% Cabernet Sauvignon) producing 90 to 100 tonneaux at about 40 hectolitres per hectare. The oldest vines are eighty years old and the average age of the plants is forty years.

The degree of de-stalking varies according to the vintage. In 1975, a hot summer with little rain, and therefore a lot of extract in the grapes, only 20% of the stalks were left on. In 1977, when there was comparatively little sun and plenty of rain and the extract was rather light, 80% were left. These are the two extremes.

The grapes are pressed in a vertical hydraulic press after being fermented for ten to twelve days. The skins are allowed to remain in contact with the *must* for twenty to twenty-five days. The malolactic fermentation may occur alongside the alcoholic fermentation, or just after, or at any time in the first year. After about twenty-five days in the fermentation vats the wine is run-off—one-third into new oak casks, one-third into one year old casks and one-third into big underground cement tanks. Thereafter, during the maturation period, the wine is circulated through the three kinds of container. Not only does this eliminate some of the vast expense of buying all new oak casks each year, but the Comte believes that maturing the whole vintage in new oak all the time makes the wine too oaky and 'woody'. After maturation, which takes between eighteen to twenty-four months, the wine is fined and bottled. In some years a second wine is made and sold under the name *Clos la Tonnelle*.

The wines have great finesse and depth of flavour and are very long lasting.

Château Tertre Daugay

The name of this property means 'hill of the look-out' and it is aptly named, being at the end of the hillside on whose slopes are the vineyards of Châteaux Ausone, Bélair, Magdelaine and Fonplégade.

It juts out in a spur overlooking the Dordogne valley. Remains of a Gallo-Roman villa of the fourth century with some fine mosaics have been found on the estate.

Previously owned by Jean-Jacques Galhaud, it was recently acquired by the Comte de Malet Roquefort, owner of Château la Gaffelière.

The methods of vinification are the same as at Château la Gaffelière. The extent of the property is 44 hectares much of which is being replanted and at the present time only 8.5 hectares are producing wine. The planting is 65% Merlot, 25% Bouchet, 8% Cabernet Sauvignon and 2% Pressac which produces an average 37 hectolitres per hectare.

After the harvesting the grapes are totally de-stalked and the *must* is fermented in tanks for ten to twelve days. The wine is then matured in oak casks. Tertre Daugay produces wines that are, on the whole, deeper in colour than those of la Gaffelière. The second wine from this property is sold under the name of *Moulin du Biguey*. The wine of Tertre Daugay is sold world-wide.

Château la Tour-Figeac

This attractive Château with lovely gardens covers an area of 15 hectares bordering Pomerol. The property was separated from the main Château Figeac in 1879 and was then split into three parts in 1882. The other two parts are both called Château la Tour-du-Pin-Figeac. The tower mentioned in its name stands on the estate and has been rebuilt during this century. The Château, which borders Cheval Blanc and Figeac, has undergone modifications.

The current owner is the Société Civile du Château la Tour-Figeac who purchased la Tour-Figeac in 1960. Michel Boutet, who also manages the Clos de l'Oratoire, Châteaux Canon la Gaffelière and Peyreau, is the manager and M Beyny has been the *Maître de Chai* for twenty-five years. The soil is mainly sand and clay with some gravel.

Thirteen.6308 hectares are planted with vines which comprise 60% Merlot and 40% Bouchet and produce 60 tonneaux per annum at 40 hectolitres per hectare.

Traditional methods of viticulture and harvesting are used and in the cellars there is up to date vinification equipment. The wine is matured in oak casks before bottling which is carried out by la Tour-Figeac staff with equipment on the property.

Château la Tour-du-Pin-Figeac (*Giraud*)

This property is essentially a single-storey farmhouse which stands on land which originally formed part of the large Château Figeac estate. Today, there are two blocks of land which both have the same name. This property belonged to the Bélivier family from 1923. In 1972 it was bought by Lucien Giraud and is now owned by his widow, Micheline and her son André Giraud. They also own Château le Caillou in Pomerol, a small family house on the main road, where they live.

The property covers more than 20 hectares, of which 9.63 are planted with vines (75% Merlot and 25% Bouchet). Production is in the region of 40 tonneaux per annum with a yield of 30 hectolitres per hectare. The soil is sandy and clayey-siliceous with some gravel and high iron-content sub-soil. Cultivation uses traditional methods and M Giraud is strongly opposed to the introduction of mechanical harvesting.

In the cellars some bottling is done by a sub-contractor and some by la Tour-du-Pin-Figeac staff.

Château la Tour-du-Pin-Figeac (*Moueix*)

This property, which adjoins Château Figeac, has no Château and was a part of the Figeac estate until 1879, when it became part of the new Château la Tour-Figeac. In 1882 this was split into three, La Tour-Figeac which comprised 16 hectares, and two parcels of 8 hectares both, confusingly, called La Tour-du-Pin-Figeac. After the last War, the property was sold by auction (1947), its previous proprietor having been sued for collaboration with the German Army. It is owned by the heirs of Marcel Moueix (A Moueix et Fils) and Armand Moueix looks after the vineyard and makes the wine.

The soil is mainly sand and clay with some gravel. There are 9 hectares of which 8.4531 are under vine (two-thirds Merlot, one-third Bouchet) which produces about 37 tonneaux. The oldest vines are sixty years old and the average age is about thirty years.

All particulars of the vinification are exactly the same as for all the A Moueix properties as detailed in the section on Château Fonplégade.

Château Trimoulet

The vineyards belonging to this Château, which is almost due north of Saint-Émilion near the border with St Georges, are very old and records can be inspected there which date back to 1773. They show that it has been owned by the same family for many generations.

Michel Jean inherited the property from his father, Pierre Jean, in 1977 and he now also performs the duties of *Maître de Chai*.

The soil is clay-silica with iron in the sub-soil. The average yield is 40 hectolitres per hectare, and the 19 hectare property has 17.55 hectares under vine, planted with 60% Merlot, 10% Cabernet Sauvignon and 30% Bouchet.

The usual Saint-Émilion vinification methods are used and cement vats are used for storage. Trimoulet have their own bottling installation and the wine is bottled on the property.

In the vineyard, traditional cultivation methods are used and M Jean is opposed to the introduction of vintaging-machines.

The wine is widely distributed in France and has a large export market; the chief overseas markets are, Belgium, Holland, Switzerland, The United Kingdom and The United States of America.

Château les Trois Moulins

This property of 5 hectares which borders Châteaux Beau-Séjour (Bécot) and la Carte was recently purchased by M Bécot and has now been absorbed into the operation of Beau-Séjour. It no longer exists as a separate property and the last vintage of Château les Trois Moulins was 1978.

Previous owners include the Duplessis-Fourcaud family, then Pierre Bargeaux, Dr G Bargeaux and the Gauthier family.

Château Troplong-Mondot

This large property, dominated by a huge water-tower, lies on a hill with particularly fertile soil about 1 kilometre east–south-east of Saint-Émilion. It belonged, in the seventeenth century, to the de Sèze family, one of whom, Raymond de Sèze, was advocate to Louis XVI. Later, in the nineteenth century, it belonged to another member of the family, M Troplong, who was Jurisconsul and President of the Imperial Senate and whose name was added to the original one, Château Mondot. The Valette family purchased the estate in 1937 from M Thienpont. Claude Valette, whose brother administers Châteaux Pavie, Pavie-Decesse and la Clusière, is the director and M Perez has been *Maître de Chai* since 1972.

In the middle of the nineteenth century, Troplong-Mondot was clearly established as one of the most distinguished growths of the area and in 1868 (second edition) of Cocks et Feret places it second after Bélair in its list of leading Saint-Émilion properties. It is not quite so highly regarded today.

There are 30 hectares of which 28.0493 are under vine (65% Merlot, 10% Bouchet, 20% Cabernet Sauvignon, 5% Pressac), producing some 125 tonneaux. The oldest vines are sixty years and the average age is thirty years.

The grapes are completely de-stalked, and then fermentation takes place in large (115 hectolitres) new stainless-steel tanks with the temperature automatically controlled at 28°C. This takes about fifteen days and the skins remain in contact with the *must* throughout. Pressing is carried out in a horizontal press, then after the malolactic fermentation the wine is run off into casks. Some casks are new each year and they are, therefore, all renewed within a period of ten years. Few of the classed growths keep their casks this long. Thereafter the wine is matured, assembled, racked and fined in the usual way, before bottling after about two years.

Château Villemaurine

This estate, which is just outside the north-eastern part of the town, takes its name from its former occupation, in the thirteenth century, by the Moors; 'Ville Maure' gradually became Villemaurine over the years. The property has the largest network of underground cellars and caves in Saint-Émilion. Records show that these were first hollowed out in the tenth century and they exist on two levels. Part of the cellars is used for storage and ageing wines in bottle (there are vintages of Château Villemaurine here dating back to 1865); other parts are hired out for receptions and similar functions. As with some of the other large cellars, the stone excavated from them was used for building in Saint-Émilion and the neighbouring villages, in Libourne and in Bordeaux.

The present owner and manager is Robert Giraud, who also owns two AC Bordeaux properties, Châteaux Cadillac and Timberlay. He bought Château Villemaurine in 1970 from Dr Jacques Vauthier, the grandson of Raoul Passemard who had owned the estate in the 1880's. In 1893 he had united the Villemaurine vineyard with one alongside it which had belonged to him for some time.

Six.7868 of the 8 hectares are planted with vines – 95% Merlot and 5% Cabernet Sauvignon which produce some 30 to 40 tonneaux at about 45 hectolitres per hectare. The oldest vines are one hundred years and the average age is about thirty years.

Monsieur Giraud uses traditional cultivation methods but has recently introduced two vintaging-machines to replace hand-picking.

The grapes are completely de-stalked and lightly crushed. Fermentation, in cement vats, lasts for fifteen to twenty days with the skins remaining in contact throughout. The temperature is controlled by running the *must* through inox stainless-steel pipes chilled with water. After pressing, the wine is kept in vats until the malolactic fermentation is completed. It is then run off into new oak casks, usually around the end of November, for maturation, racking, *assemblage* (usually in April following the vintage), fining and bottling after about eighteen months to two years.

Two 'sous marque' wines are produced under the names *Maurinus* and *Beausoleil*.

Château Yon-Figeac

This beautiful, towered Château, surrounded by trees and separate *chais*, on the sandy slopes between the eastern Côtes and the Pomerol border, is owned and operated entirely by the Lussiez brothers, Jean-Pierre and François. Their family has owned this property for more than four generations.

Of the total area of 27 hectares, 20.8986 are planted with vines. Of these 50% are Merlot, 25% Bouchet and 25% Cabernet Sauvignon, producing an average of 80 tonneaux per annum with a yield of 35 hectolitres per hectare.

The *must* is fermented and the wine matured in stainless-steel and cement vats. Oak casks are still used for the first six months of maturation and the wine is bottled by an outside bottling company which comes to the Château and performs this service on the property.

Asked about the use of harvesting-machines, Jean-Pierre Lussiez replied that they do not use one yet, but that this will probably be introduced in the future. Indeed, the layout of the Yon-Figeac vineyard is most suitable for modern cultivation methods.

All Other Properties
(including Grands Crus for 1981)

Château L'Ancien Moulin
Present owner   Gilbert Faurie
3.87 hectares
Generic Saint-Émilion

Château L'Annoucialiou
Present owner   Bruno Callegarin
4.25 hectares
Generic Saint-Émilion

Château Arnault de Jacquemeau
Present owner   Denis Dupuy
3.71 hectares
Generic Saint-Émilion

Château Austerlitz
Present owner   Gerard Audigay
5.64 hectares
Generic Saint-Émilion

Château Badette
Present owner   Daniel Arraud
8.7985 hectares
Grand Cru

Clos Badon
Present owner   Philippe Dugos
7.72 hectares
A brick-red painted house with a small vineyard close to the station.

Château Barberousse
Present owner   Jean Puyol
6.5177 hectares
Generic Saint-Émilion

Domaine de Barberousse
Present owner   M R Chaubert
0.5901 hectares
Generic Saint-Émilion

Félicien Bareige
1.0355 hectares
Sells generic Saint-Émilion in bulk only.

Château Barreau
Present owner   Edgard Valadier
1.9472 hectares
Generic Saint-Émilion

Domaine Barreau Taillefer
Present owner   Roger Grenier
0.7929 hectares
Generic Saint-Émilion

Château la Bassonnière
Present owner   Gérard Faisandier
1.1237 hectares
Generic Saint-Émilion

Château Beau Mayne
Present owner   Borde-Joinaud
1.1666 hectares
Grand Cru
Monsieur Borde-Joinaud also owns Château Couvent des Jacobins, Grand Cru Classé, to which this extra plot of vineyard is annexed.

Château Beaurang
Present owner   José Puyol
6.5793 hectares
Generic Saint-Émilion

Château Beauregard Figeac
Present owner   Denis Pueyo
2.4469 hectares
Generic Saint-Émilion
Monsieur Pueyo also owns Château la Pignone.

Clos Belle Rose
Present owner   Jean-Pierre Faurie
1.17 hectares
Generic Saint-Émilion

Château Bellevue-Figeac
Present owner   Jacques de Coninck
5.1534 hectares
Grand Cru

Château Berliquet
Present owner   Vicomte de Lesquen
8.5 hectares
Grand Cru
Situated on the plateau neighbouring Château Canon and Château Magdelaine, this Grand Cru property covers 8.5 hectares. It is owned by Patrick, Vicomte de Lesquen, in whose family it has been for generations.

Since 1978 he has bottled all his wine at the Château and has restored and re-dug all the original underground cellarage. He has also installed new oak casks.

He is a member of the Co-operative who vinify all his wine.

In 1982 he will apply for Grand Cru Classé status and, if this is granted, it will be the first Grand Cru Classé property run by the Co-operative.

Under the laws of this appellation, all vinification and bottling must be carried out at the Château and it is planned that the Co-operative will send their staff to the Château to perform this task.

The present annual out-put is 320 hectolitres.

Château Bézineau
Present owner   Jean-Roger Faure
14.15 hectares
Generic Saint-Émilion

Yvonne Blanc
0.37 hectares
Sells generic Saint-Émilion in bulk only.

Domaine du Bois de l'Or
Present owner   Jean-Marie Granet
1.4907 hectares
Generic Saint-Émilion

Château Bois Redon
Present owner   Michel Lavandier
2.18 hectares
Generic Saint-Émilion
Michel Lavandier also owns Château le Mont d'Or, Château Vachon and Vieux Château Vachon.

Domaine de la Bonté
Present owner   Robert Labonté
0.3246 hectares
Generic Saint-Émilion

Château la Boucharde
Present owner   Linette Villatte
2.4823 hectares
Generic Saint-Émilion

André Bouye
0.5019 hectares
Sells generic Saint-Émilion in bulk only.

Château la Bouygue
Present owner   Ste des Vignobles Aberlen
4.7370 hectares
Grand Cru

Château Cadet-Pontet
Present owner   Michel Mérias
4.40 hectares
Generic Saint-Émilion
Monsieur Mérias also owns Château du Rocher (Grand Cru).

Château Calendream
Present owner   Joesette Pistouley
1.65 hectares
Generic Saint-Émilion

Château Canon Pourret
This is the brand-name for the second wine of Château Franc Pourret.

Château Cantenac
Present owner   Ste des Vignobles Brunot
1   6.810 hectares
    Grand Cru
2   3.7424 hectares
    Generic Saint-Émilion
This property, owned by the Ste des Vignobles Brunot who also own Château Tour de Grenet in Lussac, has been managed by Jean-Baptiste Brunot since 1964. There are 13 hectares split into two parts (1) Grand Cru 6.810 hectares under vine and (2) Generic Saint-Émilion 3.7424 hectares under vine, planted with 90% Merlot (an unusually high proportion) and 10% Bouchet. Average age of the vines is forty years, producing some 65 tonneaux. Fermentation in cement vats lasts five to ten days and the skins remain in the *must* for some twenty-one days. The wine is bottled after two years and its chief markets outside France are Belgium, Holland and Switzerland.

Château de la Capelle
Present owner   Roger Fournial
1.2784 hectares
Generic Saint-Émilion
Fully replanted by current owner.

Château Cardinal-Villemaurine
Present owner   Pierre Carrille
9.55 hectares
Grand Cru
The second wine of this property is *Château Robin des Moines*.

The Carrille family also own Domaine de Fussignac and Château Puyblanquet-Carrille.

Château Cardoneyre
Present owner   Vignobles Raby-Saugeon
7.6178 hectares
Grand Cru
Also own Château Paradis in Vignonet.

Château Clos Carré
Present owner   Jacques Soupre
0.28 hectares
Generic Saint-Émilion
Situated at the gates of Libourne.

Domaine de la Carte
Present owner   Bernard Lomenie
0.75 hectares
Generic Saint-Émilion

Château Carteau Bas Daugay
Present owner   Henri Bideau
6.27 hectares
Generic Saint-Émilion

Château Carteau Côte Daugay

Present owner   Jacques Bertrand
12.3 hectares under vine
Grand Cru

This Grand Cru property has been owned by Jacques Bertrand since 1962. He also owns Château Franc Pipeau in St Hippolyte.

This originally formed part of the larger estate of Carteau which has been divided over the generations. It covers 14 hectares of which 12.3 are under vine planted with 50% Merlot, 30% Bouchet and 20% Cabernet Sauvignon with an average age of vine of twenty years. Of the total area under vine, 1.28 hectares are used to produce a generic Saint-Émilion.

After picking, the grapes are 90% de-stalked and fermented in cement vats for up to five days. Then allowing a further period of up to twenty-one days for maceration, the wine is matured in oak casks for eighteen months before bottling.

The average out-put is 45 hectolitres per hectare with principal markets in France, Belgium and Holland.

Château Carteau Matras

Present owner   Claude Bion
10.32 hectares
Grand Cru

This Grand Cru property is 18 hectares, 10.32 under vine for the Grand Cru and 2.30 for the other wines (70% Merlot, 20% Bouchet, 10% Cabernet Sauvignon). The oldest vines are eighty years old and the average age twenty years. They produce about 70 tonneaux.

Fermentation in cement vats is short (five to six days) and the skins stay in the *must* for eight to ten days. No new casks are used and the oldest are fifteen years old. The wine is bottled after eighteen months and is sold mainly in France.

Two other wines are produced under the labels of *Château Haut Carteau* and *Château Carteau Pindefleurs*.

Château Carteau Pindefleurs

This is a brand-name for one of the second wines of Château Carteau Matras.

Château Cassevert

This is a brand-name for the second wine of Château Grand-Mayne, Grand Cru Classé.

Castel-Sartron

0.8542 hectares
Sells generic Saint-Émilion in bulk only.

Cave Co-opérative de Gardegan

1.17 hectares
Generic Saint-Émilion.

Cave Co-opérative de Montagne

0.5225 hectares
Generic Saint-Émilion

Château Chante-Alouette

Present owner   Jacques Barbary
1.6815 hectares
Grand Cru

Château Chante-Alouette

Present owner   Alain Berjal
4.6708 hectares
Grand Cru
Also produces wine under the label of *Domaine Chante l' Alouette*

André Chatonnet

1.00 hectares
Sells generic Saint-Émilion in bulk only.

Paul Chauveau

0.3149 hectares
Sells generic Saint-Émilion in bulk only.

Claude Chevalier

0.3821 hectares
Sells generic Saint-Émilion in bulk only.

Château Cheval Brun

Present owner   Pierre Ternoy
4.1130 hectares
Generic Saint-Émilion

Château Cheval-Noir

Present owner   Henry Mähler-Besse
3.9360 hectares
Generic Saint-Émilion
High iron-content sub-soil.

Château du Clocher

Present owner   Michel Merias
2.76 hectares
Grand Cru
Monsieur Merias also owns Château Cadet Pontet.

Château du Clocher

Present owner   Robert Merias
0.5677 hectares
Generic Saint-Émilion

Château Clos Haut Plante

Present owner   Gustave Venat
0.72 hectares
Generic Saint-Émilion

Château Clos Saint-Émilion Magnan

Present owner   Simone Philippe
6.98 hectares
Generic Saint-Émilion

Château la Commanderie

Present owner   Pierre Brasseur
2.8257 hectares
Grand Cru

Château Comte des Cordes
This is the second wine of Château Fonrazade made from the young vines.

Château Cormeil Figeac
Present owner Société Civile Cormeil Figeac – Magnan (Heritiers Moreaud)
10.5 hectares
Grand Cru
This estate, consisting of 26 hectares of which 17.83 are under vine, is owned by Société Civile Cormeil Figeac – Magnan (Heritiers Moreaud). It incorporates Château Cormeil Figeac (10.5 hectares), Château Magnan (10.5 hectares) since 1979, and the rented property of Domaine Lamarzelle Cormeil (5 hectares).

The wines are vinified separately using the same equipment for each.

The vineyard is planted with 70% Merlot, 28% Bouchet and 2% Pressac. After the grapes are picked, 90% are de-stalked and after pressing are fermented in inox vats for eight days, then matured in oak casks for up to two years before bottling.

The average out-put is 26 hectolitres per hectare.

Château Côtes de Rol
Present owner Pascale Faure
4 hectares
Generic Saint-Émilion
Old farmhouse with *chai* attached. Stainless-steel vats in the front garden.

Elie Coudert
1.0010 hectares
Sells generic Saint-Émilion in bulk only.

Château Couvent des Jacobins
Present owner Pierre Semelin
0.7121 hectares
Grand Cru

Château la Croix Chantecaille
Present owner Jean-Marie Estager
0.76 hectares
Generic Saint-Émilion

Château la Croix Chantecaille
Present owner Marie-Madelaine Angle
6.82 hectares
Grand Cru
Old farmhouse set in the middle of the vineyard.

Château Croix-Figeac
Present owner Jean Guimberteau
4.0444 hectares
Generic Saint-Émilion
Modern house on the crossroads of the Saint-Émilion–Pomerol road.

Château la Croix Mazerat
This property is split into two parts:
1 *Present owner* Lucette Roubinat
0.6220 hectares
Generic Saint-Émilion
2 *Present owner* Marcel Roubinat
0.95 hectares
Generic Saint-Émilion

Château Cros-Figeac
Present owner Christian Cassagne
4.44 hectares
Grand Cru

Château Cruzeau
Present owner Luquot & Fils
4.2462 hectares
Generic Saint-Émilion

Château d'Arthus
Present owner SEV Fournier
8.2691 hectares
Grand Cru
SEV Fournier also own Château Canon, Premier Grand Cru Classé.

Henri Dattas
0.2841 hectares
Sells generic Saint-Émilion in bulk only.

Roger Dattas
0.3723 hectares
Sells generic Saint-Émilion in bulk only.

Daudier de Cassini
5.4916 hectares
Generic Saint-Émilion and Grand Cru
Sells generic Saint-Émilion in bulk, and Grand Cru in bottle.

Pierre Delage
2.0205 hectares
Sells generic Saint-Émilion in bulk only.

Jean Delas
0.93 hectares
Sells generic Saint-Émilion in bulk only.

Château Doumayne
Present owner Francis Robin
Generic Saint-Émilion
A well-maintained medium-sized house with a well in the courtyard and *chai* attached. The cellars and *chai* house the wines of Château Sansonnet (Grand Cru Classé), Clos Vieux Taillefer (Pomerol), and Domaine de la Salle which M Robin also owns.

Clos Doumayne
Present owner Roland Bel
0.90 hectares
Generic Saint-Émilion

Germaine Dubois
1.35 hectares
Sells generic Saint-Émilion in bulk only.

Paul Dubois
0.67 hectares
Sells generic Saint-Émilion in bulk only.

Domaines Dubourg
0.60 hectares
Sells generic Saint-Émilion in bulk only.

Raymond Dupuy
0.41 hectares
Sells generic Saint-Émilion in bulk only.

Madame Dussery
0.73 hectares
Sells generic Saint-Émilion in bulk only.

Emilienne Duteuil
0.43 hectares
Sells generic Saint-Émilion in bulk only.

Janine Emery
0.22 hectares
Sells generic Saint-Émilion in bulk only.

Château l'Épine
Present owner   Jean Ardouin
2.1390 hectares
Generic Saint-Émilion

Clos l'Étape
Present owner   Charles Bardon
0.50 hectares
Generic Saint-Émilion

Château Fagouet Jean Voisin
This is the brand-name for the second wine of Château Jean Voisin.

Henri Ferignac
0.73 hectares
Sells generic Saint-Émilion in bulk only.

Régis Feyzeau
0.30 hectares
Sells generic Saint-Émilion in bulk only.

Château la Fleur Chantecaille
Present owner   Guy Arpin
1.1475 hectares
Generic Saint-Émilion

Château la Fleur Cravignac
Present owner   André Beaupertuis
6.6112 hectares
Grand Cru

Château Fleur Figeac
Present owner   Jean Maison
5.26 hectares
Generic Saint-Émilion

Clos la Fleur Figeac
Present owner   Moueix Vignobles
13.3645 hectares
Generic Saint-Émilion
Moueix Vignobles also own Château La Tour-du-Pin-Figeac; Château Fonplégarde; Château Tauzinat l'Hermitage; Château Taillefer; Château Moulinet; Clos Toulifaut; Château La Croix Bellevue.
 The wine is vinified at Château la Tour-du-Pin-Figeac where the vineyards border each other.

La Fleur Gueyrosse
Present owner   Robert Simon
2.05 hectares
Generic Saint-Émilion

Château la Fleur Fonrazade
Present owner   Annick Madillac
1.6964 hectares
Generic Saint-Émilion

Château la Fleur Menissac
Present owner   Ets Jean-Pierre Moueix
5.6140 hectares
Grand Cru
J-P Moueix also own Châteaux la Clotte; Moulin du Cadet; Fonroque; la Magdelaine; and other properties in Pomerol, including part-share in Château Pétrus.

Château la Fleur Picon
Present owner   Christian Lassegues
5.68 hectares
Grand Cru

Château la Fleur Pourret
Present owner   GFA des Domaines Prats
5.8487 hectares
Grand Cru
This is another Grand Cru property of GFA des Domaines Prats who own Châteaux Cos d'Estournel and De Marbuzet in St Éstèphe, Petit-Village in Pomerol and Petit Figeac in Saint-Émilion. Gilbert Xans makes the wine and looks after the vineyards of the last two as well as this single-storey farmhouse property. There are just over 6 hectares, 5.8487 under vine (76% Merlot, 13% Bouchet, 11% Cabernet Sauvignon), average age twenty-five years, producing some 18 tonneaux. The details of vinification are exactly the same as those of Château Petit-Village.

Château Fonrazade
Present owner   Guy Balotte
9.4314 hectares
Grand Cru

This Grand Cru estate, bought by Guy Balotte in 1948 from the Comte des Cordes is about ¾ of a kilometre due east of the town. Since then it has been entirely refurbished and replanted. There are 15 hectares with 9.4314 hectares under vine, planted with 70% Merlot, 10% Bouchet, 20% Cabernet Sauvignon. The average age of the vines is twenty-five years and they produce some 50 tonneaux.

Fermentation in cement and inox vats, lasts twenty days and the skins remain in the *must* for the same length of time. The wine is bottled after two and half years.

A second wine, *Château Comte des Cordes*, named after the previous owner, is made from the young vines. The 1981 price of *Château Fonrazade* was about 30 francs per bottle.

Château Font Froide
Present owner   Archille Chagneau
5.0751 hectares
Generic Saint-Émilion

Château Clos Fortin
Present owner   Louise Semblat
0.2078 hectares
Generic Saint-Émilion

Château Fouquet
Present owner   SCE Château Fouquet
4.7209 hectares
Generic Saint-Émilion
A second wine is produced under the name of *Château la Tour Fleurus*.

Château Fougueyrat
Present owner   Daniel Nicoux
5.1807 hectares
Grand Cru
Château Fougueyrat is a small modern farm-house with *chai* attached, reached down a long drive.

Château Franc Beau Mazerat
Present owner   Annie Boyer
1.62 hectares
Generic Saint-Émilion

Château Franc Cros
Present owner   André Lafage
2.8675 hectares
Generic Saint-Émilion

Château Franc Mazerat
Present owner   Pierette Koch
1.72 hectares
Generic Saint-Émilion

Château Franc Petit Figeac
Present owner   Gilbert Dumon
4.11 hectares
Generic Saint-Émilion

Château Franc Patarabet
Present owner   Barraud et Faure
4.5895 hectares
Grand Cru

Château Franc Pourret
Present owner   François Ouzoulias
5.91 hectares
Grand Cru
Situated within 1 kilometre of the bell-tower, the area of many of the great growths of the appellation of Saint-Émilion. The soil is clayey limestone.

Part of the harvest is sold under the label of *Château Canon Pourret* and M Ouzoulias also owns Château Haut Patarabet, Grand Cru.

Rolland Fredont
0.3201 hectares
Sells generic Saint-Émilion in bulk only.

Château la Garelle
Present owner   Guy Thibeaud
8.65 hectares
Generic Saint-Émilion

Daniel Giraud
1.35 hectares
Monsieur Giraud owns 1.35 hectares of generic Saint-Émilion and also owns Château Vieux Faure.

Julia Giraud
1.0436 hectares
Sells generic Saint-Émilion in bulk only.

Micheline Giraud
1.20 hectares
Sells generic Saint-Émilion in bulk only from this plot, and she also owns Château la Tour-du-Pin-Figeac, Grand Cru Classé.

Château la Gomerie
Present owner   Marcel Lescure
2.5209 hectares
Grand Cru
Set on the crossroads, an old farmhouse with *chai* attached.

Jean Gomme
0.21 hectares
Sells generic Saint-Émilion in bulk only.

Domaine des Gourdins
Present owner   Jean-Pierre Éstager
1.4107 hectares
Generic Saint-Émilion

Château Grâce Dieu
Present owner Maurice Pauty
11.14 hectares
Grand Cru
A charming farmhouse-style Château with well-kept vineyards. Average production 400 hecto-litres.

Château la Grâce Dieu les Menuts
Present owner Max Pilotte-Xans
11.31 hectares
Grand Cru
Max Pilotte-Xans is the proprietor of this Grand Cru estate which comprises 12.5 hectares of which 11.31 hectares are under vine (60% Merlot, 35% Bouchet, 5% Cabernet Sauvignon), average age twenty years, producing some 60 tonneaux. It is situated on the main Saint-Émilion – Libourne road.

The grapes are not totally de-stalked and fermentation in cement vats lasts about twenty-one days. The wine is then bottled after eighteen months to two years, having been matured in five-year-old oak casks.

The main market for the wine is Belgium and Holland.

Château la Grâce Dieu des Prieurs
Present owner Ghislaine Laubie
This property is split into two parts:
1   5.38 hectares
     Grand Cru
2   1.36 hectares
     Generic Saint-Émilion
Located on the Saint-Émilion road at the foot of the old medieval city.

Château Grand Corbin Manuel
Present owner Pierre Manuel
11.42 hectares
Grand Cru

Domaine du Grand Faurie
Present owner René Bodet
3.5 hectares
Grand Cru

Château Grand Gontey
Present owner Jeanne Pezat
2.0697 hectares
Generic Saint-Émilion

Château le Grand Humeau
Present owner Jean-Pierre Goudineau
0.2410 hectares
Generic Saint-Émilion

Château Grand Mirande
Present owner Raymond Junet
This property is split into two parts:

1   3.89 hectares
     Grand Cru
2   4.5 hectares
     Generic Saint-Émilion

Château les Grandes Versannes
Present owner Christiane Pirabeau
1.18 hectares
Generic Saint-Émilion

François Gratadour
Owns 1.0180 hectares of generic Saint-Émilion and also owns Château Cadet-Bon, Grand Cru Classé.

Louis Grelot
0.5019 hectares
Sells generic Saint-Émilion in bulk only.

Château la Grave Figeac
Present owner Odette Ornon
Grand Cru
Situated on the border of Saint-Émilion and Pomerol, this small country-house property on the main road is the last Saint-Émilion property before entering the Pomerol appellation, opposite Château Cheval Blanc. The soil is mainly sand with a little gravel.

Château Guadet le Franc Grâce Dieu
Present owner M Siloret
3.6875 hectares
Grand Cru
This Grand Cru property lying back from the main road in the dip of the valley about a mile and a half north-west of the town, has belonged to the family of the present owner, M Siloret, since 1931. In September 1981, Eric Fournier, of Château Canon leased the vineyard. It takes the first part of its name from the Guadet family to whom it belonged from the seventeenth century; and the second from the fact that a Cistercian friary stood there from the twelth or thirteenth century. Paul Cayenave has been *Maître de Chai* since 1957, and the house is well-maintained.

There are 9 hectares of which 3.6875 are under vine (55% Merlot, 35% Bouchet, 10% Cabernet Sauvignon and Pressac), which produces some 30 tonneaux. The average age of the vines is thirty years. The percentage of the different grapes in the actual wine may vary considerably from the vineyard proportions. In very big production years when the early-ripening Merlot predominates there may be 70% to 80% Merlot in the wine (1973, 1974, 1976). In smaller production years, the overall Cabernet content in the wine may rise as high as 60% to 70% (1975, 1977, 1978).

The grapes are completely de-stalked, then pressed in an old-fashioned hydraulic press, and the juice fermented for ten to fifteen days in vats, some cement, some inox stainless-steel. The wine is then run off into casks, from two to five years old, purchased after one vintage from a Grand Cru Classé property. It is assembled (in the January or February following the vintage) racked six times, fined and bottled after twenty to twenty-two months. The entire crop is Château-bottled. Half is sold to Bordeaux *négociants*, a quarter to private customers, and a quarter is exported – mainly to Belgium and Switzerland.

Clos Geuyrosse
Present owner   Raymond Brudy
0.2072 hectares
Generic Saint-Émilion

Château Gueyrosse
Present owner   Yves Delol
This property is split into two parts:
1   5.6140 hectares
    Grand Cru
2   4.5424 hectares
    Generic Saint-Émilion
This vineyard is on the right bank of the Dordogne.

Château Gueyrot
Present owner   Frères Tour du Fayet
8.36 hectares
Grand Cru
A collection of old houses with the main property in the centre lying beneath Château Pavie.

Château Guillemin la Gaffelière
Present owner   Société Fomperier
This property is split into two parts:
1   8.3620 hectares
    Grand Cru
2   3.1872 hectares
    Generic Saint-Émilion

Clos Haut Cabanne
Present owner   Juliette Amblard
1.05 hectares
Generic Saint-Émilion

Château Haut Cadet
Present owner   Paul Petitguillaume-Sauvaître
9.4374 hectares
Grand Cru
This Grand Cru estate is sited at the extreme north of the limestone plateau of Saint-Émilion and one can still see evidence of ancient cave dwellings, some still in use in Saint-Émilion up to the nineteenth century. The present owner is Paul Petitguillaume-Sauvaître and the property has been in the family for at least four generations. Jean Bernard, the oenologist and owner of Château Matras, has farmed the vineyard and made the wine for twenty years.

There are 9.4374 hectares of vines (30% Merlot, 25% Bouchet, 45% Cabernet Sauvignon – an unusually high proportion of the last-named) producing an average of 35 tonneaux at about 31 hectolitres per hectare. The average age of the vines is twenty years.

An unusual feature of the vinification is that the wine spends a year in cement or stainless-steel vats before being transferred to casks – some new, some up to ten years old – and matured, assembled, racked and fined, before being bottled after about two years. The 1980 price was about 13 francs a bottle.

Château Haut Carteau
Present owner
This is the brand-name for the second wine of Château Carteau Matras.

Château Haut Jura
Present owner   René Andrieu
0.4920 hectares
Generic Saint-Émilion

Château Haut Jacque Blanc
Present owner   Jean-René Dupeyrou
1.61 hectares
Generic Saint-Émilion

Château Haut Jaugue Blanc
Present owner   Joseph Debacque
2.15 hectares
Generic Saint-Émilion

Château Haut la Grâce Dieu
Present owner   Jean Bernard Sabay
The property is owned by Jean Bernard Sabay who also owns Château Rozier (St Laurent-des-Combes). The average age of the vines is fifteen years. The fermentation lasts for ten to fifteen days and the wine is fermented and matured in cement tanks before being bottled after eighteen months.

Château Haut Mazerat
Present owner   Heritiers Gouteyron
10.8156 hectares
Grand Cru

Château Haut Patarabet
Present owner   François Ouzoulias
5.91 hectares
Grand Cru
Monsieur Ouzoulias also owns Château Franc-Pourret, Grand Cru.

Château Haut Plantey
Present owner   Michel Boutet
7.1095 hectares
Grand Cru
Monsieur Boutet also produces wine under the name of *Château Petit Val*; he is the *Gérant* of Château Cannon la Gaffelière, Château Peyreau and Clos l'Oratoire.

Château Haut Pontet
Present owner   Limouzin Frères
5 hectares
Grand Cru
This is a very small attractive Château situated 500 metres from the Old Walls (Vieilles-Murailles) neighbouring Châteaux Grand-Pontet and Fonroque.

Château Haut Pourret
Present owner   Madame Mourgout
2.39 hectares
Grand Cru

Château Haut Segottes
Present owner   Daniele André
7.0686 hectares
Grand Cru
A small farmhouse on the main road to Libourne adjoining Château la Grace Dieu.

Château Haut Simard
Present owner   Claude Mazière
34.2393 hectares
Generic Saint-Émilion
This Château is situated at the foot of the Saint-Émilion slopes. It is a two-storey house immediately adjacent to the station, with a small *chai* backing on to the railway-yard.

Château Haut Troquart
Present owners   Marc Herbert and Henriette Julien
2.9433 hectares
Generic Saint-Émilion

Château Haut Vachon la Rose
Present owner   André Quenouille
2.4490 hectares
Generic Saint-Émilion

Michel Huk
2.0152 hectares
Sells generic Saint-Émilion in bulk only.

Clos Jacquemau
Present owner   René Greil
0.91 hectares
Generic Saint-Émilion
A modern family house set in the vineyards.

François Janoueix
0.8079 hectares
Sells generic Saint-Émilion in bulk only from this plot. The Janoueix family own many properties in Saint-Émilion and Pomerol.

Clos Jean Faure
Present owner   Louis Feyti
0.5232 hectares
Generic Saint-Émilion

Château Jean Marie
Present owner   Guy Recapet
3.82 hectares
Generic Saint-Émilion

Château Jean Voisin
Present owner   M M Chassagnoux
11.86 hectares
Grand Cru
An impressive, turreted Château in good condition. A second wine is produced under the label of *Château Fagouet-Jean-Voisin*.

Château Clos Jean Voisin
This property has been split into two parts:
1   *Present owner*   Marie-Louise Sautarel
6.4425 hectares
Generic Saint-Émilion
2   *Present owner*   G F A Sautarel
3.0821 hectares
Generic Saint-Émilion

Raoul Joubert
0.3601 hectares
Sells generic Saint-Émilion in bulk only.

Château le Jurat
Present owner   Edward Guinaudie
This Grand Cru property set on the main road from Pomerol has a modern farmhouse and *chai*. It is owned by Edward Guinaudie, who also owns Château Haut-Corbin (Grand Cru Classé), and covers 7.95 hectares, of which 7.5 hectares are under vine, planted with 66% Merlot and 33% Cabernet Sauvignon with an average age of twenty-five years.

The grapes are picked by machine, 75% de-stalked and fermented in cement vats for up to three weeks. The wine is matured in oak casks for two years before bottling. A second wine is produced from the young vines under the name of *Le Vin d'Edouard*.

Jean Lacoste
0.9733 hectares
Sells generic Saint-Émilion in bulk only.

Roland Lacoste
0.37 hectares
Sells generic Saint-Émilion in bulk only.

Grapes arriving at Château Cheval Blanc.

Fermentation in vats at Château Figeac.

Ripe Merlot grapes awaiting vendange at Château Cheval Blanc.

Domaine Lamarzelle Cormeil
For details see Château Cormeil Figeac.

Pierre Laudu
0.84 hectares
Sells generic Saint-Émilion in bulk only.

Léopold Lavandier
1.2864 hectares
Sells generic Saint-Émilion in bulk only.

Georgette Lavigne
0.96 hectares
Sells generic Saint-Émilion in bulk only.

Jacques Lemoine
0.6154 hectares
Sells generic Saint-Émilion in bulk only.

Château Lenoir
Present owner   Léopold Couderc
5.4838 hectares
Generic Saint-Émilion

Château de Lisse
Present owner   Jean Petit
10.58 hectares
Generic Saint-Émilion
A small farmhouse property.

Clos du Louteauneuf
Present owner   Jean-Pierre Fortin
1.36 hectares
Generic Saint-Émilion

Clos la Madeleine
Present owner   Hubert Pistouley
This property is split into two parts:
1   2.00 hectares
    Grand Cru Classé
2   2.00 hectares
    Generic Saint-Émilion
He also owns Château Magnan la Gaffelière.

Château Magnan
Present owner   Heritiers Moreaud
This 10.5 hectare property is now part of Château Cormeil Figeac. For details see Château Cormeil Figeac.

Château Magnan la Gaffelière
Present owner   Hubert Pistouley
6.75 hectares
Grand Cru
Surrounded by the Premier Grand Cru Classés of Saint-Émilion. M Pistouley also owns the Clos la Madeleine, Grand Cru Classé.

Château Malineau
Present owner   Société Philippe Gouze
4.8920 hectares
Grand Cru

Louis Martin
0.3948 hectares
Sells generic Saint-Émilion in bulk only.

Pierre Martin
1.2992 hectares
Sells generic Saint-Émilion in bulk only.

Château Martinet
Present owner   De Lavaux Family
Generic Saint-Émilion
The estate consists of 25 hectares of which 15.4583 hectares are under vine. The soil is sandy, gravelly, and a high percentage of Merlot is planted. The property was the leading growth of the now extinct *Sables* appellation.
   Today, it is run by Mme. J Lavaux (née Horeau), who is related to the Saint-Genis family, who owned it for many years previously.
   Production is 35 to 40 hectolitres per hectare.

Château Matignon
Present owner   Henri Matignon
0.6399 hectares
Generic Saint-Émilion

Château Mauvezin la Gomerie
Present owner   Jeanne Dumigron
0.54 hectares
Grand Cru

Château le Mayne
Present owner   Jean Dupuy
0.2597 hectares
Generic Saint-Émilion

Château Mayne Figeac
Present owner   Jean Jaime Chambret
This property is split into two parts:
1   1.43 hectares
    Grand Cru
2   0.2560 hectares
    Generic Saint-Émilion

Château Melin
Present owner   René Debacques
10.42 hectares
Generic Saint-Émilion

Clos des Menuts
Present owner   Pierre Rivière
20.3438 hectares
Grand Cru
The vineyard lies at the gates of Saint-Émilion although their office and *caves* are situated in the town of Saint-Émilion. The sub-soil is clay-limestone and traditional methods of vinification are used, i.e., storage in oak casks for two years in vast, medieval cellars carved in the rock.
   All wine is Château-bottled.

Pierre Rivière also owns Château Grand Rivallon and Château Petit Yon, both in Saint-Émilion

Château Meylet
Present owner Michel Favard
0.89 hectares
Grand Cru

Château Meylet la Gomerie
Present owner Guy Charron
2.25 hectares
Grand Cru

Robert Mignon
0.6272 hectares
Sells generic Saint-Émilion in bulk only.

Château Milhaud Montlabert
Present owner Brieux et Fils
This property is split into two parts:
1 1.6047 hectares
   Grand Cru
2 1.2934 hectares
   Generic Saint-Émilion

Château le Moine
Present owner Raymond Tapon
2.34 hectares
Generic Saint-Émilion

Château le Mont d'Or
Present owner Michel Lavandier
1.0355 hectares
Generic Saint-Émilion
Monsieur Lavandier also owns Château Bois Redon; Vieux Château Vachon; Château Vachon.

Château Monte Cristo
Present owner Philibert Rousselot
This property is split into two parts:
1 0.3723 hectares
   Generic Saint-Émilion
2 2.48 hectares
   Generic Saint-Émilion

Château Montlabert
Present owner Château Montlabert Société Civile
11.3192 hectares
Grand Cru
This attractive property lies just over 1 mile from Saint-Émilion on the road to Libourne. The history of the Château goes back to the late eighteenth century when the owner was Monsieur Jean-Baptiste Saint Macary, but by 1845 it was in the hands of the Decazes family, Jean Michael Théodore Decazes. In 1861 the property was sub-divided and the part on which the

Château stood passed to Dr Gustave Petit. His daughter, who became Madame Stefanie, owned the Château until 1968 when a group of international investors and wine-lovers formed a syndicate to purchase the property in the name of Château Montlabert, Société Civile. The administrator is René Barnière, the *Chef du Culture* Roger Rochereau and the *Maître de Chai* M Zucchi. Behind the Château there is a beautiful park with many trees which are over one hundred years old.

There are 17.5 hectares, 11.3192 under vine (55% Merlot, 35% Bouchet, 10% Cabernet Sauvignon), average age twenty years, producing about 50 tonneaux.

The grapes are completely de-stalked and pressed in a hydraulic press.

Fermentation, in cement vats, lasts eight to ten days and the skins remain in the *must* for fifteen to twenty-one days. The wine is then run off into casks (six to eight years old) and matured, assembled, racked and fined in the usual way, before being bottled after two years. The price in 1981 was 20 to 23 francs and the main markets outside France are Belgium, The Netherlands, Denmark, Switzerland, Canada and The United States of America.

Château le Monty
Present owner Herbert Bousquet
0.2437 hectares
Generic Saint-Émilion

Château Moulin du Cadet
Present owner Gombeau Fils
2.4965 hectares
Generic Saint-Émilion
Small run-down Château.

Château Moulin du Jura
This property is split into two parts:
1 *Present owner* Armand Berlureau
   1.60 hectares
   Generic Saint-Émilion
2 *Present owner* Alain Berlureau
   2.5892 hectares
   Generic Saint-Émilion

Château Moulin Saint Georges
Present owner Alain Vauthier
6 hectares
Grand Cru
This Grand Cru property, owned and managed by Alain Vauthier, nephew of Mme Dubois-Challon of Château Ausone, lies on the slopes of Pavie facing Château Ausone. It has 6.5 hectares of which 6 hectares are under vine (50% Merlot, 40% Bouchet, 10% Cabernet Sauvignon) aver-

age age thirty years, producing 20 to 30 tonneaux. The sub-soil is rocky, covered by a few inches of clay.

Vinification is traditional, fermentation (in inox vats) lasting about fifteen days, and the *must* remaining on the skins for three to four weeks. The wine is then matured in oak casks for up to three years before bottling. It is sold direct in France, and through *négociants* to England, Belgium, Germany and Mexico. The 1981 prices are 1976: 37 francs, 1975: 55 francs, 1970: 75 francs.

Monsieur Vauthier also owns Château Jauge Blanc and Château Lucas (Lussac-Saint-Émilion).

Pierre Musset
0.4847 hectares
Sells generic Saint-Émilion in bulk only.

Bernard Oizeau
This property is divided into two parts:
1   0.1642 hectares
    Generic Saint-Émilion
2   0.1738 hectares
    Generic Saint-Émilion
Sells generic Saint-Émilion in bulk only.

Francis Paris
0.67 hectares
Sells generic Saint-Émilion in bulk only.

Château Pas Saint Georges
Present owner   Famille Prot
13 hectares
Generic Saint-Émilion
This property was originally owned by Madame Dubois-Challon of Château Ausone who sold it to the present owners Famille Prot.

The vineyards cover 13 hectares planted with 50% Merlot and 50% Bouchet. The fermentation takes place in vats for up to eight days and matured in oak casks before bottling.

The average out-put is 40 hectolitres per hectare and is marketed exclusively by Maison Dourthe.

Château Patarabet
Present owner   Eric Bordas
6.7706 hectares
Generic Saint-Émilion

Château Patris
Present owner   Michel Querre
7.38 hectares
Grand Cru
Michel Querre, cousin of Alain Querre of Château Monbusquet owns this property as well as Château Mazeyres in Pomerol. There

are 7.38 hectares of vines (66.6% Merlot, 33.3% Bouchet), average age twenty years, producing about 40 tonneaux. Fermentation, in cement and epoxy-resin vats, lasts for eight days and the skins remain in the *must* for three weeks. The wine is matured in new oak casks, which are renewed every year, and bottled after eighteen months. Outside France the main markets are Great Britain, Holland, Luxembourg, Germany, The United States and Switzerland.

Moisette Paulin
0.3964 hectares
Sells generic Saint-Émilion in bulk only.

Château Pavillon Figeac
Present owner   René de Coninck
3.40 hectares
Generic Saint-Émilion

Château Petit Bois la Garelle
Present owner   Jean Chatonnet
4.82 hectares
Generic Saint-Émilion

Château Petit Clos Figeac
Present owner   Albert Janoueix
6.78 hectares
Generic Saint-Émilion
A very small modern farmhouse set on the road to Pomerol.

Château Petit Figeac
Present owner   Société Fermieredes Domaines Prats
This property has 1.5 hectares under vine – 1 hectare of which is Merlot and the half hectare is planted with Cabernet Sauvignon.

The wine is vinified at Château la Fleur Pourret under the same technical conditions as la Fleur Pourret. The property was acquired at the beginning of the century by Fernand Ginestet and is now owned by his grandchildren under the Société Fermière des Domaines Prats.

Château Petit Franc Quet
Present owner   Jean-Pierre Quet
3.6980 hectares
Generic Saint-Émilion

Château Petit Garderose
Present owner   Jacques Henocques
3.92 hectares
Generic Saint-Émilion

Domaine du Petit Georges
Present owner   André Dusage
0.3515 hectares
Generic Saint-Émilion

Château Petit Gontey
Present owner Gérard Delbos
3.37 hectares
Generic Saint-Émilion

Clos du Petit Jauge Blanc
Present owner Georges Bigaud
3.0833 hectares
Generic Saint-Émilion

Château Petit Pin de Fleurs
Present owner Henri Bonnemaison
0.4454 hectares
Generic Saint-Émilion

Château Petit Val
This is the brand-name for the second wine of
Château Haut Plantey.

Château Peyreau
Present owner Société Civile Château Peyreau
13.4393 hectares
Grand Cru
A large, classic Château just below Château
Haut-Sarpe.

Château Peyrelongue
Present owner Jean-Jacques Bouquey
4.3348 hectares
Grand Cru
A modern house. There is also another 4.3950
hectares producing generic Saint-Émilion.

Domaine de Peyrelongue
Present owner Olivier Cassat
2.5620 hectares
Grand Cru
Olivier Cassat also owns Château Mauvezin,
Grand Cru Classé.

Domaine de Peyrelongue
Present owner Pierre Cassat
7.8798 hectares
Grand Cru
A small bungalow beside the railway.

Patrick Picaud
2.26 hectares
Sells generic Saint-Émilion in bulk only.

Château la Pignonne
Present owner Denis Pueyo
2.4469 hectares
Generic Saint-Émilion
Monsieur Pueyo also owns Château Beauregard
Figeac.

Max and Jean Louis Pineaud
4.4579 hectares
Sell generic Saint-Émilion in bulk only.

Château Pindefleurs
Present owner Micheline Dior
7.7964 hectares
Grand Cru

Château la Planète
Present owner Michel Decros
0.60 hectares
Generic Saint-Émilion

Château la Pointe Bouguey
Present owner René Bentenat
6.25 hectares
Generic Saint-Émilion

Domaine du Pont
Present owner Jean Marcel Feyzeau
0.4850 hectares
Generic Saint-Émilion

Château Pontet Clauzure
Present owner Société Marne et Champagne
10.25 hectares
Grand Cru
A small, impressive Château at the end of a long
driveway, Château Pontet Clauzure is situated
in the heart of the great growths on the high
plateau of Saint-Émilion, 200 metres from the
bell-tower. It is near the historic home of the
Girondin Gaudet at the gates of the town facing
the ruins of the Palais Cardinal and the Grandes
Murailles (Great Walls).

Robert Privat
0.63 hectares
Sells generic Saint-Émilion on bulk only.

Château Puy
Present owner Guy Thoilliez
4.75 hectares
Grand Cru
The soil is gravel and sand, and rich in iron-
oxide.
   Château Puy is well-known in the Benelux
countries, Switzerland and Great Britain.

Clos des Quatre Vents
Present owner Marcel Beaufils
0.3252 hectares
Generic Saint-Émilion

Château Queyron
This property is split into three parts:
1 *Present owner* Christian Goujou
   6.40 hectares
   Generic Saint-Émilion
2 *Present owner* Louis Goujou
   5.94 hectares
   Generic Saint-Émilion

3 *Present owner* Louis Goujou
   3.80 hectares
   Generic Saint-Émilion

Château Queyron Pindefleurs
Present owner André Fillon
9.57 hectares
Generic Saint-Émilion
Average production 400 hectolitres.

Château Quinault
Present owner Henri Maleret
This property is split into two parts:
1 3.14 hectares
   Grand Cru
2 10.22 hectares
   Generic Saint-Émilion
Château Quinault is situated at the gates of Libourne. It was owned by Baptiste Mons for many years, who completely replanted and extended the vineyard.

Clos Ratouin
Present owner Pierre Ratouin
2.0458 hectares
Generic Saint-Émilion

Château Régent
Present owner Christian Pascaud
4.03 hectares
Generic Saint-Émilion

Château Reine Blanche
Present owner Despagne Consorts
5.25 hectares
Generic Saint-Émilion

Château de Rey
Present owner Alice Carmagnac
4.4924 hectares
Generic Saint-Émilion

Dattas Reynaud
0.5603 hectares
Sells generic Saint-Émilion in bulk only.

Francis Ricco
0.2112 hectares
Sells generic Saint-Émilion in bulk only.

Château Robin des Moines
This is the brand-name for the second wine of Château Cardinal Villemaurine.

Château la Rocaille
Present owner François Florit
5.4731 hectares
Generic Saint-Émilion

Château Rochebrune
Present owner Alfred Chal
1.5 hectares
Generic Saint-Émilion
This property of 1.5 hectares is situated in the now extinct Sables area of Saint-Émilion.

The vineyard is planted with 66% Merlot and 33% Bouchet, the average age of the vines being approximately twenty-four years old.

The *Maître de Chai* M Feyzean of thirty years standing looks after the complete operation.

After the grapes are picked, they are totally de-stalked and fermented in cement vats for up to three weeks, after which the wine is matured in oak casks for two years before bottling.

Château Rocher Figeac
Present owner Max Fournier
3.7506 hectares
Generic Saint-Émilion

Château Rol
Present owner Jean Sautereau
7.2867 hectares
Grand Cru

Château Rolland Maillet
Present owner M M Rolland
3.3501 hectares
Generic Saint-Émilion
This property, like its near neighbour just across the border in Pomerol, Château La Bon Pasteur, was established at the beginning of this century by the grandparents of the present owner M M Rolland. It is right up in the northern tip of Saint-Émilion, just north-east of Château Croque Michotte.

Monsieur Rolland looks after the vineyard and the wine-making himself.

The soil is flinty clay with a sand and molasse sub-soil. There are about 5 hectares of which 3.3501 hectares are under vine (75% Merlot, 25% Bouchet) producing an average of 15 tonneaux. The oldest vines are seventy-five years old and the average age is thirty-five years.

The grapes are sometimes completely de-stalked, sometimes only 80%, depending on the year. After light crushing, the juice is fermented in cement vats for eight to fifteen days, the skins remaining in the *must* for that time and sometimes appreciably longer. After pressing, the wine spends two-thirds of its maturation time in vats and one-third in oak casks (some new, some once-used) and is racked, fined and assembled in the usual way, before being bottled after two to two and a half years. Since 1978 all the wine has been bottled at the Château.

Société Romain Maison
4.5244 hectares
Sells generic Saint-Émilion in bulk only.

Château de Roquefort
Present owner   Comte Leo de Malet Roquefort
2.60 hectares
Grand Cru
Comte Leo de Malet Roquefort also owns Château la Gaffelière, Première Grand Cru Classé, and Château Tertre Daugay, Grand Cru Classé.

Château de Roquemont
Present owner   Jean André Robineau
4.50 hectares
Generic Saint-Émilion

Château la Rose Côtes Rol
Present owner   Yves Mirande
8.38 hectares
Grand Cru
Yves Mirande owns this Grand Cru property (and a wine-shop in Saint-Émilion) which is just over a mile due north of the town on the D.122. There are 8.38 hectares of vines (60% Merlot, 15% Bouchet, 15% Cabernet Sauvignon, 10% Pressac), average age thirty years, producing some 40 tonneaux.

The fermentation, in cement vats, lasts for five to eight days and the skins remain in the *must* for fifteen to twenty-five days. The wine is bottled after eighteen months to two years. The 1981 price was 25 francs.

Château la Rose Pourret
Present owner   Bernard Warion
7.33 hectares
Grand Cru
The Château is located 1 kilometre from the town.

Château la Rose Rol
Present owner   Marie Descombe
2.10 hectares
Generic Saint-Émilion

Château la Rose Trimoulet
Present owner   Jean Claude Brisson
4.36 hectares
Grand Cru

Château la Roseraie
Present owner   Raymond Lasfargeas
3.67 hectares
Generic Saint-Émilion
A small modern house set back in the vineyard.

Daniel Rousselot
0.59 hectares
Sells generic Saint-Émilion in bulk only.

Château Roylland
Present owner   Michel Bordier
3.5 hectares
Generic Saint-Émilion

Château la Sablière
Present owner   Robert Avezou
9.0001 hectares
Generic Saint-Émilion
A small, attractive property.

Clos St André
Present owner   André Desmarty
0.6208 hectares
Generic Saint-Émilion

Clos St André
Present owner   Georges Brieux
0.6208 hectares
Generic Saint-Émilion

Château St André
This property is divided into two parts:
1   *Present owner*   Pierrette Javanaud
    0.23 hectares
    Generic Saint-Émilion
2   *Present owner*   Patrick Javanaud
    1.4752 hectares
    Generic Saint-Émilion

Château St André Corbin
Present owner   Robert Carre
1.5455 hectares
Generic Saint-Émilion

Château St Jean
Present owner   Jean-Raymond Gruge
1.36 hectares
Generic Saint-Émilion

M Sallafranque
0.3720 hectares
Sells generic Saint-Émilion in bulk only.

Château Sarenseau
Present owner   Roger Horse
7.65 hectares
Generic Saint-Émilion

Domaine de Sarpe
Present owner   Guy Chatenet
1.3353 hectares
Generic Saint-Émilion

André Sarrazin
1.80 hectares
Sells generic Saint-Émilion in bulk only.

Château Sauvenelle
Present owner   Daniele Torelli
0.70 hectares
Generic Saint-Émilion

Marie-Rose Serani
1.69 hectares
Sells generic Saint-Émilion in bulk only.

Jean Seuve
This property has two sites:
1   2.0697 hectares
     Generic Saint-Émilion
2   0.9733 hectares
     Generic Saint-Émilion
Sells generic Saint-Émilion in bulk only.

Domaine des Sommeliers
Present owner   Liliane Blanchet
0.74 hectares
Generic Saint-Émilion

Château Soutard Cadet
Present owner   Jacques Darribehaude
1.3827 hectares
Generic Saint-Émilion

Château Tarreyre
Present owner   Arlette Brissaud
2.71 hectares
Generic Saint-Émilion

Marcel Tartarin
2.18 hectares
Sells generic Saint-Émilion in bulk only.

Roger Teilhet
0.1863 hectares
Sells generic Saint-Émilion in bulk only.

Michel Terras
5.61 hectares
Sells generic Saint-Émilion in bulk only.

Marie Thomas
0.48 hectares
Sells generic Saint-Émilion in bulk only.

Marie-Thérèse Tomasina
4.37 hectares
Sells generic Saint-Émilion in bulk only, together with bottled Grand Cru.

Château Tour de Beauregard
Present owner   Illario Fritegotto
This property is divided into two parts:
1   0.37 hectares
     Generic Saint-Émilion
2   14.0260 hectares
     Generic Saint-Émilion

Château Tour Berthonneau
Present owner   Grolière & Fils
1.3548 hectares
Grand Cru

Château Tour de Corbin
Present owner   Gérard Despagne
3.8396 hectares
Generic Saint-Émilion

Château la Tour Fleurus
This is the brand-name for the second wine of Château Fouquet.

Château Tour Fonrazade
Present owner   Bezos Père & Fils
7.7560 hectares
Generic Saint-Émilion

Château Tour Grand Faurie
Present owner   Jean Feytit
10.17 hectares
Generic Saint-Émilion

Château Tour du Guetteur
Present owner   Marie Louise Andrieux
0.4000 hectares
Grand Cru
A tiny Château, less than 1 hectare, cultivated on terraces like a magnificent garden which can only be worked by hand.
   At the foot of the monument known as 'Lookout's Tower', it overlooks Saint-Émilion and its valley. It used to be the spot from which warning was given of the enemy's approach.
   Madame Andrieux also owns Château Bourron, near the Talbot monument, one of the best growths of the Côtes de Castillon.

Château Tour Monrepos
Present owner   Pierre Manuaud
0.4580 hectares
Generic Saint-Émilion

Château Tour Pourret
Present owner   Société Tour Pourret
4.5 hectares
Generic Saint-Émilion

Château Tour Saint Pierre
Present owner   Jacques Goudineau
9.35 hectares
Grand Cru
This property borders the Saint-Émilion-Montagne road, between the properties of Châteaux Trimoulet, Dassault and Vachon.
   The 9.35 hectares of vineyards are planted on clayey-siliceous soil.

Château Tour Vachon
Present owner René Rebinguet
3.4126 hectares
Grand Cru

Château Tramsou Peyroutas
Present owner Monette Bouchon
1.1615 hectares
Generic Saint-Émilion

Château Trianon
Present owner Mme Lecointre
6.17 hectares
Generic Saint-Émilion
Situated to the west of the commune of Saint-Émilion, this property lies on sandy-gravelly, siliceous soil with iron content.

Clos Trimoulet
Present owner Guy Appollot
This property is split into two parts:
1   1.0150 hectares
     Grand Cru
2   0.6647 hectares
     Generic Saint-Émilion

Château Vachon
Present owner Michel Lavandier
3.7534 hectares
Generic Saint-Émilion
Monsieur Lavandier also owns Château le Mont d'Or; Château Bois Redon; Vieux Château Vachon.

Château Valentin
Present owner Pierre Giraud
1.62 hectares
Generic Saint-Émilion

Clos Valentin
This property is split into two parts:
1   *Present owner* Bernard Leydet
     5.0326 hectares
     Generic Saint-Émilion
2   *Present owner* Leydet Vignobles
     1.0270 hectares
     Grand Cru
A run-down property with large *chai*.

Château Valentin Larmande
Present owner Raymond Mérias
6.3310 hectares
Generic Saint-Émilion

Château Verdet
Present owner Edmond Beaugier
2.10 hectares
Generic Saint-Émilion

Société Verhnes
3.68 hectares
Grand Cru

Jean-Claude Veyssière
1.7296 hectares
Sells generic Saint-Émilion in bulk only.

Château Vieille Cloche
Present owner Georges Payan
3.8850 hectares
Generic Saint-Émilion

Château Vieille Tour la Rose
Present owner Jean Ybert
7.07 hectares
Generic Saint-Émilion

Château Vieux Cantenat
Present owner Marcel Rebeyrol
This property is split into two parts:
1   3.20 hectares
     Grand Cru
2   3.07 hectares
     Generic Saint-Émilion

Vieux Château Carré
Present owner Yvon Dubost
2.6254 hectares
Grand Cru

Vieux Château Montlabert
Present owner Bernard Moulinet
0.5056 hectares
Generic Saint-Émilion

Vieux Château Pelletan
Present owner Marc Magnaudeix
3.4227 hectares
Grand Cru
Monsieur Magnaudeix also has 6.6570 hectares in adjoining St Christophe-des-Bardes under the same Château name.

Vieux Château Vachon
Present owner Michel Lavandier
1.2864 hectares
Generic Saint-Émilion
Monsieur Lavandier also owns Château le Mont d'Or; Château Bois Redon; Château Vachon.

Château Vieux Chantecaille
Present owner Lucien Moze
1.2696 hectares
Generic Saint-Émilion

Château Vieux Fonrazade
Present owner Lucette Digeos
3.59 hectares
Generic Saint-Émilion

Château Vieux Fortin
Present owner   Georges Meunier
3.72 hectares
Generic Saint-Émilion

Château Vieux Faure
Present owner   Daniel Giraud
3.1894 hectares
Generic Saint-Émilion

Château Vieux Jean Marie
Present owner   Georges Fauchier
1.2333 hectares
Generic Saint-Émilion

Château Vieux Lartigue
Present owner   SCE Château Vieux Lartigue
5.8320 hectares
Generic Saint-Émilion

Château Vieux Pin Figeac
Present owner   Janine Bosc
0.8158 hectares
Generic Saint-Émilion

Château Vieux Pourret
Present owner   SC Château Vieux Pourret
3.6699 hectares
Grand Cru
Managed by Michel Boutet who also manages Château Canon la Gaffelière; Château la Tour-Figeac; Clos l'Oratoire.

Château Vieux Rocher la Madeleine
Present owner   Gabriel Bornet
2.24 hectares
Generic Saint-Émilion

Château Vieux Rivallon
Present owner   Charles Bouquey
Grand Cru
Annual average production is 40 tonneaux and the reputation of the Château dates back a long time. Monsieur Bouquey also owns Château le Grand Faurie; Château du Roy; Château Bonnone.

Domaine Vieux Vachon
Present owner   Jean Naud
1.18 hectares
Generic Saint-Émilion

Clos Villemaurine
Present owner   Jean Brun
0.2871 hectares
Grand Cru
Owned by Jean Brun who is also the *Régisseur* of Château Grandes Murailles, Clos St Martin and Château Côte Baleau.
   The above vineyard is attached to M Brun's home and produces approximately 1,200 bottles per annum.

Le Vin d'Édouard
This is the brand-name for the second wine of Château le Jurat.

Raymond Visage
0.30 hectares
Sells generic Saint-Émilion in bulk only.

Château le Vrai Rivallon
Present owner   Jean-Daniel Bouy
1.55 hectares
Generic Saint-Émilion

Château Vray Petit Figeac
Present owner   Roger Pateau
1.4185 hectares
Generic Saint-Émilion

Henri Wery
0.3449 hectares
Sells generic Saint-Émilion in bulk only.

Château Yon Tour Figeac
Present owner   Raymond Dusseaut
5.13 hectares
Generic Saint-Émilion
Small farmhouse set back from the road to Libourne.

Vieux Château Certan. Pomerol.

THE COMMUNES OF SAINT-EMILION

St Christophe-des-Bardes

The commune of St Christophe-des-Bardes, one of the seven communes entitled to the Appellation Saint-Émilion, is some 3 kilometres east of Saint-Émilion.

The small, old-fashioned village is set high on a hillock around an eleventh-century church with its tall spire.

There are 584.89 hectares of vines and the soil is mainly clay and limestone with a stony sub-soil. The wines are generally similar in style to those of the Côtes Saint-Émilion. This commune can boast a Grand Cru Classé for part of the vineyard area of Château Haut-Sarpe is in the commune of Saint-Émilion itself and it seems to have acquired dual nationality, so to speak. Grands Crus Classés and, of course, Premiers Grands Crus Classés must be in the commune of Saint-Émilion.

The imposed minimum strength of the wine is 10° and 10.5° for Grand Cru and Grand Cru Classé with a maximum yield of 42 hectolitres per hectare.

Among the more distinguished properties of the area Château Fombrauge makes consistently good wine. Château Laroque, set in 78 hectares, is one of the oldest buildings in the entire area. It was built in the eleventh century and has been beautifully restored.

St Christophe-des-Bardes Properties

Château Barde-Haut
Present owner Jean-Claude Gasparoux
Attractive driveway leading to *chai* with property set behind.
This property is split into two parts:
1 10.2218 hectares
   Grand Cru
2 5.1359 hectares
   Generic Saint-Émilion

Michel Batard
1.5451 hectares
Generic Saint-Émilion
Sells bulk wine.

Château les Baziliques
Present owner Roger Reclus
6.1940 hectares
Generic Saint-Émilion

Château Bonneau
Present owner Marc Gouze
0.9665 hectares
Generic Saint-Émilion

Château Brun
This property has been in the hands of the Brun-Decazes family since 1500. It is currently owned by the company G F A du Château Brun, managed by Marc Brun.

The vineyard covers 5.51 hectares planted with 75% Merlot, 20% Cabernet Sauvignon and 5% Bouchet.

After picking the grapes are totally de-stalked and fermented in cement vats between eight and twelve days. Then they are matured in old oak casks for eighteen months to two years before bottling.

The main markets for the wine are France and Belgium.

A beautiful, fairly large Château set back from the road, well-preserved and cared-for with a lake behind the Château.

Albert Canard
1.96 hectares
Generic Saint-Émilion
Sells in bulk only.

Château du Cauze and Château le Bourg-du-Cauze
This Grand Cru property occupies an elevated, picturesque look-out spot, with clay-limestone, gravelly and marly sub-soil. It is owned by the Société Civile du Cauze who produce *Château de Cauze* and *Château le Bourg du Cauze* (the latter being taken up every year by J Calvert et Cie).

The vineyard covers 20 hectares of which 19.90 are under vine.

Impressive, well-maintained classic Château.

Château Cauzin
Present owner   Françoise Raynal
6 hectares
Generic Saint-Émilion

Château Champion
Present owner   Jean Bourrigaud
6.1425 hectares
Grand Cru

Château Fombrauge
This superb old Grand Cru Château, set back in its own parkland, dates back to Louis XIV and is now owned by the Heritiers Bygodt, who also own Château Maurens.

The property covers 75 hectares of which 41.9296 are under vine planted with 65% Merlot, 25% Bouchet and 10% Cabernet Sauvignon.

The grapes are totally de-stalked and fermented in cement vats, then matured in oak casks for between eighteen to twenty-four months before bottling. The average out-put is 44 hectolitres per hectare and the wine is consistently good.

Françoise Chêne
6.00 hectares
Generic Saint-Émilion
Sells in bulk.

Château Coudert
Present owner   Jean Claude Carles
24.47 hectares
Grand Cru
Also produces wine under the label of *Château Panet Grand Cru.*

Château Coudert-Pelletan
Present owner   Jean-André Lavau
This very attractive property is set in 10 hectares of which 6.0259 are under vine. It comprises the former estates of Coudert and Pelletan. The Coudert estate part, purchased in 1858 by the great-grandfather of the present owner from the Constant Roy-de-Clotte family, was enlarged in 1923 by the addition of part of the Château Sarpe-Pelletan vineyard from M Gizard.

Château Franc-Laporte
Present owner   Vve Rollet et fils
7.0868 hectares
Generic Saint-Émilion

Château Franc Pineuilh
Present owner   Jean-Paul Deson
1.3805 hectares
Generic Saint-Émilion

Château Grand-Jacques
Present owner   Jean Olivet
This property is split into two parts:
1   3.3960 hectares
    Generic Saint-Émilion
2   4.7290 hectares
    Generic Saint-Émilion

Château Guillemot
Present owner   Pierre Lavau
9.0565 hectares
Generic Saint-Émilion
Very imposing, set high on the hill. Large, turreted Château with lovely views overlooking the vineyards.

Château Haut Guillot
Present owner   Claude Castan
0.45 hectares
Generic Saint-Émilion

Château Haut-Lavallade
Present owner   Jean-Pierre Chagneau
This Grand Cru property, owned by Jean-Pierre Chagneau, covers 12.5 hectares of which 10.2731 are under vine. It has been in his family for five generations.

The vineyard is planted with 55% Merlot, 20% Bouchet and 25% Cabernet Sauvignon, the average age of the vines being thirty years.

The grapes are usually 75% de-stalked and fermented in concrete vats for approximately eight days and matured in casks for two and a half years before bottling takes place.

The wine is sold mainly in France with approximately 10% being exported, mainly to Belgium.

Château Haut-Badette

This Grand Cru property borders on to the commune of Saint-Émilion and is joined with Château Haut-Sarpe and Château Vieux-Sarpe. It is owned by M J F Janoueix who also owns Châteaux Haut-Sarpe, Vieux-Sarpe, le Câstelot, la Croix, la Croix St Georges in Pomerol. This Château was purchased by him in 1970 from Comte de Foussant de Bogeron.

The vineyard covers 4.5 hectares planted with 90% Merlot and 10% Bouchet on rootstock 101.14. The average age of these vines is thirty years and they are tended by Max Chabrerie, the *Chef de Culture* since 1971 and Paul Cazenove, the *Maître de Chai* since 1964.

The grapes are fermented in cement vats for approximately eighteen days and matured in oak casks for two years before bottling. The property produces an average of thirty thousand bottles a year.

Château Jacqueminot

Present owner   Jean Rufat
This property is split into two parts:
1   4.37 hectares
    Generic Saint-Émilion
2   7.0432 hectares
    Generic Saint-Émilion

Château Jean Guillot

Present owner   Henri Castan
3.00 hectares
Generic Saint-Émilion

Château Lapelletrie

Present owner   G F A Lapelletrie
12.31 hectares
Grand Cru
Situated on two clayey-limestone crests of the Saint-Émilion plateaus.

Château Laroque

This Grand Cru property is one of the most famous estates in the Gironde. Built in the eleventh century the feudal Château stands on the summit of a picturesque site overlooking the Dordogne valley. In the Middle ages, it was a fortress with two towers of which only one remains. There were battlements, a wide moat cut out of the rock surrounded by balustrades.

In the seventeenth century the front of the house was rebuilt, and it was completely renovated to a very high standard in 1972.

This very beautiful property stands in 78 hectares of which 43.7055 are under vine and is now owned by the Heritiers Mme Thibout, Mme Drouin and M Beaumartin. In 1964 large new *cuvées* were installed and the out-put capacity is

7,000 hectolitres. Five hundred oak casks are used for maturation but they are slowly being replaced by cement vats. The property produced 300 tonneaux in 1979. The firm of Lichine buy almost all of the wine produced at this Château.

Château Lavalade

Present owner   Pierre Gaury
This property is split into two parts:
1   4.00 hectares
    Grand Cru
2   6.73 hectares
    Generic Saint-Émilion

Jean-Louis Macaud

1.2416 hectares
Sells bulk Generic Saint-Émilion only.

Chateau Marin

Present owner   René Chêne
8.48 hectares
Generic Saint-Émilion

Château Marsolan

Present owner   Jean Cheminade
0.69 hectares
Generic Saint-Émilion

Château Millery Lapelletrie

Present owner   Michèle Macau
2.1711 hectares
Generic Saint-Émilion

Château Milon and Clos de la Curé

Present owner   Christian Bouyer
This Grand Cru property, owned by Christian Bouyer, covers 30 hectares of which 18.8616 are under vine planted with 75% Merlot, 10% Bouchet and 15% Cabernet Sauvignon. The average age of the vine is thirty-five years.

The grapes are totally de-stalked and fermented in cement vats for fifteen days and matured in vats for two years. Production averages 44 hectolitres per hectare.

Château Moreau

Generic Saint-Émilion
0.8525 hectares
Sells in bulk only.

Joseph Nicoletti

1.00 hectare
Sells bulk generic Saint-Émilion only.

Château Panet

Present owner   Jean Gipaloux
0.41 hectares
Generic Saint-Émilion

Georges Petit
0.7695 hectares
Sells bulk generic Saint-Émilion only.

Château Peymouton
Present owner   Anne Armengol
1.24 hectares
Generic Saint-Émilion

Château Peymouton Nardon
Present owner   Raymond Rufat
7.0432 hectares
Generic Saint-Émilion

Château Pierre du Maréchal
Present owner   Max Itey
0.7239 hectares
Generic Saint-Émilion

Château Plagnotte Bellevue
Present owner   Biais-Charmolue
5.8506 hectares
Grand Cru

Château Puyblanquet Carrille
This Grand Cru property is owned by Jean-François Carrille, who also owns Château Vieux Guadet, Domaine de Fussignac in Entre-deux-Mers, Château Boutisse and Château Cardinal Villemaurine.

The vineyard covers 25 hectares with 17.4928 hectares under vine planted with 70% Merlot, 20% Bouchet, 5% Cabernet Sauvignon and 5% Pressac. The grapes are generally completely de-stalked and fermented in vats. They are then matured in oak casks for up to three years prior to bottling. The wine is exported principally to The United States of America and Belgium.

Château Quentin
Present owner   Ste Château Quentin
25.59 hectares
Grand Cru

Château les Religieuses
Present owner   Pierre Coiffard
0.5390 hectares
Generic Saint-Émilion

Château Robin
Present owner   Jean-François Buzet
7.3612 hectares
Generic Saint-Émilion
Present owner   Alain Buzet
0.4775 hectares
Generic Saint-Émilion
On the main road, old family house.

Château les Rocailles
Present owner   Jean Lavdu
2.8030 hectares
Generic Saint-Émilion

Clos Rol-de-Fombrauge
Present owner   Roland Gaury
3.10 hectares
Generic Saint-Émilion

Château Rol-de-Fombrauge
Present owner   André Bonnet
3.13 hectares
Grand Cru
There is also a Château of same name, producing Generic Saint-Émilion (4.45 hectares), with the same owner.

Château la Rose Blanche
Present owner   Alain Fritegotto
4.30 hectares
Generic Saint-Émilion

Château la Rose Blanche
Present owner   André Peyramaure
4.30 hectares
Generic Saint-Émilion

Château Roucheyron
Present owner   Cazenave Garuz
2.1284 hectares
Generic Saint-Émilion

Château Saint-Christophe
Present owners   Richard et fils
8.50 hectares
Saint-Émilion Grand Cru

Clotaire Sarrazin
5.67 hectares
Generic Saint-Émilion. Sells bulk only.

Clos de Sarpe
Present owner   Yvan Beney
3 hectares
Average production 35 hectolitres

Paul Saurue
0.3679 hectares
Sells bulk generic Saint-Émilion only.

Château Tauzinat l'Hermitage
Present owners   Moueix Vignobles who also own Châteaux la Tour-du-Pin-Figeac, Clos la Fleur Figeac, Fonplégade, Taillefer, Moulinet, Clos Beauregard, Clos Toulifaut, la Croix Bellevue
1.6004 hectares
Generic Saint-Émilion
This very attractive Château dates back to 1670.

Château Toinet-Fombrauge
Present owners Ambroise et Bernard Sierra
6.5650 hectares
Generic Saint-Émilion

Château Tonneret
Present owner Albino Crestes
1.56 hectares
Generic Saint-Émilion

Château Tour St Christophe
Present owner Henri Guiter
This Grand Cru property with its terraced vineyards facing the north-west and west hills next to Château Troplong-Mondot is owned by Henri Guiter and run by his son-in-law, M Clay.

Monsieur Guiter also owns Château Tour Cazelon in Montagne.

The vineyard covers 20 hectares of which 16.44 are under vine planted with 34% Merlot, 33% Bouchet and 33% Cabernet Sauvignon producing an average yield of 110,000 bottles per annum.

François Tourriol
1.11 hectares
Sells bulk generic Saint-Émilion only.

Château Vieux Bourg
Present owner Pierre Guyonnaud
2.64 hectares
Generic Saint-Émilion

Château Vieux Bourg
Present owner René Cipière
1.32 hectares
Generic Saint-Émilion

Vieux-Château-Peymouton
Present owner Milon Hecquet
9.1101 hectares
Generic Saint-Émilion

Vieux-Château-Pelletan
Present owner Marc Magnaudeix
6.6570 hectares
Grand Cru
Also has 3.4227 hectares in Saint-Émilion.

Château Vieux Sarpe
This Grand Cru property was owned in the eighteenth-century by Comte Jacques Amedée de Carles, Lieutenant-General to the King. It is now owned by Jean-François Janoueix, owner of Château Haut-Sarpe. The property is situated on the Sarpe estates, next to Haut-Sarpe.

The vineyard covers 6.82 hectares of which 6.5 are under vine planted with 70% Merlot, 20% Bouchet, 10% Cabernet Sauvignon on 41B to 420A root-stock. The average age of the vines is twenty years.

In addition there is also a plot of generic Saint-Émilion covering 4 hectares.

After picking, the grapes are fermented in cement vats for eighteen days and matured in oak casks for two years before bottling. The average out-put is forty-eight thousand bottles a year.

Château Yon la Fleur
Present owner Jean Menozzi
3.3936 hectares
Generic Saint-Émilion

St Sulpice-de-Faleyrens

This commune of 744.31 hectares lies 3 kilometres from Saint-Émilion bordering on the Dordogne river to the east and south. St Sulpice is a small, well-maintained village; it has a very attractive twelfth-century Roman church with a gaily-coloured roof. The village now has many modern houses on the outskirts.

The generally flat land has a sandy and gravel soil in the north with iron sub-soil, whilst the south is sandy – clay fertile soil.

The minimum strength of the wine is 10° for the Saint-Émilion Appellation Contrôlée and 10.5° Grand Cru, with a maximum permitted yield of 42 hectolitres per hectare.

In keeping with the other communes outside Saint-Emilion, St Sulpice properties can only be classified as Saint-Émilion or Saint-Émilion Grand Cru. However there are châteaux whose wine is comparable with that of Grands Crus Classés properties; the most famous of these is Château Monbousquet.

St Sulpice-de-Faleyrens Properties

Château Andron de Lescours
Present owner   Jean Charvet
4.70 hectares
Generic Saint-Émilion

Justin Arnaud
0.20 hectares
Generic Saint-Émilion

Roland Auroux
1.5234 hectares
Generic Saint-Émilion
Sells bulk.

Château Baillarge
Present owner   Michel Codognotto
0.5859 hectares
Generic Saint-Émilion

Château Barrail des Graves
Present owner   Christian Descrambé
8.3779 hectares
Generic Saint-Émilion

Château Barry
Present owner   Marcel Mestadier
2.7900 hectares
Generic Saint-Émilion

Château du Barry
Present owner   Noel Mouty
This property is split into two parts:
1   3.80 hectares
    Generic Saint-Émilion
2   4.00 hectares
    Grand Cru

Pierre Bastide
0.30 hectares
Generic Saint-Émilion
Sells only bulk wines.

Château de Belle-Assise
Present owner   Yvan Brun
13.28 hectares
Generic Saint-Émilion
Set back from the road in the trees.

Château Bertinut Lartigac
Present owner   Jean Dubou
5.15 hectares
Generic Saint-Émilion

Château Bois Groulay
Present owner   Louis Lusseau
4.25 hectares
Generic Saint-Émilion

Clos Bruan
Present owner   Henriette Jarlan
0.6350 hectares
Generic Saint-Émilion

Château les Cabanes
Present owner   Jean Guy Gras
2.7796 hectares
Generic Saint-Émilion

Château le Castelot
Present owner   Jean-François Janoueix
In 1546 Henri IV, so the story goes, was forced to break his journey one day and stayed the night at this property, in a small and miserable dwelling. For his poor host's generosity, the King expressed his thanks by granting him the right to have a modern little Château built for himself on the very spot of the humble lodging. Hence the current Château and its name of 'Castelot' (Little Château).

This Grand Cru property was owned at the turn of the twentieth century by Armand Chaperon and Pierre Loubut. Then in 1979 M

Old vine at Château Trottevieille.

View of the sloping vineyards below Château Pavie.

View of the vineyards of St Christophe-des-Bardes showing the church.

Galhaud, who sadly allowed it to run down, sold it to the present owner, Jean-François Janoueix, who also owns Château Haut-Sarpe. The Château is at present being totally renovated and extensive replanting is being done in the vineyard.

The vineyard covers 5.7 hectares of which 5.5 are under vine planted with 60% Merlot, 20% Bouchet, 20% Cabernet Sauvignon grafted on to 101.14 and Riparia Gloire root-stock. The average age of vine is forty-five years.

The grapes are fermented in cement vats for eighteen days at 28°C and matured in oak casks for two years before bottling. Average out-put of 49 hectolitres per hectare produces approximately thirty-five thousand bottles a year.

1978 – 232 hectolitres
1979 – 274 hectolitres
1980 – 180 hectolitres

Château la Cavaille Lescours
Present owner   René Vigouroux
1.7550 hectares
Generic Saint-Émilion

Château la Caze
Present owner   Serge Cassin
0.37 hectares
Generic Saint-Émilion

Château la Chapelle Depagnet
Present owner   Ginette Gagnaire
7.0196 hectares
Grand Cru

Château la Chide
Present owner   Antoine Suils
4.8450 hectares
Generic Saint-Émilion

Château Concet
Present owner   Jacques Tour ou Foget
3.6825 hectares
Grand Cru

Château Côtes du Gros Caillou
Present owner   Jean Tourenne
5.4255 hectares
Generic Saint-Émilion

Arlette Coureau
6.61 hectares
Generic Saint-Émilion
Bulk wine

Château Croix Bertinot
Present owner   Christian Lafaye
7.9410 hectares
Generic Saint-Émilion

Château la Croix Daugay
This property is split into two parts:
1   *Present owner*   Jean-Claude Herve
    0.96 hectares
    Generic Saint-Émilion
2   Present owner   Jeanne Herve
    2.06 hectares
    Generic Saint-Émilion

Château la Croix Fourche
Present owner   Daniele Mallard
1.8111 hectares
Generic Saint-Émilion

Château Faleyrens
Present owner   Jacques Brisson
0.57 hectares
Grand Cru
Also has property of same name –
10.1454 hectares
Generic Saint-Émilion
Large imposing property.

Château de Faleyrens
Present owner   Roger Simon
3.53 hectares
Generic Saint-Émilion

Château Fleurus
Present owner   Raymond Barraud
1.5613 hectares
Generic Saint-Émilion

Château Flouquet
This property is split into three parts:
1   *Present owner*   Christian Bernard
    2.00 hectares
    Grand Cru
2   *Present owner*   Christian Bernard
    9.0617 hectares
    Generic Saint-Émilion
3   *Present owner*   Alain Bernard
    11.4603 hectares
    Generic Saint-Émilion

Fourniue Frères
1.86 hectares
Generic Saint-Émilion
Sells bulk only.

A Fournial
0.7462 hectares
Sells bulk generic Saint-Émilion only.

P Fournial
1.0940 hectares
Sells bulk generic Saint-Émilion only.

Jean-Claude Fournial
1.8328 hectares
Sells bulk generic Saint-Émilion only.

Château Franc-Bigaroux
Present owner   Yves Blanc
8.9428 hectares
Grand Cru Saint-Émilion
He also owns Château Haut Brisson.

Joel Gagnaire
1.3354 hectares
Generic Saint-Émilion
Sells only bulk wines.

Claude Gireaud
0.61 hectares
Sells bulk generic Saint-Émilion only.

G F A Gonzales
6.6846 hectares
Grand Cru – sold in bulk only.

Château Grand Bert
Present owner   Philippe Lavigne
6.56 hectares
Generic Saint-Émilion

Château Grand Destied
Present owner   René Thibaud
8.2802 hectares
Generic Saint-Émilion
Single-storey modern house.

Château Grand-Pey-Lescours
Present owner   G F A Heritiers Escure
23.59 hectares
Grand Cru
Formerly property of Baron Arthur de Brezets, bought by the Escure family in 1924. The Escure family also owns Cru Belle Isle-Mondotte, St Laurent-des-Combes.

Château la Grange de Lescure
Present owner   Jacqueline Pesquier
16.8738 hectares
Grand Cru

Château la Grave de Lescours
Present owner   Jean Paul Bouquey
1.16 hectares
Generic Saint-Émilion

Château Gravet
Present owner   Jean Faure
This property is owned by Jean Faure, who also owns Château de Garde (Appellation Bordeaux); it covers 25 hectares of which 17.1875 are under vine planted with 80% Merlot, 10% Cabernet Sauvignon to 10% Bouchet.

After picking, the grapes are totally de-stalked and fermented in enamel metal vats for six to eight days. Maturation takes place in oak casks for eighteen months before bottling.

Château Gros-Caillou
Present owner   Jacques Dupuy
13.6512 hectares
Generic Saint-Émilion
Very small farmhouse with out-house.

Château Haut Gravet
Present owner   Georgette Corbice
5.32 hectares
Generic Saint-Émilion

Château Haut Gros Caillou
Present owner   Paul Lafaye
5.83 hectares
Generic Saint-Émilion

Château les Hautes Jouans
Present owner   Christian Bernede
1.71 hectares
Generic Saint-Émilion

Château Haut Renaissance
Present owner   G F A Barraud-Mouty
This Grand Cru property, owned by G F A Barraud-Mouty, covers 5.5050 hectares under vine planted with 80% Merlot, 10% Bouchet, 5% Cabernet Sauvignon, 5% Bouchet with an average age of vine of twenty years.

There is also another plot of land 4.5064 hectares producing generic Saint-Émilion wines.

The grapes are picked mechanically, then totally de-stalked and fermented in stainless-steel vats for ten days and matured in concrete tanks for eighteen months before bottling.

Château les Jouans
Present owner   Henri Faure
3.3628 hectares
Generic Saint-Émilion

Château Jupile
Present owner   Regis Visage
17.8682 hectares
Generic Saint-Émilion

Château Lacaze Bellevue
Present owner   Philippe Faure
4.2360 hectares
Generic Saint-Émilion

Jean Lacroix
1.8935 hectares
Sells bulk generic Saint-Émilion only.

Château Lagresole
Present owner   Michel Decazes
2.35 hectares
Generic Saint-Émilion

Clos Landes de Gravet
Present owner   Césaire Deschamps
Previous owner   Escure
1.08 hectares
Generic Saint-Émilion

Clos Landes de Gravet
Present owner   René Brody
2.6440 hectares
Generic Saint-Émilion

Château Lescours
Present owner   S A C H Lescours
For four centuries until the end of the seventeenth century this property belonged to the Marquis de Canolle. At the time of the first Revolution it was given to Citizen Villemot, then passed to Marquis de Lur Saluces and then to Benjamin Fornerod.

This famous Grand Cru Château, with its tall imposing towers, covers 40 hectares of which 29.9258 are under vine.

It is now rather run-down. Situated near the river with a low, single-storey *chai*, it originally had a moat around it.

Château Clos Maurice
Present owner   Emile Pellerin
0.4815 hectares
Generic Saint-Émilion

Château les Maurins
Present owner   Marie Lasserre
2.84 hectares
Generic Saint-Émilion

Château les Mourins
Present owner   M Duboury
1.29 hectares
Generic Saint-Émilion

Château les Maurias
Present owner   Michel Bourée
0.95 hectares
Generic Saint-Émilion

Château Monbousquet
This magnificent Grand Cru estate can trace its history back to the sixteenth century when it belonged to François de Lescours and his descendants. In 1684 it passed into the hands of the family of de Gères and the Château was restored in the style of the period. In the eighteenth century it was transferred by marriage to the de Carles family and it was General Jacques Amadée de Carles who retired here to grow vines. He also owned Châteaux Cheval Blanc and Figeac by the time of his death in 1803. By 1850 the property was owned by the Comte de Vassal-Montvieil who increased its growing reputation. In the late nineteenth century, when *phylloxera* struck, the owners were discouraged and the vineyard was slow to recover. Little was heard of Monbousquet until Daniel Querre who, with Jean Capdemourlin, refounded the Jurade de Saint-Émilion in 1948, took it over, almost completely replanting the vineyard in 1945. Thanks to his expertise, the reputation of the wines of Monbousquet has steadily grown over the last thirty-five years. His son, Alain, is now the proprietor. The vineyard is about 2½ kilometres south-west of Saint-Émilion, in St Sulpice-de-Faleyrens, where the soil is very gravelly: a deep stony soil consisting of a mixture of iron and stones from the hill of Saint-Émilion, veined with blue clay which is also to be found in many parts of Pomerol.

The estate covers 40 hectares of which there are 27.78 hectares under vine (50% Merlot, 40% Bouchet, 10% Cabernet Sauvignon), the oldest of them thirty-five years, and the average age twenty-five years. Average production is about 130 tonneaux at 40 hectolitres per hectare.

The grapes are de-stalked but no *fouloir* is used. Fermentation lasts about eight days and takes place in cement and wooden vats. The skins remain in contact with the *must* for two weeks before being pressed in a vertical press. The wine is matured in new oak casks in a *chai* in Libourne for eighteen months with the usual *assemblage* (in March), rackings and fining, before bottling.

Château les Mauvinon
Present owner   Gilbert Lacroix
2 hectares
Generic Saint-Émilion

Château de May
Present owner   Georges Lavaud
2.96 hectares
Generic Saint-Émilion

Château Noire Vieux
This property is split into two parts:
1 *Present owner*   Bernard Xans
   2.0371 hectares
   Generic Saint-Émilion
2 *Present owner*   Alain Xans
   1.09 hectares
   Generic Saint-Émilion

Château du Moine Vieux
Present owner   Arthur Pigeon
This small property is split into two parts:
1 2.04 hectares
   Generic Saint-Émilion

2   1.10 hectares
Generic Saint-Émilion

Château Moulin de la Grangère
Present owner   Bernard Dizier
15.4266 hectares
Grand Cru
Property situated on the border of St Laurent-des-Combes. Very small two-storey, turretted property.

Château Palais Cardinal la Fuie
Present owner   Gerard Frétier
This Grand Cru property has been owned (since 1970) by Gerard Frétier, who also owns Château Haut Boutise in St Christophe-des-Bardes; it cover 20 hectares of which 13.6174 are under vine.

The vineyard is planted with 50% Merlot, 35% Bouchet and 15% Cabernet Sauvignon, with an average age of twenty-two years.

After picking, the grapes are completely de-stalked and fermented for eight days before being matured for eighteen months prior to bottling.

Out-put from 1975 to 1979:
1975 – 502 hectolitres
1976 – 609 hectolitres
1977 – 405 hectolitres
1978 – 575 hectolitres
1979 – 869 hectolitres (with an average of 47 hectolitres per hectare)

Château Moulin-de-Pierrefitte
Present owner   Jean Louis Fayard
8.9953 hectares
Grand Cru

Rino Nicoletti
1.75 hectares
Sells bulk generic Saint-Émilion only.

Château du Parc
Present owner   Vve Marie Tabarlet
2.1084 hectares
Generic Saint-Émilion

Château Perey
Present owner   Denis Martegoutes
2.0250 hectares
Generic Saint-Émilion

Château Perey Grouley
Present owner   Reni Xans
10.0402 hectares
Generic Saint-Émilion

Château Petit Faurie Quet
Present owner   Pierre Quentin
7.36 hectares
Grand Cru

Clos Petit Manvinon
Present owner   Rougene Castells
2.5554 hectares
Generic Saint-Émilion

Clos Peyrey Grouley
Present owner   Francis Campaner
1.5380 hectares
Generic Saint-Émilion

Clos Pindefleur
Present owner   Roger Toulon
0.4430 hectares
Generic Saint-Émilion

Château Plaisance
Present owner   Pierre Dubois
7.23 hectares
Generic Saint-Émilion

Château Prieuré Lescours
Present owner   Sce Prieuré Lescours
2.9860 hectares
Grand Cru

Armand Rambeaud
1.6947 hectares
Sells bulk generic Saint-Émilion only.

Georges Ripes
2.7606 hectares
Sells bulk generic Saint-Émilion only.

Raymond Ripes
1.2690 hectares
Generic Saint-Émilion
Sells bulk only.

Château Roc
Present owner   César Borde
4.5568 hectares
Generic Saint-Émilion

Château le Roudey
Present owner   Jean-Raymond Arnaud
4.4391 hectares
Generic Saint-Émilion

Château St Martine
Present owner   Micheau Palatin (who also owns Domaine Vieille Église and Monlot Capet)
3.2612 hectares
Grand Cru

Château St Martial
Present owner   Armand Dupeyrat
3.2612 hectares
Grand Cru

Château St Valéry
Present owner   Jean Claude Faure
1.6282 hectares
Generic Saint-Émilion

Clos St Vincent
Present owner   Pierre Ripes
2.5310 hectares
Generic Saint-Émilion

Château la Sablonerie
Present owner   Robert Lavigne
9.24 hectares
Generic Saint-Émilion

Claude Simon
3.53 hectares
Sells bulk generic Saint-Émilion only.

Michel Soulard
5.90 hectares
Sells bulk generic Saint-Émilion only.

Gerrard Sylvain
This property is divided into two parts:
1   0.6587 hectares
2   0.5791 hectares
Sells bulk generic Saint-Émilion only.

Château les Trois Ormeaux
Present owner   Edward Desgals
2.96 hectares
Generic Saint-Émilion

Château Verdot
Present owner   Yves Guillemon
6.00 hectares
Generic Saint-Émilion
Small run-down farmhouse.

Vieux Château de Jouans
Present owner   Jean Claude Faure
7.2190 hectares
Generic Saint-Émilion

Château les Vieux Maurins
Present owner   Marcel Goudat
7.1118 hectares
Generic Saint-Émilion

St Hippolyte

This commune of 268.49 hectares is located 2 kilometres east of Saint-Émilion. The soil is clay–limestone on the hilly slopes and sand and gravel to the west with fertile sandy–clay soil in the east.

The tiny residential village, with its small town-hall and little church set high on a hill on its outskirts, is surrounded by vineyards and a number of very attractive Châteaux; among the better known are Château de Ferrand, Château Lassegue and Château Capet-Guillier.

In keeping with its appellation, Saint-Émilion, the minimum strength of the wine is 10° Saint-Émilion, 10.5° Grand Cru with a maximum yield of 42 hectolitres per hectare.

St Hippolyte Properties

Château Bourney
Present owner   Monique Vytters
5.6215 hectares
Grand Cru

Irène Bouyer
2.8872 hectares
Generic Saint-Émilion
Sells bulk.

Château Capet
Present owner   François Madrolle
11.0062 hectares
Grand Cru

Château Capet-Guillier
It is a very attractive, turreted property set in its own parkland. This Grand Cru property, situated on the crossroads near St Étienne-de-Lisse, used to be part of the 'maison noble et seigneurie de Capet' (noble house and family of Capet) which belonged to Comtesse de Guerchy, née d'Harcourt, and her brother, the Marquis of Bevron. The Taillade family, who owned Château Lassegue, purchased this property in 1763. At the end of the eighteenth century, the Taillade family owned the whole line of the slopes in the commune of St Hippolyte.

When the property was split between the four children, the present property, Capet-Guillier, was separated from that of Lassègue and fell to the eldest son, an ancestor of the Charmolie, then Guillier families.

For two-hundred years Château Capet-Guillier has been in the hands of the same family. Now it is owned by the Société Château Capet-Guillier.

This property has 13.82 of its 20 hectares under vine planted with 60% Merlot, 35% Bouchet and 5% Cabernet Sauvignon. After the grapes are picked, they are generally de-stalked and fermented in cement vats for approximately fifteen days and matured in oak vats for two years before bottling.

The second wine of this property is bottled under the name of *Tour de Capet*.

Château Destieux
Present owner   GFA Destieux
7.7810 hectares
Grand Cru

Château de Ferrand
Present owner   Marcel Bich
26.0499 hectares
Saint-Émilion Grand Cru
Has for several centuries belonged to the family of the Marquis de Mons de Dunes, who inherited it from the Betoulaud and the Ferrand families, mentioned in the history of Saint-Émilion as far back as the thirteenth century.

The very handsome, large Château with two wings and courtyard is set high on a hill with exceptional views. This Grand Cru property covers 26.0499 hectares of vines.

Château Franc Pipeau
Present owner   Jacqueline Bertrand
4.5 hectares
Average production 156 hectolitres.

Château Gaillard
Present owner   Jean-Jacques Nouvel
16.7060 hectares
Grand Cru

Château Lassègue
Present owners   Elaine and Jean-Pierre Freylon
This very attractive Grand Cru property with its turreted Château is set high on a hillock beneath the church and covers 23 hectares of which 21.5325 are under vine. These are planted with 50% Merlot, 30% Bouchet and 20% Cabernet Sauvignon.

It was owned by the Baudry family for several centuries, the present related owners are Elaine and Jean-Pierre Freylon.

After picking, the grapes are completely de-stalked, crushed and fermented in inox-lined vats for fifteen days. The wine is then matured in cement vats for two years before bottling.

Out-put from 1975 to 1979:
1975 – 1,039 hectolitres
1976 – 1,265 hectolitres
1977 –   956 hectolitres
1978 – 1,153 hectolitres
1979 – 1,423 hectolitres

Château Maurens
Present owner   Bygodt (who also owns Château Fombrauge)
18 hectares
Within the Maurens estate, a vineyard with particularly chalky soil was established in 1908, which is very famous and known as the Clos des Sarrasins. There is a small farmyard house, set back from the road up a hill.

Château la Melissière
Present owners   Patrick Bernard and Jeanne Bernard
This property is divided into two parts:
1   *Present owner*   Patrick Bernard
    1.8500 hectares
    Grand Cru
    2.9430 hectares
    Generic Saint-Émilion
2   *Present owner*   Jeanne Bernard
    4.6600 hectares
    Generic Saint-Émilion

Château Monlot-Capet
Present owner   Paulette Ichon
Generic Saint-Émilion.

Château Monlot-Capet
Present owner   Palatin Micheau
7.30 hectares
Grand Cru

Château Pailhas
Present owner   Michel Robin
14.2045 hectares
Generic Saint-Émilion.
The Vineyard is planted with mainly Merlot.
   Old sprawling farmhouse with attractive gardens, on left as one is leaving St Hippolyte, with *chai* on the right.

Château Pipeau Menichot
Present owner   Marc Dubois
9.1620 hectares
Generic Saint-Émilion

Domaine Vieille Église
Present owner   Constant Palatin
11.8095 hectares

Château Villot
Present owner   Paul Lagrange
0.6035 hectares
Generic Saint-Émilion

St Laurent-des-Combes

This commune, situated 2 kilometres from Saint-Émilion, covers an oblong of vineyards covering 242.21 hectares on predominantly clay–limestone soil surrounding a tiny residential village with an old church set high on a hill, and a railway station.

   There are several Grand Cru properties and a Grand Cru Classé, Château Larcis-Ducasse, which has part of its property in Saint-Émilion, and is thus able to claim Grand Cru Classé status.

   The minimum imposed strength is 10° and 10.5° for Grand Cru and Grand Cru Classé with a maximum yield of 42 hectolitres per hectare.

St Laurent-des-Combes Properties

Château Baladoz
Present owner   M de Schepper
3.7422 hectares
Grand Cru

Château Barbeyron
Present owner   Jean Claude Bassilieaux
3.66 hectares
Grand Cru

Château Clos la Barde
Present owner   Jacques Bailly
4.5250 hectares
Grand Cru

Château de la Barde
Present owner   Michel Bergey
3.62 hectares
Grand Cru

Château Beard
Present owner   Robert Goudichaud
6.7171 hectares
Grand Cru
Attractive property and gardens.

Château Beard la Chapelle
Present owner   Richard Moureau
14.6990 hectares
Average yield 500 hectolitres.

Château Bellefont-Belcier

This vineyard was completely re-established by Pierre Faure and since then the property was passed to his son, M le professeur Jean-Louis Faure, then to his daughter Mme Labusquière, and in 1953 to grandson, M le docteur Labusquière.

Today this very attractive Grand Cru property, which is situated on the slopes below Côtes Pavie, is run by Jean Labusquière and covers 17 hectares of which 12.8046 are under vine planted with 60% Merlot, 20% Bouchet and 20% Cabernet Sauvignon.

After picking, the grapes are totally de-stalked and fermented in cement vats for ten to fifteen days, after which the wine is matured in cement vats for eighteen months.

The principal market is France, but approximately 30% is sold to Belgium.

Château Bellefont Belcier Guillier

Present owner   Philippe Guillier
4.47 hectares
Grand Cru
This owner also owns Château la Garelle.

Château Bellisle Mondotte

Present owner   Heritiers Escure
4.54 hectares
Grand Cru

Château Belle Nauve

Present owner   Carmen Chatonnet
4.4475 hectares
Generic Saint-Émilion

Albert Benard

0.26 hectares
Sells bulk generic Saint-Émilion only.

Jean Borie

0.5571 hectares
Sells bulk generic Saint-Émilion only.

Château de Candale

Present owner   Jean Dugos
2.2450 hectares
Grand Cru

Château Chante l'Alouette

Present owner   Paul Castera
1.9136 hectares
Grand Cru

Château la Croizille

Present owner   M JS Marin Audra
4.95 hectares
Grand Cru
This owner also owns Château Claymore and Château Blanchou in Lussac and two others

outside the area. Set high on a hill. Small, single-storey property.

Château Franc-Rosier

Present owner   André Joussamme
2.78 hectares
Generic Saint-Émilion

Château la Garelle

Present owner   Philippe Guillier
4.13 hectares
Generic Saint-Émilion
This owner also owns Château Bellefont-Belcier-Guillier. Grand Cru

Château Godeau

Present owner   Société Civile du Château Godeau
Grand Cru
Five hectares, of which 3.05 are under vine. Situated on the top of a hill known as the 'Rôte-Boeuf'. The Château is at present being rebuilt. Average production 66 hectolitres.

Château Grand Nauve

Present owner   Joseph Castan
5.6060 hectares
Generic Saint-Émilion

Château Haut Gueyrot

This property is split into two parts:
1   *Present owner*   Jean-Claude Gombeau
     3.2390 hectares
     Generic Saint-Émilion
2   *Present owner*   Jean-Marcel Gombeau
     4.33 hectares
     Generic Saint-Émilion
Small farmhouse.

Raymond Lafont

0.3463 hectares
Sells bulk generic Saint-Émilion only.

Roland Masse

2.0320 hectares
Sells bulk generic Saint-Émilion only.

Château Mondotte-Bélisle

Present owner   René Chaput
5.53 hectares
Grand Cru

Château Napoléon

Present owner   Ste Pages
1.2434 hectares
Generic
Also produces wine under the name of *Château les Terres Rouges*.

Château de la Nauve
Present owner   Michel Veyry
9.22 hectares
Generic Saint-Émilion

Château la Nauve
Present owner   Maurice Courrière
2.1410 hectares
Generic Saint-Émilion

Château la Nauve
Present owner   Madeleine Simars
1.2350 hectares
Generic Saint-Émilion

Francis Périer
4.3578 hectares
Sells bulk generic Saint-Émilion

Château Pipeau
Present owner   Pierre Mestreguilhem
22.1420 hectares
Grand Cru
Small, renovated limestone Château near the station with a large, attached *chai*.

Jacqueline Roche
3.9255 hectares
Sells bulk generic Saint-Émilion only.

Château Rochebelle
Present owner   Georges Faniest
2.2026 hectares
Grand Cru

Château Rozier
Present owner   Jean Bernard Saby
This attractive Grand Cru property lying on the crossroads, is owned by Jean Barnard Saby who also owns Château Hauchat in Fronsac, Château Reindent Bordeaux Supérieur and Château Haut le Grace Dieu St Émilion Grand Cru. This property covers 25 hectares of which 17.2685 are under vine and planted with 66% Merlot, 33% Bouchet.

The harvest is picked by a mechanical harvester, totally de-stalked and then fermented in cement vats for ten to fifteen days. Maturation takes place in oak casks for up to two years before bottling.

The principal markets for this wine outside France are Belgium, Germany and The United States of America.

Château le Sable
Present owner   Ste le Richelieu
3.7483 hectares
Generic Saint-Émilion

Château le Sable
Present owner   Jean Darribeaude
11.45 hectares
Grand Cru

Château le Tertre Rôteboeuf
Present owner   François Mitjavile
4.1034 hectares
Grand Cru
Small, attractive old farmhouse set high on the hill.

Vieux Château Haut Beard
Present owner   Jean Riboulet
2.7952 hectares
Generic Saint-Émilion

St Pey-d'Armens

This commune is situated 12 kilometres south-east of Saint-Émilion. It covers an area of 389.61 hectares of sandy, fertile soil with some clay in the north. The sub-soil is gravel in the south-east, sand in the south-west and sand–clay in the north.

The small residential village, lying on the N.316, is built around a picturesque church and a café and bar.

Being outside Saint-Émilion itself, the classification is restricted to Saint-Émilion (10° minimum) and Grand Cru Saint-Émilion (10.5° minimum) with a maximum permitted yield of 42 hectolitres per hectare.

St Pey-d'Armens Properties

Château Bonnet
Present owner   Roger Bonnet
This Grand Cru property, set back from the main road, is owned by Roger Bonnet and has been handed down from father to son for over six generations. It covers 20 hectares of which 18.8300 are under vine planted with 60% Merlot, 20% Bouchet, 15% Cabernet Sauvignon, 5% Pressac, the average age of vines being twenty years.

The grapes are totally de-stalked and fermented in stainless-steel tanks for approximately eight days and matured in oak casks for two years before bottling.

André Bouyer
0.3635 hectares
Generic Saint-Émilion
Sells in bulk only.

Château Clos Gerbaud
Present owner   Jean Selosse
2.30 hectares
Generic Saint-Émilion

Robert Desport
0.76 hectares
Generic Saint-Émilion
Sells in bulk only.

Château la Fôret Aubert
Present owner   Alain Aubert
1.9000 hectares
Generic Saint-Émilion

Château Fourney
Present owner   M Rollet
Since 1729 through successive generations, the Rollet family have owned land in Saint-Émilion.

This very attractive old Château, with large parkland and gardens was purchased during the last decade. It used to belong to the Meynot family.

The large estate has 39.2997 hectares under vine, the *chais* and 2 hectares of vines are in the commune of St Pey-d'Armens, the main part of the vineyard being in the commune of St Étienne-de-Lisse.

Monsieur Rollet also owns the Château la Fourquerie in Côtes de Castillon. This Grand Cru property is owned by Vignobles Rollet who also produce wine under the name of *Château du Vieux Guinot*.

Château le Frèche
Present owner   Henri Domezil
3.7156 hectares
Generic Saint-Émilion

Château Gerbaud
Present owner   Jean Massis
2.6253 hectares
Generic Saint-Émilion

Roger Goursaud
2.6253 hectares
Sells bulk generic Saint-Émilion.

Château Guérin Bellevue
Present owner   Arlette Dartigue
14.3 hectares
Generic Saint-Émilion

Château Haut Barreyse
Present owner   René Itey
0.6845 hectares
Generic Saint-Émilion

Robert Laguillon
0.11 hectares
Bulk generic Saint-Émilion

Château Lespinasse
Present owners   Pierre and Roger Bentenat
1   1.67 hectares
    Grand Cru
2   4.8572 hectares
    Generic Saint-Émilion
Situated on the main road. Small farmhouse.

Château le Maine
Present owner   Pierre Veyry
5.3340 hectares
Generic Saint-Émilion
Small old-fashioned farmhouse.

Pierre Musset
3.7319 hectares
Sells bulk Grand Cru Saint-Émilion only.

Société Noyeraies d'Aquitaine
2.4432 hectares
Sells bulk generic Saint-Émilion only.

Château Petit Prince
Present owner   Joseph Biais
2.1907 hectares
Generic Saint-Émilion

Château Reynaud
Present owner Aline Terras
3.9346 hectares
Grand Cru
Small farmhouse.

Château Saint Hubert
Present owner Ste Vignobles Aubert
2.6100 hectares
Grand Cru

Château Saint-Lô
Present owner Ste du Château St Lô
8.65 hectares
Generic Saint-Émilion
They also produce a wine under the name of
Château Gros. Big, sprawling old-fashioned
French farmhouse with two turrets.

Château de Saint Pey
Present owner Jean-Pierre Musset
18.43 hectares
Grand Cru

Château de Saint Pey
Present owner Maurice Musset
9.2350 hectares
Situated on the borders of St Pey-d'Armens and
St Étienne-de-Lisse.

Jean-Pierre Seguinel
This property is split into two parts:
1   2 hectares
    Grand Cru
2   1.72 hectares
    Generic Saint-Émilion
Sells bulk wine only.

Michel Guy Seguinel
This property has two plots of vineyard:
1   1.8162 hectares
    Grand Cru
2   1.9521 hectares
    Generic Saint-Émilion
Sells bulk wine only.

Château Sicard
Present owner Guy Duboudin
5.0210 hectares
Generic Saint-Émilion

Château Vieux Peyrouquet
Present owner J Jaques Cruchet
2.3339 hectares
Generic Saint-Émilion

Paul Vivien
0.2051 hectares
Sells bulk generic Saint-Émilion only.

Vignonet

This commune of 330.22 hectares lies 4 kilometres south of Saint-Émilion and is the most southerly commune within the Saint-Émilion appellation.

The small village bordering the Dordogne river centres around a very old picturesque church.

The soil is sandy-gravelly to a depth of 6 metres, becoming more sandy to the north with some clay to the south and west.

The minimum strength allowed under the appellation is 10° Saint-Émilion 10.5° Grand Cru, with a maximum yield of 42 hectolitres per hectare.

Many growers in this region produce generic wines which are sold in bulk.

Vignonet Properties

Château le Barrau du Maréchal
Present owner Pierre Barbe
0.66 hectares
Generic Saint-Émilion

Château Belles-Graves
Present owner Gaec Dangin
This property is split into two parts:
1   2 hectares
    Grand Cru

2   8.68 hectares
    Generic Saint-Émilion

Yvol Bergerie
Generic Saint-Émilion
Sold in bulk.

Château du Bois
Present owner   Raymond Lenne
This property is split into two parts:
1   0.58 hectares
    Grand Cru
2   1.5385 hectares
    Generic Saint-Émilion

Bouladou-Roy
2.80 hectares
Generic Saint-Émilion
Sold in bulk.

Château Burlis
Present owners   Jean Corbière & Christian
Corbière
1.85 hectares & 0.3940 hectares
Generic Saint-Émilion
Only sells bulk wines.

Château Caillou d'Arthus
Present owner   Jean-Paul Salvert
This property is split into two parts:
1   0.5530 hectares
    Grand Cru
2   3.33 hectares
    Generic Saint-Émilion

Hector Chenard
0.74 hectares
Generic Saint-Émilion
Sells only bulk wines.

Terzo Cocetta
0.3615 hectares
Generic Saint-Émilion
Sells only bulk wines.

Marcelle Crouzet
4.9696 hectares
Generic Saint-Émilion
Sells only bulk wines.

Gilberte Gintrac
1.2080 hectares
Sells bulk generic Saint-Émilion only.

Château Haut-Brisson
Present owner   Yves Blanc
9.3312 hectares – 50 tonneaux
Grand Cru
This owner also owns Château Franc Bigaroux.

Château Haut-Graves-d'Arthus
Present owner   Gérard Musset
4.78 hectares – 40 tonneaux
Generic Saint-Émilion
Situated at the edge of the Saint-Émilion and
Vignonet communes. Also produces a second
wine under the name of *Moulin des Graves*.

Château Haut-Graves-Rouy
Present owner   Guy Bouladou
This property is split into two parts:
1   4.20 hectares
    Generic Saint-Émilion
2   1.23 hectares
    Generic Saint-Émilion

Château Haut-Peyroutas
Present owner   Labécot et fils
This property is split into two parts:
1   2.17 hectares
    Generic Saint-Émilion
2   1.20 hectares
    Grand Cru

Château La Haut-Rouchonne
Present owner   Jean Couder
6.16 hectares
Generic Saint-Émilion

Clos Joly
Present owner   Etiene Faugeras
2.8695 hectares – 15 tonneaux
Generic Saint-Émilion

R Lantignac
0.69 hectares
Sells bulk generic Saint-Émilion only.

Château Moulin-Bellegrave
Present owner   Max Perier
This property covers 14 hectares and is split into
two parts:
1   8.0240 hectares
    Grand Cru
2   3.10 hectares
    Generic Saint-Émilion
These vineyards also produce a wine called
Château des Graves.
   The vineyard is planted with 75% Merlot, 15%
Bouchet and 10% Cabernet Sauvignon.
   After the grapes are picked, they are 90% de-
stalked and fermented in stainless-steel vats for
up to three weeks and matured in oak casks for
up to thirty months before bottling.

Château du Paradis
Present owners   Société des Vignobles Raby-
Saugeon
13.2730 hectares
Grand Cru
Owned by this family for five centuries. They

also own Château la Grave (5 hectares), Château Corboueye, both in Vignonet and Château la Cateau, in Saint-Émilion.

Château Guillemin-de-Gorre and Beau-Rivage in the communes of Sainte-Terre and Cabara, make up in total 15 hectares which produces a very good 'Bordeaux Supérieur'.

All these vineyards give full yield. The average age of the vines are between ten and thirty years old. producing appoximately 200 tonneaux, vinified in the modern cellars of the Château du Paradis.

Very well-kept vineyards.

Château Peyroutas
Present owner   Jean Bernard Gagnerot
4.30 hectares
Generic Saint-Émilion

Château Peyroutas
Present owners   Mmes Baye et Dupin de Beyssat
4.32 hectares – 25 tonneaux
Generic Saint-Émilion

Marie-Thérèse Pradel
2.8695 hectares
Sells bulk generic Saint-Émilion only.

Château Quercy
Present owner   Charles Duchartre
5.38 hectares – 20 tonneaux
Generic Saint-Émilion
Very imposing property.

Château Rose d'Arthus
Present owner   Jean Claude Arnaud
5.31 hectares
Generic Saint-Émilion

André Roux
0.55 hectares
Sells bulk generic Saint-Émilion only.

Gilles Roux
2.16 hectares
Sells bulk generic Saint-Émilion only.

Bernard Roy
1.23 hectares
Sells bulk generic Saint-Émilion only.

Émile Salvador
4.9686 hectares
Sells bulk generic Saint-Émilion only.

Château Taillefer
Present owner   Bernard Videau
Generic Saint-Émilion – 20 tonneaux

Château Teyssier
Present owner   Gérard Colin
8.7391 hectares
Grand Cru
Very attractive, small Château which is well-maintained.

Jacques Thibaud
0.2180 hectares
Sells bulk generic Saint-Émilion only.

Robert Thibeaud
0.67 hectares
Sells bulk generic Saint-Émilion only.

Jean Valadier
1.55 hectares
Sells bulk generic Saint-Émilion only.

Château Val-d'Or
Present owner   Roger Bardet
9.8415 hectares
Grand Cru

Bernard Videau
8.4228 hectares
Sells bulk generic Saint-Émilion and also under the label of Château Destieu.

St Étienne-de-Lisse

In the nineteenth century this commune was known locally as St Estèphe de St Émilion and used to come under the jurisdiction of Saint-Émilion.

It is located 5 kilometres east of Saint-Émilion at the end of a line of hills bearing its name. It is in this commune that the imposing Château de Pressac stands. On the outskirts of the village, on a hill, the attractive village church is situated.

This area, covering 405.15 hectares, is mainly clay–limestone soil on the slopes, with a sub-soil of stone and iron, whilst the plain is sand with some clay in the sub-soil.

In keeping with other communes, the appellation is restricted to Saint-Émilion 10° minimum and Grand Cru Saint-Émilion 10.5° minimum with a maximum permitted yield of 42 hectolitres per hectare.

St Étienne-de-Lisse Properties

Château Barbey
Present owner Anne-Marie Ollivier
0.4608 hectares
Generic Saint-Émilion

Mauricette Bersac
2 hectares
Sells bulk generic Saint-Émilion only.

Château Bonneau
Present owner Alain Bonneau
5.8605 hectares
Grand Cru

Château de Bray
Present owner Yves Grall
3.60 hectares
Generic Saint-Émilion

Château du Calvaire
Present owner Jean-Pierre Cisterne
9.6572 hectares – 50 tonneaux
Generic Saint-Émilion

Château Canterane
Owned by the Ouy family for more than two centuries. Managed by M A Trabut-Cussac. This property is split into two parts:
1 7.00 hectares
   Generic Saint-Émilion
2 2.74 hectares
   Grand Cru

Château la Chapelle
This property is split into two parts:
1 *Present owner* Denis Celier
   1.7592 hectares
   Generic Saint-Émilion
2 *Present owner* René Celier
   1.20 hectares
   Generic Saint-Émilion

Domaine de Clotte
Present owner Alain Maynard
0.6248 hectares
Generic Saint-Émilion

Château Côtes-Bernateau
This property is split into three parts:
1 *Present owner* Régis Lavau
   2 hectares
   Grand Cru
2 *Present owner* Régis Lavau
   8.5588 hectares
   Generic Saint-Émilion
3 *Present owner* Jacqueline Lavau
   1.4720 hectares
   Generic Saint-Émilion

Château Côtes Puy Blanquet
Present owner Daniel Bertoni
7.76 hectares
Generic Saint-Émilion

Château les Demoiselles
Present owner Rémy Daut
5.38 hectares (part of which is in St Hippolyte)
Generic Saint-Émilion

Antoine de Vecchia
0.2052 hectares
Sells bulk generic Saint-Émilion only.

Château la Fagnouse
Present owner Madame Anne Marie Coutant
This lovely old Château, set in attractive surroundings and owned by Madame Anne Marie Coutant, is one of the oldest in the commune. There are 7.5 hectares of which 7.1195 are under vine. The vineyard is planted with 90% Merlot and 10% Cabernet Sauvignon with an average age of vine of thirty-five years.

After picking, the grapes are totally de-stalked and fermented in cement vats for fifteen days, and matured for two years before bottling.

The average out-put is 35 hectolitres per hectare and the property enjoys Grand Cru status.

Château Faugères
Present owner Philippe Esquissaud
10.12 hectares
Generic Saint-Émilion

Château Fleur de Lisse
Present owner   Michel Minnielle
This property is split into two parts:
1   2.65 hectares
    Grand Cru
2   1.85 hectares
    Generic Saint-Émilion

Château Foutenelle
Present owners   Bigarrette Frères
1.6628 hectares

Éliane Garnier
2.9723 hectares
Sells bulk generic Saint-Émilion only.

Château Grand Champ
Present owner   Jean Blanc
1.9094 hectares
Grand Cru

Château Haut-Bardoulet
Present owner   Jacques Baraize
3.8962 hectares
Grand Cru

Château Haut-Rocher
Present owner   Jean de Monteil
This attractive, classic Grand Cru Château is
owned by Jean de Monteil.
   The property covers 14.5 hectares, of which
13.2 are under vine (60% Merlot, 20% Cabernet
Sauvignon, 20% Bouchet).
   The grapes are totally de-stalked and fermented in cement tanks for eight to ten days and
then matured in tanks for eighteen months prior
to bottling.

Château Haut-Veyrac
Present owner   Maurice Claverie
7.0322 hectares
Generic Saint-Émilion

Château Jacques-Blanc
Present owner   Pierre Chouet
21.0366 hectares – 125 tonneaux
Grand Cru
Just outside the village of St Étienne-de-Lisse.
Well-kept, attractive Château.

Domaine de Lacares
Present owner   Monique Ducousso
0.38 hectares
Generic Saint-Émilion

Château Lapeyre
Also produces wine under the name of *Château
Guinot.*
This property is split into three parts:
1   *Present owner*   H. Tauziac
    3.51 hectares
    Grand Cru

2   *Present owner*   H. Tauziac
    1.77 hectares
    Generic
3   *Present owner*   Simone Tauziac
    7.46 hectares
    Grand Cru

Château Laurenceau
Present owner   Bruno Laporte
8.0485 hectares
Grand Cru

Abel Laurent
0.5730 hectares
Sells bulk generic Saint-Émilion only.

Gisèle Lavandier
0.73 hectares
Sells bulk generic Saint-Émilion only.

Château Mayne Vieux
Present owner   Gilbert Ducher
3.9910 hectares
Generic Saint-Émilion

Château Mont-Belair
Present owner   Fernand Denamiel
This property is split into two parts:
1   0.72 hectares
    Generic Saint-Émilion
2   11.4666 hectares
    Generic Saint-Émilion
Set high on a hill. Family house.

Château la Mouleyre
Present owner   Geneviève Beaucousin
4.8680 hectares
Generic Saint-Émilion

Château la Mouleyre
Present owner   Pierre Roques
8.8111 hectares
Grand Cru
Château la Mouleyre is part of the de Savoie
estate, which covers over 40 hectares in all.
   The Château Savoie Cru bears the Appel-
lation *Bordeaux Supérieur, Côtes de Castillon.*
   Clayey, limestone soil.

Pierette Muscat
1.7020 hectares
Sells bulk generic Saint-Émilion only.

Paul Pallaro
0.4388 hectares
Sells bulk generic Saint-Émilion only.

Château Perey
Present owner   P. Martegoutes
1.0541 hectares
Generic Saint-Émilion

Château Petit-Mongot
Present owner Jean Decamps
5.40 hectares
Grand Cru

Château de Pressac
Present owner G.F.A. Jacques Pouey (Gérant)
Several Châteaux in France bear this name: two
in the Gironde, one at Daignac and the other at
St Étienne-de-Lisse. The latter, set in its own
parkland, is situated on a high wall overlooking
the valley, the village and the church. It used to
be an impressive building, dating from the fifteenth century and, according to local tradition,
flanked by twenty-seven towers. The ruins of
some of their old walls can still be seen.

The main body of the building, rebuilt in
seventeenth century, occupies the main promontory. It is a heavy, inelegant construction, in
quite a bad state of repair; to the north the valley
drops away. The perimeter wall must have at
one time covered the whole of the tip of the
promontory, and there are still the remains of
walls and towers of the previous exterior
defences. To the east and south there are walls in
relatively good condition and some damaged
towers, broken by horizontal loop-holes and
crowned with ivy. The roof forms a whole
which still retains a certain grandeur.

In front of the Château there is an avenue and
some trees. To the side there are garden areas.
The Château de Pressac is surrounded by a
property of 40 hectares, meadows, land and
woods. There are 24.11 hectares under vine
which produce 60 to 75 tonneaux of Grand Cru
wine, and 1.50 hectares of generic Saint-Émilion.

Château Pistouley
Present owner Paul Fressinneau
2.0020 hectares
Generic Saint-Émilion

Château les Places
Present owner Claude Fritegotto
1.0909 hectares
Generic Saint-Émilion

Château Puy-Blanquet
Present owner Roger Jacquet
20.1548 hectares – 110 tonneaux
Grand Cru
Set on a hill in woodland. Lovely setting.

Château du Rocher
This Grand Cru property is owned by Baron
Stanislas de Montfort in whose family it has
been since the sixteenth century.

The property covers 15 hectares of which
12.84 hectares are under vine. The grape
varieties here are 50% Merlot, 25% Bouchet,
20% Cabernet Sauvignon and 5% Pressac. The
average age of the vines is twenty-five years
with the oldest being eighty years.

Château Rocher Bellevue
Present owner Rudiger Geens
This property is split into two parts:
1 7.5988 hectares
   Grand Cru
2 2.50 hectares
   Generic Saint-Émilion

Château la Rose Pressac
Present owner Franck Barthome
7.3927 hectares
Generic Saint-Émilion

Jean-Claude Roux
1.3565 hectares
Sells bulk generic Saint-Émilion only.

Michel Guy Seguinel
0.63 hectares
Sells bulk generic Saint-Émilion only.

Château la Tour de Pressac
This ancient Grand Cru property is owned by
Les Heriteurs d'André Povey who also own
Châteaux Vieux Larguet and Cadet.

The *Chef de Culture* is M Marly, who has been
employed at the property since 1977.

The vineyard covers 50 hectares of which 35
are under vine planted with 30% Merlot, 30%
Bouchet, 30% Cabernet Sauvignon and 10%
Pressac. The average age of the vines is twenty
years.

The grapes are completely de-stalked and
fermented in cement vats for approximately ten
days and then matured in oak casks for two
years prior to bottling. The average out-put is
35 hectolitres per hectare, fetching 13,000
francs per tonneaux.

Château St Charles
Present owner Jean-Pierre Hibert
0.73 hectares
Generic Saint-Émilion

Château Tertre de la Mouleyre
0.96 hectares
Sells bulk generic Saint-Émilion only.

Château Tour Puy-Blanquet
This property is split into two parts:
1 *Present owner* Daniel Lapoterie
   5.8422 hectares
   Generic Saint-Émilion

2   *Present owner*   Marcel Lapoterie
    2.9211 hectares
    Generic Saint-Émilion

Château Trapaud

Present owner   André Larribière
Well-kept traditional Grand Cru estate covering
14 hectares of which 12.0025 hectares are under
vine.

Château la Tuilerie

Present owner   Christian Fargeot
2.9490 hectares
Generic Saint-Émilion

Château Veyrac

Present owner   Robert Bellanger
12.7023 hectares
Generic Saint-Émilion

Clos Viranon

Present owner   Jean Lafaye
This property is split into two parts:
1   3 hectares
    Grand Cru
2   2.5947 hectares
    Generic Saint-Émilion

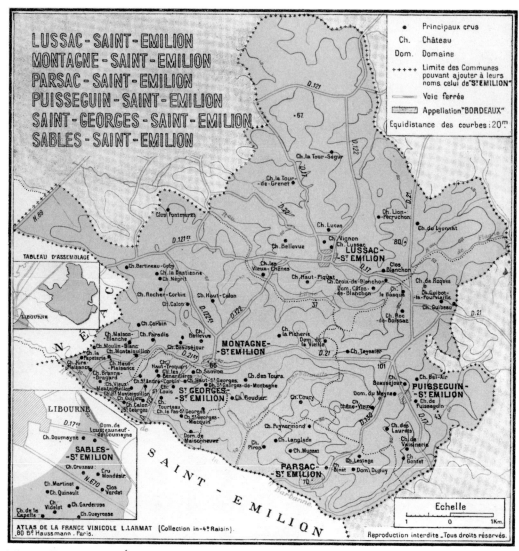

The satellites of Saint-Émilion. It should be noted that Parsac and Sables no longer have their own appellations.

THE SATELLITES OF SAINT-ÉMILION

For many years these six satellite villages situated north of Saint-Émilion were involved in a battle with Saint-Émilion, who always refused to accept them within their appellation.

They were finally granted, in 1936, their own individual appellations and were allowed to suffix the name of Saint-Émilion. Parsac no longer exists as an appellation and is now included in Montagne: likewise Sables is now part of Saint-Émilion and its own appellation no longer exists.

The wines produced from these satellite villages are similar in style to those of Saint-Émilion but generally do not rise to their quality, although there are some notable exceptions such as Châteaux St Georges, Roudier and Lyonnat.

The minimum permitted strength of the wines is 10.5° and the maximum permitted yield is 42 hectolitres per hectare.

Lussac-St Émilion

When approaching Lussac you cannot fail to see to the south of the village a hill with a wooded summit, The Tertre de Picampeau, where there is a monument from the Gallic period, a witness to the ceremonies practised by the community established here before the Christian era.

But it was in the Gallo-Roman period that the first vines covered the slopes of Lussac, which owes its name to the first owner of a Roman villa called 'Luccius', whose land 'Lucianus' formed the parish of Lussac with its original boundaries.

Numerous remains brought to light by the growers and archeologists – including amphoras and pruning-knives – prove the existence of sizeable vineyards at this time.

Barbarian invasions subsequently sacked the entire region and the vine returned to its wild state until the twelfth century when the establishment of Citeaux by the Benedictines gave a considerable boost to the region. In his historical study of Lussac, Mr J A Garde says:

> 'The Benedictines re-established cultivation of the lands of Lussac where the vine is king. The Monastery grew up at the place known as Faise. The Abbot Commander who bore the title Baron de Lussac, lived in the Château la Tour Ségur, the luxurious residence in which the Abbot received important guests such as the Archbishops of Bordeaux who carried the reputation of the wines of Lussac as far as the Court of England.'

Towards the middle of the eighteenth century, the Abbot of Faise was Joseph de Secondat de Montesquieu, brother of the famous writer. The latter sometimes passed through Lussac where, as an informed wine-grower, he was studying agricultural methods in the area and attested the high quality of the Abbot's wines.

A document of 23rd November, 1726, shows the presence of Montesquieu at the Château la Tour where he signed as witness an agreement between his brother the Abbot, and Drivet du Lyonnat.

By the time of the Revolution, the vineyards of Lussac covered quite a sizeable area. Under the Empire the slump in wines following the wars which closed export out-lets was felt severely. The citizens of Lussac then became travellers to find new markets for their wines.

Today this satellite commune, with its small thriving village, lies 12 kilometres north-east of Saint-Émilion and comprises 1,050 hectares of which 940 hectares are under vine. In 1981 there were two-hundred and twelve growers, twenty of whom bottle their wine at the Château, and fifty-six of whom are members of the Co-operative. Many sell their wine in bulk.

The land here is some 30 to 35% cheaper than in the communes entitled to the full Appellation Saint-Émilion, at around 300,000 francs per hectare (1981). The minimum permitted strength is 10.5°; the basic maximum yield (42 hectolitres per hectare) is the same as that required by the Saint-Émilion Appellation Contrôlée.

The soil on the slopes in the south-east part of the commune is limestone and clay, similar to that of the Côtes area of Saint-Émilion. The best Lussac wines come from this area; their style resembles the Côtes Saint-Émilion wines and the best are capable of improving over a long period in bottle. Château Lyonnat has perhaps acquired the most notable reputation for making fine-quality wine.

A little further north there are banks of limestone, in the west a high gravelly plateau, in the north-west stony soil with iron or clay and sand, and still further north mostly clay or loam.

A little white table wine is made, mostly in the north of the commune, from Sémillon, Sauvignon and Ugni Blanc, for local consumption.

Out-put of Lussac-St Émilion in hectolitres since 1950 was:

1950 – 26,485		1967 – 25,735	
1951 – 14,544		1968 – 13,032	
1952 – 17,505		1969 – 16,864	
1953 – 30,594		1970 – 42,994	
1954 – 17,801		1971 – 23,827	
1955 – 28,431		1972 – 36,274	
1956 – 7,814		1973 – 58,639	
1957 – 7,954		1974 – 40,718	
1958 – 15,814		1975 – 35,286	
1959 – 13,698		1976 – 45,784	
1960 – 17,347		1977 – 15,153	
1961 – 8,606		1978 – 43,540	
1962 – 35,364		1979 – 57,590	
1963 – 21,463		1980 – 32,847	
1964 – 32,936		1981 – 42,307	
1965 – 20,898		1982 – 61,237	
1966 – 26,490			

Union des Producteurs de Puisseguin-et Lussac-St Émilion

This Co-operative covers the districts of Puisseguin and Lussac. It was formed on April 24th, 1937, and started with the 1938 vintage.

There are one hundred and twenty grower-members covering 395 hectares. They produce some 20,000 hectolitres of Lussac and 10,000 hectolitres of Puisseguin a year, and have the capacity to handle over 78,000 hectolitres of wine.

The wines are fermented and matured in cement vats and refrigerated before bottling.

The amount of wine from Lussac produced by the Co-operative represents over 40% of the total wine, and its members own almost 50% of the total hectares under vine of that commune.

Most of the wine is sold in France but about 25% is exported, mainly to Holland, Denmark and Switzerland.

The Châteaux vinified in the Co-operative are the following:

Châteaux	Present owners
Château la Tour Ségur	M Robert Garrigues
Château la Garenne	M Jacques Chasselinat
Château Bois Tiffray	M Bertrand Le Comte Du Pouget
Château le Piquat Montroc	M Maurice Gorge
Château la Chevallière	Mesdames Mayen/Thimouy
Château Taureau	M Raymond Laborie
Château Roc de Jamard	M Yvan Sanchou
Château Haut Pagaud	M Marius Lacroix (and Son)
Château la Rose	M Jean Abadie
Château les Vieux Chênes	M Michel Debes
Château les Adams	Madame France Debes
Château Pichon	M Claude Bonnin
Château Lagrange	G F A René Boidron
Château Haut Drouillard	M Marcel Boudot
Château Girard Tiffray	G F A Paul Goiset
Château Verdu	Messieurs Gaury/Dubos

The following are the members of the Co-operative who sell their grapes to be vinified under generic Lussac or brand-names of the Co-operative:

Name	Size of vineyard in Hectares
Claudine Bonamy	5 HA 12
Gilbert Bonamy	3 HA 33
Michel Boudyo	8 HA 27
Lucien Peytour	2 HA 91
Jean Autier	5 HA 80
Pierre Autier	5 HA 06
Christian Barraud	2 HA 93
Jean Boibelet	2 HA 42
Pierre Boireau	4 HA 28
Philippe Bonnin	5 HA 08
Claude Bonhomme	5 HA 62
Robert Boudot	2 HA 29
Pierre Bourdeau	2 HA 40
Mario Buoro	5 HA 52
Denis Chaignaud	7 HA 95
Maryse Chambon	3 HA 16
Jean Chibrac	4 HA 96
Louis Corazza	8 HA 17

Name	Size of vineyard in Hectares
Pierre David	4 HA 19
Gabriel Duchartre	4 HA 00
Joël Dumas	2 HA 36
Pierre Dumons	6 HA 03
Duverger	6 HA 72
Benjamin Gaiotto	7 HA 91
Jean Gallot	5 HA 58
GFA Domaine de Lagrange	16 HA 95
Paul Goizet	13 HA 95
Marcel Gorry	3 HA 03
Labatut	2 HA 72
Marcel Laporte	2 HA 73
Henri Madrid	3 HA 04
Francis Martin	6 HA 74
Cesar Raichini	5 HA 22
Gerard Moreau	2 HA 89
Jean Paret	4 HA 11
Michel Porcher	3 HA 29
Michel Picard/Dupouget	11 HA 96
Fernand Poudret	5 HA 92
Odile Sarrazin	3 HA 92
Roger Trepaud	3 HA 51
Marcel Vauthier	3 HA 36
Jean Vergnaud	4 HA 53
Bernard Lacroix	4 HA 52
Henri Rabiller	2 HA 75
Marcel Lescure	2 HA 95

Lussac Properties

Château des Aubaredes
Present owner M Sublett

Château les Adams
The present owner is Madame France Debes, a member of the Co-operative, which produces her wine. The vineyard has 9.5 hectares.

Château de Barbe-Blanche
No-one can be sure of the origin of Barbe Blanche (white beard), King Henri IV, an inveterate gourmet and owner of many estates, was particularly fond of the Barbe Blanche wine which was already being produced by the Gallo-Romans. Remains of the Gallo-Roman period can be found in the ground.

The monks of the nearby Abbaye de Faize tended the vines with the greatest care and, in 1382, their Prior, Guillaume IV Panare, sent several casks to the court in England.

The name of Montesquieu appears in the history of Barbe Blanche and in a note dated 16th March, 1762, Abbé Lecomte de la Tresne, commendatory of the Royal Abbey of Faize, wrote down certain methods of cultivation which are still used today.

At the time of the French Revolution, Barbe Blanche appears as part of the National Heritage and was sold as such.

Today the 15 hectare vineyard with its very attractive Château is owned by André Bouvier. He purchased the property in 1964 from the Cassat family in whose hands it had been since 1815.

The clay and limestone soil is planted with 50% Merlot, 25% Bouchet and 25% Cabernet Sauvignon, and all the wines are Château-bottled.

Château Belair
Present owner Mme Jean Roi
Situated in the north-east of the commune, this property covers 29 hectares with 18 under vine,

5 hectares of which are planted with new vines.

From 1890 the Châteaux Belair, la Tour de Grenet and Lyonnat belonged to the Baudou family and then passed down to Gabriel Roi, the nephew of Mme Baudou.

The present owner is Mme Jean Roi, the widow of Gabriel Roi.

The vineyard is planted with 70% Merlot, 20% Bouchet and 10% Cabernet Sauvignon which, when picked, are totally de-stalked and fermented in cement vats for three to four weeks. Then with one fining of egg-whites, the wine is matured in oak casks for up to two years.

A second wine is produced under the label of *Château la Gravette*.

Château Bel-Chouteau
Present owner   M Mallet

Château de Bellevue
Present owner   Charles Chatenoud
This Château, set back behind a long driveway from the D.122 just as one enters the village of Lussac is owned by Charles Chatenoud. The property is situated on the summit of the southern slopes of Lussac. It covers 15 hectares of clay/limestone soil and a limestone sub-soil, with 11.6 hectares under vine, planted with 65% Merlot, 30% Bouchet and 5% Cabernet Sauvignon.

The grapes are normally totally de-stalked and fermented in cement vats for up to seven days. After one fining with bentonite, the wine is then put into bottle after approximately eighteen months. The out-put in hectolitres per hectare since 1975 are:

1975 – 30	1978 – 38
1976 – 58	1979 – 55
1977 – 20	

Château Bellevue-Poitou
Present owner   Jean Emile Blanc
The present owner, Jean Emile Blanc, has created this property piece by piece over the last thirty-two years. Situated on almost flat clay/limestone land, it covers 35 hectares of which 25 are under vine with 15 hectares planted with Merlot, 8 hectares with Bouchet and 2 hectares with Cabernet Sauvignon. The grapes are totally de-stalked and fermented in cement vats for approximately eight days. Then, after one fining with egg-whites, the wine is matured in vats for three to four years before bottling.

It has recently been decided that the wines will, in future, only be sold in bulk to the trade.

Château de Blancheu
The present owner of this very small property is M J S Marin-Audra, who also owns Château Claymore.

Domaine de Blanchon
Present owner   M Ducharte

Château Bois-Tiffray
The present owner, Le Comte Bertrand de Pouget, is a member of the Co-operative which produces his wine.

Château des Bruges
Present owner   Mme Claudine Bonamy
This Château lies in both Lussac and Puisseguin. It is owned by Mme Claudine Bonamy, a member of the Co-operative which produces her wine.

Château Busquet
Present owner   Dominique Robin
His family also own Château Sansonnet, Grand Cru Classé, Domaine de la Salle, Châteaux Doumayne, Gontet Robin and Clos Vieux Taillefer. Château Busquet is 10 hectares.

Château Canon Chaigneau
Present owners   G F A Canon Chaigneau

Domaine du Calvaire
Present owner   Serge Coudsoy

Château Chambeau
Present owner   M Bordes

Château Champs de Jamard
Present owner   M Roudière

Château Cailloux les Martins
Present owner   M d'Anthony

Château le Chevallière
The present owners are Mesdames Mayen/Thimouy, members of the Co-operative which produces their wine.

Château Chéreau
Present owner   M Silvestrini
This Château, partly situated on the slopes, covers 19 hectares of which 10.5 are under vine. The property was owned by M Mercadier who sold it in 1941 to M Londex who in turn sold it to the present owner M Silvestrini in 1958.

The vineyard is planted with 75% Merlot, and 25% Cabernet Sauvignon.

Seventy-five per cent of grapes are de-stalked and fermented for approximately three weeks in cement vats and then pressed. After one fining, the wine is matured in old casks.

This property produces on average 50 ton-neaux per annum with approximately 41 hecto-litres per hectare.

The production in hectolitres from 1975 to 1979 was:

1975 – 386	1978 – 395
1976 – 645	1979 – 604
1977 – 144	

The wine is sold in bulk and in bottle.

Château Chouteau
Present owner   M Rogerie
2 hectares under vine.

Château Claymore
Present owner   M J S Marin Audra
This property on the slopes of the plateau covers 38 hectares of which 20 are under vine. It is owned by M J S Marin Audra who also owns Château de Blancheu in Lussac and Château Canon Chaigneau in Lalande-de-Pomerol.

It is planted with 63% Merlot, 20% Bouchet, 15% Cabernet Sauvignon and 2% Pressac on clayey soil with a heavy clay sub-soil.

The grapes when picked, are totally de-stalked and fermented for up to twelve days in cement *cuvées*. One fining with egg-white before maturing in cement tanks and bottling after two years.

The output in 1978 was 40 hectolitres, and in 1979 – 836 hectolitres.

Domaine du Courlat
The ownership has now passed from M J-B Audy to his daughter, Mme Bounotte.

Château aux Cousins
Present owner   Gabriel Seize

Château Croix de Blanchon
The present owner is Georges David, who also owns Château Haut-Larose.

Château la Croix de Chouteau
Present owner   Raymond Coudroy

Château Croix de Rambeau
Present owner   M Trocard

Château la France Grand Bersam
Present owner   Marcel Chassagne
This property, owned by Marcel Chassagne, is situated on undulating hillsides covering 20 hectares of which 6 are under vine.

The vineyard is planted with 80% Merlot and 20% Cabernet Sauvignon.

After total de-stalking the grapes are fermented in cement vats for up to twenty-five days and matured in stainless-steel vats for two years before one fining with egg-whites and then bottling.

The out-put in 1978 was 40 hectolitres, and in 1979 – 23 hectolitres.

The wine is mainly sold to private clients.

Château la Garenne
Present owner   Jacques Chasselinat
21.3 hectares
The present owner is Jacques Chasselinat, a member of the Co-operative, which produces his wine.

Château Girard Tiffray
Present owner   Paul Goiset (who is a member of the Co-operative which produces his wine)
13.95 hectares

Clos Girondon
Present owner   M Gantzer

Château Grand Bersan
Present owner   M Duvergnon

Château la Grande-Clotte
Present owner   Mme Peyrat-Chèze

Château les Grandsjays
Present owner   Jean Boireau
Situated on gravel, clay and iron soil, this property, owned by Jean Boireau since 1964, covers 66 hectares of which 44 are under vine.

The vineyard is planted with 62.5% Merlot, 2.5% Bouchet and 35% Cabernet Sauvignon.

The grapes are completely de-stalked and the fermentation takes place in cement tanks for up to five days, after which it is matured in concrete vats for between eighteen months to two years.

It is then fined once with gelatine before bottling.

The out-put in hectolitres over the last few years was:

1975 –	1,269
1976 –	1,715
1977 –	979
1978 –	1,843
1979 –	2.461

Château la Grenière
Present owner   Jean Paul Dubreuil
This property situated on a plateau in the north of the commune is owned by Jean Paul Dubreuil whose grandparents bought it from the Hingues family in 1941.

It covers 8 hectares of which 7 are under vine planted with 60% Merlot, 15% Bouchet and 25% Cabernet Sauvignon.

After the grapes have been totally de-stalked they are fermented in cement vats for up to ten days and matured in oak casks for eighteen months prior to bottling.

The out-put from this vineyard has been:

1975 – 22 hectolitres
1976 – 32 hectolitres
1977 – 16 hectolitres
1978 – 24 hectolitres
1979 – 46 hectolitres

Château la Haut Claymore
Present owner D D Devaud

Château Haut Drouillard
Present owner Marcel Boudot, a member of the Co-operative, which produces his wine.
10.8 hectares

Château Haut Jamard
Present owner Mme Charpentier

Château Haut-Larose
Present owner Georges David
Georges David also owns Château Croix-de-Blanchon in this commune. He has fully replanted the vineyard which is situated in the northern part of Lussac.

Château Haut Milon
Present owner M Boireau

Château Haut Pagaud
Present owners Marius Lacroix and Fils (members of the Co-operative which produces their wine)

Château Haut Pichon
Present owner M Seignat

Château Haut-Piquat
Present owner J P Rivière

Château Lagrange
Present owner René Boidron (a member of the Co-operative which produces his wine)

Château Lucas
This property has belonged to the Vauthier family since the sixteenth century. It was then that the Abbé de Montbalin gave this growth to the Lord of Lavignerie in recognition of good and loyal service.

Now this vineyard also produces the red wines of Château Rouzaud, Château la Filiberte and Château des Millonieres and white wines of la Tour-de-Lucas – reserved for certain regular customers.

The property lies on the outskirts of Lussac and although fairly small, the Château is attractive and well-kept.

Château de Lussac
The estate of Château de Lussac covers 35 hectares of which 16 hectares are under vine.

Planted 50% with Cabernet Sauvignon, 25% Merlot and 25% Pressac.

The Château itself is an eighteenth-century Château, well-maintained, lying just on the outskirts of Lussac, under the ownership of GFA Château de Lussac and run by the Marquis de Sercey.

Château Lyonnat
Present owner Jean Milhade
Situated on a hill in the south-east of the commune, this property covers 60 hectares of which 45 are under vine with 60% Merlot, 20% Bouchet, 18% Cabernet Sauvignon and 2% Pressac, grown on clay/limestone soil.

Fifty percent of the vineyard was replanted in 1970 and there are still 4 hectares of one hundred-year-old vines.

The present owner, Jean Milhade, is the President of the Syndicat de Lussac and in 1961 acquired the Château which had previously been owned by the Bandou family since 1895. At one time it belonged to the brother of Montesquieu, Abbot of Faise, whose jurisdiction covered most of Lussac.

Monsieur Milhade also owns Château Recougne (Bordeaux Supérieur) and Château Sergant and Château les Annereaux in Lalande de Pomerol.

After the grapes are picked, they are totally de-stalked and fermented in concrete vats lined with epoxy resin for up to ten days.

The wine is matured for two and a half to three years in oak vats before bottling.

Wines produced from this Château are of high quality and generally considered to be the finest in Lussac.

The out-put in hectolitres from 1975 to 1979 was:

1975 – 200	1978 – 22
1976 – 210	1979 – 220
1977 – 40	

Clos Lyonnat
Present owner Luciene Sagnebe
This property bordering Château Lyonnat in the south-east of the commune was owned by the Boudou-Roi family since 1890 and sold to the present owner Luciene Sagnebe in 1961.

The vineyard covers 20 hectares planted with 50% Merlot and 50% Cabernet Sauvignon.

After the grapes are picked they are totally de-stalked and fermented in cement vats.

Maturation takes place in oak vats and the wine is bottled after three years.

The out-put in hectolitres from 1975 to 1979 was:

1975 – 86
1976 – 176
1977 – 18
1978 – 130
1979 – 50 (due to *coulure*)

Château Lyon Perruchon
Present owner   M Thezard

Château Malidure
Present owner   M Oust

Château Mayne Blanc
Present owner   M Bouchaud

Château Moulin Noir
Present owner   Alain Dupuy
2.2 hectares

Château les Murailles
Present owner   Marc Vergniol

La Petite Clotte
Present owner   M Madrid
8 hectares

Château Petit-Refuge
Present owner   M Turbet-Delof
This property of 10 hectares, of which 6.5 hectares are under vine set on clayey soil, is planted with 33% Merlot, 33% Bouchet and 33% Cabernet Sauvignon.

The present owner is M Turbet-Delof who produces approximately 240 hectolitres per annum.

Château Pichon
Present owner   Claude Bonnin – a member of the Co-operative which produces his wine.
22.3 hectares

Château le Piquat Montroc
Present owner   Maurice Corge (who is a member of the Co-operative which produces his wine)
13 hectares

Château le Pont de Pierre
Present owner   Bernard Vergniol

Château Roc de Jamard
Present owner   Yvan Sanchou (who is a member of the Co-operative which produces his wine)
2.7 hectares

Château Roc de Perruchon
Present owner   M Chollet

Château la Rose
Present owner   Jean Abadie (who is a member of the Co-operative which produces his wine)
7 hectares

Château les Rochers
Present owner   M Garem

Château la Rose Peyroli
Present owner   Michel Debes (who is the owner of Château les Vieux Chênes)

Château St Pierre
Present owner   M Monboeut

Château de Tabuteau
Present owner   Jacques Bessou

Château St Pierre de Rambaud
Present owner   M Abanades

Château Taureau
Present owner   Raymond Laborie
The present owner Raymond Laborie is a member of the Co-operative which produces his wine.
16.2 hectares

Château Tertre-de-Perruchon
Present owner   H Laporte

Château La Tour-de-Grenet
Present owner   Jean Baptiste Brunot
This property is set on top of one of the highest hills in the commune with the vines planted on the clayey-limestone slopes.

It originally belonged to the Badou family who sold it to Jean Baptiste Brunot, the present owner, in 1970.

There are 33 hectares of which 25 are under vine planted with 70% Merlot, 25% Bouchet and 5% Cabernet Sauvignon. Many of the vines are one hundred years old.

After the grapes are picked, they are totally de-stalked and fermented in cement *cuvées* for up to twelve days.

The wine is matured in oak casks for two years before bottling.

The out-put in hectolitres from 1975 to 1979 was:

1975 – 33
1976 – 46
1977 – 14
1978 – 54
1979 – 66

Château la Tour-de-Ségur
Present owner   Pierre Berjal
When the benedictines of Citeaux established themselves at Lussac, they gave renewed standing to the cultivation of vines. Their Abbé

(or Abbot) held the title of Abbé de Faise and Baron de Lussac. He lived in the Château la Tour. The wines produced there were already thought well of since in 1382 the Archbishop of Bordeaux bought 2 tonneaux of his wine of Lussac from the Abbé de Faise, to send to the Court of England 'pro quodam magnato concilio regio'. From 1724 to 1754, the Abbé de Faise was Charles-Louis-Joseph de Segondat, Baron of Montesquieu, brother of the famous philosopher, who often came to visit him at Château la Tour. Thus one finds the famous signature as witness to an agreement signed on November 23rd, 1726, between the Abbé, his brother and Drivet du Lyonnat.

The name of Segur appears twice in the history of the Château. First, in the sixteenth century there appears a Lord of Segur who, to make amends for murdering a monk while out hunting in the forest of Faise, made a gift of alms to the Abbé de Faise in the form of his manor.

Again in the nineteenth century, we find the Segur family in the Château la Tour and it is probably in the tranquility of this Park that the famous Comtesse de Segur wrote part of her works.

The property is now owned by Pierre Berjal who also owns Château le Chatelat, Chante l'Alouette and Clos St Valery. It is a superb property of 15 hectares with its ancient tower overlooking the moat. The vineyard is planted with 33% Merlot, 33% Cabernet Sauvignon and 33% Bouchet. There is also a long rectangular lake and a chapel in the grounds.

Château la Tour Ségur
Present owner   M Garrigues
8.8 hectares

Château Verdu
Present owner   Gavry-Dubos (a member of the Co-operative which produces his wine)
16.8 hectares

Château Vieux Busquet
Present owner   M Pinnaud

Château les Vieux-Chênes
Present owner   Michel Debes, who also owns La Rose-Peyroli.
He is a member of the Co-operative which vinifies all his wine under the Château label. The 12.2 hectare property itself is located on the southern slopes of the commune on clayey-limestone land.

Château Vieux Fournay
Present owner   Roger Albert
This Château owned by Roger Albert is set on clayey-limestone soil and is planted with 33% Merlot, 33% Bouchet and 33% Cabernet Sauvignon.

After picking the grapes are totally de-stalked and fermented and matured in cement vats before bottling.

Château Vieux Rocs
Present owner   M Vilain

Puisseguin-St Émilion

This satellite commune, whose village is dominated by the church in the main square, is situated some 9 kilometres north of Saint-Émilion.

The name Puisseguin was derived from the Celtic word 'sea-gwin' which means strong wine, with the prefix 'Puy' which means hill.

Around 800 BC a Lord of Seguin who had distinguished himself in the service of Charlemagne came to live here. It is known that at the end of the twelfth century the titled lands of Puy-Seguin, as it was then called, were owned by the Dame Seguin who ordered the construction of the church which has a magnificent Roman doorway. Catherine of Navarre, sister of King Henri IV, lived in the Château de Puisseguin for a time. All that remains of the Château today is the octagonal tower which stands at the entrance to the village.

Puisseguin has 603.16 hectares under vine divided between one hundred and ten growers. Fifty of the growers, whose land covers 127.29 hectares, belong to the Co-operative, which is jointly run with the growers of Lussac. The remaining sixty growers, whose land covers 475.87 hectares, are all members of the Syndicate to whom they have to present their wines each year for tasting to obtain the appellation which entitles them to sell their wines in bulk with a small proportion bottled at the Château.

As with the other hyphenated satellite communes, Puisseguin-St Émilion was granted its own appellation in 1936. The minimum permitted strength is 10.5° and basic maximum yield is 42 hectolitres per hectare.

The soil is clay–limestone on a stony and molasse sub-soil and the wines are somewhat similar to the wines of the Côtes Saint-Émilion.

No new oak casks are used in this region and most wine is fermented and matured in cement vats.

The out-put in hectolitres from 1950 was:

1950 – 25,680	1967 – 21,465
1951 – 15,039	1968 – 10,198
1952 – 16,238	1969 – 9,350
1953 – 29,595	1970 – 27,492
1954 – 17,483	1971 – 16,624
1955 – 27,701	1972 – 20,859
1956 – 6,798	1973 – 34,709
1957 – 6,008	1974 – 24,785
1958 – 13,308	1975 – 21,949
1959 – 11,806	1976 – 27,626
1960 – 18,326	1977 – 11,152
1961 – 7,888	1978 – 28,184
1962 – 27,865	1979 – 33,795
1963 – 16,809	1980 – 22,519
1964 – 24,688	1981 – 25,140
1965 – 15,085	1982 – 35,832
1966 – 20,162	

Union des Producteurs de Puisseguin et Lussac-St Émilion

This Co-operative covers the areas of Lussac and Puisseguin. The Puisseguin Châteaux that have their wines vinified by the Co-operative are:

Châteaux	Owners
Château Côtes de Mouchet	Francis Laulla
Château les Agasseaux	Gaston Beney
Château des Bruges	Claudine Bonamy
Château du Roy	G F A Bonnot
Château Côtes de Saint Clair	Jean Paul Dupeyrat
Château Bayens	Maurice Grumiaux
Château Champs-de-Naya	Vve Mariaud
Clos l'Église	Monique Balineau

The remaining members listed below have their wine vinified under the generic labels of *Roc de Puisseguin* and *Puisseguin-St Émilion*.

Names

Axel Arnault
Gerard Barde
Pierre Bastaire
Jean Pierre Beaudu
Pierre Berthon
Gilbert Bonamy
Jeanine Bonamy
Michel Boudyo
Raymond Debrie
Robert Delbouscas
Desville
Marie Joseph Dornat
Jean Pierre Dufour
Roger Durou
Vve Emile
Mario Farot
Claude Galineau
Vve Galineau

André Goujou
Lallemand
Joseph Lamoureux
Micheline Laulla
Joseph Laulla
Étienne Laurent
Jacques et Jean Marie Lenier
Philippe Mounet
Roger Mounet
Adrienne Nouet
Lucien Peytour
Claude Pissorin
Jean Jacques Poitou
Pierre Raillard
Fernand Remy
Vve Rontin
Saint Gerard
Ste Sublett
Vve Touzeau

Château Pétrus. Pomerol.

Puisseguin-St Émilion Properties

Château les Agasseaux
Present owner   Gaston Beney
Member of the Co-operative which produces his wine.

Château le Basque
Now part of Château le Brandat

Château Bayens
Present owner   Maurice Grumiaux
A member of the Co-operative which produces his wine.

Clos Beauséjour
Present owner   Francis Bassic
5.11 hectares

Château Beauséjour
Present owner   Annick Dupuy
17.1 hectares
An attractive property surrounded by trees, opposite the Town Hall.

Château Belair
Present owner   Robert Adoue
11.25 hectare vineyard in one single block, situated in the centre of the clayey-limestone plateau of the commune of Puisseguin. Monsieur Adoue is currently the President of the Syndicate of Puisseguin-Saint-Émilion.

Château Bernat
Present owner   Bruno et Christian Laporte
5.77 hectares

Château le Bernat
Present owner   Germaine Frugier
4 hectares

Château le Brandat
Present owner   GFA du Brandat
1.00 hectares
Imposing old classic Château at the end of a driveway of trees.

Château des Bruges
Present owner   Claudine Bonamy (a member of the Co-operative which vinifies the wine)

Château le Cabanne
Present owner   Victor Marcadet
3.8 hectares

Château Cassat
Present owner   Joseph Paludetto
26.19 hectares

Paul Celerier
0.50 hectares
Only sells wine in bulk.

Château le Chay
Present owner   Raoul Berny
12.95 hectares

Château Champ des Moines
Present owner   Espérance Berny
4.34 hectares

Château Champs-de-Naya
Present owner   Vve Mariaud is a member of the Co-operative which vinifies her wine.

Château Chêne-Vieux
Present owner   SCE Foucard et Fils
9.82 hectares
This very imposing three-storey property is set back from the road, next to the football pitch.

Château Côtes du Fayan
Present owner   Guy Poitou
4.9 hectares

Château Côtes de Mouchet
Present owner   Francis Laulla
A member of the Co-operative which vinifies his wine.

Château Côtes de Saint Clair
Present owner   Jean-Paul Dupeyrat
A member of the Co-operative which produces his wine.

Château Croix de Justice
Present owner   Jean-Marie Estager
1.55 hectares

Château la Croix de Mouchet
Present owner   Primo Grando
4.01 hectares
Set back from the main road, this imposing property has fine views of the vineyards.

Château Durand Laplaigne
Present owner   Jacques Bessou
12.1 hectares

Château Durand Moureau
Present owner   Jean Sublett
29.30 hectares
This property is part of the estate of Château Roc de Boissac.

Château le Fayan
Present owner Philippe Mounet
3.48 hectares

Château Fongaban
Present owner Ste Civile Fongaban
6.53 hectares

Château Gontet-Robin
Present owner Jean-Loup Robin
11.74 hectares
The same family own Château Sansonnet, Grand Cru Classé, and Château Doumayne, Clos Vieux Taillefer, Domaine de Salle and Château Busquet.

Château Grand-Rigaud
Present owner Guy Desplat
2.28 hectares

Michel Guenant
0.23 hectares
Only sells wine in bulk.

Château Guillotin
Present owner Jacques Moritz
2.19 hectares

Château Guillotin
Present owner Olindo Pasquon
0.70 hectares

Château Hermitage la Carenne
Present owner Ghislain Dupuy
7.29 hectares

Château Haut-Bernon
Present owner Jean-Marie Estager
The two vineyards of Château Haut-Bernon (9.81 hectares) and Château la Croix-de-Justice (4 hectares) both belong to Jean-Marie Estager.

Henri Lacoste
0.48 hectares
Only sells wine in bulk.

Château Langlais
Present owner Alain Dupuy
5.10 hectares

Cru Larimondi
Present owner Raymond Marvel Berthon
4.44 hectares

Château des Laurets
Present owner Famille Bourlon
This was originally two properties: Château Guibeau and Château la Fourvieille. They also produce wine under the labels of *Châteaux Guibeau, Guibot la Fourvieille, la Fourvieille* and *Guibeau-la Fourvieille.*

Château des Laurets
Present owner SCE des Laurets et de Malengin
Together with the feudal Château Malengin (Parsac), the Château des Laurets forms a large property with an area of 160 hectares. Vineyards occupy 26.89 hectares which stand in the large superb-looking, well-kept estate.

The estate is owned by SCE des Laurets et de Malengin, and run by M Bechau Lafonta.

Clos l'Église
Present owner Mme Monique Galineau
1.5 hectares
Small modern farmhouse lying on the outskirts of Puisseguin. A member of the Co-operative which produces and markets all the wine.

Château Léonard
Present owner Henri Saure
6.23 hectares
Small two-storey modern farmhouse.

Ley et Fils
0.06 hectares
Sells only bulk wine.

Jules Massoubre
0.82 hectares
Sells only bulk wines.

Château du Mayne
Present owner Pierre Raymond
8.23 hectares

Guy Millet
0.16 hectares
Sells only bulk wines.

Château de Mole
Present owner Michel Lenier
11.24 hectares

Château du Moulin
Present owner Guy et Jean-Claude Chanet
11.85 hectares Situated opposite the Co-operative. A modern property.

Château Moulin des Laurets
Present owner Lionel Mounet
9.83 hectares

Château Moulins Listrac
Present owner Jean-Charles Lalande
9.25 hectares

Château Moulin Noir
Present owner Jean Rolland
2.2 hectares

Château la Muchique
Present owners　André Godrie who owns 0.45 hectares, and Jean Godrie who owns 0.23 hectares.

Château Ormeau-Vieux
Present owners　Alain Cyren-Arvis and Didier de Coly
6.16 hectares

Château la Pavillon
Present owner　Francine Lamay
1.93 hectares

Château la Plagne
Present owner　Jean Pierre Duvergnon
5.34 hectares

Château Pocci le Menn
Present owner　G F A Vignobles Pocci le Menn
3.46 hectares
Only sells wine in bulk.

Albert Poivert
1.95 hectares
Only sells wine in bulk.

Giu Privat
0.37 hectares
Only sells wine in bulk.

Château de Puisseguin
Present owner　Jean Robin
Large estate with 19.03 hectares under vine.

Château Puynormond
Present owner　Madeleine Massoubre-Lamarque
0.36 hectares

Château Quint
This is part of the estate of Château Roc de Boissac consisting of 29.90 hectares owned by Jean Sublett.

Clos des Religieuses
Present owner　Jean Marie Leynier
3.61 hectares

Château Rigaud
Present owner　Josette Taix
5.93 hectares

Côtes de Rigaud
Present owner　Jean Guimberteau
2.34 hectares

Château la Rose
Present owner　André Boireau
6.50 hectares

Château de Roques
Present owner　Michel Sublett
This Château, owned by Michel Sublett, is situated in its own little hamlet. It is a large walled Château with its own moat and consists of 14.71 hectares.

Château Roc de Boissac
Present owner　Jean Sublett
29.30 hectares

Cru la Rose
Present owner　Gaston Marchesseau
0.98 hectares

Cru la Roseraie
Present owners　Henri Descombes and J Claude Brisson
8.66 hectares

Château du Roy
Present owner　G F A Bonnot, a member of the Co-operative, which produces the wine.

Château Saint Clair
Present owner　Michel Berny
3.84 hectares

Château Soleil
Present owner　Jean Soleil
11.57 hectares
New, modern family home.

Château Teillac
Present owner　Jean-Pierre Lejet
17.27 hectares

Château Teyssier
Present owners　SCE Domaines Château Teyssier
14.18 hectares

Château la Tour Guillotin
Present owner　Arthur Lorenzon
14.87 hectares (which lie set back from the road)
The house is an old rambling, turreted farmhouse with out-buildings.

Château Vaisinerie
Present owner　Michel Sinet
10.67 hectares

Château du Vieux Moulin
Present owner　J Sublett and children

Montagne-St Émilion

This satellite commune, about 4 kilometres north-east of Saint-Émilion, has approximately 1,200 hectares under vine, owned by two-hundred and fifty growers. It is on high ground, as its name suggests, and the village itself is set around an attractive eleventh-century church.

The soil to the east and in the centre is clay and limestone on the slopes, known locally as the uplands. In the south, west and north-west there is sand and clay on the plain known as the lowlands. The sub-soil is limestone and molasse with some gravel.

The Co-operative has sixty members and produces wine under the brand-name of *La Tour Mont d'Or*.

The President of the Syndicate Viticole of Montagne is Gérard Despagne; he recently succeeded M Yerles of Château des Tours who had held the office for the past twelve years and has been Mayor of Montagne since 1971.

The appellation Montagne-St Émilion, by the decree of December 5th, 1972, now includes wines made from vines grown on specified land in the communes of Parsac-St Émilion and St Georges-St Émilion.

The minimum permitted strength is $10.5°$ and the basic maximum yield 42 hectolitres per hectare.

Out-put of Montagne-St Émilion in hectolitres since 1950:

1950 – 38,908	1967 – 31,002
1951 – 20,877	1968 – 16,678
1952 – 24,679	1969 – 18,702
1953 – 41,984	1970 – 50,844
1954 – 28,033	1971 – 25,077
1955 – 38,034	1972 – 33,084
1956 – 8,099	1973 – 75,054
1957 – 9,161	1974 – 59,254
1958 – 19,262	1975 – 43,855
1959 – 16,709	1976 – 59,394
1960 – 29,982	1977 – 23,097
1961 – 12,326	1978 – 53,429
1962 – 44,750	1979 – 76,010
1963 – 22,372	1980 – 43,617
1964 – 45,255	1981 – 53,322
1965 – 27,268	1982 – 76,522
1966 – 30,152	

Montagne-St Émilion Properties

Jean Alphonso
2.14 hectares

Ginette Ancelin
0.20 hectares

Château Arriailh Beauséjour
Present owner Lucien Laporte
12.53 hectares
This property has been in the family since 1820. It is situated on the highest slopes in the commune.

Pierre Aurier
1.55 hectares

Francis Auge
0.08 hectares

Château Barreaud
Present owner   Robert Laydis
13.76 hectares

Château Baudron
Present owner   Nelson Guimberteau
7.37 hectares

Château Bayard
Present owner   Jeannine Latorre
8.36 hectares

Château Bayard
Present owner   Société Christian Bruno Laporte
24.84 hectares

Château Bayard
Present owner   Société Philippe Gouze et Fils
13.81 hectares

Château Bayard
Present owner   Angélo Nicoletti
6.45 hectares

Heritiers Baye Dupin
2.55 hectares

Château Beaudron
Present owner   Henry Demur
5.45 hectares

Lucien Beauvilain
2.43 hectares

Lucien Beauvilain
(Métayer de Alban Baroy) 1.49 hectares

Château Bèchereau
Present owner   Jean Michel Bertrand
5.41 hectares

Roland Bel
0.94 hectares

Château la Bergère
Present owner   Pierre Yerles (whose family also owns Château des Tours)
5.46 hectares

Château Berlière
Present owner   Société René Michel Guillon
4.77 hectares

Château Berlière
Present owner   Georges Demur
4.90 hectares

Château Berlière Chêne Vert
Present owner   Felix Demur
5.46 hectares

Armand Berlureau
1.36 hectares

Raoul Berny
0.25 hectares

Château Bertin
Present owner   Francis Arvouet
3.56 hectares

Château Bertin
Present owner   Société Guy Arpin
9.48 hectares

Château Bertin
Present owner   Société Arvouet Sandias
6.16 hectares

Château Bertineau
Present owner   Angélo Vedelago
9.17 hectares

Château Bertineau
Present owner   Société Larnaudie
6.60 hectares

Société Bertineau-Quancard
2.50 hectares

Jean Michel Bertrand
(Métayer de Indivision Leglise)
1.17 hectares
Also has 2.49 hectares (Métayer de Jean Leglise)

Château Biquette
Present owner   Yvette Bertin
9.35 hectares

Château Bonde
Present owner   Gilles Dignac
5.78 hectares

Château Bonneau
Present owner   Maurice Marchand
6.18 hectares

Château Bonneau
Present owner   Marc Gouze
6.41 hectares

Château Bonneau
Present owner   Alain Despagne
10.11 hectares

Château Bourg
Present owner   Edgard Gineste
6.25 hectares

Château le Bourg
Present owner   Robert Gaury
6.15 hectares

Château Calon
Present owner   Yves Gros
5.99 hectares

Château Calon
Present owner   Jean Michel Faure
6.34 hectares

Château Calon
Present owner   Jean Noël Boidron (who also owns Château Corbin-Michotte, Grand Cru Classé)

Well-situated on the high slopes with fine views of the region. It is a very attractive estate of 22.09 hectares: 70% Merlot, 15% Bouchet and 15% Cabernet Sauvignon.

Robert Cally
0.22 hectares

Château Cap d'Or
Present owner   Vignobles Rocher Cap de Rives
4.07 hectares

Jacky Carré
0.54 hectares

Robert Carré
1.62 hectares

Château Cazelon
Present owner   Jean Fourloubey
3.10 hectares

Claude Chagneau
Present owner
0.85 hectares

Philippe Chanloup
0.85 hectares

Henry Chanloup
1.22 hectares

Château Chéreau
Present owner   Aurélien Silvestrini
4.77 hectares

Château la Clotte
Present owner   Alain Reygondeau
3.65 hectares

Château Colas Nouet
Present owner   Jean Claude Fabris
8.35 hectares

Claude Constantin
0.76 hectares

Château Corbin
Present owner   François Rambeau (who occupies this large farmhouse property).
20.01 hectares

Denis Corre
4.90 hectares

Château Coucy
Present owner   G A E C Maureze
17.54 hectares

René Courty
6.49 hectares

Germaine Darnajou
0.30 hectares

Michel Deley
1.12 hectares

Jean Desuergne
0.38 hectares

Marc Dufour
0.20 hectares

Paul Dumain
0.77 hectares

Gylain Dupuy
0.39 hectares

Francette Duret
1.20 hectares

Château Église de Parsac
Present owner   Philipe Bel
4.95 hectares

Ernest Escarpe
1.11 hectares

Antoine Fabris
1.04 hectares

Louis Fabris
1.51 hectares

Château Faizeau
Present owner   Geneviève Raynaud
8.73 hectares

Château Farguet
Present owner   Annie Andouard
4.24 hectares
Wines distributed exclusively by Dulong Frères. 60% Merlot, 25% Bouchet, 15% Cabernet Sauvignon. Average yield 25,000 bottles.

Mario Favot
2.25 hectares

Joseph Fayemendy
0.61 hectares

David Fernandel
3.21 hectares

Château Fontmurée
Present owner   Simonnet Père et fils
10.24 hectares

Château Fontmurée
Present owner   Jacques Fourgeaud
5.75 hectares

Société Georges Fortin
0.64 hectares

Louis Gaurel
1.89 hectares

Société Georgette Gaston Jean Page
0.39 hectares

Francisco Gil
0.40 hectares

Château Gillet
Present owner   Gilbert Cally
9.19 hectares

Château Gillet
Present owner   Jacques Darribehaude
4.12 hectares

Château Gillet Bayard
Present owner   Michel Darnajou
9.63 hectares

Marc Gimanaze
3.88 hectares

Château la Giraude
Present owner   Lucien Beauvilain (Métayer de René Rolland)
4.06 hectares

Château Goujon
Present owner   Henry Garde
6.71 hectares

Château Goujon
Present owner   Agricole Lycée
18.28 hectares

Gaston Goureaud
3.18 hectares

Jean Guillou
0.32 hectares

Bernard Guimberteau
0.66 hectares
This grower also owns another nearby vineyard of 2.28 hectares.

Michel Guimberteau
2.79 hectares

Château Guitard
Present owner   Guy Buzet
5.78 hectares

Château Haute Faucherie
Present owner   Yvette Audinet
9.15 hectares

Château Haute Faucherie
Present owner   Lucien Saint Gaudens
2.86 hectares

Château Haute Faucherie
Present owner   Pierre et André Durand
6.80 hectares

Château Haute Grave
Present owner   Société Civile Château Haute Grave
1.78 hectares

Yvonne Henry
0.90 hectares

Château les Jaye
Present owner   René Leonard Labert
7.20 hectares

Léopold Jourdan
0.53 hectares

Château le Jura
Present owner   Alain Berlureau
3.49 hectares

Château le Jura
Present owner   Violette Delol
6.84 hectares
This Château lies on the borders of Pomerol and Saint-Émilion, separated by the la Barbane stream.

Château Labatut
Present owner   Jean Pierre Lazzarini
3.93 hectares

Château Labatut
Present owner   Adrienne Danflous
3.84 hectares

André Lacoste
0.71 hectares

Jean Lacour
2.61 hectares

Château Lamaçonne
Present owner   Paul Maule
8.87 hectares

Château Lamaçonne
Present owner   Lucien Moze
4.79 hectares

Château Lamaçonne
Present owner   Claude Lateyron
12.99 hectares

Francine Lamy
2.89 hectares

Château Langlade
Present owner   François Bodet
6.60 hectares

Fernand Lasserre
1.30 hectares

Pierre Laudu
1.23 hectares

Château Lestage
Present owner   Micheline Lavaud
7.04 hectares

Robert Leyney
1.22 hectares

Château Maison Blanche
Present owner   Gérard Despagne
27.65 hectares
This very attractive Château is set behind white
fencing and surrounded by well-kept vineyards.
It is situated on land once occupied by the
Seigneury of Corbin.

Château Maisonneuve
Present owner   Marcel Guenant
5.21 hectares

Château Maison Neuve
Present owner   Michel Coudroy
15 hectares

Château Maisoneuve Parsac
Present owner   Ismaël Candidat
4.53 hectares

Château Marchand
Present owner   Micheline Duverneuil
6.59 hectares

Château Marchand
Present owner   Yves Claude Naud
6.01 hectares

Paul Marchand
1.23 hectares

Château la Marche St Denis de Piles
Present owner   Maurice Carrere
6.14 hectares

Société Marin Audra Claymore
2.05 hectares

Moïse Martin
0.33 hectares

Jules Massoubre
1.83 hectares

Jacques Mourneaud
0.50 hectares

Château Mirande
Present owner   Louise Lafougerie
1.74 hectares

Château Mirande
Present owner   GFA Fanon Floret
6.89 hectares

Château Mirande
Present owner   André Floret
6.27 hectares

Château Mirande
Present owner   Raymond Edgard Tapon
10.62 hectares

Château Léonard Mouchet
Present owner   Henry Saure
7.20 hectares

Château Montaiguillon
This property, covering 42 hectares of which
24.9 are under vine, has a very large, well-kept
farmhouse owned by M Amart, Société Viticole
Montagne-St-Émilion, who produces wine
under the labels of *Châteaux Montaiguillon* and
Vieux Montaiguillon, Appellation Montagne and *St
Georges-St-Émilion.*
   The vineyard is planted with 50% Merlot and
50% Cabernet Sauvignon, producing a high
yield which is fermented in cement *cuvées* and
matured in oak casks and inox *cuvées.*

Château Mouchet
Present owner   Primo Grando
11.74 hectares

Château Mouchet
Present owner   Guy Desplat
4.50 hectares

Château Moulin de Trançon
Present owner   Simonne Dupeyrat
1.49 hectares

Joseph Moze
2.18 hectares

Château Musset
Present owner   Michèle Gadenne
6.88 hectares

Château Musset
Present owner　Société Joseph Dominique Nicoletti
6.27 hectares

Château Musset
Present owner　Albert Poivert
Albert Poivert, who also owns another nearby vineyard covering 1.33 hectares, owns this Château of 3.06 hectares.

Fany Nicoletti
3.01 hectares

Château Négrit
Present owners　Indivision Lagardere
11.74 hectares

Robert Ouvrard
2.65 hectares

Pierre Pallard
3.93 hectares

Château la Papeterie
Present owner　Estager Indivision
5.24 hectares
This property borders onto Pomerol, Saint-Émilion, Néac and Montagne.

Château Paquillon
Present owner　Michel Rivière
6.14 hectares

Château Paradis
Present owner　Frères Malleret
6.18 hectares

André Paret
0.66 hectares

Château Parsac
Present owners　Société Binet et Bodet Latour
11.99 hectares

Vve Maria Petit
0.39 hectares

Château Petit Mangot
Present owner　GAEC Descomps
5.88 hectares

Château Petit Moulin
Present owner　Charles Grosdidier
3.26 hectares

Château Piron
Present owner　Rémy Fressinneau
6.13 hectares

Château Plaisance
Present owner　Larribière Despagne
19.60 hectares

This property has been in the Larribière family since 1935. It is a lovely old Château and borders on Saint-Émilion and Pomerol.

Château Plaisance
Present owner　Robert René Eresue
10.54 hectares

Château Plaisance
Present owner　Jean Paul Deson
4.82 hectares

Jean Marie Poivert
3.88 hectares

Gérard Poirier
0.15 hectares

Roger Privat
0.12 hectares

Château du Puy
Present owner　Marie-Thérèse Villesuzanne
7.60 hectares

Château Puynormon
Present owner　Paul Massoubre
3.73 hectares
There are also 6.31 hectares owned by Massoubre Lamarque.

Jean Pierre Quet
0.26 hectares

Société de Réal
0.85 hectares

Yves Reygondeau
Present owner
0.12 hectares

André Ribette
0.33 hectares

Jean Rivière
2.04 hectares

Able Rocher
1.38 hectares

André Rongieras
0.94 hectares

Château le Roquet
Present owner　Lucien Durand
7.54 hectares

Château Roudier
This magnificent Château is situated on the slopes of St Georges and Montagne. The property covers 42 hectares of which 26.79 are under vine, many of great age, belonging to Jacques Capdemourlin, the owner of Château Balestard-la-Tonnelle, and Château Cap de Mourlin, Grands Crus Classés.

The method of production undertaken by the *Maître de Chai*, Maurice Beaudu, is of the same high standard as at Château Balestard-la-Tonnelle and all the wine here is Château-bottled.

Production in hectolitres from 1975 to 1980:

1975 – 29	1979 – 65
1976 – 46	1980 – 24
1977 – 19	
1978 – 26	

Château Saint André Corbin

Present owner   Jean-Claude Berrouet (who is the wine-maker at Château Pétrus and all the other J-P Moueix properties in Saint-Émilion and Pomerol).
4.99 hectares

Château Teyssier

Present owners   GFA Durand Teyssier
19.48 hectares

Château des Tours

This magnificent Château dating from the fourteenth century was restored by Viollet-le-Duc and is set in 95 hectares of land, 67.16 of which are under vine, leaving approximately 28 hectares of beautiful parkland.

The present owner, GFA Louis Yerles, bought the property in October 1957. Having lived in Algeria, the proprietor moved to des Tours in 1964 and spent over three-million francs restoring the Château and installing ultra-modern vinification equipment.

The grape varieties planted are 60% Merlot, the balance being Bouchet and Cabernet Sauvignon. When picked, the grapes are crushed within half-an-hour after being completely de-stalked. The *must* is fermented in cement *cuvées* for up to three weeks. The wine is then transferred to other cement *cuvées* for maturation before bottling. The equipment used is the most up-to-date and can be operated by three people. Fermentation can be stopped or started and is temperature-controlled at the press of a button. The second wine of des Tours is sold under the name of *Château Chapelle-des-Tours*. The wine is exported to Belgium and The Netherlands.

Château la Tour-Musset

Present owner   H. Guiter (who also owns Château Tour St Christophe in St Christophe-des-Bardes where all the wine is produced)
Wine is also produced under the name of *Château Tour Cazelon*.

Château Vieille des Landes

Present owner   Henry Chadouteau
4.76 hectares

Gérard Vialle

1.60 hectares

Marcel Villegente

2.05 hectares

Ginette Zely

0.13 hectares

Montagne-St Émilion.

St Georges-St Émilion

This small satellite commune 3 kilometres north of Saint-Émilion, bordered on the north, west and east by Montagne, covers approximately 300 hectares of vineyards centred around a small village and farmhouses with an imposing twelfth-century church and the magnificent eighteenth-century Château St Georges. Château St Georges was built by Victor Louis, who designed the famous theatre in Bordeaux.

The soil is generally fertile, having clay and limestone with a stony sub-soil on the slopes and reddish sandy clay with a clay–iron sub-soil on the plateau and valley.

The appellation St Georges-St Émilion is granted to those properties within the delimited area of St Georges but according to the decree of December 5th, 1972, they may also use the Montagne-St Émilion appellation if they choose, as well as the Co-operative. Out of the thirty growers, sixteen decided to retain the St Georges appellation. Their properties cover 151.3 hectares producing, on average, 8,000 to 8,500 hectolitres per annum. The remainder use the Montagne appellation as a proportion of their property is in Montagne. As a result of this, they have to renew their application each year. A number of the proprietors have purchased jointly a mechanical harvester.

Monsieur Menguy has been the President of the Syndicate of St Georges growers since 1971. The minimum strength of the wine is 10.5° and the maximum yield is 42 hectolitres per hectare.

The out-put in hectolitres from 1950 is:

1950 –	7,668	1967 –	8,282
1951 –	5,748	1968 –	3,716
1952 –	5,909	1969 –	4,784
1953 –	8,614	1970 –	10,928
1954 –	4,358	1971 –	4,446
1955 –	8,330	1972 –	7,484
1956 –	1,674	1973 –	10,252
1957 –	2,156	1974 –	7,378
1958 –	3,990	1975 –	5,647
1959 –	4,176	1976 –	7,878
1960 –	6,281	1977 –	4,001
1961 –	2,601	1978 –	6,659
1962 –	11,079	1979 –	9,509
1963 –	4,772	1980 –	5,724
1964 –	9,171	1981 –	5,568
1965 –	5,807	1982 –	9,054
1966 –	7,533		

St Georges-St Émilion Properties

Château Belair-Montaiguillon
Present owner Pocci-Lemenn
10 hectares
This property faces the northern slopes of Saint-Émilion and was protected from the bad frosts of 1956.

Château Bellone
Present owner François Corre (who also owns Château Macquin-St Georges et Domaine de Maisonneuve)
   Château Bellone is 16 hectares producing up to 800 hectolitres.

Château Bellevue St Georges
Present owner M Gaury
5.5 hectares producing up to 260 hectolitres

Château au Bourg
The owner, M P Barroy died and the property now no longer exists.

Château Calon St Georges
Present owner Jean Noel Boidron (who also owns Château Corbin-Michotte) administers Château Corbin-Michotte) Grand Cru Clâsse (80% Merlot, 10% Bouchet, 10% Cabernet Sauvignon).
5.5 hectares producing up to 260 hectolitres

Château Cap d'Or
Present owner M Geens
14 hectares producing up to 800 hectolitres

Château la Croix-St Georges
Present owner Jean de Conninck
6.5 hectares producing up to 290 hectolitres
This property is separated from the commune of Saint-Émilion by the stream, La Barbanne.

Château Divon
Present owner Jean-René Andrieu
4 hectares producing up to 210 hectolitres

Château Guillou
This was a brand-name of Château Bellone, which is no longer used.

Château Haut-Guillou
This was the brand-name for wines of Château Bellone, which is no longer used.

Château Haut St Georges
Present owner Baye-Dupin
2.80 hectares producing up to 160 hectolitres

Château Haut Troquart
Present owner M Tourriol
2.5 hectares producing up to 140 hectolitres

Château Macquin-St Georges et Domaine de Maisonneuve
Present owner François Corre (who also owns Château Bellone)
This joint property was formed by Albert Macquin at the end of the last century. The first 25 hectares came from the break-up of Château-St Georges. These then were joined with an old bordering vineyard known as 'Maisonneuve', both in the commune of St Georges. Monsieur Macquin was one of the leading exponents and experts in American stock-grafting after *phylloxera*.

Château le-Pas-St Georges
Present owner E Prot
12 hectares producing up to 625 hectolitres

Château Pavillon St Georges
Present owner M A de Conninck
0.5 hectares producing up to 30 hectolitres

Château Roc de Troquart
Present owner M Visage
2.4 hectares producing up to 130 hectolitres

Château St André-Corbin
Present owner Robert Carré
17 hectares producing up to 950 hectolitres
   It is said that poet Ausonius, from whom Château Ausone takes its name, also had a villa on the site of this property. Certainly excavations in 1843 revealed Gallo-Roman remains of great value.

Château St Georges
The Château itself, sited on the top of a hill overlooking the plateau of Saint-Émilion, is a most beautiful and imposing building. It is some two miles north of the town of Saint-Émilion and was built in 1774 by the architect Victor Louis who built the famous theatre in Bordeaux; perhaps one should say that the former feudal castle was rebuilt, retaining the original four corner towers.
   Excavations in 1843 proved that this was the site of a spectacularly luxurious villa of the Gallo-Roman period and among other discoveries were the remains of a swimming pool, baths, marble mosaics and some very beautiful statues.
   We know that Château St Georges and its estate were sold to Jean Barbot by King Henri IV on October 27th, 1602, for one thousand five-hundred pounds 'principal' and seventy-five

pounds for the 'droit de vinage', or viticultural rights. The purchaser also acquired the title of Baron. Soon the estate passed into the hands of the Rabar family when a Barbot daughter married the Marquis of Rabar. Subsequent Rabar owners were César (b. 1668), Pierre (d. 1739), and another César. In 1770 the estate passed to Guillaume Ignace de Bouchereau when he married a Rabar daughter. He was the last Baron of St Georges and it was he who commissioned Victor Louis to rebuild the Château. In 1818 he sold the property to a financier, Louis Boitard, who had done well out of the Revolution. In the latter part of the nineteenth century the property declined under the ravages of *oidium, phylloxera* and mildew and changed hands several times until in 1891 it was purchased by Pétrus Dubois who reconstituted the vineyard by grafting French vines on to American root-stock. His son, also Pétrus Dubois, is the present owner and cultivates 50 hectares with a planting of 60% Merlot, 20% Cabernet Sauvignon and 20% Bouchet.

The *must* is fermented in sixteen new stainless-steel vats. After pressing the wine is matured in oak casks of which there are some 3,000 in the cellars. It has two rackings and one fining before being lightly filtered and then bottled.

The lovely old cellars contain bottles dating back to 1926 and during the Second World War the wine was put into tins and sent to prisoners of war.

The wine is of a consistently high standard and probably the best of the group of communes entitled to hyphenate their names with Saint-Émilion.

Château Samion
This is another brand-name for *Château Cap d'Or*.

Château Troquard
Present owner   M Marcès
4.60 hectares producing up to 260 hectolitres

Cru Troquard
Since the death of M Canteloube, wine is no longer produced here.

Château Vieux-Guillou
Present owner   Paul Menguy
8 hectares producing up to 450 hectolitres

Sables-St Émilion

This area which borders the town of Libourne used to have its own appellation until a law, passed on December 24th, 1973, and confirmed by official permission of the Ministry of Agriculture in 1975, entitled it to the appellation Saint-Émilion. Henri Matignion, former vice-president of Sables-St Émilion and now a member of the Council of Saint-Émilion told us that they had been working for some years to be included in either the Pomerol or Saint-Émilion appellation. An attempt to be absorbed into Pomerol, which seemed the more logical alternative as the wines are more similar in style and character to Pomerols, and the area is more closely contiguous with Pomerol, was unsuccessful some years earlier. Monsieur Matignion said that despite the appellation, *négociants* treat their wines as if they were buying Pomerol. When the change was made several properties wished to remain autonomous, as the sixteen St Georges properties had when St Georges was officially absorbed into Montagne, but this was not allowed; and there is no longer an appellation Sables-St Émilion. The last vintage to be called by that name was 1973. The minimum permitted strength of Sables-St Émilion was 10.5° and the part of the agreement entitling the area to the Saint-Émilion appellation was that none of the properties were eligible to apply by tasting for Grand Cru status. This seems to have been relaxed as in recent years Châteaux Quinault, Gueyrosse, Mayne-Figeac and Vieux-Château-Carré, for example, have applied and been accepted.

The former Sables vine-growing area is gradually being reduced in size as the town of Libourne expands southward. The main Châteaux survive but a number of the smaller owners have left or been taken over.

This group of properties produced 6,000 hectolitres in 1979, 4,900 in 1980 and 5,000 in 1981. About 60% of the wine is sold in bulk and 40% in bottle.

The best-known properties are Châteaux Martinet, Quinault, Gueyrosse, Vieux-Château-Carré and Mayne-Figeac. Here, too, is the beautiful house and private estate of M J-P Moueix, part-owner of Château Pétrus and owner/administrator of a number of other leading properties in Saint-Émilion and Pomerol.

As its name suggests, the soil is mainly sandy, layers of sallecaceous soil of various thicknesses lying on a gravel sub-soil. The wines are rather similar in style to the lesser Pomerols and the wines of Lalande.

Out-put in hectolitres since 1950:

1950 – 5,683	1962 – 7,003
1951 – 3,330	1963 – 2,646
1952 – 4,140	1964 – 7,024
1953 – 5,994	1965 – 4,413
1954 – 4,543	1966 – 5,626
1955 – 7,121	1967 – 6,602
1956 – 10	1968 – 2,655
1957 – 1,101	1969 – 3,977
1958 – 2,798	1970 – 8,039
1959 – 3,559	1971 – 4,844
1960 – 4,428	1972 – 5,379
1961 – 2,583	1973 – 7,508

Parsac-St Émilion

This small region surrounds a very old tiny village dominated by an eleventh-century church perched high on a hill. It is about 5 kilometres north-east of Saint-Émilion.

The area used to have its own Appellation Contrôlée, but under a decree dated December 5th, 1972, the growers now use the appellation of Montagne-St Émilion as well as its Co-operative. The last vintage declared under the Parsac-St Émilion appellation was 1974, and there is no longer any such appellation.

The wine had to have a minimum strength of 11° and a maximum yield of 42 hectolitres per hectare. The soil, like that of Puisseguin, is clay and limestone on a stony and molasse sub-soil. The wines resemble the lesser wines of the Côtes Saint-Émilion.

The most important property in the region is Château de Musset, a very attractive Château set high on a hill.

Out-put in hectolitres since 1950:

1950 – 6,820	1963 – 3,017
1951 – 4,273	1964 – 7,615
1952 – 3,232	1965 – 4,533
1953 – 6,686	1966 – 6,641
1954 – 4,063	1967 – 4,871
1955 – 6,213	1968 – 2,976
1956 – 696	1969 – 3,511
1957 – 1,012	1970 – 9,339
1958 – 2,562	1971 – 5,040
1959 – 2,006	1972 – 6,792
1960 – 4,121	1973 – 371
1961 – 2,279	1974 – 195
1962 – 7,339	

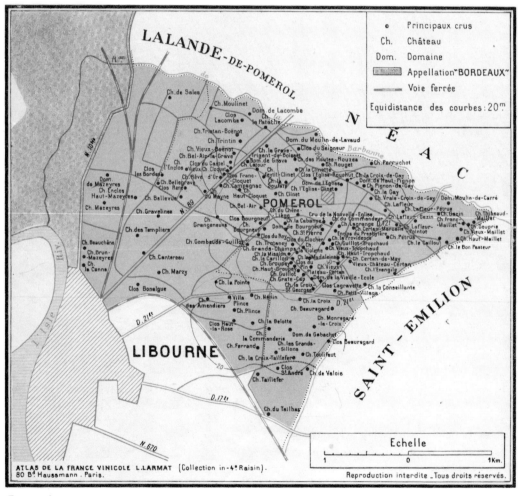

Pomerol.

POMEROL

General

This is the smallest of the fine-wine areas of the Gironde and consists of a plateau about 130 feet at its highest part in the area of Château Pétrus and Vieux-Château-Certan and gently sloping in a series of tiny undulations down towards the outskirts of Libourne. It is very intensively planted with vines (some 785 hectares – 725 in production) and lies immediately north-east of the old town of Libourne and starting from its very outskirts.

It is only 4 kilometres long and 3 wide, and virtually the whole area is suitable for vine-growing (that is, excluding the low-lying marshy area) and is planted with vines.

It is essentially an area of small properties and there are few of the grand houses so characteristic of the Médoc. There is no town; merely a number of villages, or rather hamlets, of which Catusseau, on the D.21 between Châteaux Nenin and Petit Village, is the largest. The others include Pomerol itself, with its church surrounded by vines, the two Moulinets, Grand and Petit, Pignon and la Patache.

This comparatively tiny plot of fine wine-growing country is divided up between one hundred and seventy-two growers who have to declare their harvest, according to the Ministry of Agriculture regulations, in order to qualify for the Appellation Contrôlée Pomerol. They do not, however, have at this stage to specify any 'marques deposées', or second wines that they may sell under another label. These have to be separately registered according to the regulations of the Ministry for Trade and Agriculture. The official tasting which the wines have to undergo to qualify for the Appellation is arranged by the Syndicat Viticole de Pomerol and controlled by the INAO.

Of these one hundred and seventy-two 'declarers', one hundred and sixteen of whom are members of the Syndicat, only two have properties of more than 25 hectares, Châteaux de Sales (much the largest with 45) and Nenin. The rest are as follows:

    Owners of 20 to 25 hectares – 3
    Owners of 16 to 20 hectares – 1
    Owners of 10 to 15 hectares – 14
    Owners of 6 to 10 hectares – 23
    Owners of 3 to 6 hectares – 33
    Owners of 1 to 3 hectares – 45
    Owners of less than 1 hectare – 51

Thus well over half the owners have properties of less than 3 hectares and almost a third have less than one.

Since the limits of the area are officially established by the ruling of the civil court of Bordeaux in 1928, the area under vine has gradually increased. In 1936 it was 350 hectares; by the mid-1940's it had increased to 625 hectares. By the early 1970's it was 700 and has now risen to 785 hectares.

The annual production has increased accordingly. The average for the period 1942 to 1956 was 20,000 hectolitres; for the period 1957 to 1969 it was 25,000 hectolitres. It is now

THE WINES OF SAINT-ÉMILION AND POMEROL

29,000 hectolitres where it will probably stay for, as we have seen, almost every available hectare is now planted with vines.

The harvest figures from 1950 to 1980 in hectolitres have been as follows:

1950 – 28,017	1967 – 30,033
1951 – 18,682	1968 – 13,291
1952 – 20,713	1969 – 18,606
1953 – 32,949	1970 – 39,284
1954 – 20,326	1971 – 21,333
1955 – 32,089	1972 – 22,060
1956 – 112	1973 – 41,720
1957 – 6,999	1974 – 37,856
1958 – 16,316	1975 – 21,110
1959 – 16,169	1976 – 33,445
1960 – 22,553	1977 – 13,543
1961 – 13,086	1978 – 27,216
1962 – 29,808	1979 – 36,188
1963 – 28,808	1980 – 23,283
1964 – 37,536	1981 – 23,720
1965 – 24,547	1982 – 38,626
1966 – 27,499	

In 1956, after the great frost had devastated the vineyards in February, a mere 112 hectolitres of wine were produced and much replanting had to be done.

About half the annual production goes to the home-market and the main importers of Pomerol are Belgium, The Netherlands, The United States of America, Scandinavia and Great Britain.

Between 1978 and 1979 the official marketing figures were as follows: total 28,264 hectolitres (8,696 sold from the property and 19,568 through trade-channels). Of these 13,820 went to the home-market and 14,444 to foreign-markets as follows:

Belgium	6,207 hectolitres
The United States of America	2,526 hectolitres
Denmark	1,275 hectolitres
The Netherlands	1,219 hectolitres
Great Britain	1,006 hectolitres
Germany	855 hectolitres
Switzerland	781 hectolitres
Other countries	571 hectolitres

Between 1980 and 1981 27,608 hectolitres of Pomerol were sold (17,925 through the trade and 9,673 direct by the growers). The home-market took 16,880 hectolitres and 10,728 were exported (808 went to Great Britain). At the end of August, 1981, the stocks held by growers (two harvests) amounted to 59,159 hectolitres; stocks held by merchants in the Gironde were 19,961 hectolitres.

This relatively tiny out-put, and the fact that there is no possibility of appreciably increasing it, accounts in part for the rather high prices of Pomerol wines which tend to be more expensive than those of the Médoc, Graves and Saint-Émilion. Another consideration is the fact that their main market consists of three wealthy countries: France itself, Belgium and The United States of America. Château Pétrus nowadays often commands higher prices than the Médoc first growths and Vieux-Château-Certan and la Conseillante are usually on a par with the Médoc second growths and Figeac just across the border in Saint-Émilion. Over 80% of Pomerol wine is bottled by the grower.

There is no official classification of Pomerol wines but Château Pétrus is universally acknowledged as the best, and certainly commands the highest prices. It was the first Pomerol wine to achieve international honours when it won a gold medal at the 1878 Paris Exhibition.

The 1853 edition of Franck's *Traité sur les Vignes du Médoc* mentions Pomerol briefly and names only one property, Château de Curtan. As we have seen, the early editions of Cocks et Feret include Pomerol under the general heading of Saint-Émilion wines and the 1868 edition lists seventeen leading properties which it calls '*Crus bourgeois et premiers artisans*'. It is headed by Vieux-Château-Certan and includes Châteaux Trotanoy, Pétrus and la Conseillante. These are followed by fourteen '*deuxième crus, artisans et paysans*' and we are told that there are also about twenty small owners producing 2 to 6 tonneaux, selling second or third growths. In the 1893 edition thirty-one first growths are listed and twenty-five second growths.

The following ten properties would probably be included in most contemporary authorities' selection of outstanding growths:
(in alphabetical order)

  Château la Conseillante
  Château l'Évangile
  Château la Fleur
  Château la Fleur Pétrus
  Château Gazin
  Château Nenin
  Château Petit Village
  Château la Pointe
  Château Trotanoy
  Vieux-Château-Certan
   Other properties with claims for inclusion in the 'first division' would be:
Château Beauregard
Château Bourgneuf
Château Certan-de-May
Château Certan-Giraud
Château Certan Marzelle
Clos l'Église
Château l'Enclos
Château la Croix
Château la Croix-de-Gay
Château Lagrange
Château la Tour Pomerol
Château le Gay
Château Mazeyres
Château Moulinet
Château Clos-René
Château Rouget

The Confrérie des Hospitaliers de Pomerol

Like most of the great French wine districts, Pomerol has its own Confrérie or wine brotherhood. The Hospitaliers de Pomerol take their name from a famous hospital or hostel built in the area, reputedly on the site of the present Château Beauregard, by the Knights Hospitalers of St John of Jerusalem in the twelfth century. It was built on the route of one of the most celebrated pilgrimages, to St James at Santiago de Compostella, to shelter the pilgrims on their way. They also built a Romanesque Church which was destroyed at the end of the nineteenth century.

The old boundary stones that used to mark the limits of the domaine of the Commanderie des Hospitaliers can still be seen. They have a Maltese cross carved on them and the present day Confrérie has this same emblem (with a scallop-shell at the centre) embroidered on its robes to commemorate their predecessors of the Middle ages. There are thirty male grower members.

The aim of the Hospitaliers is to promote and to protect the reputation of the wine and vineyards of Pomerol. On the first Sunday in June every year they hold a special spring ceremony to celebrate the flowering of the vines and to glorify the hopes of the harvest. The ceremony ends with a tasting of the wines.

'La vinée' is the name of a special blend of the wines of various properties which is given to guests of the Hospitaliers on this occasion.

Decree of December 8th, 1936

Article 1 – The right to use the Appellation Contrôlée Pomerol is held only by those wines which, in accordance with the conditions stated hereunder, have been harvested on land in the commune of Pomerol, and on that part of the commune of Libourne (Gironde) established by the ruling of the civil court of Bordeaux on December 29th, 1928, bounded on the north by the river Barbanne, on the east by the borders of the commune of Pomerol, on the south by the stream Taillas, on the west by the trunk road N.10 bis and the railway-line from Libourne to Bergerac, a total of 350 hectares 29 ares. (This ruling, by taking the railway-line as the south-west border, actually annexed a small parcel of Sables-St Émilion to Pomerol.) Within the production area thus defined, those parcels of land located in the naturally wet and marshy levels shall be excluded from the right to use the 'Appellation Contrôlée Pomerol'.

The boundaries of this production area shall be entered on the surveyors' plans of the communes in question, by experts appointed by the Managing Committee of the National Committee of appellations of origin and the plan thus prepared shall be registered with the Town Hall of the commune of Pomerol, before July 1st, 1937.

Article 2 – Only those wines shall have the right to the 'Appellation Contrôlée Pomerol' if made from vines of the following stock, to the exclusion of all others: Cabernet, Bouchet, Malbec or Pressac, Merlot.

From the harvest of 1961 onwards, any producer of 'Appellation Contrôlée' wine defined by this decree who owns plots of land containing hybrids within his property located in the area described, may not claim the right to use this appellation.

View of the vineyards of Saint-Émilion.

The Confrérie des Hospitaliers de Pomerol.

Article 3 – Those wines having the right to use the 'Appellation Contrôlée Pomerol' shall only be made from *must* containing 178 grammes of natural sugar per litre before any additions, and with a minimum alcoholic content of 10.5° after fermentation.

Article 4 – (modified February 8th, 1948) – Base-yield is fixed at 40 hectolitres per hectare of vines in production. (These provisions were completed by decrees Nos. 74.872 of October 19th, 74.958 modified of November 20th, and 75.842 of September 8th)
– classification ceiling: 20%
– increase percentage established in Article 6 of the above main decree No. 74.872: 60% of annual yield for 'appellation "Bordeaux" '.
The young vines may only be counted in the surface-area planted, from and including the fourth year's leafing.
(Completed December 8th, 1954.) In addition, those producers of 'Appellation Contrôlée Pomerol' wines who own or operate vineyards producing wine under any other 'Appellation Contrôlée' may not show a per hectare yield in their vintage declaration which is greater for 'Appellation Contrôlée Pomerol' wines than that of other appellation wines, excepting with official dispensation granted after enquiry by the National Institute of Appellation of Origin.

Article 5 – With a period of one year, proposals aimed at regulating the pruning of vines producing 'Appellation Contrôlée Pomerol' wines shall be submitted to the National Committee of Appellation of Origin by the Syndicat Viticole et Agricole de Pomerol (A. February 15th, 1947).

Article 6 – Vinification shall be in accordance with local practice. All oenological practices allowed under current law and regulations are allowed for 'Appellation Contrôlée Pomerol' wines.

Article 7 – Those wines, which, under the terms of this decree have the right to use the 'Appellation Contrôlée Pomerol' may not be declared after the harvest, offered to the public, despatched, put on sale or sold unless in the harvest declaration, in advertisements, on brochures, labels or any form of container, the above-mentioned appellation of origin is accompanied by the words 'Appellation Contrôlée' in very clear form.

Article 8 – The use of any indication or any sign which may lead the purchaser to believe that a wine has the right to use the 'Appellation Contrôlée Pomerol' when it does not conform with all conditions required in this decree shall be prosecuted under the general laws relating to fraud and to the protection of appellation of origin. (L. August 1st 1905, articles 1 and 2; May 6th 1919, article 8; d. August 1st 1905, articles 1 and 2; L. May 6th 1919, article 8; D. August 1921, article 13), without prejudice to any kind of fiscal sanctions which may be applicable.

Pomerol Properties

M Aubert
0.60 hectares
Sells bulk wine only.

Marcel Barbier
Has two properties:
1   0.86 hectares
2   0.57 hectares
Sells bulk wine only.

Charles Bardeon
0.28 hectares
Sells bulk wine only.

Château la Bassonnerie
Present owner   Gerard Faisandier
3.08 hectares
A second wine is produced under the name of
Domaine de René.

Château Beauchêne
This is another brand-name of the wine produced from Clos Mazeyres.

Château Beaulieu
Present owner   André Boireau
0.98 hectares

Château Beauregard
This estate, which is just south of Petit Village
and quite close to the border of Saint-Émilion,
takes its name from its seventeenth-century
owner, Bernard de Beauregard, who also built
the Château. In the eighteenth century the
property passed to Jèrôme de Chaussade de
Chandos and it remained in the hands of his
family until the end of the nineteenth century.
At the beginning of the eighteenth-century, fire
destroyed much of the upper part of the
building and it was rebuilt in 1745 in the style of
the day. A replica of the Château called Mille-
Fleurs can be seen on Long Island, New York,
built by the American architect Mr Coffin in
1932 who visited Pomerol just after the First
World War. Recent owners have been Durand
Desgranges until 1920, Ms Chavaroche and Le
Coq until 1922, and from then until the present
day, by the Clauzel family. Madame Clauzel's
family have been established in Pomerol since
the seventeenth century and were the proprietors of Château Trotanoy from 1610 to
1935. Paul Clauzel, co-proprietor with his
sisters, is currently (1980) President of the

Hospitaliers de Pomerol. He also owns Château
Graves Guillot which is bottled at Château
Beauregard. Monsieur Zucchi of Vieux-
Château-Certan and Châteaux l'Évangile and
Montlabert is *Maître de Chai*.

The soil is gravel, sandy-gravel with a little
clay and some iron-content in the sub-soil. The
extent of the vineyard is 13.06 hectares (48%
Merlot, 44% Bouchet, 5% Cabernet Sauvignon, 3% Pressac) which produce from 46 to 65
tonneaux at around 31 hectolitres per hectare.
The oldest vines are seventy years and the
average age is thirty-six years.

The grapes are completely de-stalked and
crushed with fermentation, in cement vats,
lasting about eight days. The skins remain in
contact with the *must* for three weeks, before
being pressed in a horizontal Lorsa press. After
the malolactic fermentation the wine is run off
into oak casks, one third of which are new each
year. The *assemblage* takes places any time
between the end of the malolactic fermentation
and the March following the vintage and
thereafter the wine is matured for twenty-four
to twenty-eight months with the usual rackings
and finings before bottling. A second wine is
made and sold under the name *Domaine des
Douves*.

Clos Beauregard
Present owner   Heritiers Marcel Moueix
This vineyard was originally part of Château
Beauregard. It has 4.38 hectares planted with
73% Merlot, the balance being Bouchet. The
wine is vinified at Château Taillefer, which is
owned by the Heritiers Marcel Moueix along
with the Châteaux Fonplégade, la Tour-de-Pin-
Figeac, and Moulinet. The methods of vinification are the same as those of the other A
Moueix properties.

Château Beauséjour
Present owner   Ste Combezoux Cosset
1.92 hectares

Château Beauséjour Tour Maillet
Present owner   Yves Lagardère
2.21 hectares

Château Beausoleil
Present owner   Mme Rambard
3.51 hectares
Small, old-fashioned farmhouse.

Château Bel-Air
Present owner Mme Sudrat & Fils
12.67 hectares
Large property set on the crossroads to Pomerol in sight of the Pomerol church. Classic French-farmhouse.

Château Belle-Brise
Present owner Michel Lafage
1.43 hectares

Château Bellegrave
Present owner Jean Bouldy & Fils
5.79 hectares

Château Bellevue-Montviel
This property, just south of Clos René, belongs to Robert Brieux and has been in his family for several generations.

The soil is mainly gravel with some iron-content in the sub-soil. There are 8 hectares of vines (60% Merlot, 25% Bouchet and 15% Cabernet Sauvignon) producing some 35 tonneaux at 38 to 40 hectolitres per hectare. The oldest vines are fifty years and the average age is thirty years.

The grapes are de-stalked, crushed and the fermentation (in cement tanks) takes five or six days, with the skins left in the *must* for eight to ten days. After the pressing the wine is matured for two-thirds of its time in cement vats and one-third in casks up to ten years old before being bottled after about twenty months. A second wine, *Domaine de Montviel*, is produced from the young vines.

Château la Bible
Present owner Bernard Cubillier
0.19 hectares

Clos Boého
Present owner Jean-Roger Musseau
0.56 hectares

Château Bois de Plince
Present owner M Veyssière
0.42 hectares

Château le Bon Pasteur
This property, like its near neighbour just across the border in Saint-Émilion, Château Rolland Maillet, was established at the beginning of this century by the grandparents of the present owner Mme Geneviève Rolland. It is near the eastern-most corner of the commune south of Gazin and next to Haut Maillet. Madame Rolland looks after the vineyard and the wine-making herself.

The soil is flinty-gravel on clay sub-soil. There are about 9 hectares of vines (75%

Merlot, 25% Bouchet) producing an average of 25 tonneaux. The oldest vines are seventy-five years and the average age is thirty-five years.

The grapes are sometimes completely de-stalked, sometimes only 80% depending on the year, and crushed. The juice is fermented in cement vats for eight to ten days, the skins remaining in the *must* for that time and sometimes appreciably longer before pressing. The wine spends two-thirds of its maturation time in vats and one-third in oak casks (some new, some used once), and is racked, fined and assembled in the usual way and bottled after two to two and a half years. Since 1978, all the wine has been bottled at the Château.

Château Bonalgue
Present owner Bourotte/Barbeyron
2.44 hectares

Château de Bourgueneuf
Present owner Edmond Meyer
It takes its name from the former 'holding' on which it is situated. It is an old vine-grower's house which has been enlarged and is still being altered. Part of the cellars are to be found at the Moulin de Lavaud, which is owned by the Domaine, on the edges of the stream la Barbanne, on the Pomerol side. There are 4.85 hectares of vineyard.

Château Bourgneuf-Vayron
Charles and Xavier Vayron are the proprietors of this estate which formerly belonged to Malle de Gombault, who sold it to the Vayron family in 1831. The story goes that on one occasion when the wines at Bourneuf-Vayron were being served, a Marshall of France proposed a toast to them saying 'They deserve the cross'. The proprietors tend the vineyard and make the wine themselves. A vintaging-machine has now been purchased and will be used for the first time on the 1982 vintage.

The soil is a mixture of gravel, gravel-clay and sand. There are 9.2 hectares of which 8.65 hectares are under vine (80% Merlot, 20% Bouchet) producing about 40 tonneaux. The oldest vines are fifty years and the average age is thirty years.

The grapes are de-stalked and crushed. Then fermentation, in cement tanks, lasts ten to fifteen days when the skins remain in contact with the *must* before pressing. After *assemblage*, usually in December, there are the usual rackings and fining but the wine is matured in glass-lined cement vats; no casks are used. It is bottled after about twenty months, three-quarters being sold to the wholesale trade and one-quarter direct to private customers.

Pierre Brisson
0.17 hectares
Sells in bulk only.

André Buget
0.31 hectares
Sells in bulk only.

Château la Cabanne
This newly-renovated estate is right in the geographical centre of the commune just to the east and north of Château Bourgneuf. Its name, which probably goes back to the fourteenth century, comes from 'Cabane' which is a hut in which serfs and small-holders lived in those days; Châteaux la Cabanne, Trotanoy and Clinet belonged at that time to the Bourgneuf estate. Previous owners include Claude Louis de Combaud, Leonard Bulle – barrister, Lieutenant-General of the Seneschal and Mayor of Libourne in 1750 – the Berthomieu de Meynot family and the Destrilles family. In 1966, Jean-Pierre Estager, the present proprietor, succeeded François Estager. Monsieur Estager is in charge of the wine-making and his cellar staff have been with the family for fifteen to twenty-five years.

The soil is gravel and clay with some iron in the sub-soil. There are 10 hectares of vines (60% Merlot, 30% Bouchet, 10% Pressac) producing some 45 to 50 tonneaux at about 40 to 42 hectolitres per hectare. The oldest vines are forty years and the average age is around twenty-five years.

The grapes are completely de-stalked and crushed and the juice is fermented in enamelled cement vats. The fermentation and contact of skins with the *must* are on the long side. There are three rackings before the *assemblage* which usually takes place in February. The wine is matured in oak casks, a third of which are renewed each year, and there are the usual further rackings and finings before it is bottled after about eighteen months in cask. The main markets outside France are Belgium, Switzerland and The United States of America. A second wine, *Domaine de Compostelle*, is produced in some years.

Château le Caillou
This small, family house is situated on the main road away from the vineyard. It had belonged to the Belivier family of Pomerol for more than a century. It owes its name to a description of the area in which it is sited, used in a survey.

The Domaine de la Combe and Clos Lacombe were annexed in 1905 giving a total of 6.75 hectares of vineyards, 75% Merlot, 25% Bouchet. Châteaux Soulate, Tropchaud and Clos Tropchaud were also purchased from the Belivier family but have now all been absorbed into Château le Caillou. The property is presently owned by the widow of Lucien Giraud and the house is lived in by his son, André.

Château Cantereau
Present owner   Marcel Bertrand
It has been in the family of this owner for more than a century. Re-constituted after 1920.

Château Carillon
Present owner   Grelot & Fils
2.92 hectares

Château du Castel
Present owner   Robert Cazemajou
2.35 hectares

Château Certan-de-May (also known as de-May-de-Certan)
4.68 hectares – 20 tonneaux

Château Certan-Giraud
Situated on the highest part of the famous plateau of Certan in Pomerol. A vineyard of 6.84 hectares borders those of the most famous growths. To the east lies Château Pétrus, to the south Vieux-Château-Certan, and to the west Château Certan-de-May.

In 1955 it became the property of the Giraud family who already owned Château Corbin in Saint-Émilion. They also produce wine under the labels of *Château Certan-Marzelle* and *Château Clos du Roy*.

Château Certan-Marzelle
This is a brand-name of *Château Certan-Giraud*.

Château du Chêne-Liège
Present owner   André Niarfex
1.93 hectares

Château Clinet
Present owner   Georges Audy
Situated 100 metres to the south-west of the church in Pomerol. 6.39 hectares under vine. A vintaging-machine has been purchased and was used for the first time on the 1982 vintage.

Château Clos Belair
Present owner   Jacques Lespine
2.36 hectares

Clos du Clocher

This property is on the Pomerol plateau 300 yards south of the famous church from whose steeple it takes its name. It was purchased in 1924 by Jean-Baptiste Audy, whose son, Jean Audy, is the present proprietor (strictly-speaking, the manager on behalf of the GFA des Ets J B Audy).

The soil is gravel-clay with an iron-bearing sub-soil. There are 6 hectares of vines (70% Merlot, 30% Bouchet) producing from 135 tonneaux (1980) to 316 (1976) at an average of 36 hectolitres per hectare. The oldest vines are twenty-four years and the average age is seventeen years.

After the grapes have been completely de-stalked and the juice is fermented for about eight days in glass- or plastic-lined cement vats, the skins remain in the *must* for up to three weeks before pressing. The wine is racked, fined and assembled in the usual way but spends a third of its maturation time in new oak casks, a third in one-year-old casks and a third in cement vats before being bottled after eighteen months to two years. All the wine is sold through Ets J B Audy, *négociants* in Libourne.

A second wine is produced under the name of *Château Monregard-Lacroix*.

Château Clos-du-Roy

This is a brand-name for Château Certan-Giraud.

Clos des Litanies

This tiny property, a little more than three-quarters of a hectare, is next to Château la Croix and belongs to Joseph Janoueix.

The proportion of planting is the same as at Château la Croix (60% Merlot, 20% Bouchet, 20% Cabernet Sauvignon) but it has the distinction of being an 'Appellation Pomerol Contrôlée' wine which is vinified in Saint-Émilion, for the wine is actually made, by special dispensation, in the cellars of another of M Janoueix's properties, Château Haut-Sarpe, Grand Cru Classé Saint-Émilion.

Château la Commanderie

This estate is about in the centre of the triangle of land south of the D.21. Its name is said to originate from the beginning of the thirteenth century when the Knights of St John of Jerusalem, a very powerful military and religious organisation, set up their Commanderie here. The Société de Château la Commanderie are the present owners and M Dé is the manager. It was purchased from M Leonaidon in 1957.

The soil is gravel and sand. There are 5.87 hectares of vines (65% Merlot, 35% Bouchet) producing some 20 tonneaux. The oldest vines are fifty years and the average age eighteen years. The grapes are completely de-stalked and crushed and the juice is fermented in stainless-steel vats with floating covers. After pressing and the malolactic fermentation, the wine is racked, assembled and fined in the usual way and matured in oak casks before being bottled after about two years. In some years, a second wine, *Le Priourat* is made.

Château du Commandeur

Present owner Raynaud-Ardurat (who also owns Château la Croix de Gay)

Château la Conseillante

This famous property, whose name originates from a Councillor of the Parliament of Bordeaux, lies at the eastern edge of Pomerol, on the boundary with Saint-Émilion and surrounded by Petit Village, Vieux-Château-Certan, l'Église and Cheval Blanc. Since 1871 it has been owned and run by the Nicolas family; the present proprietor, who has been in charge since 1970, is an insurance broker in Libourne. Before that it had long been the property of the Princeteau family, one of whose members was the well-known painter of that name and teacher of Toulouse-Lautrec. The house itself is a late-eighteenth-century, single-storey building of the type known as 'petit maison Girondine', and the doors of the *chai* are made from the old oak fermentation vats. Lucien Chaucherie has been *Maître de Chai* for twenty-eight years.

The soil of the vineyard is clay, gravel and sand with a sub-soil rich in iron. There are 13 hectares, 12 of which are under vine (45% Merlot, 45% Bouchet, 10% Pressac) which produce between 30 and 60 tonneaux at anything from 20 to 42 hectolitres per hectare according to the vintage. Monsieur Nicolas considers that the Pressac is essential to the character of his wine. The oldest vines are some one hundred-year-old Merlot and the average age is forty-five years. As at Figeac, minimum use is made of anti-pest treatments in the vineyards.

The grapes are completely de-stalked and crushed. Fermentation, in eight inox stainless-steel vats, is controlled when necessary by water poured down the sides cooling by evaporation, and lasts for six to eight days. The skins are left in contact with the *must* for at least three weeks before pressing. The stainless-steel tanks were introduced instead of the old wooden vats in

1971 to facilitate the very important control of temperature during the fermentation. As soon as the malolactic fermentation is over the wine is assembled and run off into oak casks (half of them new for each vintage) for maturing, racking and fining before *assemblage* when the wine is put into the large vats for three to seven days before being bottled after about two years. All the wine has been bottled at the Château since 1961.

Château la Croix-Taillefer
Present owner Mme Anglet-Rietsch
1.5 hectares

Château la Croix Toulifaut
This property which absorbed the former Château la Lamberte is 2 hectares in extent and is owned by M J F Janoueix. The proportions of the grape varieties and the vinification methods are the same as in the other Janoueix properties in Pomerol. Like Clos des Litanies, it is a Pomerol A C wine vinified in Saint-Émilion, for the wine is actually made at Château Vieux Sarpe, yet another Janoueix property.

Château la Croix des Templiers
Present owner Yves Lamarche
2.76 hectares

Château du Couvent
Present owner Edward Fillandean
2.29 hectares

Château Deltour
Present owner Marcel Thouraud
1.62 hectares

Domaine Dubourg
Run by Mme Gillet
0.66 hectares

M Duthil
Sells only in bulk.

Château Côte l'Église
This property was formerly owned by M Bellanger (1863–1914). The present owner is Jacques Forton. It is split up into twenty-one separate parcels of vines totalling 7 hectares on four different types of sub-soil. The wine is all vinified together.

The grape varieties are 65% Merlot, 25% Cabernet Sauvignon, 10% Bouchet. Some of the wine is sold under different brand-names: *Les Haute Rouges* (exclusively to Belgium), *La Fleur des Rouges* and *La Fleur Cloquet*. Monsieur Forton has experimented with a vintaging-machine but had trouble with oil from the machine getting into the juice of the grapes.

Châteaux la Croix, la Croix St Georges
These properties comprise a vineyard area of 14 hectares on either side of the D.21 near the junction with the D.121 and a little west of Petit-Village. The Société Civile J Janoueix owns them as well as Châteaux le Gabachot, Prieuré Pomerol and la Fleur Tropchaud in Pomerol, and Haut-Sarpe, Vieux Sarpe, de Sarpe, Haut Badette and Côte Maurejon-Badette in Saint-Émilion. Messieurs Horeau, Nadeau and Henin were the three previous owners of Château la Croix before it was purchased by the S C Janoueix in 1960. G Gastesoleil owned Château la Croix St Georges before selling it to the S C Janoueix in 1974. Max Chabrène has been *Chef de Culture* since 1971 and Paul Cazanove *Maître de Chai* since 1964.

The soil is gravelly-sand, gravel and clay with iron in the sub-soil. The make-up of the vineyards is 60% Merlot, 20% Bouchet, 20% Cabernet Sauvignon and the average annual production is 60 tonneaux at around 39 hecto-litres per hectare. The oldest vines are eighty years and the average age is thirty-five years.

The grapes are completely de-stalked and after light crushing in a *fouloir* are fermented for about eighteen days in wood and enamel-lined cement vats. The skins remain in contact with the *must* for three to four weeks before pressing. The wine is then run-off in oak casks up to four years old, and is racked, assembled in March, fined and matured before being bottled after two years. A second wine is made, *Le Gabachot*.

Château la Croix du-Casse
Present owner M Audy (on behalf of the Société Civile du Château la Croix du Casse)
8.43 hectares.

Château la Croix de Gay
Present owners Ardurat-Raynaud
11.43 hectares
The Château has been owned by this family for many generations. They also own Château le Commandeur.

Set right on the main road: large family house.

Clos l'Église
The Moreau family have owned this imposing thirteenth-century property for more than forty years. The present owner, M Moreau, is a surveyor by profession. The property lies just north of the church in Pomerol and takes its name from the old church built by the Knights' Templers in the thirteenth century which stood on the site of the present cemetery. Patrice Ducher has been *Maître de Chai* since 1940. The

Moreau family also own Château Plince.

The soil is gravel and clay with an iron-bearing sub-soil. There are 5.94 hectares of vines (60% Merlot, 20% Cabernet Sauvignon, 20% Bouchet) producing 20 to 25 tonneaux at around 30 hectolitres per hectare. The oldest vines are eighty years and the average age is thirty years. These old vines give a lot of extract to the wine.

The grapes are completely de-stalked and crushed and the juice is fermented for fifteen to twenty-one days in cement vats, the skins remaining in the *must* for that period before pressing. The wine is then run off into oak casks (three years old on average) and racked, assembled, fined and matured in the usual way, before being bottled after about two years. They have purchased a vintaging-machine and it was used for the first time on the 1982 vintage.

Clos l'Église
This small property, owned by Gerard Vialle since 1968, covers 2 hectares with an average age of vine of twenty years.

Fermentation takes place in cement *cuvées* and the wine is matured in oak casks for two years before bottling. Some of the wine is sold in bulk.

Domaine de l'Église
This ancient property, close to the church at Pomerol, is one of the oldest in the commune; it was purchased from Simon Landard in 1973 by the Casteja family, who also own Château Batailley, Beausite, Trottevieille and others in the Gironde. It can trace its history back to the era of the Knights of St John of Jerusalem when there was a leper hospital in Pomerol. At that time it was called 'Porte Rouge'. Philippe Casteja and M Preben Hansen are the joint proprietors. As at Trottevieille, Jean Brun is the *Maître de Chai*.

The soil is of varied make-up but is predominantly deep gravel with some gravelly clay. There are 7 hectares of vines (75% Merlot, 25% Bouchet) producing 30 to 35 tonneaux. The average age of the vines is twenty-five years.

The grapes are completely de-stalked and crushed and the juice is fermented in stainless-steel and cement vats. The skins are left in contact with the *must* of twelve to twenty days before pressing. The wine is matured partly in vats and partly in casks and assembled, racked and fined in the usual way, before being bottled after sixteen months to two years. The wine is sold exclusively through the firm of Borie Manoux.

Château l'Église-Clinet
This property, which is just to the north-west of Pétrus on clay and gravel soil with an iron sub-soil, takes its name from a nearby twelfth-century church destroyed at the end of the last century. It has belonged to the family of the present owner, Mme G Durantou, for several centuries. Pierre Lasserre and his grandson, Jean-Marie Garde of Clos René and Moulinet-Lasserre, make the wine.

There are 4½ hectares of vines (60% Merlot, 30% Bouchet, 10% Pressac) producing about 20 tonneaux. The oldest vines are one hundred years. The methods of vinification are exactly the same as for Clos René and Moulinet-Lasserre.

Château Élysée
Present owner Armand Berlureau
1.91 hectares

Château l'Enclos
This property, immediately to the north of Clos René, belongs to the Société Civile du Château l'Enclos (Mme Carteau, Mme Marc and her daughter, and Mme St Martin) and has been in Mme Carteau's family for over a century. Mme Marc has managed it since the death of her husband in 1971.

The soil is gravel and flinty gravel with a clay and gravel sub-soil. There are 10.5 hectares of vines (80% Merlot, 19.25% Bouchet, 0.25% Pressac) producing some 40 tonneaux at an average of 35 hectolitres per hectare. The oldest vines are forty-six years and the average age twenty-five years.

The grapes are usually completely de-stalked and crushed and the juice is fermented in cement enamel-lined tanks before pressing. The wine is then run off into oak casks, some new each year, and assembled, racked, fined and matured in the usual way, before being bottled after about twenty months.

Château Enclos-Haut-Mazeyres
Present owner Mme de Pedro-Souille
6.80 hectares

J M Estager
0.23 hectares
Sells bulk only.

Château l'Évangile
This property, which has been in the hands of the Ducasse family for more than one hundred and twenty years, lies on the border with Saint-Émilion very close to Château la Conseillante and Vieux-Château-Certan. Louis Ducasse has

owned it, with his sister, for over sixty years. He has no sons and the estate will pass eventually to his nephews. The house was built in 1750 and partly rebuilt in 1960. Monsieur Zucchi of Vieux-Château-Certan, and Châteaux Beauregard and Montlabert, is *Maître de Chai*.

The soil is gravel, sand and clay with some iron in the sub-soil. There are 13 hectares of vines (two-third Merlot, one-third Bouchet) producing 45 to 70 tonneaux and around 50 hectolitres per hectare. After the great frost of February, 1956, 8 hectares had to be completely replanted.

The grapes are completely de-stalked and crushed and the juice is fermented for two to three weeks in epoxy-lined cement vats, the skins remaining in the *must* throughout that period before pressing. The wine is matured in oak casks, two-thirds of which are new each year, and assembled, racked and fined in the usual way, before being bottled after about two years.

Château Fagnard
Present owner M Barbeyron
0.5 hectares

Aubert Fahre
0.38 hectares
Sells bulk wine only.

Raymond Faure
0.84 hectares
Sells bulk wine only.

Château la Femilleraie
Present owner Guy Janoueix
0.38 hectares

Château Ferrand
This property which is in the southern part of Pomerol, about three-quarters of a mile south to south-east of Château Plince, is owned by the Société Civile du Château Ferrand and run by Fernand Gasparoux. His family purchased it in 1935 from M Doublet. The previous owner was M Seraphin who had inherited it from his employer, M Goutier, a Libourne architect.

The soil is sandy with some gravel and clay but it is the iron-bearing sub-soil (from which it takes its name) which is said to give the wine its character. There are 12 hectares of vines in full production (about 60% Cabernet Sauvignon and Bouchet and 40% Merlot, but with a few Pressac vines) producing about 80 tonneaux. The vineyard was entirely destroyed by the great frost of 1956 so the oldest vines are twenty-five years. There is a regular programme of uprooting, resting the soil and replanting.

The grapes are usually completely de-stalked and crushed. Fermentation, in lined cement vats, varies in length according to the temperature and the skins are left in the *must* for a further ten days after it has finished before pressing. In January the wine is assembled and put into glass-lined metal tanks where it is racked every two months and filtered once. (It is not usually fined except in years when the wine is exceptionally tannic, such as 1975.) It is then transferred to oak casks of various ages to mature until it is ready for bottling. In poor years the wine is not sold under the name of the Château but as *Clos l'Étoile, A C Pomerol*.

There is another small property of 3 hectares, on the Pomerol plateau near the famous church, which belongs to M Gasparoux. It used to be part of three other properties: Clos de la Vieille École, Clos des Amandiers and Château Haut Pignon. The wine called *Château Haut Ferrand*, is made in the cuvier and *chai* at Château Ferrand and the same methods of vinification and maturation are used. Production is about 10 tonneaux. It is regarded as superior to the wine of *Château Ferrand*.

Château Ferron
Present owner Madame Vve Ernest Jean
2.00 hectares

Château Feytit-Clinet
This small farmhouse property lies a little to the south of the N.89 about $2\frac{1}{2}$ miles north-east of Libourne, next to Château Latour-à-Pomerol. Like its neighbour, it has been owned by the same family for many years but has its wine made and sold by the firm of J-P Moueix. The owners are the heirs of the Tane-Domergue family.

The soil is gravel and clay with an iron-bearing sub-soil. There are $6\frac{1}{2}$ hectares of vines (90% Merlot, 10% Bouchet) producing some 25 tonneaux at around 40 hectolitres per hectare. The oldest vines are seventy years and the average age is thirty-two years.

The vinification and maturation, as at all the J-P Moueix properties, is exactly as described under Château Pétrus, except that here two to four-year-old casks are used.

Château Feytit Guillot
Present owner Jean Lureau

Domaine de la Fleur
Present owner Raymond Visage
1.38 hectares

Château la Fleur Boého
Present owner Joseph Golin
0.51 hectares

Château la Fleur Cloquet

This is another brand-name for *Château Côte l'Église*.

Château la Fleur-Pétrus

This property is in the eastern part of the Pomerol plateau close to Châteaux Pétrus and Gazin. In the 1920s it was the property of the Pineau family whence it passed to M Garret and in 1952 the firm of J-P Moueix acquired it. The official proprietor is the Société Civile du Château la Fleur-Pétrus.

It is well-sited in one of the best parts of the Pomerol plateau on gravel and clay soil with an iron-bearing sub-soil. There are 7.49 hectares of vines (75% Merlot, 25% Bouchet) producing some 30 tonneaux at around 40 hectolitres per hectare. The oldest vines are thirty-five years and the average age is twenty-six years so a large proportion of the vineyard has been replanted since the firm of J-P Moueix took over and it seems probable that the quality of the wine has gradually improved. It is certainly one of the finest Pomerols.

The vinification and maturation, as at all the J-P Moueix properties, is exactly as described under Château Pétrus, except that here two to four-year-old casks are used.

Château la Fleur-des-Rouzes

This is another brand-name for *Château Côte l'Église*.

Château la Fleur-du-Gazin

This property lies in the eastern part of Pomerol between the famous Châteaux from which it takes name: Lafleur and Gazin. Between the Wars it was owned by M Bedin and it is now the property of Maurice Borderie. He rents part of it to the firm of J-P Moueix who make the wine.

It is well-sited on clay and gravel soil with iron-bearing sub-soil. There are just over 7 hectares of vines (70% Merlot, 30% Bouchet) producing some 30 tonneaux at around 40 hectolitres per hectare. The oldest vines are thirty-eight years and the average age is twenty-nine years.

The vinification and maturation, as at all the J-P Moueix properties, is exactly as described under Château Pétrus, except that here two to four-year-old casks are used.

Château lafleur-du-Roy

Present owner   Yvon Dubost
2.68 hectares

Château la Fleur Treyssac

Present owner   Paul Chauveau
1.26 hectares

Château Franc Beaulieu

Present owner   M Bertrande
0.24 hectares

Château Franc-Grand-Moulinet

Now part of Château Moulinet Lasserre.

Château Franc-Maillet

Present owner   Guy and Gerard Arpin
5.44 hectares

Rolland Fredont

0.53 hectares
Sells wine in bulk only.

Château la Ganne

Two generations of the Lachaud family had already been proprietors of this estate before the present owner, M Dubois-Lachaud. The main part of the vineyard lies between the N.10 and the railway which runs north from Libourne and is enclosed by Châteaux Mazeyres and Beauchêne; there is a further parcel of land the other side of the railway in the part of Pomerol sometimes called 'Le Grand Moulinet'. Monsieur Dubois-Lachaud looks after the vineyard and the wine-making himself.

The soil is gravel on a sub-soil containing iron. There are about 5 hectares of vines (70% Merlot, 25% Bouchet, 5% Cabernet Sauvignon) producing an average of 22 tonneaux at around 40 hectolitres per hectare. The oldest vines are forty years and the average age is twenty years.

The grapes are completely de-stalked and crushed and the juice is fermented in lined cement and stainless steel vats for about twelve days. The skins remain in contact with the *must* for twenty-one days before pressing. The wine is then racked, fined, assembled and matured, before being bottled about two and a half years after the vintage.

Château le Gay

The present owners of this attractive Château which lies on the main road are Mlles Thérèse et Marie Robin, who also own Château Lafleur. It used to be called the Gay Manor, in the time when it belonged to the Bechade family. It constantly produced and still produces good quality wine. There are 13.15 hectares of which 11 hectares are under vine.

Château Gazin

This famous and imposing Château is most attractive and is set back off the main road, surrounded by vines. It is situated in the extreme eastern part of Pomerol, in sight of the Pomerol church and is a near neighbour of Château Pétrus. Indeed, 5 hectares of Gazin's vineyard were sold to its famous neighbour in 1969 and are now part of the Pétrus vineyard. The 1868 edition of Cocks et Feret lists it as fourth among the leading growths calling it Rouget et Gazin, owner M Fabue. Originally known as the Domaine des Templiers, it has belonged to the family de Bailliencourt, called Courcol, for several generations. The present proprietor is M Étienne de Bailliencourt dit Courcol. Monsieur Gagnerot has been *Régisseur* for twenty-five years and M Forrest *Chef de Culture* for ten years.

The soil is gravel and clay with an iron-bearing sandstone sub-soil, typical of the best parts of Pomerol. There are 23 hectares of well-kept vines (about two-thirds Merlot and a third each Bouchet and Cabernet Sauvignon) producing some 100 tonneaux at about 35 hectolitres per hectare. The oldest vines are forty years and the average age twenty-five years. Gazin is one of the first of the well-known properties to use a vintaging-machine.

The timing of the fermentation, contact of skins with the *must*, the occurrence of the malolactic fermentation all vary from year to year. After the *assemblage* the wine is matured in oak casks, some new, some up to fifteen years old to be further racked, fined and matured, before being bottled after about two years.

Château Gombaude-Guillot

Suzanne and Henri Laval and their children own this property which is just west of Trotanoy and south of Bourgneuf. It previously belonged to M Amédée and Charlotte Darbeau, then to their niece, Mme Laval (née Darbeau) who inherited it in 1954. The *Maître du Chai* is M T Zucchi.

The soil is gravel and sand with some iron in the sub-soil. There are 6.75 hectares of vines (33% Merlot, 33% Bouchet and 33% Pressac) producing about 24 tonneaux. The oldest vines are ninety years and the average age thirty-five years.

The grapes are completely de-stalked and crushed and fermentation (in glass-lined cement vats) usually takes between eight and ten days. After the pressing, maturation takes place partly in casks and partly in stainless-steel tanks and there are the usual rackings, *assemblage* and fining, before bottling after eighteen months to two years. The family market the wine themselves and virtually all of it is sold to private clients.

Château Groupey
Present owner   Lucien Moze
4.42 hectares

Château Grands Champs
Present owner   Mme Giraud
0.54 hectares

Château Grand-Moulinet
Present owner   Pierre Julion
0.89 hectares

Château les Grands-Sillons
Present owner   Mme Colette Dignac
2.24 hectares

Château Grands-Sillons-Gabachot
Present owner   Vve François Janoueix
2.96 hectares
Located near the village of Catusseau-Pomerol.

Château Grange-Neuve
Present owner   Gros & Fils
6.13 hectares
Situated in the west of the commune, between the village and the Route Nationale. Modern house with *chai* behind it, white-washed and with Virginia creepers.

Clos Grangeneuve
Present owner   Mme Augeron
0.91 hectares
Small single-storey, well-maintained house.

Château Grate-Cap
Present owner   Albert Janoueix
10.34 hectares
The name of Grate-Cap, the site on which the cellars and vats are situated in the middle of the vineyard, comes from a Latin expression, 'gratum caput', meaning an assembly of vines producing a delicious wine.

Monsieur Janoueix also owns the Château la Mission in Pomerol and the Clos des Graves and the Domaine du Haut-Pomerol. In Saint-Émilion he owns Château Mouton-Bland and Petit-Clos-Figeac.

Clos de la Gravette
Present owner   M Chanlot
0.25 hectares

Château Graves Guillot
Present owner   Paul Clauzel (who also owns Château Beauregard)
0.92 hectares

Château Graves de Maillet
Present owner   Jean Dulan
0.56 hectares

Château la Grave-Trigant-de-Boisset
This property, with its attractive house set
among trees, is just south of the N.89 some 4
kilometres north-east of Libourne and immediately north of Latour à Pomerol. It is an
ancient estate owned in the late-nineteenth-
century by M Dubourg and subsequently his
widow. Madame Edgard Bouché was later
proprietor for many years and now Christian
Moueix, son of Mr J-P Moueix, owns it. The
'Trigant de Boisset' is the name of another
former owner.

It is well-sited on a favourable part of the
Pomerol plateau and has an unusually gravelly
soil with the iron-bearing sub-soil characteristic
of the area. There are just under 8 hectares of
vines (90% Merlot, 10% Bouchet) producing
some 35 tonneaux at around 40 hectolitres per
hectare. The oldest vines are thirty-five years
and the average age is twenty-five years.

The vinification and maturation, as at all the
J-P Moueix properties, is exactly as described
under Château Pétrus except that here two to
four-year-old casks are used.

Château Guillot
Present owner   Luquot & Fils
4.68 hectares – 30 tonneaux

Château Guillot-Tropchaud
André Arnaud is the proprietor of this small
property, a little west of Pétrus and it has
belonged to his family for some years. The soil is
mainly sandy with some iron in the sub-soil.

There are 8.75 hectares of vines (60% Merlot,
39% Bouchet with some Cabernet Sauvignon
and 1% Pressac) producing anything from 7 to
19 tonneaux according to the year. The oldest
vines are forty years and the average age twenty-
five years.

The grapes are completely de-stalked and
crushed and the juice is fermented in cement
vats for five or six days. The skins are left in
contact with the *must* for a further six or seven
days before pressing. After the malolactic
fermentation, the wine is assembled, racked and
fined in the usual way. Some is kept in vats to be
sold in bulk while the remainder is kept in casks,
some as old as fifty years, to mature before being
bottled at least eighteen months after the
vintage.

Château Haut Bellevue
Present owner   M Reyrel
0.52 hectares

Château Haut Cloquet
François de Lavaux bought this property, a
little east of Clos René, the other side of the
N.89 in 1971 from the Foyard family. He is
descended from two ancient families, Beylot
and Horeau, who have been involved in the
Bordeaux wine trade since 1740. The area under
vine is 5.03 hectares of gravel and clay soil with
some iron in the sub-soil. The de Lavaux family
also owns Châteaux la Renaissance and St Pierre
in Pomerol and Martinet in Saint-Émilion.

Château Haut-Maillet
Pierre Delteil, whose family have been the
proprietors for many years, owns this small
property which is near the extreme eastern tip of
the commune, on the Saint-Émilion border
about half a mile south–south-east of Gazin.

The soil is gravel and clay with a brown free-
stone sub-soil. Monsieur Feyti has been *Maître
de Chai* for more than twenty years. There are
5.48 hectares of vines (80% Merlot, 20%
Bouchet) producing an average of 20 tonneaux
at around 35 hectolitres per hectare. The oldest
vines are fifty years and the average age thirty
years.

The grapes are completely de-stalked and
crushed and the juice is fermented in cement
vats. The skins are left in contact with the *must*
for several days after the fermentation is
completed. After pressing, the wine is then
racked for the first time and spends part of its
maturation time in casks and part in cement vats
with the usual rackings, fining and *assemblage*,
before being bottled after about twenty months.

Château Haut Pignon
Present owner   M Barbeyron
0.44 hectares

Château des Hautes Rouzes
This is another brand-name of *Château Côte
l'Église*, exclusive to Belgium.

Château Haut-Tropchaud
Present owner   Jean Mathias
1.14 hectares

Château des Jacobins
Present owner   Henri Matignon
1.3 hectares

Château la Loubiere
Present owner   Claude Rivière
1.85 hectares
This property has been owned by Marie Claude

and Claude Rivière since 1977 and covers 2.2 hectares of which 1.85 are planted with very old vines, mainly Merlot, the average age of which is fifty years.

After fermentation in inox-lined vats the wine is matured in oak casks which are renewed every two years before being Château-bottled. Out-put from 1977 to 1979:

1977 – 42 hectolitres per hectare
1978 – 63 hectolitres per hectare
1979 – 70 hectolitres per hectare

Dom de Lacombe
Now part of Château le Caillou.

Château Lafleur
Present owners Mlles Thérèse and Marie Robin, who also own Château le Gay.
4 hectares (in one block)
Gravel soil with a little clay. (Motto – 'Qualité passe quantité': Quality surpasses quantity.)

Château Lagrange
Another of the J-P Moueix properties, this lies a little west of Pétrus. Formerly owned by the Société Civile des vignobles du Grand-Corbin, then the SC de Château Lagrange, it is now under the official proprietorship of Establishment, Jean-Pierre Moueix.

The soil is mainly gravel with a sub-soil of iron-bearing clay. There are 8.25 hectares of vines (90% Merlot, 10% Bouchet) producing some 20 tonneaux at around 40 hectolitres per hectare. The oldest vines are fifty years and the average age is twenty-eight years.

The vinification and maturation, supervised by Jean-Claude Berrouet, the J-P Moueix oenologist, is exactly as that described under Château Pétrus except that no new casks are used. The casks here are two to four years old.

Jean André Lagrave
0.75 hectares
Sells bulk only.

Mme Lagrave-Berthier
0.65 hectares
Sells bulk only.

Château la Lamberte
Now part of Château Croix Toulifaut.

Claude Lateyron
0.40 hectares
Sells bulk only.

Château Latour à Pomerol
This famous estate, with its attractive ivy-covered house and small central tower, lies just to the south of the N.89, some 4 kilometres north-east of Libourne. It has been owned by the family of Mme Edmond Loubat, the famous former owner of Pétrus, for several centuries and the present proprietor is her niece Mme Lily Lacoste. Since 1917 it has incorporated another former vineyard of considerable reputation, les Grandes Vignes. The wine is made and sold by the firm of J-P Moueix.

It is well-situated on a gravel out-crop with iron-bearing sub-soil. There are just under 8 hectares of vines (80% Merlot, 10% Bouchet, 10% Pressac). It is the only one of the Moueix properties to grow a proportion of Pressac. It produces some 30 tonneaux at around 40 hectolitres per hectare. The oldest vines are fifty years and the average is thirty-six years.

The vinification and maturation, as at all the J-P Moueix properties, is exactly as described under Château Pétrus except that here two to four-year-old casks are used.

Château Lucie Taulifaut
Present owner René Debacque
0.33 hectares

Château la Madeleine
Present owner M Fontaneaud

Château Margot
Present owner M Chevrier
0.75 hectares

Château Marzy
Present owners Société Civile Romain Maison
Set back in the vines. Attractive property with Normandy roof.

Château du Mayne
This is another brand-name for *Château Rêve d'Or*.

Château Mazeyres
This attractive property is a little north of Libourne between the N.10 and the railway. In the Château itself there is an impressive collection of Gallo-Roman pottery found buried in the vineyard. The estate, formerly the property of Baron de Susbielle, was acquired by the Querre family in 1909. The present proprietor is Michel Querre on behalf of the Société Civile Heritiers Christian Querre. Christian Durond has been vineyard manager and oenologist for one year and Jean-Claude Musseau has been *Maître de Chai* for twenty years.

The soil is sand and gravel with some iron-bearing clay in the sub-soil. There are 9 hectares of vines – exactly half the area of the estate – (67% Merlot, 33% Bouchet) producing an average of 45 tonneaux at around 45 hectolitres per hectare. The vineyard was completely devastated by the great frost of 1956 and the oldest vines are twenty-four years, the average age being twenty years.

The grapes are completely de-stalked and crushed and the juice is fermented in steel and cement vats, lined with epoxy resin, for about seven days and the skins remain in contact with the *must* for fifteen to twenty-one days before pressing. The wine is then run off; one-third into new oak casks, two-thirds into vats. It is assembled, racked, fined and matured in the usual way, before being bottled after about eighteen months. The main markets outside France are Belgium, The Netherlands, Luxembourg, Germany, Switzerland, The United Kingdom and The United States.

Clos Mazeyres
Present owner Leymarie & Fils
9.62 hectares
They also produce wine under the label of *Château Beauchêne*. The family also own Château Bonet in Canon Fronsac and part of Clos Vougeot in Burgundy.

Pierre Meillan
0.59 hectares
Sells bulk wine only.

Château Monbrun
This property is owned by Mme Vve Cabireau et Paul Dubois who also produce wine under Château Mouton-Mazeyres, which is exclusively planted with Merlot and Bouchet. Production of this growth is 15 tonneaux from 2.25 hectares.

Château Monregard-la-Croix
This is another brand-name for *Clos du Clocher*.

Château Moulinet
This is the second most northerly estate of Pomerol next to its neighbour, Château de Sales, and is separated from Lalande de Pomerol by the Barbanne. It is one of the largest domaines in Pomerol. Between 1894 and 1925 it belonged to Raymond de Seguin, who had inherited it from his uncles: M M Dufresne (Bordeaux dealer) and Hippolyte Danglade (former Mayor of Libourne). On the death of M de Seguin, his descendants inherited it: Jean de Seguin, Mme Vve Lesne de Molaing, the Countess of Carrère, the Countess Arnaud de Castelbajac. It was then owned by Mme de Castelbajac, a member of this old Libournais family, who sold it in 1971. The Société de Domaine de Moulinet is the present proprietor and Armand Moueix is the Adminis-

trator and responsible for the vineyard and wine-making. Since 1971 there has been much replanting and modernisation, including a new *chai* with stainless-steel vats.

There are 17.7153 hectares under vine (67% Merlot and 33% Bouchet) producing some 65 tonneaux. The oldest vines are sixty years and the average age is thirty years.

A vintaging-machine was used for the first time on the 1981 vintage but otherwise all the particulars of vinification are exactly the same as for all the A Moueix properties, as detailed in the report on Château Fonplégade, Saint-Émilion, except that here the Blanchère system of fermentation is not used at present, although it is planned to introduce it in the near future.

Château Moulinet-Lasserre
Present owner Jean-Marie Garde
4.52 hectares
See Clos René.

Ginette Musseau
0.53 hectares
Sells bulk wine only.
She is also cook/housekeeper at *Château Mazeyres* and her husband is the *Maître de Chai*.

Château Nenin
This property lies on the southern slope of the plateau of Pomerol between the outskirts of Libourne and the village of Catusseau. The proprietor is M Despujol whose family have owned it since the middle of the nineteenth century. Pierre Esben is the *Régisseur*.

The 45 hectare estate is one of the largest in Pomerol. Thirty are devoted to vines (50% Merlot, 30% Bouchet, 20% Cabernet Sauvignon) and average production is around 100 tonneaux at 36 hectolitres per hectare. The oldest vines are sixty years and the average age is twenty-five years. The soil is appreciably more gravelly than that of the other properties in this part of Pomerol.

A vintaging-machine was used for the 1982 vintage.

The grapes are completely de-stalked and crushed. Fermentation is done in cement vats and lasts for ten to fifteen days at a controlled temperature, the skins remaining in contact with the *must* throughout before pressing. Malolactic fermentation follows immediately and the wine remains in the vats for a further four to eight weeks before being transferred to oak casks, some of them new, for maturation and the usual rackings and fining. There are two *assemblages*, one of the young wines shortly after the malolactic fermentation, the other at the end of the maturation period just before bottling, after eighteen months to two years. A second wine is made from the young vines, and sold under the name *Château St Roch*.

Château de la Nouvelle-Église
Present owner M J Servant (who also owns Château la Violette)
2.43 hectares
A new church has recently been built on the highest point of the commune to which a large contribution was made by Château de la Nouvelle-Église. It is situated literally between the presbytery and the church and beside the girls' school.

Jean Pageot
0.18 hectares
Sells bulk only.

Château la Patache
Present owner Pierre Thibeaud
1.65 hectares

Clos du Pelerin
Present owner Paul Boutin
3.32 hectares

Château Petit Beauséjour
Present owner M Vinzent
0.67 hectares

Château Petit Clos Taillefer
Present owner Gilbert Favrie
0.27 hectares

Château Petit Plince
Present owner Mme Chaulet
2.79 hectares
Very small farmhouse.

Château Petit-Village
This property, which in recent years has been consistently among the best Pomerols, lies between the village of Catusseau and Vieux-Château-Certan and la Conseillante and its soil is the typical clay and gravel of that part of the plateau. The origin of the name is uncertain – though some think that it refers to the original site of the village of Pomerol. It was purchased in 1919 from M Heron by Fernard Ginestet who also owned Châteaux Margaux and Cos d'Estournel in the Médoc, la Fleur Pourret, Marbuzet, Petit Figeac in Saint-Émilion and later de Taste in St Croix du Mont.

In 1971 the estates were divided between M Ginestet's son, Pierre, who took Margaux, and his daughter, Mme Jean Prats, who received the others. The Prats family own these properties and Bruno Prats, the youngest of Mme Prats' three sons manages Petit-Village. Gilbert Xans is the *Régisseur*.

There are 11 hectares of vines (80% Merlot, 10% Bouchet, 10% Cabernet Sauvignon) producing some 40 tonneaux at about 30 hectolitres per hectare. The oldest vines are thirty-three years and the average age is twenty-four years. Much replanting was necessary after the disastrous frost of February 1956 when the vineyard was very hard-hit.

The grapes are completely de-stalked and very lightly crushed. The *cuvier* was renovated in 1976. Fermentation, which lasts from ten to twenty days, takes place in stainless-steel vats with epoxy lining before the pressing in a very modern Vaslim circular fibre-glass press. The wine is then transferred to cement vats for the malolactic fermentation. The skins are left in contact with the *must* for ten days to three weeks according to the vintage. The wine is then run into oak casks (one-third of them new each year) for maturation, *assemblage* (in the January following the vintage), racking, fining and bottling, after about two years.

Château Pétrus
This is undoubtedly the most famous of the Pomerol estates and its wines are the most expensive, matching and sometimes exceeding the prices of Cheval Blanc and the Médoc first growths. It was the property of the Arnaud family for over one hundred years until they made it into a company at the time of the First World War. In the mid-1920s Edmond Loubat acquired part of the property and after his death his widow gradually bought up the rest. Madame Loubat, by her energy and personality, combined with the excellence of the wine, had much to do with contributing to Pétrus the great reputation which it has now. She died in 1961 and now the ownership of the shares of the Société Civile du Château Pétrus is divided between her niece, Mme L-P Lacoste and Jean-Pierre Moueix. Michel Gillet has been *Régisseur* of Pétrus and all the other J-P Moueix properties since 1977. Jean Veyssière has been. *Maître de Chai* of Pétrus since 1947 and the other J-P Moueix properties since 1967. The distinguished oenologist, Jean-Claude Berrouet, who is responsible for making the wine of all the J-P Moueix properties, has been in charge of the vinification of Pétrus since 1964.

There is a pleasant but unpretentious building dating in its present form, from the late nineteenth century, with a statue of St Peter, from whom the estate takes its name, wielding an enormous key (to the gates of heaven) and sitting in a boat surrounded by large stone fish to remind one of his piscatorial origins. Saint Peter and his key also appear on the label.

The vineyard is small, about 11.5 hectares of vines, and before 1969, when 5 hectares were acquired from the neighbouring Château Gazin, had been a mere 6.5. The make-up of the top-soil is unique in the area for it is virtually all clay (with some sand) as opposed to the more usual gravel–sand, or gravel–clay mixture. There is some gravel in the five ex-Gazin hectares. The sub-soil is also clay. This, combined with the very unusually high proportion of Merlot in the vineyard (95% to 5% Bouchet), probably has much to do with the extraordinary intensity and richness of colour, bouquet and flavour. The oldest vines are over eighty years and the average age is forty years. After the terrible frost of 1956, Mme Loubat did not replant but decided to leave the vines to recover in their own time, hence the high proportion of old vines. Usually some 40 tonneaux of wine are produced at around 40 hectolitres per hectare. The J-P Moueix 'army' of over one hundred pickers manages to complete the vintaging in about four days despite picking only in the afternoons to avoid the morning dew.

The grapes are de-stalked (though in some years 20% of the stalks may be allowed to remain) and crushed and fermentation, in unlined cement tanks, usually lasts some four to six days but may take much longer. The skins remain in contact with the *must* for two to three weeks before pressing. The wine is then run off into casks, new each year, and made especially for the Château by the firm of J-P Moueix; it is assembled after two months, racked every three months, fined in the second winter and bottled after twenty months, two years or longer. Until 1973 the wine was bottled cask by cask, but since then the various casks have been assembled in stainless-steel vats before bottling to avoid cask variation.

Château Phébus
Present owner André Fernandez

Clos le Picassou
Present owner Henri Darnajou
1.15 hectares

Château Pignon Larroucaud
Present owner Mme Largeteau
0.26 hectares

Cru Pignon-Larroucaud
Present owner André Durandet
0.27 hectares

le Pin
This little property is next door to Vieux-Château-Certan and the GFA Château du Pin is the proprietor. It was previously owned by Mme Laubie, from 1924 to 1979 and is now managed by Jacques Thienpoint of Vieux-Château-Certan.

The soil is gravel and clay with iron in the sub-soil. There is 1 hectare of vines (88% Merlot, 12% Bouchet) producing about $3\frac{1}{2}$ tonneaux at an average of 32 hectolitres per hectare. The oldest vines are forty years and the average age is twenty years.

The grapes are de-stalked and crushed and the juice is fermented in stainless-steel vats for eight to fifteen days, the skins remaining in the *must* for that period before pressing. Then the wine is run off into oak casks (four years old for the 1979 and 1980 vintage; new from 1981 onwards) and assembled, racked, fined and matured in the usual way, before being bottled after eighteen months to two years.

Clos Pleville
This name no longer exists. All the wine is now under the label of *Château Ste Marie*.

Château Plince
This small, classic-looking Château lies just south of la Pointe and the D.21 and north-west of la Commanderie. The site was originally a marsh called Plemse and around 1800 the property was called Château Pleince. The Moreau family, who also own Clos l'Église have owned the property since 1940, before which the Rouchut family had been the owners for many years. Patrice Ducher has been *Maître de Chai* since 1940.

The 10 hectare property has some 8.35 hectares under vine planted with 70% Merlot, 15% Bouchet, 15% Cabernet Sauvignon producing some 35 tonneaux at around 37 hectolitres per hectare. The oldest vines are forty years and the average age is twenty years. The soil has a high content of sand.

The grapes are completely de-stalked and crushed; the juice is fermented in cement vats for fifteen to twenty-one days, the skins remaining in the *must* for that period before pressing. The wine spends the first six months of its maturation period in vats and the last eighteen in oak casks (average age five years) and is assembled, racked and fined in the usual way. They used a vintaging-machine for the 1982 vintage.

Clos Plince
Present owner   Philippe David
1.05 hectares

Clos Plince
Present owner   Mme Martorell
1 hectare

Clos Plince
Present owner   Maltord-Moncassin
1 hectare

Château Plincette
Present owner   Coudreau
2.5 hectares
Managed by J P Estager.

Château la Pointe
This is one of the largest estates in the area and has long been one of the best-known. It is mentioned in the 1868 Cocks et Feret as being among the leading growths of the region and it sold for the same price as the fifth-growth Médocs, very high for this then little acclaimed area. A M Grandet owned it in those days. Later it was purchased by a Swiss businessman, M Ducolon, who already owned Château la Serre in Saint-Émilion. Both these properties were purchased in 1949 by Paul Delahoutre, a Bordeaux *négociant*. He did much to restore the vineyard, which had become rather run-down during the War, and the *chai*. The two properties then passed to his father's father-in-law, then his father, and Mr Delahoutre was succeeded by his son-in-law, Bertrand d'Artfeuille. His immediate predecessor as proprietor was M Montauroy. The attractive house with Virginia-creeper on the outside was built under the Directoire and in the style of the time and there is a small park and a tree-lined drive. It is set back from the D.21 on the left about 1.5 kilometres from Libourne. Monsieur L David is the *Maître de Chai*.

The soil is sand and gravel with an iron-bearing sub-soil. The property has 25 hectares of which 21 are under vine (70% Merlot, 30% Bouchet) producing between 50 (1977), 120 (1978), 120 (1979), 100 (1980) and 80 (1981) tonneaux at an average of 41 hectolitres per hectare. The oldest vines are thirty-five years and the average age is twenty-five years.

The grapes are completely de-stalked and crushed and the juice is fermented in cement and stainless-steel vats for about fifteen days; the skins remain in contact with the *must* for three weeks before pressing. The wine is then run off into oak casks (one-third new each year, two-thirds up to five years old) and assembled, racked, fined and matured in the usual way, before being bottled after eighteen months to two years. The grape varieties are vinified separately and assembled after one year. A vintaging-machine has been purchased and will be used for the first time on the 1982 vintage.

Château Pont-Cloquet
Present owner   Henri Duffau
1.44 hectares

Château Prieurs-de-la-Commanderie
This is another brand-name for *Château Saint André*.

Château la Providence
Present owner   Jean Dupuy
2.66 hectares

Mme Vve Ransan
3 hectares
Sells bulk wine only.

Château Ratouin
Present owner   Serge Ratouin
2.17 hectares
This property was originally called 'Château l'Angélus' but M Ratouin had to change it as it caused confusion with the Grand Cru Classé in Saint-Émilion of the same name.

Domaine des Remparts
Present owner   Estager-Angle
3.22 hectares

Clos René and Château Moulinet-Lasserre
Although these are listed as two properties the wine is all made together; two-thirds of it is bottled as Clos René and one-third Moulinet-Lasserre. The joint proprietors are M Pierre-Lasserre and his grandson, Jean-Marie Garde, though M Lasserre is named as proprietor on the Clos René label and M Garde on that of Moulinet-Lasserre. He also owns Château la Mission in Lalande. The wine is vinified at Clos René. The property, which is about 2 kilometres north of Libourne, has been in the hands of the Lasserre family for six or seven generations. The house was built at the end of the nineteenth century and the *chai* and *cuvier* were rebuilt in 1947.

There are 15 hectares under vine (70% Merlot, 20% Bouchet, 10% Pressac) producing about 80 tonneaux in all at around 45 hectolitres per hectare. The oldest vines are fifty years. The soil is a mixture of gravel, sand and some clay.

Work in the vineyards at vintage time.

Wine maturing in oak barrels at Château Beauregard (Pomerol).

Fermentation vats at Château Pétrus.

The grapes are completely de-stalked and crushed by a Mabille *fouloir-égrappoir*. Fermentation, in cement vats lasts for about ten days with the skins in contact with the *must* throughout and the temperature controlled before pressing in a vertical press, also a Mabille. Then, after the malolactic fermentation, the wine is run off into oak casks, some of which are new each year, assembled after a month, and matured, racked and fined in the usual way, before bottling after about two years.

Clos René has made consistently fine wine over the last thirty years and its reputation has increased accordingly.

Domaine de René
This is another brand-name for *Château la Bassonerie*.

Château la Renaissance
Present owner François de Lavaux (who also owns Châteaux Haut Cloquet and St Pierre, both in Pomerol, and Château Martinet in Saint-Émilion)

Christian Renie
0.25 hectares
Sells bulk wine only.

Château Rêve d'Or
Present owners Vigier & Fils
6.71 hectares
They also produce wine under the label of *Château du Mayne*.

Château Riffat
Present owner M Lamarche

Château Robert
Present owner M Frances
4.12 hectares of well-kept vineyards.

Château Rocher-Beauregard
This small property is just less than 1 kilometre south-west of Château Beauregard. The Tournier family has owned it and Château Rocher Figeac in Saint-Émilion for several generations. The present proprietor is Max Tournier.

The soil is sand and gravel with a sub-soil of iron-bearing clay. There are 2.46 hectares of vines (Merlot, Bouchet and Cabernet Sauvignon) producing about 9.5 tonneaux. The vines range from six to fifty years old.

The grapes are completely de-stalked and crushed and the juice is fermented in cement vats before pressing. It is matured partly in vats and partly in oak casks and assembled, racked and fined in the usual way, before being bottled after about two years.

Château la Rose Figeac
Present owners Despagne-Rapin
4.20 hectares
They also produce wine under the label of *Château Trintin*.

Château Rouget
Present owner François Brochet
One of the oldest domaines in Pomerol, it belonged to M Bayonne, a longtime Mayor of the town, up until 1804. In one of the first editions of Cocks et Feret, this growth was classified fourth immediately after Vieux-Château-Certan, Château Trotanoy and Château Pétrus. It is listed there as *Rouget et Gazin*, and as owned by M Fabre.

The property covers an area of 26 hectares of which 14.82 are under vine situated near the village which surrounded the former village.

Monsieur Brochet also owns the old Château of the Templars, Clos des Templiers, whose vinyards adjoin those of the Château Rouget. The Château Rouget itself is an ivy-clad, single-storey building set back through the vines.

Château les Rouzes-Clinet
Present owner Régis Bose
3.52 hectares

Château Saint André
Present owner Mme Jacqueline Evrard
3.05 hectares
A second wine is produced under the name of *Château Prieurs de la Commanderie*.

Clos St André
Present owner André Desmarty

Château Sainte Marie
Present owner Jacques Pélotier
4.46 hectares

Château St Pierre
This property is a little to the south of the church at Pomerol and just less than 1 kilometre west of Pétrus. It was purchased in the 1950s by M Horeau, father of the present owner Mme J de Lavaux. The de Lavaux family also own Château la Renaissaince and Château Haut Cloquet in Pomerol and Château Martinet in Saint-Émilion. Monsieur Passebon assists Mme de Lavaux with the wine-making.

The soil is predominantly gravel on a sub-soil of sand and clay with traces of iron. There are 2.74 hectares of vines, with a preponderance of Merlot, producing some 10 tonneaux at 30 to 35 hectolitres per hectare. The average age of the vines is twenty years.

The grapes are completely de-stalked and crushed, the complete fermentation averages about three weeks during which time the skins remain in contact with the *must* before pressing. The wine is matured partly in vats and partly in oak casks and is assembled, racked and fined in the usual way, before being bottled usually in the spring of the second year after the vintage.

Château de Sales

This, by far the largest of the Pomerol estates and the biggest producer, lies approximately 2.5 kilometres almost due north of Libourne between the road to Paris (RN.10) and the road to Perigeux (RN.89). It has the unusual distinction of not having been sold since the middle of the sixteenth century. It was at this time that a rich Libourne family, Sauvanelle, adopted the title 'Seigneurs de Sales'. The house and gardens were much altered in the eighteenth century after Jeanne de Sauvanelle married her cousin Jacques Desygues. The family was dispersed during the Revolution but managed to regain possession soon afterwards when Pierre Desaygues de Sales, returning from abroad, made his nephew Alexandre de Liage heir to the estate. Alexandre's grandchildren, the Marquis de Folin, Ambassador of France, and his sister, Madame de Lambert, later became co-proprietors and the property is now in the hands of Henri de Lambert assisted by his son Bruno who holds the National Diploma of Oenology. The owners are officially the heirs of the Liage family.

The estate with its fine house, gardens and woods is 90 hectares of which 47 are under vine (70% Merlot, 10% Bouchet, 20% Cabernet Sauvignon) producing about 180 tonneaux at around 42 hectolitres per hectare. The oldest vines are thirty-five years. After the frost of February 1956 three-quarters of the estate had to be replanted over the next three years. The normal cycle of replanting is 1 hectare per year. The soil is sand and gravel with some iron in the sub-soil. De Sales is revolutionary indeed in being the first major property in the entire area to use a 'vintaging machine' instead of hand-picking; now others are following suit. The time and labour-saving involved can be imagined, some of the rows of vines being 800 metres long.

The grapes are completely de-stalked in a Coq *fouloir-égrappoir* and crushed before being pressed in a horizontal press that can be operated either manually or automatically. Fermentation, in cement vats, lasts from three to six days

controlled by water-cooling when necessary. The skins are left in contact with the *must* from two to four weeks depending on the amount of juice in the grapes and the amount of tannin in the pips and skins. After the malolactic fermentation the wine is assembled and run off into oak casks. An interesting feature of the wine-making here is that M de Lambert uses no new oak casks at all but buys them second-hand from other leading properties after they have matured one wine. This is not simply to cut costs but because he feels that new wood imparts too much tannin and a 'woody' or 'oaky' taste to the wine. The wine is then matured, racked and fined in the usual way, and bottled between sixteen months and two and a half years after the vintage. After the tasting of the various *cuvées* and the *assemblage* only the very best wine goes on to become Château de Sales; a second wine is sold as *Château Chantalouette, Pomerol*, and in some years a third, *Château de Délias, Pomerol*. Ninety-eight percent of de Sales is sold to five *négociants* in Bordeaux and Libourne, with J-P Moueix taking more than half.

Two stories are related by Bruno de Lambert to visitors at the Château. The first is about the mural on the ceiling on the main reception room. When his grandfather was celebrating his marriage it was decided to commemorate the occasion by painting a Michaelangelo-style fresco. Madame, however, decided that the artist's example of the painting, which still exists in the form of a small oil-painting, was too risqué for those days, as one lady was shown with her dress draped below her bosom; and so the ceiling was painted portraying clouds instead.

The second story relates to events at the time of the French Revolution when M de Lambert's ancestors lived at Château de Sales. During the Revolution the family had to flee the Château and on their eventual return they found that everything in the house – all the paintings, carpets, their furniture, etc – had been ransacked and destroyed and the place was totally empty. At the turn of this century one of M de Lambert's great aunts was playing in the attic above the out-houses (where the dome is) and when told to come down immediately by her mother as the floor was thought to be extremely dangerous, she replied that she was perfectly safe as the floor was covered with carpets. The servants were hastily ordered to move the carpets and when laid out in the courtyard they were found to be the original tapestries which, although slightly chewed by rats, have since been restored and now hang in the house again as they did before the Revolution.

Clos de Salles
Present owner Jean Avril
1.18 hectares

Château la Soulate
Now part of Château le Caillou.

Château du Tailhas
Present owners Nebout & Fils
Vineyard covers 9.77 hectares. Its eastern boundary is the border with Saint-Émilion.

Château Taillefer
This property lies just south of Château Beauregard and close to the border of Saint-Émilion. The Château was built in 1872 and belonged to a rich Parisian family who used it as a country house and not as a vineyard and it has a superb garden. In 1926 it was sold to the Moueix family and its present proprietors are the heirs of Marcel Moueix (A Moueix et Fils). Armand Moueix is responsible for the care of the vineyard and the making of the wine. The grounds now house the headquarters of A Moueix et Fils and the grandmother and mother of Bernard Moueix and his brother Jean-Michel live at the Château.

There are 25.35 hectares under vine (66% Merlot, 34% Bouchet) which produce about 90 tonneaux. The oldest vines are sixty years and the average age is thirty years. The *cuvier* was rebuilt in 1961.

All the particulars of the vinification are exactly the same as for all the A Moueix properties as detailed in the report on Château Fonplégade, Saint-Émilion. A second wine of the property is produced under the label *Clos Toulifaut*.

Domaine Tour du Roy
Present owner Paul Chanlot

Château Trintin
This is another brand-name for Château la Rose-Figeac.

Château Tristan
Present owner Mme Simone Cascarret
3.89 hectares
Small farmhouse.

Château Tropchaud
Now part of Château le Caillou.

Clos Tropchaud
Now part of Château le Caillou.

Château Tropchaud l'Église
Present owner Jean Estrade
0.62 hectares

Château Troques
This property no longer produces wine.

Château Trotanoy
This property, which is about half-a-mile north of the little village of Catusseau and lies on the western slope of the Pomerol plateau, was owned by the Giraud family for over two hundred years. For much of the early part of this era it was known as Pomerol-Giraud, Cru-de-Trotanoy. The 1898 Cocks et Feret entry claims that thanks to intelligent cultivation and the use of insecticides from the beginning of the *phylloxera* invasion, Trotanoy had managed to preserve all their old vines without grafting on to American root-stocks. Then the estate covered 25 hectares split up in several separate plots. By 1929 it was down to 11 hectares and it is now a fraction under 8. It was purchased in 1953 by the firm of J-P Moueix. Jean-Jacques Moueix lives in the attractive house and with his cousin Christian Moueix and oenologist Jean-Claude Berrouet helps to supervise the making of the wine. Apparently the name 'Trotanoy' comes from the soil of the vineyard: the mixture of gravel and deep clay that can become so hard in a hot, dry summer that it is 'trop ennoye' – too hard to work.

There are just over 7 hectares of vines (85% Merlot, 15% Bouchet) producing up to 35 tonneaux at around 40 hectolitres per hectare. The oldest vines are eighty years and the average age is thirty-four years. As at Pétrus, the Moueix 'army' of pickers work only the afternoons and on dry days at Trotanoy so that no moisture accompanies the grapes to the *chai*.

All the details of the vinification and maturation are as detailed under Château Pétrus except that only one-third of the casks are new each year.

Trotanoy is generally agreed to be consistently among the very finest Pomerols alongside Vieux-Château-Certan and occasionally challenging Pétrus itself.

Château la Truffe
Present owner Jean Paul Garde
2.34 hectares

Château de Valois
Present owner Jacques Leydet
6.76 hectares
Set on the border of Saint-Émilion and Pomerol. The old farmhouse is situated on a side road.

Château Vieille École
This property no longer produces wine.

Clos de la Vieille Église
Present owner   Robert Luçon
1.28 hectares

Vieux Château Boéno
Present owner   GFA Château Haut-Surget
1.14 hectares

Vieux-Château-Certan
This property, which enjoys a reputation second only to that of its famous neighbour, Pétrus, is close to the border of Saint-Émilion and adjacent to l'Évangile and la Conseillante. The word 'Certan' is said to be derived from an old French word meaning 'desert', the soil being so poor here that the local peasants were exempt from paying taxes. Perhaps because of this the property was planted with vines earlier than many of its neighbours. It is part of an estate owned in the sixteenth-century by the De May family, and there is documentary evidence (Marion, *Collection de Documents sur l'Histoire de la Révolution Française*) to show that in 1796, the domaine de Certan was producing wine comparable in price (and therefore presumably in quality), with the top Médoc properties, which is very remarkable for this period when Pomerol prices were generally far lower than those of the Médoc. After the Revolution one of the family emigrated and part of the property had to be sold off to refund the emigré's portion. Then in 1858 it was purchased by a Parisian, Charles de Bousquet, who rebuilt the Chartreuse-style house in its present form, though the shorter of the two towers is at least one hundred years older. The family, however, retained one part of the estate. Georges Thienpont, a Belgian wine-merchant who had recently bought Château Troplong-Mondot, acquired the property in 1924. The present proprietor, his son, Leon Thienpont-Thevelin, became the first member of the family to live in the house when he moved there in 1966. The official owner is the Société Civile du Vieux-Château-Certan (Heritiers de Georges Thienpont). Monsieur Zucchi has been *Maître de Chai* since 1970, a post he also holds at Châteaux l'Évangile and Beauregard as well as Château Montlabert in Saint-Émilion. His predecessor, M Belerier, had held the post for thirty years, following his father and grandfather.

The soil is gravel and clay with traces of iron in the sub-soil. There are 13.5 hectares of vines (50% Merlot, 25% Bouchet, 20% Cabernet Sauvignon and 5% Pressac) producing some 70 tonneaux at around 40 hectolitres per hectare. These percentages have been maintained since 1924 and are likely to remain unchanged. In general Merlot is planted where the clay predominates and the two Cabernets and Pressac in the more gravelly soil. The oldest vines are fifty years and the average age is about twenty-five years. Two-thirds of the vines were destroyed in the great frost of February 1956 and had to be replanted.

The grapes are completely de-stalked and crushed in a Coq *fouloir-égrappoir*. Fermentation is carried out in oak vats (a new *cuvier* and *chai* were built in 1972), but M Thienpont says that he retained the oak for reasons of tradition not because he thought that it made better wine than cement or stainless-steel. There are eight oak fermentation vats with open tops. For the five days or so of the first fermentation the 'cap' of skins rests about one foot down under a wooden grille. Then the vat is covered with a tarpaulin and *remontage* goes on for ten to fifteen days before the pressing in a programmed Garnier press, and the wine is pumped into a stainless-steel tank for the malolactic fermentation. The stainless-steel tank is used only for this and for the *assemblage* (usually in January). The wine is matured in oak casks, about one-third new each year, and racked and fined in the usual way, before being bottled, usually in the July of the second year after the vintage. All the wine has been bottled at the Château since 1950 except for a small amount in 1959. In poor years a 'sous marque' is produced, under the name of *La Gravette*.

The comparatively high proportion of Cabernet Sauvignon means that the character of the wine is slightly atypical of the area combining Pomerol richness with something of the finesse and backbone of the Médoc.

Outside France the main markets are Belgium, The United Kingdom, The United States of America, Japan and Australia.

Vieux Château Bourgneuf
Present owners   Larthoma et Fils
4.80 hectares
Also known as 'Clos Bourgneuf'. The Château is a newly-constructed house.

Vieux Château Cloquet
Present owner   Pierre Boyer
2.38 hectares

Vieux Château Haut Graves Beaulieu
Present owner   Jean Riboulet
0.09 hectares

Château Vieux-Maillet
Present owner   Louis Feytit
2.74 hectares

Vieux Cru Perruchet
Present owner   Mme la Baronne Guichard (who also owns Château Vraye Croix de Gay in Pomerol, Château Siaurac (Lalande de Pomerol) and Château Prieuré (Grand Cru Classé, Saint-Émilion)).

Château Vieux Pressac
Present owner   Jean Hollet
0.80 hectares

Château Vieux Taillefer
Present owner   René Fontanaud
2.66 hectares
He also owns a further 0.53 hectares whose wine is sold in bulk.

Clos Vieux Taillefer
Present owner   M Robin (who also owns Châteaux Sansonnet and Doumayne in Saint-Émilion)
There is no Château on this 1 hectare property and the wine is vinified at Sansonnet and matured at Doumayne.

Château la Violette
This property, which is set in the middle of the hamlet of Cattuseau in Pomerol on the main road, consists of several small plots of vines mostly on the Pomerol plateau near the famous church, but some lie further south near the vineyards of Château Nénin. The property belongs to Mme Jodeau-Servant, who also owns Château la Nouvelle-Eglise, and takes its name from the aroma of violets which the bouquet of its wine is said to evoke.

The soil is sand and gravel with an iron-bearing sub-soil. There are 3.26 hectares of vines (1 hectare Bouchet, the rest Merlot) producing some 15 tonneaux at around 40 hectolitres per hectare. The average age of the vines is twenty-five years.

The grapes are completely de-stalked and crushed and the juice is fermented in cement and stainless-steel vats for fifteen to twenty days during which time the skins are left in contact with the *must* before the pressing. The wine is then run off and matured partly in vats, partly in oak casks and assembled, racked and fined in the usual way, before being bottled about two years after the vintage. It is sold mainly to private customers.

Château Vraye-Croix-de-Gay
Present owner   Mme la Baronne Guichard (who also owns Châteaux Cru Perruchet in Pomerol, Siaurac in Lalande de Pomerol and le Prieuré in Saint-Émilion)
It lies a little to the north of Pétrus and east of the church of Pomerol.

The soil is sand and gravel with an iron-bearing sub-soil. There are 3.66 hectares of vines producing 4.25 (1977) to 14 (1979) tonneaux.

The vine-planting and method of making the wine are exactly as for Château Siaurac.

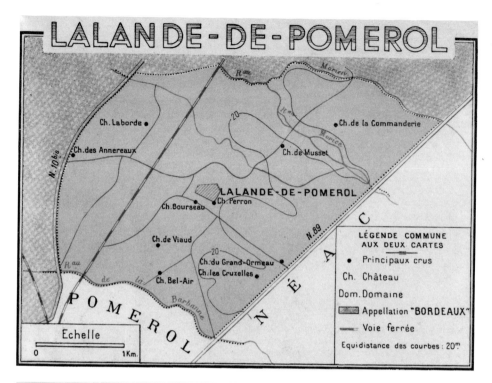

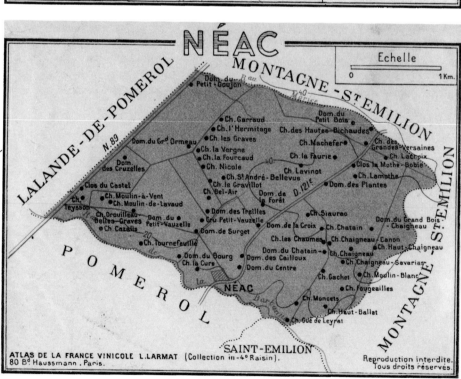

Lalande-de-Pomerol. It should be noted that Néac no longer has its own appellation.

LALANDE-DE-POMEROL

General

Situated 6 kilometres north-east of Libourne is the picturesque village of Lalande with its thirteenth-century church, which once belonged to the Templars, surrounded by 976 hectares of vineyards, of which 81 hectares are young vines not ready to be used to make wine.

During the eleventh century the Knights of St John of Jerusalem founded in the vicinity of the present village of Catussau a home and hospital combined, for the pilgrims coming to and from St James de Compostella and it was they who introduced the cultivation of the vine to the district. The Seigneurs of Barbane, Grailly and Castillon made numerous gifts of land to the Knight-Hospitaliers and these constitute the vineyard areas.

The area is quite flat with varied soil. To the north it is fertile sand and gravel, to the north-east gravel, to the east and south a heavy soil mixed with gravel. The sub-soil is gravel with white sand.

In 1954 the area of Lalande was merged with Néac, a small village spread around an attractive church set on a hill overlooking fields and valleys, which had hitherto had its own Appellation. The reason for the union was that the vines of Néac were less known and consequently sold at a lower price. The wines from these two areas were mainly sold in bulk to *négociants* but now quite a number of properties are bottling at the Châteaux. The Appellation Lalande de Pomerol requires the wine to have a minimum strength of 10.5° and a maximum yield of 40 hectolitres per hectare. Monsieur Trocard has been the President of the Syndicate for the past eighteen years.

The total out-put from this area, in hectolitres, has been:

1950 – 7,153	1967 – 20,661
1951 – 5,621	1968 – 20,919
1952 – 4,335	1969 – 14,526
1953 – 9,799	1970 – 37,327
1954 – 13,707	1971 – 17,364
1955 – 22,759	1972 – 20,947
1956 – 60	1973 – 38,956
1957 – 3,156	1974 – 36,151
1958 – 8,310	1975 – 22,452
1959 – 9,472	1976 – 37,361
1960 – 12,204	1977 – 11,304
1961 – 6,756	1978 – 28,394
1962 – 22,816	1979 – 45,355
1963 – 20,780	1980 – 24,249
1964 – 26,549	1981 – 32,661
1965 – 21,275	1982 – 45,871
1966 – 29,324	

Lalande-de-Pomerol Properties

Château Alainjo
Present owner René Ambeau

Château l'Alouette
Present owner J Louis Boutin

Château des Annereaux
In the sixteenth century this Château and its vineyard was already in the hands of the Annereau family, who have handed it down through direct descendants to the Malescot family. In the eighteenth century they were, with the Trigants, an extremely influential family, having a councillor in the Parliament of Bordeaux, Jurat members and King's Lieutenant in the Libourne Praesidium. The ownership then passed to the grandchildren and great-grandchildren of Mme Soehnée (née Malescot), representing the twelfth and thirteenth generations of continuous ownership of this domaine. The owner at that time, Mme Ponsot, played an important part in the reconstitution of the vineyards by the introduction of American root-stock which began in 1876.

The vineyard now covers 35 hectares and is owned by Indivision Hessel Milhaude. Jean Milhaude also owns Châteaux Lyonnat in Lussac and Serguent in Lalande.

Jean-Claude Anquetil
Sells wine in bulk.

Château des Arnauds
Present owner Pierre Godineau

Aubert Frères
Sell wine in bulk.

Mauricette Augeron
Sells wine in bulk.

Pierre Aurier
Sells wine in bulk.

Château les Baraillots
Present owner Lionel Boireau

Yvette Barraud
Sells wine in bulk.

Château Bechereau
Present owner Michel Bertrand

Roland Bel
Sells wine in bulk.

Château de Bel-Air
Formerly the property of the Beauchaine-Nicholas-Redeuilh family, this property is now owned by P et J P Musset. Twelve hectares are under vine. The property has established a reputation for making consistently fine wine.

Château Belle Graves
Present owner Mme Théallet

Château la Belle Rose
Jean Lacour is the owner of this property which lies on gravel soil. There are 2 hectares of vines (100% Merlot), the oldest vine being eight years. The grapes are not de-stalked; fermentation lasts for two weeks and takes place in wood and cement vats.

J-C Berrouet
He is the oenologist for all the J-P Moueix estates and personally has a small holding in Lalande.

Claude Bertin
Sells wine in bulk.

Château de Bertineau
Present owners SCE de Bertineau

Georges Biais
Sells wine in bulk.

Domaine Bienaimé
Present owner Abel Guimberteau

J Émile Blanc
Sells wine in bulk.

Albert Blanchet
Sells wine in bulk.

Château le Bon Pasteur
Present owner Genevieve Rolland

Château Bois de Laborde
This is the property of Angelo Vedelago, who also owns Château Mothe de Bertineau. There are just over 12 hectares of young vines (Merlot and Cabernet Sauvignon), none older than seven years.

Fermentation, in wooden vats, usually takes about ten days and the skins remain in contact with the *must* for three weeks before pressing. The wine is then racked off into five-year-old casks and racked, fined and matured in the usual way.

Domaine Bois de la Borde

This is another small property with young vines and belongs to Joseph Callegarin. There are 0.75 of a hectare of vines (50% Merlot, 50% Cabernet Sauvignon) none older than six years. Seven hectolitres were produced in 1977, 27 in 1978, 47 in 1979 and 30 in 1980.

Fermentation, in cement vats, lasts ten days and the skins are left in the *must* for three weeks. The wine is then racked off into five-year-old casks and racked, fined and matured in the usual way.

Château la Borderie Mondésir

Present owners   Rousseau et Fils

Regis Bosc

Sells bulk wine.

Château Bouquet de Violette

Present owner   Gaston Gauthier

Château du Bourg

Present owners   Sautarel et Fils (who also own Château Tournefeuille in Lalande de Pomerol)

Château Bourseau

This very attractive and well-maintained Château right in the heart of Lalande de Pomerol and adjacent to the church, belongs to the GFA Château Bourseau, which represents the heirs of the oenologist, Jean Bernard, the previous owner, who is still responsible for the wine-making. They also own Château Croix de Bourseau and Château Croix de Viaud. The house is the former residence of the local priest and a Maltese cross on the front door is a reminder that the Templars once had a monastery in Lalande. Former owners include M Nadaud, Ms Dumesnil and Passemard and the widow Passemard.

The soil is predominately gravel. There are 10 hectares of vines (60% Merlot, 20% Bouchet, 20% Cabernet Sauvignon) producing up to 50 tonneaux at about 30 hectolitres per hectare. The vines are all about twenty-five years old as the whole vineyard had to be replanted after the great frost of 1956.

The grapes are completely de-stalked and crushed and the juice is fermented in inox-lined stainless-steel vats for about fifteen days; the skins remain in the *must* for the same time before pressing. An unusual feature is that the wine is kept in the vats for a whole year, being racked several times, before being assembled and transferred to four-year-old oak casks (usually from Château Matras) for the second year of its maturation. Much of the total production is sold for export to The United Kingdom, The United States of America, Germany, The Netherlands, Denmark and Belgium. In 1980 the price was about 17 francs per bottle. A second wine is produced called *La Croix de Bourseau*.

Gaston Breuil

Sells wine in bulk.

E J Brochet

Sells bulk wines.

Château Brouard

Present owner   Claude Bonhomme

Arnaud Byais

Sells bulk wine.

Domaine de la Cabane

Present owner   Gaston Barbeyron

Léo Cablot

Sells bulk wine.

Domaine du Caillou

Present owners   Champseix et Fils (who also own Château Vieux Chevrol and Clos la Treille)

Château Canon-Chaigneau

Present owner   M J S Marin-Audra (who also owns Château Tour Canon, Tour Chaigneau, Grand Cormier in the area and, in addition, Châteaux Claymore and Blanceau in Lussac and Château la Croizelle in St Laurent-des-Combes)

Château Cardinal Viaud

This small property is in the centre of Lalande near the church which is depicted on the label. It belongs to Roger Champagne (not to be confused with Pol!).

The soil is sand and gravel. There are 2 hectares of vines (30% Merlot, 36% Bouchet, 34% Cabernet Sauvignon) which may produce up to 13 tonneaux in a big year. All the vines are ten years old.

The grapes are completely de-stalked and crushed and the juice is fermented in cement vats for some three weeks, the skins remaining in the *must* for the first eight days before pressing. After the usual racking, fining and maturation, the wine is bottled after eighteen months.

Maurice Carrère

Sells bulk wine.

Reine Casenoube

Sells bulk wine.

Château du Castel

Present owner   Robert Cazemajou

Château Castel Viaud
Present owners R et C Courty (who also own Château Changrolle)

Domaine de Cazelys
Present owner Maxime Piaud

Château du Centre
Present owner André Ceron

Château des Cerfs
Present owner G Vauvrecy

Château Chaigneau
Present owner Clouis Guillon

Clos Chambrun
Present owner J R Chollet

Domaine Champs de Lalande
Present owner Marcel Audubert

Château Changrolle
Present owners R et C Courty (who also owns Château Castel Viaud)

Gabriel Chansard
Sells bulk wines.

Clos Chante Gatonne
Present owner Jean Diard

Clos du Chapelain
Present owners Société Civile de l'Enclos

Château Chatain
Present owners Société Civile le Château Chatain

Château Chatain-Pinaud
Present owner Palatin-Pinaud (who also owns Château du Jard)

Robert Château
Sells bulk wine.

Château les Chaumes
Present owner Alain Vigier
10 hectares

Château Chevrol-Belair
Present owner Guy Pradier

Château de la Commanderie
Doctor Henri Roland Lafon is the manager of this property on behalf of the G F A du Château la Commanderie. It lies on gravel, sand and clay soil. There are 17.5 hectares of vines (40% Merlot, 20% Bouchet, 40% Cabernet Sauvignon) producing some 65 tonneaux. The oldest vines are twenty-five years and the youngest five years.

The grapes are completely de-stalked; fermentation in cement vats lasts eight to ten days

and the skins remain in the *must* for twelve to sixteen days before pressing.

Claire Courteau
Sells bulk wine.

Château la Croix
Present owners Arnaudet & Colombel

Château la Croix Bellevue
Present owner Heritiers Marcel Moueix
Situated just inside Lalande de Pomerol separated from Château Moulinet by a small stream. There is a high proportion of Cabernet Sauvignon. Some wine is vinified at Château Moulinet by the same methods as at all the A Moueix properties.

Château la Croix Blanche
Present owner Maurice Vigier

Château Croix de Bourseau
Present owner Gaboriaud-Bernard (who also owns Château Bourseau and Château Croix de Viaud

Château la Croix Chaigneau
Present owner Georges Boireau

Château Croix Chenevelle
Present owner Daniel Bedrenne

Château Croix des Moines
Present owner Paul Larthomes

Château la Croix des Moines
Jean Louis Trocard owns this property which lies on gravel and sand soil with an iron-bearing sub-soil. There are 7.25 hectares of vines (60% Merlot, 35% Bouchet and Cabernet Sauvignon and 5% Pressac) producing about 35 tonneaux in a good year. The oldest vines are thirty-five years and the youngest five years.

The grapes are two-thirds de-stalked and crushed and the juice is fermented in cement vats for a week and the skins remain in contact with the *must* for three weeks before pressing. The wine is then racked off into oak casks (one to five years old) and assembled, racked, fined and matured in the usual way, before being bottled after about two years. Outside France the main markets are Belgium, Luxembourg, Germany and Switzerland.

Château la Croix-Perron
Present owner Jean Aiguesparses

Château la Croix Saint André
Present owners Carayon & Fils (who also own Château la Forêt and Château la Croix St Louis.) Situated opposite the Marie in Néac on the corner of D 21. Attractive single-storey, well-

maintained property with a lovely view of Néac church.

Château la Croix St Jean
Present owner   Raymond Tapon

Château la Croix St Louis
Present owners   Carayon & Fils (who also own Châteaux la Croix St André and la Forêt)

Château Croix de Viaud
Present owners   Gaboriaud-Bernard (who also own Château Bourseau and Croix de Bourseau)

Château les Cruzelles
Present owner   Christian Richon

Château Dallau
Present owner   Vette Bertin

Pierre Delteil
Sells bulk and bottled wine.

J André Dubois
Sells bulk wine.

Pierre Dubois
Sells bulk wine.

Albert Dubos
Sells bulk wine.

Yvon Dubos
Sells bulk wine.

Jean Dulau
Sells bulk wine.

Remy Dussort
Sells bulk wine.

Clos de l'Église
Present owner   Camille Berry (who also owns Clos des Grand Moines in Lalande)

Morbert Egreteau
Sells bulk wine.

Mme Vve & JP Estager
Sells bulk wine.

Jean Estrade
Sells bulk wine.

Château l'Étoile de Salles
Madame Dubois is the owner of this property. The soil is gravel with an iron-bearing sub-soil. There are 5 hectares of vines (60% Merlot, 15% Bouchet, 15% Cabernet Sauvignon, 10% Pressac) producing some 19 tonneaux at about 40 hectolitres per hectare. The oldest vines are thirty years.

The grapes are 80% de-stalked and crushed. The juice is fermented for about twenty days in cement vats and the skins remain in the *must* for twenty-five days before pressing. Later the wine is transferred to oak casks (some new, some up to five years old) and is assembled, racked, fined, matured and bottled after two and a half years.

Château de l'Évêché
Present owner   Gerard Chaumet

Antoine Fabris
Sells bulk wine.

Gerard Faisandier
Sells bulk wine.

Edmond Fillaundeau
Sells bulk wine.

Château la Fleur
Present owners   Albert & Richon

Château la Fleur Châtain
Present owner   Robert Courty

Château la Fleur Galvesse
Present owner   J L Hollet

Château la Fleur Lambarret
Present owner   René Ollet

Château la Fleur St Georges
Present owner   Jean de Robillard (who also owns Château de Rosaire)

Château la Fleur Vauzelle
Present owner   Mollet-Fourreau (who also owns Château Haut Surget)

F & R Fonrede
Sells bulk wine.

Château la Forêt
Present owners   Carayon & Fils (who also own Châteaux la Croix St André and la Croix St Louis)

Louis René Fortin
Sells bulk wine.

Pierrett Forton
Seels bulk wine.

Château Fougailles
Present owner   Estager Frères

Château Franc Vauzelle
Present owner   Jean du Bourg

Château Gachet
Present owner   Pierre Brisson

Domaine des Galvesses Grand-Moine
Present owner   Guy Chanet

Château des Garaudières
Present owners   Société Civile Nonoy (who also own Châteaux Garraud and Treytine)

Château Garraud
Present owners Société Civile Nonoy (who also own Châteaux des Garraudières and Treytins)

Paul Gauthier
Sells bulk wine.

Château les Gazelles
Present owner Robert Merlet

Lucien Giraud
Sells bulk wine.

Yves Giraud
Sells bulk wine.

Château du Grand Bossuet
Present owner Pierre Petit

Château le Grand Cardinal
Present owner André Malescot

Château Grand Cormier
Present owner M J S Marin-Audray (who also owns Châteaux Canon Chaigneau, Tour Canon and Tour Chaigneau)

Château du Grand Moine
Present owners Mme MC Pommier

Château des Grands Moines
Present owners Marc & Michel Tarendeau

Clos des Grand Moines
Present owner Camille Berry (who also owns Clos de l'Eglise in Lalande).

Domaine du Grand Moine
Present owner Jean Casenoube

Château Grandes Nauves
Present owner Jean Christian Grezel

Château Grand Ormeau
Present owner M Vidal

Domaine du Grand-Ormeau
Present owner Jean Paul Garde

Domaine de la Grande Pièce
Present owner Roger Faure

Château la Grande Taillis
Present owner André Pichot

Clos la Grave
Present owner Casimir Bouyge

Château Graves des Annereaux
Present owner Paul Boujut

Château Graves de Brouard
Château du Grand Moine
Present owner Mme Marie Charlotte Ponnier
The soil is sand and gravel. They comprise 7.25 hectares of vines (60% Merlot, 40% Bouchet)

producing from 10 to 23 tonneaux. The oldest vines are sixty years and the youngest eight years.

The grapes are entirely de-stalked and crushed and the juice is fermented in cement or wooden vats for eight to ten days, the skins remaining in the *must* for that time before pressing. Afterwards the wine is matured in casks, from one to four years old, and bottled after two years, having undergone the usual *assemblage*, rackings and fining. Sixty percent of the total production is sold in France, 25% exported to The Netherlands, 10% to Belgium and 5% to Luxembourg.

Château la Gravière
Château Lavaud la Maréchaude
Madam Simone Cascarret, also proprietress of Château Tristan in Pomerol, owns these properties which adjoin the commune of Pomerol which lies just the other side of the Barbanne.

The soil is gravel and sand with a clay sub-soil. There are a little over 5.5 hectares of vines (50% Merlot, 20% Bouchet, 25% Cabernet Sauvignon, 5% Pressac) producing some 25 tonneaux. The oldest vines are thirty-seven years and the youngest three years.

The grapes are completely de-stalked and crushed and the juice is fermented in cement vats for eight days, the skins remaining in contact with the *must* throughout before pressing. Later the wine is transferred to oak casks (three to six years old) and is assembled, racked, fined and matured, before being bottled after eighteen months to two years. Some is exported to Belgium.

Château les Graves de Goujon
Present owner Henri Chanloup

Château Graves Lavergne
Present owner Bernard Besse

Château les Graves de Lavergne
Present owner André Rivière (who also owns Château Haut Châtain)

Pierre Gricolat
Sells bulk wine.

Château Gromel Bel Air
This property, owned by René Delmon, lies on limestone, clay and sandy soil and comprises 3 hectares of vines which produce wine entitled to the Appellation Lalande-de-Pomerol, and 7 hectares producing Bordeaux Supérieur. The vines are 70% Merlot and 30% Bouchet and Cabernet Sauvignon and an average of 13 tonneaux of Lalande-de-Pomerol AC is made.

The oldest vines are thirty years and the youngest two years old.

The grapes are not de-stalked and after crushing the juice is fermented in cement vats for twelve days with the skins remaining in the *must* for that period before the pressing. After the malolactic fermentation the wine is racked off into oak casks (from four to eight years old) and assembled, racked, fined and matured, before being bottled after two years.

Château Guimberteau
Present owner J B Guimberteau

Henri Hamon
Sells bulk wine.

Clos Haut-Bocage
Present owner Guy Blanc

Château Haut-Caillou
Present owner Jean Alphonso

Château Haut Chaigneau
Present owner André Chatonnet (who also owns Château Tour Standre)

Château Haut-Châtain
André Rivière is the owner of this property which is on sand and clay soil. He also owns Château les Graves de Lavergne.

There are 10 hectares of vines (65% Merlot, 15% Bouchet and 20% Cabernet Sauvignon) producing some 36 tonneaux. The oldest vines are fifty years.

The grapes are completely de-stalked and crushed and the juice is fermented for ten days in cement vats, the skins remaining in contact with the *must* throughout before pressing. The wine is then run off into ten-year-old oak casks and assembled, racked, fined and matured in the usual way, before being bottled after about two and a half years. Ninety percent of the total production is sold in France, 10% goes to Belgium.

Château les Hautes Conseillants
Present owner Leopold Figeac

Château Haut Gallvesses
Present owner Villegente Frères

Château Haut Goujon
Present owner Henri Garde

Château Haut Graves Marchesseau
Present owner Robert Jean Luçon

Château Haut-Laborde
Jean Vergne

Château Haut-Surget
Present owner Mollet-Fourreau (who also owns Château la Fleur Vauzelle)

Château les Hautes Tuileries
Present owner Pierre Bourotte

Chateau du Jard
Present owners Palatin-Pinaud (who also own Château Châtain-Pinaud)

Guy Jean
Sells bulk and bottled wine.

Magdelaine Jollivet
Sells bulk wine.

Château Laborde
Present owner Jean Marie Trocard who is the president of the Syndicate of Hallande.

Château Lafaurie
Present owner Roger Thaillet

Louis Laine
Sells bulk wines.

Yves Lamarche
Sells bulk wine.

Annie Largeteau
Sells bulk and bottled wine.

Château Latour Colombier
Present owner Jean Biais

Gisèle Laujais
Sells bulk wine.

H Pierre Laujais
Sells bulk wine.

Château Lavaud Marechaude
Present owner Mme Cascaret (who also owns Château la Gravière)

Michel Lavaye
Sells bulk wine.

Château Lavinot-Lachapelle
Present owner André Deval

Robert Leney
Sells bulk wine.

Bernard Londin
Sells bulk wine.

Irène Lureau
Sells bulk wine.

Domaine Maison Blanche de Queyron
Marc Berteau owns this tiny property which formerly belonged to the Arnaud family. There are 0.75 hectares of vines (70% Merlot, 30%

Bouchet and Cabernet Sauvignon) producing an average of 1.75 tonneaux. The oldest vines are sixteen years.

The grapes are not de-stalked and after crushing the *must* is fermented in cement vats for ten to fifteen days before the pressing. Later the wine is run off into oak casks (average age five years) and assembled, racked, fined, matured and bottled after two years.

Château Marcel Bertineau
Present owner   Marcel Jayle

Château de Marchesseau
Christian Renie owns this property which has belonged to his family since 1880. The soil is gravel and clay. There are 9 hectares of vines (50% Merlot, 25% Bouchet, 20% Cabernet Sauvignon, 5% Pressac) producing some 40 tonneaux in a good year at around 40 hectolitres per hectare. The oldest vines are forty years.

The grapes are completely de-stalked and crushed and the juice is fermented in inox-lined cement vats for six to ten days with the skins remaining in the *must* throughout before pressing. Later the wine is run off into oak casks (three to ten years old) and assembled, racked, fined, matured and bottled after two years. Most of the wine is sold in France but about 8% is exported to Belgium, The Netherlands and Switzerland.

J Bernard Martin
Sells bulk wine.

Château Martinet
Present owner   François de Lavaux

Pierre Melin
Sells bulk wine.

Château la Mission
Pierre Lasserre and JM Garde are the proprietors and they also own Clos René in Pomerol where the wine is vinified. It has been in the family for one generation.

Château des Moines
Present owners   H Darnajou & Frères

Clos des Moines
Present owner   Étienne Martin

Château Moncets
Baron LG and ME de Jerphanion are the owners of this property which has been in this family for over one hundred years. It is near the south-eastern tip of the Néac area, near the border with Montagne-St Émilion. The soil is gravel and clay. There are 17 hectares of vines

(66% Merlot, 33% Bouchet, 1% Cabernet Sauvignon) producing about 66 tonneaux at around 40 hectolitres per hectare. The oldest vines are seventy-four years.

The grapes are completely de-stalked and crushed; the juice is fermented in wood and cement vats for five to fourteen days and the skins remain in the *must* for eight to ten days before being pressed. Later the wine is run off into oak casks (three to twelve years old) and assembled, racked, fined, matured and bottled after fifteen to twenty months.

Domaine de Montbiel
Present owner   R. Brieux

Michel Monteil
Sells wine in bottle and bulk.

Château Mothe de Bertineau
Present owner   Angélo Vedelago (who also owns Château Bois de Laborde).

Château Moulin à Vent
Present owners   Société Immobile des Vignobles Pierre Couffin

Château Moulin-de-Lavaud
Paul Marengo owns this property whose soil is sand and gravel. There are just under 5 hectares (40% Merlot, 50% Bouchet, 10% Cabernet Sauvignon) producing around 20 tonneaux. The oldest vines are sixty years.

The grapes are completely de-stalked and crushed and the juice is fermented in cement vats and the skins remain in contact with the *must* for two to three weeks before pressing. The wine is then transferred to oak casks (average age ten years) and assembled, racked, fined, matured and bottled after two years.

Château Moulin de Salles
Present owner   Marc Albert

Château de Musset
Present owner   Yvonne Foucard

André Roger Niarfeix
Sells wine in bulk and bottle.

Château Nicole
Present owner   Prévôst-Garat (who also owns Château Trianon Beauséjour)

Daniel Nicoux
Sells bulk wine.

Château des Ormeaux
Present owner   Yvonne Petit

Château Perron
Present owner Michel Massonie (who also owns Château Pierrefitte)
12 hectares of vineyard

Domaine de Petit Bois
Present owner Daniel Larnaudie

Clos la Petite Croix
Present owner Louis Zero

Pierre Peyronneau
Sells bulk wine.

Domaine du Pont des Guestres
Present owner J R Rousselot

Charles Pommier
Sells wine in bulk and bottle.

Gaston Privat
Sells bulk wine.

Château la Prunerie
René Martin is the owner of this property in succession to his father. The soil is sand and gravel. There are 2.5 hectares of vines (50% Merlot, 30% Bouchet, 10% Cabernet Sauvignon, 10% Pressac) producing about 8 tonneaux. The oldest vines are twelve years.

The grapes are not de-stalked and after crushing the juice is fermented in cement vats for about two weeks, the skins remaining in contact with the *must* for all that time before pressing. The wine is later transferred to oak casks (average age ten years) and is assembled, racked, fined and matured before being bottled after about eighteen months. Belgium is the main export market.

Pierre J Quet
Sells bulk wine.

Lucien Rabier
Sells bulk wine.

Domaine de Réal
Present owners Société Civile Immobilier Réal

Château de Roquebrune
Present owner Roger Guinjard

Château de Rosaire
Present owner Jean de Robillard (who also owns Château le Fleur St Georges)

Clos les Sabines
Present owner Serge Ratouin

Château le Sabloire du Grand-Moine
Present owner René Vedrenne

Domaine du Sablot
Present owner Pierre Turpeau

Andrée Sabourin
Sells wine in bulk and bottle.

Château Saint André Bellevue
Present owner André Gouzou

Château St Jean de Lauaud
Present owner Louis Feytit

Château Saint Louis
Present owner Heritiers Hautier

Château Saint Michel
Present owner Marcel Lacaze

Château Saint Paul
Present owner Elie Arvouet

V Sartran
Sells wine in bulk.

J G Sautreau
Sells wine in bulk.

Château Sergant
Present owner Jean Milhade (who also owns Château Lyonnat in Lussac and Château des Annereaux in Lalande)

Jean Seynat
Sells wine in bulk and bottle.

Château Siaurac
Baronne Guichard, also proprietor of Château Vraye Croix de Gay in Pomerol and Château le Prieuré-Grand Cru Classé Saint-Émilion, owns this: one of the better-known properties in the area. It is a very large beautiful and imposing property in need of repair. The soil is sand-clay and clay-gravel. Jacques Rougier has been the *Maître de Chai* and *Régisseur* since 1977. There are 23 hectares of vines (55% Merlot, 40% Bouchet, 5% Cabernet Sauvignon) producing some 80 tonneaux.

The Château which is set well-back behind the trees has many acres of parkland. The grapes are 80% de-stalked and crushed and the juice is fermented in cement vats for about six days, the skins remaining in contact with the *must* for three months before being pressed. It is matured first in cement vats and then in oak casks and is assembled, racked, fined and matured before being bottled after eighteen months to two years.

Château du Temple
Present owner Gérard Audigay

J P Tarendean
Sells bulk wine.

Clos Templiers
Present owner   Edmond Meyer

Château Teysson
Present owner   Françoise Dumas
16 hectares (of which 10 are under vine).

Marc Thibeaud
Sells bulk wine.

Pierre Thibeaud
Sells bulk wine.

Château des Treilles l'Embarre
Present owner   Daniel Rebeyrol

André Tridat
Sells bulk wine.

Château des Tourelles
Present owner   F Janoueix

Château Tour Canon
Present owner   M J S Marin-Audray (who also owns Châteaux Canon Chaigneau, Tour Chaigneau and Grand Cormier)

Château Tour Chaigneau
Present owner   M J S Marin-Audray (who also owns Châteaux Canon Chaigneau, Tour Canon, and Grand Cormier)

Château Tour Colombier
Jean Biais owns this property whose soil is sand and gravel. There are 3.5 hectares of vines (70% Merlot, 20% Bouchet, 10% Cabernet Sauvignon) producing around 16 tonneaux. The oldest vines are thirty-one years.

The grapes are not de-stalked and after the crushing the *must* is fermented for ten to fifteen days in cement vats before the pressing. Later the wine is run off into oak casks of varying ages and assembled, racked, fined, matured and bottled after about eighteen months. Some of the wine is exported to Belgium.

Château Tournefeuille
Present owner   Sautarel et Fils who also own Clos-Jean-Voisin in Saint-Émilion and Château de Bourg in Pomerol. This Château is situated on a clayey-gravel soil, unique in Néac, facing the great Pomerols only a few metres away.

Château Tour St André
Present owner   André Chatonnet (who also owns Château Haut Chaigneau)

Château Trianon Beauséjour
Present owner   Prévôst-Garat (who also owns Château Nicole)

Clos la Trielle
Present owners   Champseix et Fils (who also own Château Vieux Chevrol and Domaine du Caillou)

Château Treytins
Present owners   Société Civile Nonoy (who also own Châteaux Garraud and Garaudières)

Clos des Tuileries
Present owner   Fernard Merlet et Fils

Henri Vacher
Sells bulk wine.

A Vedelago
Sells bulk wine.

B Vergnol
Sells bulk wine.

Viaud Grand Chambellan
Present owner   Michèle Mallet (who also owns Château de Viaud)

Château de Viaud
Present owner   Michèle Mallet (who also owns Viaud Grand Chambellan)

Clos de Viaud
Present owner   Roger Faucher

Domaine de Viaud
Present owner   Maurius Bielle

Château Vieux Brouard
Present owner   Jean Mamelat

Château Vieux Chaigneau
Monsieur Berlureau has been the owner of this property since 1977. The soil is predominantly clay. There are 5.25 hectares of vines (55% Merlot, 25% Bouchet, 20% Cabernet Sauvignon) producing about 25 tonneaux. The oldest vines are thirty years.

The grapes are completely de-stalked and crushed and the juice is fermented for about eight days in reinforced concrete vats, the skins remaining in contact with the *must* for about fifteen days before being pressed. The wine is then run off into oak casks (between ten and thirty years old) and assembled, racked, fined, matured and bottled after two years. Most of the wine is sold in France but some is exported to Belgium.

Vieux Château Châtain
Present owner   André Lafaye

Château Vieille Forge
Present owner   Georges Lavaud

Vieux Domaine de Bertineau
Present owner   Lucienne Hattinguais

Vieux Château Gachet
Present owners   Guy et Gérard Arpin

Clos Vieux Laborde
Present owner   Marc Vacher

Château Vieux Noyer
Present owner   Rémi Marlon

Château Voselle
Present owner   Joseph Golin

Château Yveline
This is the property of Ms J and Y Durand and its soil is clay and limestone. There are 4 hectares of vines (60% Merlot, 25% Bouchet, 10% Cabernet Sauvignon, 5% Pressac) producing some 14 tonneaux and at an average of 33 hectolitres per hectare. The oldest vines are eighty years and the youngest six years old.

The grapes are completely de-stalked and crushed and the juice is fermented in cement vats for eight days, the skins remaining in contact with the *must* for three to four weeks before being pressed. The wine is later run off into oak casks (from two to ten years old) and assembled, racked, fined, matured and bottled after two years. The export markets include Belgium and The United Kingdom.

Clos René. Pomerol.

Tasting Notes and Comments on Vintages from 1900 to 1982

We include this chapter both for general interest and to serve as some sort of guide for buyers, especially those interested in older vintages. The notes are arranged according to vintages, starting in 1900, and the date of each tasting is given. We hope that the notes will help to dispel the idea that Saint-Émilions and Pomerols are essentially quick-developing and short-lived wines. It should also be noted that the difference in climatic conditions and the fact that the predominantly Merlot and Bouchet grapes are picked earlier in these areas mean that there can be appreciable difference in quality between Saint-Émilion and Pomerol, and the Médoc; as, for instance in 1950, 1964 and 1971.

Of course, it can only be a very general indication. There are always exceptions: there are some rather disappointing wines in otherwise fine vintages and some surprisingly pleasant ones in bad years. Vinification methods vary, especially the length of *cuvaison*, and this may greatly affect the longevity of the wine. Conditions of storage can also make a great difference and a bottle kept all its life in ideal cellaring conditions is likely to be better after twenty years or so than one which has travelled a lot and changed hands (and temperatures) several times.

Finally, in old age, the condition of each individual cork may cause some variation even between bottles that have been identically cellared all their lives.

The notes are those of a distinguished Master of Wine, Patrick Grubb, Head of Sotheby's Wine Department, the authors Jeffrey Benson and Alastair Mackenzie and Dr Christopher Davenport Jones.

Tasting Notes

1900   A very hot summer producing a very big crop. Excellent weather conditions.
Pavie – tasted 1973
   Medium depth, pale colour with orange rim
   Light, sweet, old Merlot nose
   Still fruity and sweet with old dry finish
Pomerol Lafitte (Scottish-bottled) – tasted 1976
   Medium depth of colour with brown rim
   Surprising amount of fruit and sweetness on the nose
   Light-weight but a good bottle

1901   Mixed, variable weather. There was a lot of rot in the vineyards.

1902   Variable weather conditions resulting in light wines. Vintage late September producing a medium to large crop.
Ausone – tasted 1973
   Medium depth of colour with brown rim
   Old mushroom nose with underlying sweetness
   Still some fruit but faded quickly
l'Évangile – tasted 1975
   Pale colour with brown rim
   Sweet, old vegetable nose
   Dried-out but still a sweet finish

1903   Frost in the spring reduced the harvest. A poor summer resulting in unbalanced wine.

1904 A good summer with good conditions. Excellent vintage producing good quality, long-lived wines.

Ausone – tasted 1979
Medium depth of colour with brown rim
Nice Merlot nose, light
Still sweet, lovely rich old wine

Cheval Blanc – tasted 1978
Light in colour with brown rim
Light, sweet nose, signs of age
Still quite fruity, but dry finish with acidity

la Gaffelière – tasted 1980
Deep depth of colour with brown rim
Old nose, but still rich and sweet
Still there with fruit and sweetness, drying on finish

1905 Good conditions throughout the year somewhat spoilt by rain during the vintage.

1906 Good conditions throughout the year. Very hot summer resulting in wines of high quality.

Canon – tasted 1976
Deep colour with brown rim
Nice, rich, sweet Merlot rot on nose
Still quite rich with dry finish

1907 Good conditions throughout the year giving a large crop.

Cheval Blanc – tasted 1974
Pale depth of colour with orange rim
Madeira nose
Passed its prime but still some sweet fruit, dry finish

1908 Fair conditions throughout the year, producing average crop of reasonable wines.

1909 Good conditions until heavy rains in August and September but improved towards the vintage, producing a fair crop of average wines.

1910 Very poor conditions throughout the year. Improved in September producing a late harvest of indifferent wines.

Clos Fourtet – tasted 1972
Pale in colour with a brown/orange rim
Thin, sweet nose
Drying out but still some fruit in centre

1911 Bad start to the year but weather improved. The year produced a small crop of good quality wine.

Cheval Blanc – tasted 1977
Very old brown colour
Little nose
An interesting wine. Not bad or unpleasant but is not particularly appealing. Has fruit and tannin.

Cheval Blanc – tasted 1980
A good bottle with soft sweet fruit good length and finish

Figeac – tasted 1975
Deep in colour and brown on rim
Ripe, quite rich nose showing age
Still quite a lot of fruit, sweet centre with dry finish

Clos Fourtet – tasted 1974
Very deep colour with brown rim
Quite sweet, violet nose, showing oxidation
Holding quite well, dry finish

Magdelaine – tasted 1975
Medium depth of colour with brown rim
Old agreeable Merlot nose
Still quite a lot of fruit but dry firm finish

Nenin – tasted 1973
Deep in colour and with brown rim
Nice soft sweet nose
Losing fruit but a nice bottle of wine with sweet soft centre

1912 Quite good conditions throughout the year except for August, but still produced a large crop of quite good wines.

1913 Poor conditions throughout the year apart from just before the harvest producing a fairly large crop of indifferent wines.

1914 Good conditions throughout the year. A very hot August. An average crop of good quality.

Beauséjour – tasted 1974
Deep in colour with a brown rim
Age showing above some sweetness
Still holding with quite a lot of sweetness, nice long finish

1915 Very poor conditions throughout the year apart from vintage time resulting in poor quality wines generally.

1916 Good conditions throughout apart from a rainy spring, producing a good crop of reasonable wines, some fairly good, some harsh.

Cheval Blanc – tasted 1966
  Bright red
  Beautiful nose
  Full of flavour – fruit but developed acetic smell

1917   Good conditions throughout; hot summer, resulting in good quality, light-weight wines.

Cheval Blanc – tasted 1974
  Medium colour with brown rim
  Old nose with sweet, violet undertones
  Well-balanced, still fruity and sweet, long finish

Cheval Blanc – tasted 1982
  Mid and brown
  Soft, sweet old Merlot nose
  Still quite fruity with long sweet finish

Figeac – tasted 1979
  Medium colour with brown rim
  Lovely old rich toffee nose
  Still a lot of fruit, fine dry finish

1918   Fine conditions throughout. A good crop, fair quality.

Ausone – tasted 1975
  Medium colour with brown rim
  Lovely sweet rich violet nose
  Still a lot of fruit in the centre but drying quite a lot on the finish

Cheval Blanc – tasted 1972
  Good medium depth of colour with brown rim
  Old nose, but still rich and sweet
  Although old and tired, still fruity, with sweet, dry finish

1919   Variable conditions. Average crop, some good wines and some light wines produced.

1920   Excellent conditions until July to August which was cold and wet reducing crop substantially. Then a good September producing good quality wines.

Ausone – tasted 1977
  Very pale in colour
  Trace of sweetish nose
  Theoretically totally over the top but, in fact, quite drinkable. Very light in fruit, slightly sweet

Ausone – tasted 1978
  Good deep, brown colour
  Nice sweet, violet nose, but showing age
  Well-balanced fruit and sweetness, dry finish

Canon – tasted 1982
  Mid and brown
  Lovely old sweet Merlot nose
  Still has lots of fruit, slightly dry finish

Cheval Blanc – tasted 1975
  Pale in colour with brown rim
  Dried-out nose, slightly fruity centre
  Light, still fruity centre but drying finish

Cheval Blanc – tasted 1981
  Pale in colour with brown rim
  Old sweet, perfumed nose
  Drying out but still soft sweet centre

Cheval Blanc – tasted 1982
  Mid/pale and brown
  Good old rich deep Merlot
  Lots of centre sweet and rich finish

Clos Fourtet – tasted 1980
  Very pale, russet red
  Beautiful, very delicate rose petals and strawberry nose
  Very sweet, lovely, but showing age and fades quickly

Gazin – tasted 1979
  Medium depth of colour with brown rim
  Old mushroom nose but not unpleasant
  Drying out with some fruit in centre

1921   Very hot year, spring frosts. Good summer resulting in very good wines with lasting power.

Ausone – tasted 1975
  Medium depth of colour with brown rim
  Delicate, scented rose-petal nose
  Good depth of fruit, good finish but drying out

Canon – tasted 1974
  Medium depth of colour with brown rim
  Superbly rich violet nose
  Lots of sweet fruit, good finish but slightly drying out

Canon – tasted 1982
  Pale/mid and brown
  Good old rich Merlot nose
  Well-balanced, good, full-bodied finish

Cheval Blanc – tasted 1973
  Deep rich colour, browning
  Lovely ripe rich Merlot rot
  Holding very well with a lot of fruit and sweetness, lovely long finish

Cheval Blanc – re-tasted 1975
  Superbly rich and fine, high alcohol

Cheval Blanc – tasted 1982
  Mid and brown
  Lovely old burnt sugar nose
  Still holding very well with lots of fruit in centre

Long sweet finish

Clos Fourtet – tasted 1978
Deep colour with brown rim
Old rich Merlot, violet nose with slight signs of age
Still a lot of sweetness, dry finish

Clos Fourtet – tasted 1982
Pale/mid and brown
Old sweet violet nose
Rich, ripe, still lots of fruit, drying finish

1922   Wet summer, large vintage. Variable quality.

Vieux-Château-Certan – tasted 1973
Quite a deep colour, browning
Quite sweet, rich, violet nose, showing age
Still a lot of fruit but fading fast

1923   Wet spring, but good warm summer producing good quality wines. Average yield.

Clos René – tasted 1973
Medium depth of colour with brown rim
Showing age but still soft sweet Merlot nose
Still holding fruity centre, dry finish

1924   Poor spring, rain in August, but superb conditions throughout the vintage, producing good quality wine.

Cheval Blanc – tasted 1975
Medium depth of colour with orange/brown rim
Lovely sweet, old Merlot nose
Showing age but still sweet and fruity

Cheval Blanc – tasted 1982
Mid and brown
Good rich ripe old Merlot
Well-balanced still holding very well with rich finish

Clos René – tasted 1973
Good deep brown colour
Still sweet and quite rich with acidity
Drying out but still a lot of fruit in the middle

La Grange à Pomerol – tasted 1981
Pale orange
Old mushroom nose
Totally dried-out, undrinkable

Château Nenin – tasted 1982
Mid and brown
Quite old sweet nose
Still quite fruity but fading fast

1925   Poor conditions, a lot of rain producing a large crop of below average wines.

Cheval Blanc – tasted 1975
Pale in colour with orange rim

Old Madeira-type nose, still some fruit
Over the top and dried-out but still quite fruity

1926   Cold spring, poor flowering. Very hot dry summer producing small crop of very good wines.

Cheval Blanc – tasted 1974
Medium depth with brown rim
Lovely rich sweet chocolate nose
Full, fruity, very rich and sweet
Long, luscious finish

Cheval Blanc – tasted 1982
Mid and brown
Lovely old rich violet nose
Still has lots of fruit, fine firm finish

la Gaffelière-Naudes – tasted 1979
Medium pale in colour with brown rim
Light soft violet Merlot nose
Still a lot of fruit but fading fast, dry finish

1927   Very poor vintage. Rain throughout picking, producing poor-quality wine, average crop.

1928   Perfect conditions throughout, producing superb quality and good crop. Better than the Médoc.

Ausone – tasted 1974
Deep in colour with brown rim
Lovely rich violet nose
Soft, sweet, rich, wonderful finish

Canon – tasted 1974
Medium colour with brown rim
Light pleasant Merlot nose

Cheval Blanc – tasted 1973
Medium depth of colour with brown rim
Lovely rich soft sweet nose
Good fruit and body, slightly drying on finish

Cheval Blanc – tasted 1982
Quite deep and brown
Lovely sweet old violet nose
Good depth of fruit, slightly drying on finish

Figeac – tasted 1974
Good deep colour with brown rim
Lovely old rich Merlot, rotting nose
Good extract, still a super wine

Nenin – tasted 1978
Good brown deep colour
Quite a rich old nose
Slightly drying out in the centre but holding well

Pavie – tasted 1973
Good, rich, deep colour with brown rim
Superb rich violet nose
Lots of fruit and depth, long finish

Vieux-Château-Certan – tasted 1980
  Deep colour with brown rim
  Big deep smell
  Lots of extract and flavour, slightly spicy,
  very fine and rich

1929 Very good conditions throughout. Very
      hot summer producing very good wines
      and average crop.
Ausone – tasted 1980
  Good deep colour
  Rich, sweet, caramel nose
  Good fruit and body, dry finish
Belair – tasted 1975
  Medium depth of colour with brown rim
  Nice fruit with some age
  Drying out but still very drinkable
Bel-Air (Lalande de Pomerol) – tasted 1982
  Deep and very brown
  Old mushroom nose but a lot of sweet depth
  underneath
  Still sweet and rich with immense con-
  centration on the finish
Canon – tasted 1975
  Medium/deep colour with brown rim
  Quite light on the nose but delicate fruit
  Nice body, light centre, firm finish
Cheval Blanc – tasted 1975
  Lovely, rich, deep colour with brown rim
  Huge, sweet nose – superb
  Long, rich, full-bodied, superb finish
Cheval Blanc – tasted 1982
  Mid and brown
  Lovely rich ripe Merlot nose
  Still holding well with firm fruity finish
Roudier – tasted 1982
  Very deep colour with brown rim
  Lovely, old, rich, chocolate, vegetable nose
  Superb, rich, deep, lots of fruit, long, super
  finish
Rouget – tasted 1976
  Great depth of colour with brown rim
  Mature nose showing signs of age
  Hard big wine, fair amount of residual fruit, a
  delight to drink but slightly past its prime
Rouget – tasted 1978
  Full depth of colour
  Fresh clarety nose
  A remarkable wine, tasting as though ten to
  twenty years old
  Perfectly preserved, quite dry and full-
  bodied, classic and perfect claret. Exceptional
Rouget – tasted 1980
  Good deep colour with brown rim
  Superb, rich, full-bodied, sweet nose

Hardly any signs of age. Superb balance, rich
finish fading after twenty minutes

1930 Bad weather conditions throughout the
      year producing poor quality and quan-
      tity.

1931 Poor spring but good summer produc-
      ing average crop of below average
      quality.
Cheval Blanc – tasted 1979
  Pale in colour with brown rim
  Old decaying, Merlot nose but still pleasant
  Still holding, fruity centre with very dry
  finish
Cheval Blanc – tasted 1982
  Mid and very brown
  Old mushroom nose
  Still quite fruity and sweet with dry finish

1932 Poor conditions throughout the year
      producing poor quality wine and below-
      average crop.

1933 Not very good weather but good in
      patches, producing some good wines.
      Below-average crop.
Canon – tasted 1978
  Pale depth of colour with brown rim
  Old, sweet, Merlot nose
  Dried-out, slightly sweet finish
Cheval Blanc – tasted 1973
  Pale in colour with brown rim
  Nice sweet, chocolate, light nose
  Quite sweet, light centre, nice finish
Cheval Blanc – tasted 1982
  Pale and brown
  Quite sweet nose
  Fairly fruity, lacks centre now, firm quite
  fruity finish
la Fleur Pétrus – tasted 1978
  Deep in colour with brown rim
  Superb rich, sweet, Merlot nose
  Good rich, sweet fruit, faded after twenty
  minutes of opening

1934 Good conditions producing good qual-
      ity wines, with a large crop.
Ausone – tasted 1974
  Good deep colour with brown edge
  Lovely soft, Merlot nose
  A lot of fruit, still holding well
Canon – tasted 1981
  Medium depth of colour with brown rim
  Slight mushroom nose, and sweet fruit
  Full, fruity, amazingly young palate

Cheval Blanc – tasted 1975
  Medium depth of colour with brown rim
  Light, but sound, rich nose
  Good fruit, long, fruity, sweet finish
Cheval Blanc – re-tasted 1978
  Pale in colour
  Rich, cheesy nose
  Very rich, perfect balance, full, marvellous
  finish

1935 Poor conditions with a lot of rain, producing a lot of below-average wines.

1936 Poor weather conditions but sun during the vintage, producing below-average crop and indifferent wines.
Cheval Blanc (half-bottle) – tasted 1976
  Soft wine, very old, weak and really finished, almost cabbage water
la Fleur Pétrus – tasted 1975
  Medium depth of colour with brown edge
  Nice, sweet, old nose
  Quite rich centre, very nice wine
la Fleur Pétrus (Magnum) – tasted 1981
  Medium depth of colour with brown edge
  Good, rich, truffle nose
  Round, soft, good fruit, slightly drying on finish but a super wine
Nenin – tasted 1976
  Pale colour with brown rim
  Old cabbage nose
  Dried-out, over the top

1937 Dry summer with lack of rain. Good harvest, average quantity, producing hard, tannic wine with high acidity.
Ausone – tasted 1971
  Medium depth of colour with brown rim
  Lovely rich truffle nose
  Good fruit and body, slightly drying on finish
Cheval Blanc – tasted 1978
  Deep brown/red in colour
  Good fruity, sweet nose and acidity
  Hard with light centre, drying finish, still holding
Cheval Blanc – tasted 1982
  Deep and brown
  Good rich deep violet nose
  Firm, fruity dry finish
Figeac – tasted 1976
  Medium depth of colour with brown edge
  Nice soft, Merlot nose showing age
  Quite rich and fruity, dry, firm finish
la Fleur Pétrus – tasted 1978
  Medium depth of colour with brown rim

Good fruity, sweet nose still holding
Nice, sweet, fruity wine, faded fast to a very dry finish

1938 Late vintage, below-average quantity and quality, producing light wines with high acidity.
Cheval Blanc – tasted 1976
  Rather pale, poor colour
  Quite good nose
  Light in fruit, acidity showing through, rather odd style
Cheval Blanc – tasted 1982
  Mid/pale and brown
  Old mushroom dank nose
  Dried-out with acidity on finish

1939 Variable summer with rain producing large quantity, light-weight but quite well-balanced wines.

1940 Well-balanced weather throughout the year, producing average crop, reasonable quality, mostly faded now.
la Fleur Pétrus – tasted 1973
  Medium depth with brown rim
  Still quite fruity but old nose
  Losing fruit very quickly, dry finish

1941 Wet spring, good summer. Small quantity of below-average wines.

1942 Good spring and summer but poor conditions during the harvest, producing a small crop of light, indifferent wines.
la Fleur Pétrus – tasted 1973
  Pale depth of colour, brown rim
  Old cabbage nose
  Lost fruit, dry finish
la Fleur Pétrus (Magnum) – tasted 1981
  Medium depth, brown edge
  Slight acidity but good, old nose
  Dried-out, but just there in the centre

1943 Good conditions throughout producing average crop of good well-balanced wine.
Cheval Blanc – tasted 1970
  Beautiful nose
  Still very fruity
  Fat with perfect balance
Cheval Blanc – tasted 1975
  Medium red colour with brown rim
  Old, interesting chocolate nose
  Still holding but faded fast in the glass

Cheval Blanc – tasted 1982
  Mid/deep and brown
  Lovely soft sweet violet nose
  Still holding well, good fruit and finish
Croix de Gay – tasted 1976
  Pale brown tawny in colour
  Nice, rather slight nose, quite sweet
  Dry, light style of wine with sweet finish
  Old-style wine in fairly good shape. Obviously a light-weight wine.
Croix de Gay – tasted 1978
  Mid-pale colour with brown rim
  Peppery nose with high acidity
  Dry, fairly fruitless
Figeac – tasted 1981
  Colour very pale to dark
  Nose slightly metallic to full grapey
  Lack of flavour to full overblown
la Fleur Pétrus – tasted 1973
  Pale in colour with brown edge
  Light, sweet nose with age
  Losing fruit and centre, dry finish

1944 Hot summer with some rainfall producing large crop of unbalanced quality, variable from Château to Château.
Beau-Séjour (Fagouet) – tasted 1981
  Pale in colour with brown rim
  Quite delicate, light, still fruity
  Showing a lot of signs of age but still holding
Beau-Séjour (Fagouet) – tasted 1982
  No decanting time given
  Medium colour, brown edge
  Only a slight bouquet, old plums
  A very light-weight wine, mean, watery, retaining a trace of fruit, just Merlot in style. Remarkable in that it showed no signs of old age such as acidity or oxidisation, as though much younger

1945 Crop vastly reduced by May frosts. Very hot, dry summer producing superb long-lasting wine.
Ausone – tasted 1973
  Very deep in colour and browning at edge
  Huge, sweet, soft nose
  Very rich, luscious, well-balanced wine
Canon – tasted 1980
  Big rich brown/red colour
  Superb, soft, sweet Merlot rot nose
  Massive fruit and sweetness, luscious finish
la Carte – tasted 1980
  Very deep red with brown rim
  Concentrated truffle/violet nose
  Lovely balance, rich, full, superb finish

la Carte – tasted 1982
  Opaque and brown
  Slight volatile acidity but fruity chocolate nose
  Lots of fruit and depth
  Has rich finish and high alcohol
Cheval Blanc – tasted 1975
  Deep red in colour with brown rim
  Big deep, rich concentrated nose
  Lovely rich sweet wine, long full finish
Cheval Blanc – tasted 1982
  Deep brown
  Full fruity sweet rich nose
  Lots of fruit, long sweet finish
Corbin d'Éspagne (LB Berry Bros) – tasted 1982
  Very deep in colour with brown rim
  Lovely rich violet nose, immense concentration
  Huge weight in the mouth, a lot of fruit, lovely rich finish
la Dominique – tasted 1952
  Deep colour
  Fine nose
  Clean palate, quite pleasant, but still tannic
Figeac – tasted 1975
  Deep rich brown colour
  Lovely full rich ripe Merlot nose
  Lots of rich fruit, superb balance, lovely finish
la Gaffelière-Naudes (Magnum) – tasted 1980
  Good deep colour with brown rim
  Elegant, closed-up, no signs of age
  Quite shy, but rich fruit, needs two hours decanting time as still firm and tough
Gazin – tasted 1978
  Very deep colour, brown edge
  Powerful nose, slightly tart, prickle
  Very rich and lots of tannin, but fruit there. Needs another twenty years. Later – develops well.
Gazin – tasted 1978
  Classic 1945 colour, dark mahogany
  Deep rich lovely old clarety nose
  Requires some decanting time – 1 hour given in this case
  Initial acidity as seen in so many 1945's. This disappears
  Great depth of flavour, full of character, real style of 1945
  Very refined and cedary. Very fine bottle
Magdelaine – tasted 1976
  Very deep red with brown rim
  Good rich, ripe Merlot nose with slight signs of age
  Slightly drying out but still a lot of sweetness

Pavie – tasted 1952
   Raspberry nose
   Smooth velvety, very fruity and good length
Pétrus – tasted 1973
   Very deep red
   Rich, sweet, a lot of extract
   A lot of fruit, rich centre, tannic finish
Pétrus – tasted 1980
   Very deep red, tawny edge
   Slight dank smell, very strong extract of flavour
   Superb meat, very rich and elegant
de Sales – tasted 1978
   Deep red with brown rim
   Full blown violet/truffle nose
   Slightly drying out on finish but lots of centre
Soutard – tasted 1980
   Deep red with brown rim
   Old rather Médocain nose but very concentrated
   Plenty of flavour, quite hard on the finish
Soutard – re-tasted 1982
   Deep red with brown rim
   Lovely rich chocolate nose
   Superb, rich, fruity wine, long finish

1946 Wet year with quite hot summer. Poor conditions during vintage, producing small crop of variable quality from poor to mediocre.
Beau-Séjour (Fagouet) – tasted 1980
   Deep red with brown rim
   Rich, deep, chocolate, truffle nose with acidity
   Drying out, palate not as promising as the nose
   High acidity on finish
Cheval Blanc – tasted 1956
   Very dark in colour
   Lovely fruity, velvety nose
   Rich round, perfect balance, short finish

1947 Excellent conditions throughout the year producing superb wine of long-lasting quality, better than 1945 and 1949 in Saint-Émilion.
Ausone – tasted 1974
   Very deep in colour with brown rim
   Lovely rich sweet nose
   Superb balance of fruit, good extract, long finish
Ausone – tasted 1975
   Big, deep colour with brown rim
   Superbly rich ripe Merlot nose
   Very full, long, fruity wine

Balestard-la-Tonnelle – tasted 1980
   Deep red in colour with brown rim
   Very soft and rich, no signs of age
   Sweet, soft, very good depth and extract, long rich finish, high alcohol
Balestard-la-Tonnelle – re-tasted 1981 and 1982
   Same as above
Belair – tasted 1978
   Very unyielding, tough and slightly dried tannic wine
   Very interesting and a pleasure to drink
Belair LB – tasted 1981
   Very deep in colour with brown rim
   Rich deep truffle nose
   A very good bottle, lovely rich sweet fruit and long finish
Canon (Magnum) – tasted 1979
   Deep in colour
   Very full nose
   Fat and nice, lovely wine
Canon – tasted 1980
   Very deep colour with brown rim
   Deep rich mature nose, violets
   Big rich flavour, long finish, a lovely wine
la Carte – tasted 1980
   Deep in colour with brown rim
   Light, violet nose
   Soft, attractive, silky with tannin
   Faint burnt after-taste
Cheval Blanc – tasted 1964
   Delicately perfumed nose
   Beautiful, full, well-balanced, still length and lots of potential
Cheval Blanc – tasted 1975
   Very deep opaque
   Superb, rich, full, powerful, violet bouquet
   Very rich, full-bodied, sweet, superb wine, very long finish
Cheval Blanc – tasted 1976
   Dark in colour
   Huge wine with great depth and very tannic, so much so that it had dried out and made it like Dow – medicinal port style, hence, did not drink easily, far too hard
Cheval Blanc – tasted 1976
   Tremendous colour hardly showing any age
   Nose a little closed
   Very full fat wine, good balance of tannin, great length
Cheval Blanc (Belgian-bottled) – tasted 1978
   Good colour with brown rim
   Tight, ungiving nose
   Sweet, quite soft but drying out
Cheval Blanc (Belgian-bottled) – tasted 1978
   Tawny oxidised edge
   Beautiful, rich, sweet wine

Great fruit and tannin, excellent follow through
Slightly acetic nose

Cheval Blanc – tasted 1978
Deep in colour with brown rim
Good soft rich nose
Very rich, a lot of extract, full finish with tannin

Cheval Blanc – tasted 1978
Deep colour
Closed nose
Very rich, smooth, lovely sweet and rich

Cheval Blanc (Magnum) – tasted 1978
Very deep purple/red
Slightly earthy nose
Top sweetness, tannin and fruit, enormously rich, great depth, needs time

Cheval Blanc – tasted 1980
Very dark
Huge plummy nose, very powerful
Very rich and full of fruit, goes on with great length

la Croix de Gay (half-bottle) – tasted 1975
Pale in colour
Caramel, rich nose
Lovely wine, very sweet, quite light in fruit, perfect old claret

Croque-Michotte – tasted 1955
Very strong colour
Lovely raspberry nose
Good, fruity, full-bodied

de Ferrand (L B Hedges & Butler) – tasted 1959
A nice little wine but not exciting, hard sharp finish

la Fleur Pétrus – tasted 1975
Medium colour with brown rim
Good rich truffle nose with signs of age
Good depth of fruit, still a lot of centre, drying on finish

la Fleur Pétrus – re-tasted 1981
Still the same as above but drying more on finish

Figeac – tasted 1973
Very deep in colour with brown rim
Superb, rich, chocolate nose
Enormous fruit and depth of extract, very long finish

Fonroque – tasted 1980
Medium depth of colour with brown rim
Good, soft, fruity
Slightly light centre, high acidity on finish

la Gaffelière-Naudes (Magnum) – tasted 1980
Very deep in colour with brown rim
Enormous depth of fruit, sweet and smooth
Fully-developed, amazing rich, sweetness, excellent balance, long superb finish

Gazin (LB) – tasted 1981
Deep colour with brown rim
Very deep rich, chocolate, superb, no signs of age
Rich, very full, long superb finish and centre

Mazeyres – tasted 1978 and 1980
One had two hours decanting, the other none. Both were similar
Dark, concentrated colour
Lovely big clarety nose, waxy
Nice balance, good fruit, perfect old maturity, typical old claret, tasting of bees-wax

Monbousquet – tasted 1977
Strange wine, very unyielding and dried-out somewhat, leaving rather tough backbone. Similar to some other 1947's in hardness. Lacks style

Nenin – tasted 1980
Deep colour with brown rim
Lovely, truffle, mature Merlot nose
Lots of fruit, soft, rich, long finish

Pavie – tasted 1960
Light red colour
Good nose
Big and fruity with some acidity and tannin

Pétrus (Belgian-bottled) – tasted 1978
Deep colour with brown rim
Light-weight, lacks depth, slightly dry finish

Pétrus (Belgian-bottled) – tasted 1978
Huge, deep colour
Fantastic rich nose
Outstanding rich taste, supple, far better than Belgian-bottled Cheval Blanc

Pétrus – tasted 1980
Very strong red with tawny edge
Great farmyard smell
Lovely, sweet palate, dry after-taste

Rouget – tasted 1976
Lovely purple colour, hardly any brown
Nose full and slightly sweet and perfumed
Lovely fruity wine, great balance, sweetish and perfect maturity, dries on finish

Rouget – tasted 1978
Superb depth of colour, well-matured
Good soft perfumed nose
Very fruity, soft, perfect balance, long finish

Trottevieille (BB) – tasted 1981
Deep in colour with brown rim
Deep and rich, slight volatile acidity
High acidity, overpowering, a deep rich sweet wine

Haut-Sarpe – tasted 1982
Fine, bright, dark, mature, red colour
Firm rather tannic wine, losing its fruit now and drying out somewhat, rather austere
Now a shadow of its potential but still drinks

well as an interesting old claret entering its 'final stage'

1948   Very hot spring, warm summer with a lot of rain producing below-average quantity, quite good quality.

Belair – tasted 1980
 Medium colour with brown rim
 Old mushroom nose, sweet underneath
 Quite nice fruit, good depth of fruit and acidity, nice long finish

Cheval Blanc – tasted 1959
 Overloaded with acid, but had some fruit, still holding something

Cheval Blanc – tasted 1975
 Deep colour with brown rim
 Soft, sweet, chocolate nose
 Good, rich, fruit and balance, nice soft finish

Cheval Blanc (Magnum) – tasted 1978
 Deep colour
 Lovely delicate nose, better than first growths
 Drying finish, good wine

Cheval Blanc – tasted 1982
 Mid and brown
 Fruity, quite intense violet nose
 Good fruit but high acidity on finish

la Conseillante – tasted 1979
 Good, deep, rich colour
 Full, mature, ripe, Merlot rot, similar to Pinot Noir
 Good, full, mature, good rich finish

Pétrus – tasted 1980
 Very strong tawny red
 Farmyard smell
 Starts with a little fruit and then breaks up

Peyreau – tasted 1975
 Deep colour with brown edge
 Tight, tough nose
 Quite fruity, but slightly sour, unbalanced palate

Peyreau – tasted in 1977
 Bit unbalanced in some respects. Not really mature either
 Rather awkward wine

Plince (L B Brooks Boodle) – tasted 1954
 Quite pleasant, but not a great wine

1949   Spring ruined by *coulure*, very hot dry summer, small quantity but good quality.

Chauvin (B B Calvet) – tasted 1954
 Very well-developed and balanced. Clean and fruity

Chauvin (B B Calvet) – tasted 1954
 Has more body and is far more attractive

Cheval Blanc – tasted 1978
 Deep colour with brown rim
 Very soft, sweet, rich nose
 Lovely, rich, chocolate. Long finish

Cheval Blanc – tasted 1960
 Good colour
 Nose deep velvety
 Full and quite good balance. Fattish, finished roundly

Clos Fourtet (Magnum) – tasted 1982
 Very deep colour with brown rim
 Rich, sweet, ripe Merlot nose
 Masses of ripe fruit, slightly drying on finish

l'Évangile – tasted 1981
 Very deep colour with brown rim
 Lovely, rich, sweet, chocolate, showing age
 Slightly drying out, but still a lot of sweet fruit in the centre

Gazin – tasted 1981
 Pale colour with brown rim
 Madeira nose but sweet
 Drying out but still fruity in centre

Gravet (B B Calvet) – tasted 1954
 Pleasant nose
 Rather light wine, lacks fruit

Gravet (E B) – tasted 1955
 Good colour but light
 Nice fruity nose
 Round and full but finishes a little sharply

Pétrus – tasted 1975
 Deep colour with brown rim
 Lovely rich, deep, truffle nose
 Lots of fruit, still deep and rich, long finish

Pétrus – tasted 1980
 Strong russet red
 Powerful nose
 True claret style, more Médoc except for sweetness
 Gorgeous fruit, drying out towards finish

Peyreau – tasted 1975
 Lovely colour, dark concentrated red
 Good firm nose with acidity
 Slightly immature, firm wine with plenty of tannin and some acidity, good fruit, quite tough

la Tour-du-Pin-Figeac (E B Avery) – tasted 1959
 Dark red colour
 Sweet big nose
 Good big wine with some tannin. Nice balance

Vignonet (L B) – tasted 1980
 Deep colour with brown rim
 Rich, soft, sweet nose
 Lovely depth of fruit, well-balanced finish

1950 Good spring and hot summer. Some rain during the vintage resulting in an abundant crop of variable quality. Some Saint-Émilions excellent, for example *Figeac*.

Cheval Blanc – tasted 1973
Nose soft and slightly acetic at tail
Fruit and some depth, but drying out

Cheval Blanc (LB J. Lyons) – tasted 1981
Pale in colour, brown rim
Oxidised, well past its best

Cheval Blanc – tasted 1982
Mid/pale and brown
Light-weight, quite fruity nose
Some fruit in centre, dry finish

la Commanderie – tasted 1952
Very harsh

la Commanderie – tasted 1952
Fruity, heavy nose. Slightly bitter

Croque-Michotte (E B) – tasted 1955
Very good colour
Good fruity nose
Lovely and full, but on the hard side at finish

Croque-Michotte (E B) – tasted 1956
Light red colour
Nice nose
Pleasantly fruity, round, supple and clean

Figeac – tasted 1980
Deep colour
Vegetable nose
Very full of fruit, excellent, slight leafy taste, good length

Figeac – tasted 1980
Good depth of colour with browning rim
Superbly rich, almost Pinot Noir
Strong, full, excellent balance, excellent fruit

la Fleur Pétrus – tasted 1975
Medium colour with brown rim
Nice rich, sweet, violet nose, showing age
Nice fruit and centre, slightly drying on finish

la Fleur Pétrus – tasted 1981
Good deep colour with brown rim
Old toffee, truffle nose
Drying out but good rich centre

la Gaffelière-Naudes– tasted 1982
V/deep and brown
Good rich pine-kernel nose
Lots of fruit and body, good finish

le Gay (LB Averys) – tasted 1981
Deep colour with brown rim
Superb depth of fruit
Rich, full finish

Gazin – tasted 1952
Sweeter than some others of this vintage
No great depth

Pétrus – tasted 1959
Nice nose
Good fat wine, fruit drops a little at the finish

Pétrus – tasted 1973
Deep colour, browning rim
Good thick, rich nose, some acidity showing
Good fruit, slightly light centre and finish

Peyreau – tasted 1980
Very dark colour
Pleasant old claret nose
Rather light-weight, fruit gone, hence now rather past it but drinks well all the same, not tannic

Soutard – tasted 1980
Very deep in colour with brown rim
Remarkable nose
Rather like a fine old St Éstephe. Very good texture, weight and balance, in perfect condition, no trace of age

Soutard – re-tasted 1981
Superb

Vieux-Château-Certan – tasted 1976
Good deep colour with brown rim
Lovely, rich, well-balanced truffle nose
Sweet, rich, lovely chocolate finish

1951 Poor vintage, too much rain and cold, not enough sunshine. Late vintage, resulting in poor, thin, acidic wines. Much better in Saint-Émilion than the Médoc.

Cheval Blanc – tasted 1959
Pale red
Soft, round, a little sweet, but very light

Cheval Blanc – tasted 1974
Quite pale and an orange rim
Quite fruity and soft but with high acidity
Faded but a pleasant light-weight wine

Cheval Blanc – tasted 1982
Pale and brown
Quite sweet old nose
Drying out fast

1952 A success in Saint-Émilion and Pomerol. Warm spring, good summer with some rain. Not good vintaging conditions which were cold and rainy resulting in below-average quantity, but good quality. Now fading in most instances.

Ausone – tasted 1962
Pale russet colour
Nose delicate and old
Fair fruit, soft, but falls away. Not long to live

Ausone – tasted 1976
Good colour with brown rim
Soft, sweet, fruity nose
Slightly drying out on the palate

Ausone (Belgian-bottled) – tasted 1978
Lovely tawny colour
Very delicate cedar nose
Superb fruit and fat

Ausone – tasted 1978
Nice firm tannic nose
Big wine, lots of tannin, creamy despite its toughness, opens up into a real Saint-Émilion. Good

Ausone (L B half-bottle) – tasted 1981
Medium, deep colour, brown rim
Slightly oxidised nose but still fruity
Delicate but drying out

Belair (B B) – tasted 1953
Nice nose, full and fruity

Belair – tasted 1953
Fresh nose rather thin wine

Belair (E B) – tasted 1978
Highly mature, sweet, rich style, tasting very well at present

Cheval Blanc – tasted 1979
Good deep, rich colour with brown edge
Lovely, sweet, chocolate nose
A lot of depth and fruit, good balance, long firm finish

Cheval Blanc – tasted 1981
Deep colour with brown edge
Thick, rich, soft, sweet, violet nose
Very good, rich balance, lovely finish

Cheval Blanc (L B Harveys) – tasted 1981
Quite pale colour with brown rim
Light, sweet, chocolate nose
Light-weight, lacks charm and body, high acidity on the finish

Cheval Blanc – tasted 1982
Deep and brown
Lovely rich deep violet nose
Lots of fruit and lovely long finish

Clos Fourtet – tasted 1977
Good deep colour with orange rim
Strong, sweet, rich nose
Well-balanced, slightly high acidity but good fruit

Clos Fourtet – tasted 1978
Darkish, lovely colour, mature rim
Nice stylish, clarety nose
Medium maturity, a very nice wine indeed, lovely fruit
Much more typical of a Médoc wine

la Croix Figeac (B B) – tasted 1953
Round, but rather watery

la Croix Figeac – tasted 1953
Big robust and fruity, quite nice

Figeac (B B) – tasted 1953
Quite nice and fruity but rather thin finish

la Fleur Pétrus – tasted 1981
Deep colour, brown rim
Witchazel nose but rich and sweet
Rich and deep but drying quickly

la Fleur Pomerol – tasted 1979
Good colour, brown rim
Good soft, sweet Merlot
Well-balanced, good fruit, slightly light centre, good finish

la Gaffelière-Naudes – tasted 1979
Medium colour, brown rim
Good soft, Merlot nose
Well-balanced, good fruit, slightly light finish

la Gaffelière-Naudes (B B) – tasted 1953
Nice nose, but a little thin with a dusty nose

la Gaffelière-Naudes (Magnum) – tasted 1966
Excellent, deep colour, fruity and very fine

la Gay – tasted 1959
Quite a fruity nose, softish, but lacks depth

Gomband-Guillot (B B) – tasted 1953
Lovely nose, fruity, round and plenty of body

Magdelaine – tasted 1979
Brown colour
Totally oxidised
Fruit dried-out

Magdelaine – re-tasted 1981
Better bottle although showing a lot of age on the palate

Magdelaine – re-tasted 1982
Same as 1981 above

Nenin – tasted 1979
Deep colour, brown rim
Good sweet, chocolate, Merlot nose
Good depth of fruit, nice finish with tannin

Pétrus – tasted 1974
Deep colour, orange rim
Tight, closed, sweet nose
A lot of extract, good balance, long finish

Pétrus – tasted 1980
Pale, russet red
Fine nose
Very supple, fat and fruity, good follow

Trotanoy – tasted 1976
Deep colour, red/brown rim
Deep, rich nose
Elegant with great finesse, good, rich finish

1953 Superb vintage. Variable spring with some frost. Superb hot summer, some rain in September. Late harvest in good conditions.

Cheval Blanc – tasted 1971
    Very deep fine colour
    Elegant nose, almost creamy
    Very big fine flavour, smooth, slightly burnt after-taste
Cheval Blanc (E B – Corney & Barrow) – tasted 1977
    Deep red, brown edge
    Very leafy/blackcurrant nose
    Huge wine with great depth
Cheval Blanc – tasted 1979
    A very big wine, very stylish and a trace closed, almost to the point of detracting from the wine. Not showing the usual metallic style, nor burgundian, nor sweet
Cheval Blanc – tasted 1980
    Good deep colour with brown rim
    Deep, rich, truffle nose
    Great finesse, slightly dumb and unforthcoming, but great depth and extract
Figeac – tasted 1982
    Deep colour with brown edge
    Rich, deep, violet nose
    Great depth of fruit, rich centre
    Slightly dry finish
la Fleur Pétrus – tasted 1976
    Deep in colour, brown rim
    Lovely, rich, truffle nose
    Good depth of fruit, long finish
la Fleur Pétrus – tasted 1981
    Good, dark colour, brown rim
    Lovely, rich, soft, chocolate nose
    A lot of depth, soft, superb wine
la Gaffelière-Naudes – tasted 1982
    Quite deep with brown rim
    Delicate, sweet, rich nose
    Charming and sweet, slightly drying on finish
Gazin (E B Hedges & Butler) – tasted 1980
    Tawny/red
    Perfumed
    Lovely, fruity, almost sweet but good length
Magdelaine – tasted 1979
    Medium in colour, brown rim
    Oxidised nose
    Dried-out fruit
Magdelaine – re-tasted 1981
    Slightly better bottle but still dried-out
Pavie – tasted 1975
    Very deep colour with orange rim
    Superb, full, fruity, sweet nose
    Excellent fruit and a lot of depth
Pétrus – tasted 1963
    Great depth of colour
    Superb balance, great
Pétrus – tasted 1967
    Nose develops into true clarety nose. Big

liquid, trace acetic, typical full claret, lacks definition, drinks nicely
Pétrus – tasted 1980
    Good strong red
    No nose
    Still some tannin, no fruit, drying out
Vieux-Château-Certan – tasted 1978
    Lovely, rich, deep colour with brown rim
    Superb, sweet, rich, chocolate nose
    Long, full, well-balanced, long finish

1954 Cold spring and summer and rain. Sun in September, rain during the vintage, resulting in low crop, generally poor-quality wines, with the odd exceptions.
Cheval Blanc – tasted 1959
    Fattish, but straight, flowery nose. Good colour
    Has body and fruit but lacks any great depth
Cheval Blanc – tasted 1976
    Very mature colour
    Sweet rich nose
    Very rich wine, sweet, big and highly mature. Very pleasant but this was a personal liking being a bit overdone
    A little burgundian in style, almost mushroomy
Cheval Blanc (half-bottle) – tasted 1978
    Good deep colour, browning at edge
    Green, stalky, some fruit and sweetness
    Odd dryness, fruitless, some tannin and acidity
Cheval Blanc – tasted 1981
    Deep colour, brown rim
    Oxidised nose, very chocolatey
    Quite thin with high acidity, very thin finish
Cheval Blanc – tasted 1982
    Pale and orange
    Dried-out completely
la Gaffelière-Naudes (half-bottle) – tasted 1978
    Remarkably full, big wine for year. Tasting very pleasant at present

1955 Variable spring, good hot summer, rain in September, resulting in good yield of excellent quality, some now fading.
Ausone – tasted 1978
    Good, deep colour with brown rim
    A lot of fruit and sweetness
    Quite rich, good centre, slightly dry finish
Beau-Séjour (Fagouet) – tasted 1980
    Brownish red
    Thin, old burgundy nose
    Rather unpleasing in the mouth
    Thin, and acidity on finish

Canon (St Georges) – tasted 1976
Very unusual wine. Incredibly soft and unclarety in many respects, yet has enough body to last a good while
Canon (Magnum) – tasted 1980
Very deep colour, brown rim
Very rich, superb chocolate, Merlot
Huge, a lot of alcohol, rich, sweet
Still tannin on the finish
Cap de Mourlin – tasted 1980
Very fine red
Nice, but unexciting, very tannic finish
Cap de Mourlin – tasted 1980
Medium depth of colour, brown rim
Good, deep, rich, sweet, violet
Superb fruit, rich, sweet, long finish
Cheval Blanc – tasted 1976
Good depth with brown rim
Lovely rich, soft nose
Superb, rich, delicious
Cheval Blanc – tasted 1976 (2nd bottle)
A little flat and tired at the finish
Cheval Blanc – tasted 1978
Very refined, classic claret, perfect maturity
The Merlot is so concentrated and well-made that it is like Cabernet. Delicious and suave
Cheval Blanc (Belgian-bottled) – tasted 1978
Huge colour
Nose sweet
Very powerful, great richness and tannin
Cheval Blanc – tasted 1980
Still deep centre, tawny edge
Very fine perfume, real Saint-Émilion
Slightly acetic on nose
Excellent fruit and depth, beginning to dry out a little
Cheval Blanc – tasted 1980
Good depth, brown rim
Good fruit and acidity
Quite soft and sweet, slightly lacking depth. Drying on the finish
Cheval Blanc – re-tasted 1981
Fading in the glass
Cheval Blanc – tasted 1982
Mid/deep and orange
Nice rich deep Merlot nose
Good fruit and balance in centre
Quite high acidity on finish
Clos Fourtet – tasted 1975
Very black colour
Superb fat wine with tannin, balanced. Fabulous
Clos René – tasted 1978
Deep colour, very brown rim
Merlot sweetness, and rotting vegetation

Full-bodied, rich and sweet, high alcoholic finish
Clos René – tasted 1979
Light nose
Lovely old-style claret retaining some tannin and still well-knit. A sort of text-book old Pomerol with firm, hard, earthy fruit. Very pleasant (deteriorated progressively after opening)
Clos René – tasted 1982
Very deep in colour, brown rim
Truffle, sweet, Merlot nose
Superbly rich, lovely long finish
la Commanderie (LB Harveys) – tasted 1977
Average colour
Delicate, nice fruity nose
Wine is of delicate style, well-balanced, still in youthful form. Develops in glass and sweetness shows
Corbin-Michotte – tasted 1975
Smells of clotted cream
Medium-weight wine, showing acidity but with a good style
l'Évangile – tasted 1978
Good, dark red
Fine fruity nose
Very full of fruit and meat, slight toughness at finish
Lasts well. More perfume develops on nose later
Figeac – tasted 1975
Deep, black red
Great fruit on nose
Almost hint of sweetness
Latour à Pomerol (LB Averys) – tasted 1977
Opens up slowly, nicely mature wine, quite full ultimately, and well-balanced. Tastes younger
Latour à Pomerol (LB Averys – half-bottle) – tasted 1979
Sweet, rich, burgundian-style nose
Big fruity wine, drinks very nicely, dry finish with glycerine
Martinet – tasted 1972
Brown
Dried-out, completely over the top
Undrinkable
Moulin St Georges Pavie – tasted 1979
Lovely russet red
No nose
Very elegant and fruity, rather short finish
Pavie – tasted 1959
Rather oily nose
Some fruit but has little depth
Pavie – tasted 1977 (decanted three hours)
Deep colour, brown rim

Lost almost all fruit
Dried-out due to over-decanting
Pavie – tasted 1978
Brick-red colour
Good nose
Full of fruit, finished hard. Opened out later
Pétrus (LB Harveys) – tasted 1976
Lovely colour
Nice, slightly sweet, clarety nose
Nice wine to drink, showing slight vegetabley aspect of Merlot, perfect maturity. Possibly lacking positive definition
Pétrus – tasted 1980
Lovely garnet red
Fine, slightly metallic
Good fruit, slightly acetic. Very good
Vieux-Château-Certan (half-bottle) – tasted 1979
Huge depth of colour with slight tawny edge
Superb cedarwood with almost hint of prunes
Lovely balance of fruit with still some tannin kept under by the fat. Still sweet.

1956 Poor year. A very bad spring with snow. Saint-Émilion and Pomerol were hit very badly killing many vines, up to 80% in some vineyards. This resulted in a very small crop from most Châteaux.
Ausone – tasted 1977
Quite deep with brown rim
Thin, acidic nose, some fruit
Light-weight, lacks fruit and centre, dry finish

1957 Warm spring, then heavy frost, following by a poor summer. Some sun at vintage time, resulting in small quantity and general poor quality. There were some exceptions.
Cheval Blanc – tasted 1976
Spritzig – characteristic of most 1957's. Ignoring this aspect, wine is quite big, heavy but not very appealing
Cheval Blanc (1st bottle) – tasted 1979
Dried out, over the top
Cheval Blanc (2nd bottle) – tasted 1979
High acidity, fruit fading fast
Cheval Blanc – tasted 1980
Pale/medium in colour, brown rim
High acidity, fruit drying out fast
Oxidised finish
Clos Fourtet – tasted 1977
Light in colour with orange edge
Thin, acidic nose, lacks fruit
Light-weight, no centre, short finish

Gazin – tasted 1974
Typical wine of 1957, having the 'spiked' or prickly taste
Very average wine which might benefit by decanting
Troplong-Mondot – tasted 1982
Mid/deep and v/brown
Violet Merlot and alcohol
Soft, drying in centre
Stalky chaptalised finish and acidity

1958 Variable spring. A good summer resulting in good crop of variable wine. Some wine can be very nice and soft.
Ausone – tasted 1980
Medium depth of colour, brown rim
Nice chocolate, Merlot, sweet nose
Good fruit, nice balance, sweet finish
Capbern (Dutch-bottled) – tasted 1982
Wine totally past it, acetic and finished
Cheval Blanc – tasted 1980
Medium colour, brown rim
Nicely-balanced nose, sweet caramel
Good fruit and weight, sweet finish
Cheval Blanc – re-tasted 1981
Same as above
la Gaffelière-Naudes – tasted 1980
Quite deep colour with brown rim
Subdued, subtle, lovely nose
Good fruit, slightly light centre, but lovely finish
Pétrus – tasted 1975
Medium depth of colour, orange rim
Quite rich and sweet with acidity
Seems to lack charm, light centre, short finish

1959 Very good spring and very hot summer with some rain at the start of the vintage, resulting in good yield and excellent quality. Some wines lack acidity and are now fading.
Ausone – tasted 1978
Deep colour with orange rim
Superb, rich, truffle nose
Lots of fruit, good balance, tight finish
Ausone – re-tasted 1982
Deep colour with brown rim
Rich, ripe nose
Full, ripe, fruity wine, good finish
Canon (Magnum) – tasted 1980
Mid-deep in colour with brown rim
Good fruity nose, slightly closed
Elegant wine slightly light centre, but good fruity finish
Canon (Magnum) – tasted 1979
Pale russet colour

THE WINES OF SAINT-ÉMILION AND POMEROL

Finely perfumed
Nice roundness, complete, ready, a little light on finish
Capet (Dutch-bottled) – tasted 1982
Deep in colour, brown rim
Slight volatile acidity but good Merlot nose
Good fruit holding well, firm, dry finish
Cheval Blanc (Avery-bottled) – tasted 1975
Paling, not very intense colour
Slightly restricted nose
Smooth, soft wine, fairly sweet, not very intense. Bit burgundian and rather ferrous
Cheval Blanc – tasted 1982
Mid/deep and brown
Sweet nose and acidity
Quite a lot of sweet fruit
Spoilt by high acidity on finish
Clos René – tasted 1977
Dry wine lacking fruit and sweetness, hence bit past it
Nose fades early. Quite an interesting wine
Curé-Bon La Madeleine – tasted 1976
Rather undistinguished and drying out
Domaine de la Clotte (LB) – tasted 1980
Fairly pale
Light, soft, caramel nose
Light of fruit and centre, fading fast
Domaine de la Clotte (LB Corney & Barrow) – tasted 1982
Good dark colour
Very little nose
Drinks very well, a light easy style of wine with firm backbone, drying a little, old Merlot flavour, very pleasant
la Dominique – tasted 1978
Very nice wine, well-knit and trace of sweetness
l'Éveche – tasted 1981
Pale, medium depth of colour, brown rim
Dusty, dry, medicinal nose
Drying out, lost most of its fruit
Franc Bigaroux – tasted 1982
Medium depth of colour, brown rim
Soft, violet, Merlot nose
Slightly light on palate, but well-made and long finish
Figeac – tasted 1980
Deep colour, brown rim
Overpowering, lovely sweet, rich bouquet
Superb, rich depth of sweetness, very long finish
Gombaude-Guillot – tasted 1974
Dark wine
Big fruity, clarety nose
Big, rich wine, showing well, pleasant

Pavie – tasted 1979
Big, deep colour, orange rim
Superb, full, sweet
Lots of extract and fruit, excellent wine
Pétrus – tasted 1974
Deep colour with brown rim
Lovely, rich, Merlot rot
A lot of depth and extract, long rich finish
Pétrus – tasted 1980
Brick red
Bit chalky, dusty
Lacks great style, slight port tang
Rouget – tasted 1976
Very mature wine, showing typical dryness of the 1959's
A bit past its prime now, but drinks nicely
la Serre – tasted 1980
Deep colour, brown rim
Good ripe, chocolate, Merlot
Lots of fruit, good balance, fruity finish
Vieux-Château-Certan (half-bottle) – tasted 1980
Good red colour
Very fine, elegant mature bouquet
Fine character in mouth, gentle mellow complexity, lovely wine with great elegance

1960 Good spring, but wet summer resulting in average crop of below-average wines.
Ausone – tasted 1981
Medium depth of colour, brown rim
Old brown nose, smells of brown sugar
Thin, lacks fruit and centre, light finish
Cheval Blanc – tasted 1978
Quite big one for 1960, lacking a degree of refinement
No problem of overmaturity
Cheval Blanc – tasted 1980
Medium depth of colour, brown rim
Light-weight and now beginning to fade
Cheval Blanc – tasted 1982
Mid and brown
Old mushroom nose
Lost most of its fruit dry finish
Figeac – tasted 1970
Good red colour, brown rim
Big, beautiful nose and taste with marked blackcurrant Cabernet flavour
Figeac – tasted 1976
Medium depth, orange rim
Light but fruity nose
Still holding but fading slightly, lacked centre
Figeac – tasted 1981
Medium depth, brown rim
Lovely ripe Merlot nose, like toffee
Fruit now fading on finish

le Gay (L B Averys) – tasted 1981
  Pale in colour, orange rim
  Light, sweet
  Very light, lacks finish
Gazin – tasted 1981
  Medium depth, brown rim
  Nice deep, truffle nose
  Quite rich but thin centre, nice fruity finish
Gazin – tasted 1980
  Deep colour, brown rim
  Lovely deep, truffle nose
  Good body and depth
  Light centre, but well-balanced finish
Grand-Barrail – tasted 1978
  Quite a lot of weight, fairly similar to Cheval Blanc 1960, but more identifiable and better style
Pavie – tasted 1978
  Medium colour with brown rim
  Quity fruity but light
  Light-weight, but a pleasant bottle of wine
Pétrus – tasted 1980
  Deep russet red
  Muddy, earthy nose
  Soft, fruity, but very short, bit watery
Soutard – tasted 1978
  Firm, big wine with lot of weight, good style and quite good for year, but showing a rather harsh side

1961 Some frost in the spring and some rain which reduced the flowing. A very hot summer and very dry, resulting in small quantity but excellent quality.
Ausone – tasted 1961
  Browning at edges
  Beautiful, soft, grapey nose
  Almost sweet on palate, lovely
Belair – tasted 1981
  Deep in colour, brown rim
  Good, rich, sweet nose
  Full, rich fruit, good firm finish
Canon la Gaffelière – tasted 1981
  Very deep colour, brown rim
  Violets and truffles, soft and full
  Rich, plenty of fruit, good long finish
Cheval Blanc – tasted 1980
  Deep colour, brown rim
  Superb, deep, rich nose
  Very concentrated, superb, rich, long finish
Cheval Blanc – tasted 1982
  Deep and brown
  Lovely rich extract of violets
  Immense fruit and flavour, perfect balance and finish

Certan – tasted 1981
  Very deep colour
  Volatile acidity, but rich, deep truffle
  Volatile acidity, with long finish
Château le Couvent – tasted 1982
  Quite deep and brown
  Vegetable nose and acidity
  Good fruit but high acidity on finish
Clos l'Église – tasted 1978
  Deep colour, brown rim
  Good, rich, iron nose
  A lot of fruit, good soft finish
Clos Fourtet – tasted 1975
  Good red colour, brown edge
  Round, rich, full, perfumed nose
  Rather thin in the mouth, disappointing after such a good bouquet
  High acidity, unbalanced
Clos Fourtet (half-bottle) – tasted 1978
  Dark colour, mature rim
  Closed nose, trace of Saint-Émilion
  Wine still immature, strong, acidity present, fruit not in preponderance, hence dull at present
Clos Fourtet – tasted 1980
  Deep in colour – brown rim
  Sweet nose, slightly medicinal
  Drying out on palate
Clos Fourtet – re-tasted 1982
  Quite deep colour, brown rim
  Light, dry nose
  Lost most of its fruit, dry finish
Clos René – tasted 1975
  Deep colour, brown rim
  Rich, creamy nose
  Full, rich flavour
Clos René – tasted 1977
  Very deep colour
  Powerful nose
  A lot of fruit with length. Some tannin still underneath, excellent
Dassault – tasted 1981
  Very deep colour, brown rim
  Enormous depth of fruit and concentrated violets
  Superb, rich, lovely fruit, very long finish
la Gaffelière-Naudes – tasted 1980
  Deep in colour, brown rim
  Good, ripe, violet nose
  Excellent balance and finish, a rich and sweet wine
la Gaffelière-Naudes – re-tasted 1982
  Same as above
Gazin (L B Lebegue) – tasted 1978
  Good, brick red, browning colour
  Fairly fruity nose

Very big wine, well-balanced, immature, trace earthy

Gazin – tasted 1979
Deep, red colour and brown rim
Big, soft nose
Creamy, big fruity wine with tremendous texture

Gazin – re-tasted 1981
Still same as above

Gazin – tasted 1979
Deep in colour, brown rim
Good ripe, forward, violet nose
A lot of finesse, fruit, lovely finish

Gazin (EB Hedges & Butler) – tasted 1981
Very deep colour
Huge nose
Very big chewy wine with lovely depth and length

Grand Pontet – tasted 1973
Deep colour, orange rim
Slightly musty nose, but good fruit
Good rich fruit, good balance, tannic finish, well-made

l'Évangile – tasted 1979
Very deep with brown rim
Lovely, truffle nose, mature
Ripe, rich fruit, long finish

Figeac – tasted 1981
Very deep colour, brown rim
Superb, rich, violet nose
Lots of fruit, ripe, long finish

Figeac – re-tasted 1982
Still the same as when tasted in 1981

la Fleur (Lalande) (EB Lebegue) – tasted 1979
Dark, immature colour
Nose develops, soft heavily-scented
Initially spritzig, benefits by decanting. Fairly tough yet has balanced softness. Perfectly drinkable but will last for years. Represents sort of aromatic Pomerol/Graves. Lacks the tannin to characterise 1961. Ultimately becomes more Merlotish, almost Lafite-like

Fombrauge – tasted 1973
Deep in colour, orange edge
Soft, velvety, violet nose
Full of fruit and still a lot of tannin
Good finish

Magdelaine – tasted 1979
Medium deep colour, brown rim
Almond nose
Dried-out, unpleasant finish, perhaps bad bottle

Magdelaine – tasted 1979
Deep colour, brown rim
Good, soft, Merlot, showing age

Good fruit in centre, but drying on finish

Magdelaine – tasted 1981
Good deep colour
Rich, violet nose, sweet
Lovely rich, soft wine with tannin

Nenin (LB Justerini & Brooks) – tasted 1975
Very dark colour, intense, orangey, with brown rim
Cabernet nose
Big, fairly mature, just drinking nicely – too plump for Margaux style
More like Pauillac, etc

Nenin (LB Grants) – tasted 1976
Very pleasant wine to drink. Full and lot of fruit, lot of tannin but quite forward, drinking well, and quite soft

Nenin (EB) – tasted 1977
Very big earthy wine. Trace sweet, fruit just showing

Pavie – tasted 1978
Light, red, browning. Smell of dried leaves, bit metallic
Good fruit and meaty, drying out

Pavie – tasted 1980
Very deep with brown edge
Lovely soft, rich, sweet nose, immense concentration
Superb depth, full, rich , excellent

Pavie – re-tasted 1981
Still same as tasted in 1980

Pavie (half-bottle LB) – tasted 1980
Good colour
Lovely, Merlot, rotting vegetation
Slightly fading on finish but good centre and balance

Petit Village – tasted 1976
Fairly mature colour
Good fruity nose, mature Merlot
Slightly light centre with some tannin on the finish

Pétrus – tasted 1980
Very deep with brown rim
Rich mature, ripe, Merlot/truffle
A lot of concentrated fruit, very long, sweet finish

Pétrus – tasted 1980
Russet red
Very fine delicate nose, sweet strawberries
Super, sweet wine with perfect balance

la Pointe – tasted 1982
Very deep, brown rim
Lovely, rich, truffle, sweet and ripe
Superbly, rich centre, lovely fruit, solid chocolate finish

de Sales (LB Justerini & Brooks) – tasted 1976
Lovely nose, trace of violets and wood

Big maturish wine, lots of tannin but style has developed nicely

la Serre – tasted 1982
Deep colour, brown rim
Lovely deep, rich toffee
Rich, great depth, great wine

Tertre Daugay (LB Justerini & Brooks) – tasted 1981
Quite deep colour, brown rim
Dumb but deep and rich
Quite soft, chocolate taste, slightly drying on finish

Troplong-Mondot (EB Lebegue) – tasted 1976
Still very dumb, backward and needing a lot of time
Not good yet

Troplong-Mondot (LB Lebegue) – tasted 1982
Very deep colour, brown rim
Delicate, rich, deep, concentrated nose
Lovely, delicate fruit, well-balanced wine

Trotanoy – tasted 1980
Deep colour, brown rim
Good deep, concentrated violet nose
A lot of fruit in centre, good firm finish

Vieux Château Calon (Montagne) (EB) – tasted 1975
Browning. Good wine, still not fully mature

Vieux-Château-Certan – tasted 1981
Deep in colour, brown rim
Slighty faded nose
Sweet but fading

1962 A cold spring, a good summer but late harvest, resulting in a good crop of good quality wine but not as good as the Médoc.

l'Arrosée – tasted 1981
Medium depth of colour, brown rim
Dry, dusty nose
Quite fruity and sweet, drying out

Ausone – tasted 1974
Medium depth of colour, orange rim
Light, fresh, fruity, sweet nose
Not a lot of depth, light finish

Ausone – tasted 1982
Medium depth of colour, brown rim
Delicate chocolate nose
Sweet, light-weight, dry finish

Ausone – tasted 1976
Very nice wine. Very stylish, trace of sweetness, lovely claret

Belair (Lussac) – tasted 1981
Medium depth, brown rim
Dusty, leafy, showing age
Drying out on finish

Bellegrave (LB Harveys) – tasted 1981
Deep colour, brown rim
Old nose showing age
Sweet but lacks centre, drying out on the finish

Bourgneuf Vayron – tasted 1980
Nice deep colour, brown rim
Good solid, iron nose
Good fruit and balance, slightly fading now

Brun – tasted 1981
Medium depth, brown rim
Quite soft and sweet
Nice fruity centre, drying on finish

Canon – tasted 1979
Good deep colour, brown rim
Nice balance, light-weight nose
Light in centre but good firm finish

Canon – re-tasted 1982
Deep colour, brown rim
Tight, well-balanced nose
Dry, slightly stalky but good ripe finish

Cheval Blanc – tasted 1978
Considerable depth of colour, mature rim
Difficult nose to describe. Quite a lot of fruit still but drying out, presumably past its best. Not typical of the Château's usual style. Pleasant, not great, but fair

Cheval Blanc – tasted 1980
Deep colour, brown rim
Good deep, fruity, violet nose
Soft, chocolate, sweet wine, good finish
A lot of finesse

Cheval Blanc – tasted 1981
Deep colour, orange rim
Lovely rich nose with superb extract and depth
Good depth, rich fruit, nice chocolate finish

Cheval Blanc – tasted 1982
Mid and brown
Light dry sweet nose
Dry, losing fruit, fading on finish

Clos-des-Jacobins – tasted 1977
Nice full colour
Superb classic Merlot nose
Very nice wine at peak of maturity, rather Médoc in style

Clos-des-Jacobins – tasted 1978
Good deep colour, brown rim
Good soft, oaky nose
Good fruit, tight centre, will improve

Clos-des-Jacobins – tasted 1979
Good deep colour, brown rim
Good mature, oaky, soft nose
Good, deep, fruit, centre well-balanced, nice finish

Clos Fourtet (L B Godfrey & Duchène) – tasted 1981
    Medium depth of colour, brown rim
    Quite leafy and showing age
    High acidity, lacks fruit, drying out
la Conseillante – tasted 1979
    Fairly dark, mature rim
    Nose opened up progressively, slightly sweet, rather closed initially, fruity and sweet, sugary
    Quite tannic and acidity showing, drying out now, rather closed style, rather burgundian in style, bit dull
Figeac – tasted 1971
    Good red colour, orange rim
    Gentle, soft, round nose
    Very attractive, creamy taste with a touch of Cabernet characteristic
    A lovely wine
Figeac – re-tasted 1982
    Similar to above but fading on the finish
Figeac (half-bottle) – tasted 1976
    Good deep colour, orange edge
    Soft, lovely Merlot rot
    Slightly light centre but good finish and balance otherwise
Figeac (half-bottle) – re-tasted in 1978
    Same as above
Figeac – tasted 1981
    Medium colour, brown rim
    Nice, rich, sweet, mature Merlot
    Lovely balance and superb rich fruit
la Fleur Pétrus – tasted 1978
    Pale in colour, brown rim
    Nice, fresh, fruity nose
    Quite light-weight, thin finish
la Fleur Pétrus – tasted 1981
    Medium depth of colour, brown rim
    Good soft, truffle nose
    Quite light centre, dry finish
Fonplégade (LB) – tasted 1976
    Deep in colour, pink rim
    Soft violet nose
    Full, round, light, slight tannin but acidity
Gazin (L B Wine Society) – tasted 1971
    Deep red in colour, brown rim
    Big, rich, round, smooth, almost chocolate nose
    Strong unsubtle but full of power and character and richness
Gazin (LB Harveys) – tasted 1981
    Medium colour and brown rim
    Nice, soft, violet nose
    Sweet, soft, good centre and finish
Gazin (LB Justerini & Brooks) – tasted 1981
    Medium colour and brown rim

Deep, rich, chocolate, truffly nose
Nice, rich deep, iron taste, slightly drying on finish
Gaffelière-Naudes – tasted 1968
    Very pale russet
    Light in fruit and tannin
Gaffelière-Naudes – tasted 1964
    Pleasant but very light, with fruit
Gaffelière-Naudes – tasted 1980
    Good colour, with brown rim
    Soft, sweet, Merlot nose
    Well-balanced, good fruit and body
    Slightly dry on finish
Gaffelière-Naudes – re-tasted in 1981 & 1982
    Still same as above
Grand Pontet (LB Justerini & Brooks) – tasted 1981
    Deep colour, brown rim
    Slightly stalky
    Quite fruity, but drying slightly on the finish
Lyonnat – tasted 1977
    Full mature colour
    Nice sweet mature nose
    Interesting wine, very full in fruit, nice balance, beautifully mature, holding remarkably well
Lyonnat – tasted 1975
    Delicate soft wine rather like a Margeaux area wine
Lyonnat – tasted 1979
    Good deep colour, browning on rim
    Mature, Merlot nose
    Nice fruit, good weight, nice soft chocolate finish
Magdelaine – tasted 1979
    Medium depth of colour, brown rim
    Faded nose
    Losing fruits, dry finish
Magdelaine – tasted 1981
    Good deep colour
    Lovely, rich, Merlot, sweet nose
    Soft, full, sweet, chocolatey wine, well-made
Pavie – tasted 1981
    Good, deep colour
    Nice, delicate, violet nose
    Good fruit and balance, slightly light finish
Pétrus – tasted 1978
    Very poor after fair bit of decanting. More like *Côte Rotie*.
Pétrus – tasted 1980
    Beginning to brown
    Soft, slight metallic nose
    Very supple, supper wine, goes on and on
Pétrus – tasted 1980
    Deep in colour, brown rim
    Dumb, shy bouquet

Although a big wine, it lacks subtlety, dumb finish

la Pointe – tasted 1978
Very deep colour, brown rim
Lovely mature, ripe Merlot
Lots of fruit and superbly rich finish

Château Ripeau (Magnum) – tasted 1982
Deep and brown
Old acidic nose with some sweetness underneath
Drying out with high acidity

de Sales (Dutch-bottled) – tasted 1974
Good colour
Fairly fruity nose
Average flavour at first but poor finish

de Sales – tasted 1975
Dark colour
Firm nose
Very full wine, very clarety, little nose

de Sales (LB Hedges & Butler) – tasted 1976
Lovely colour, orange maturity
Rather light in fruit and body with excess acidity
Tends to ease on opening to a pleasant wine with good style

de Sales (LB) – tasted 1976
Good deep colour with orange edge
Good chocolate nose and Merlot rot
Good depth and balance, slightly light centre, but strong finish

Soutard – tasted 1980
Good red colour, brown rim
Lovely generous, well-developed, mellow nose
Beautiful, mellow, almost sweet, elegant, mature, faint herbal taste

Taillefer (half-bottle) – tasted 1982
Light style of wine, now a bit dry and losing its fruit, but drinking pleasantly still

Trotanoy – tasted 1977
Good deep colour, browning slightly on rim
Strong oaky, sweet, almost like Pauillac
Superb, rich, fruit and oak, excellent balance, good finish

Trotanoy – re-tasted 1980
Same as above but just beginning to dry on the finish

1963 A poor vintage. Cold and wet causing rot, below-average crop producing light, thin wine.

1964 Warm spring, and hot dry summer. Success in Saint-Émilion and Pomerol as early picking before the rains.

Ausone – tasted 1976
Deep colour, orange rim
Lovely rich, tight, sweet nose
Good body and extract, a lot of fruit, still to open up

Ausone – re-tasted 1982
Medium depth of colour, brown rim
Delicate, sweet nose
Full, well-balanced, at its peak

Beauregard – tasted 1980
Very deep, red, tinged with brown
Attractive, restrained nose
Lovely, full, gentle flavour, sweet, long-lasting, superb balance

Canon – tasted 1980
Very deep colour, brown rim
Very big, rich nose
Lovely, rich, superb depth, a lot of finesse

Canon – re-tasted 1981
Same as above

Canon la Gaffelière (LB Hedges & Butler) – tasted 1974
Good colour, rich nose, improves on opening. Seems to be rather insipid in some respects but is quite pleasant
Some richness, smooth and rounded

Canon la Gaffelière – tasted 1977 and 1980
Initially wine is fizzy. Settles after one hour.
Dark in colour. Soft, fruity nose
Rather clumsy flabby liquid, bit anonymous, lot of fruit still.
Resembles a younger wine

Canon la Gaffelière – tasted 1974
Medium depth of colour
Very rich full round nose
Very full, rich taste, almost sweet, markedly burgundian character

Cheval Blanc – tasted 1977
Deep colour, brown rim
Voluptuous, fruit and richness on nose
Very full, burgundian character, touch of herbs, soft and velvety
Long finish

Cheval Blanc – tasted 1978
Sweet, fruity nose, very soft
Big, soft, very full-bodied wine, almost mature
Has typical metallic character

Cheval Blanc – tasted 1981
Quite deep colour, brown rim
Lovely, rich, deep, elegant, violet nose
Good depth of fruit, slightly drying on finish

Cheval Blanc – tasted 1982
Mid and brown
Lovely sweet violet nose
Lots of fruit, a fine wine at its peak now

Clos Fourtet – tasted 1979
  Medium depth of colour, brown rim
  Good, soft, fruity, nose but not as rich as most 1964's
  Quite disappointing, light, lacks body and finish

Clos Fourtet – tasted 1982
  Medium depth of colour, brown rim
  Quite sweet, violet nose with slight volatile acidity
  Good balance, slight acidity on finish

Clos Roi de Fombrauge – tasted 1969
  Deep colour, pink rim
  Good depth of fruit, soft nose
  Quite light centre, firm finish

la Conseillante – tasted 1980
  Deep colour, orange rim
  Lovely, rich, Merlot, rotting vegetation
  Full, deep, excellent balance, long full finish

Curé-Bon la Madeleine – tasted 1975
  Old wine, fully mature

Figeac – tasted 1979
  Deep, red colour, brown rim
  Quiet but elegant nose
  Big, round, dark taste, rich velvety texture. Grip at end. Great vinosity, overwhelming, and massive rather than subtle, but very fine

Figeac – tasted 1980
  Deep colour, brown rim
  Deep, mature Merlot, a lot of extract
  Very rich, ripe Merlot, well-balanced, lovely fruity, long finish

Figeac – re-tasted 1982
  Same as when tasted in 1980

la Fleur Pétrus – tasted 1977
  Medium red colour
  Attractive elegant, perfume of pinks
  Good balance, fair fruit, elegant but lightweight

la Fleur Pétrus – tasted 1979
  Deep in colour, brown rim
  Good, sweet, ripe nose
  Good fruit, balance and finish

la Fleur Pétrus – tasted 1981
  Good deep colour, brown rim
  Lovely, soft, rich and sweet
  A lot of fruit and depth, great wine

Fonplégade – tasted 1980
  Deep red
  Fair character on nose, slight hint of volatile acidity
  Slightly unbalanced, drying finish

Gazin (LB Grants) – tasted 1974
  Fine dark colour
  Fruity nose

Rather Médocain style wine, pleasant to drink

Gazin (LB Hedges & Butler) – tasted 1975
  Dark wine
  Not much nose. Very big immature hard wine which needs much time. Tannin predominates, bit earthy, unyielding wine

Grand Corbin Despagne – tasted 1972
  Very deep colour
  Lovely, rich, sweet nose
  Full fruity, tannin, tight finish

Grangeneuve (LB Hedges & Butler) – tasted 1974
  Purple in colour
  Tannic, thin, immature
  Improved on opening with better qualities showing

Grangeneuve – tasted 1974
  Deep colour, brown rim
  Big full nose
  Very fruity flavour, and tannin

Lassègue – tasted 1976
  Big wine. Bit sharp on opening, but is all right

Lyonnat – tasted 1980
  Medium colour, tawny rim
  Light but mature, sweet Merlot
  Lightweight, lacks centre, fruit fading

Magdelaine – tasted 1970
  Good, deep red colour
  Slight but fruity nose
  Big, attractive taste, good structure and tannin

Monbousquet – tasted 1978
  Russet red
  Stalky, bit closed-in on nose
  Some fruit, chewy but hollow, watery finish

Monbousquet – tasted 1980
  Quite deep colour, brown rim
  Soft, sweet, good depth of fruit
  Quite rich, soft, delicate, chocolate, good firm finish

Moulin St Georges (Magnum) – tasted 1982
  Deep colour, brown rim
  Rich, violet nose
  Lots of fruit, well-balanced finish

Nenin – tasted 1976
  Deep colour, orange rim
  Lovely rich, sweet, truffle nose
  Huge extract and fruit, very good finish

Pavie (EB Hedges & Butler) – tasted 1974
  Fairly rich wine, lot of sweetness and fruit
  Nose of emulsion or ripe melons
  Crème brûlée
  Almost old burgundian

Pavie – tasted 1974
  Very deep colour

Deep, round nose, touch of compost
Great, big, dark flavour, very firm finish
Pavie – tasted 1976
Very nicely-developed wine
Good Saint-Émilion style in very good shape
Not sweet
Pavie – tasted 1976
Fairly light with mature rim
Soft, but light nose
Fruit fading slightly and acidity showing through
Pavie – tasted 1981
Good deep colour
Lovely soft rich nose
Good fruit, excellent balance and finish
Pétrus – tasted 1974
Very deep colour with pink rim
Big, deep nose, slightly-burnt characteristics
Huge flavour and extract, but still closed, immense tannin, very weighty wine, a very long way to go
Pétrus – tasted 1975
Very dark
Slightly rich sweet nose
Huge wine, still totally immature
Extremely concentrated with abundant fruit
Too young to show much sign of identification
Pétrus – tasted 1980
Very fine deep red
Nose pallid
Very tough, seems to lack some fruit. Not as fat as I remember it
la Pointe – tasted 1974
Very dull, biggish, clumsy wine
Would benefit by good bottle age
Rouget – tasted 1975
Big, dark wine
Showing reasonable style, not yet mature and not yet drinkable
de Sales – tasted 1976
Fairly full, slightly immature colour
Stalky, quite big, typical claret, not showing any signs of its age, more like Médoc wine
la Serre – tasted 1981
Medium colour, brown rim
Good, strong, violet nose
Soft, sweet, lightish centre, but nice round finish
Soutard (Magnum) – tasted 1981
Very deep colour, brown rim
Lovely rich, ripe Merlot
Very full, lovely balance, long finish, a superb wine

la Tour-du-Pin-Figeac (EB half-bottle) – tasted 1976
Fine refined Bordeaux nose
Tastes of young, good-quality Médoc wine
la Tour-du-Pin-Figeac (half-bottle) – tasted 1976
Good colour, slightly browning
Good soft nose, violets and some acidity
Slightly light centre, but nice balance, acidity on finish
Trotanoy – tasted 1976
Deep red, brown rim
Mature, classy nose
Good balance, lovely texture, real class, good long finish and tannin
Trotanoy – re-tasted 1981
Just starting to fade now
Trottevieille – tasted 1973
Good, deep colour with slight pink edge
Quite fruity but with a medicinal smell underneath
Not a lot of fruit, light centre
Vieux-Château-Certan – tasted 1970
Good, deep red
Smooth, fruity nose
Very full and rich, velvety texture, good fruity finish
Vieux-Château-Certan – tasted 1974
Very nice wine, rich, very clarety
Vieux-Château-Certan – tasted 1975
Good red
Warm generous nose, elegant and well-perfumed
Find depth of flavour, very pleasing texture, beautifully rounded wine

1965 Wet throughout the year resulting in a very poor vintage with a lot of rot, and a small crop.

1966 A fine spring, a dry summer with a hot September resulting in a very good vintage of fine wine.
l'Angélus – tasted 1974
Browning
Well-balanced, fairly fruity, tasting moderately well only
Fully mature, lacks some finish and body
Ausone – tasted 1978
Deep colour, orange rim
Superb, rich, Merlot, nose
Lovely, sweet, rich, well-balanced wine
Balestard-la-Tonnelle – tasted 1981
Very deep colour, brown rim
Good, deep, rich, truffle nose
Tough, tannic, good fruit, long finish

Balestard la Tonnelle – re-tasted 1982
   Same as above
Beauséjour (Duffau-Lagarrosse) – tasted 1980
   Very deep colour, youthful appearance
   Good, rich, Merlot rot
   Very deep, good balance, long finish, well-
   made
Bellevue-Figeac – tasted 1982
   Pale colour, brown rim
   Soft, over-sweet nose
   Light, lacks centre and finish
Bezinau – tasted 1975
   Very tannic
   Light though and not ready
Canon (LB Grants) – tasted 1978
   Nice semi-mature wine, rather Pomerolish
Canon – tasted 1980
   Quite dark colour
   Dry, toffee nose
   Tastes of toffee as well, bit insipid and lacking
   style
   Seems to improve in the glass and develops
   into quite a nice wine similar to Belair 1966
   Seems to be typical of the 1966's – rather
   disappointing
Canon – tasted 1980
   Deep colour, pink edge
   Good, deep, attractive nose with finesse
   Very big concentration of fruit
   Lots of tannin still, a long way to go, one of
   the better 1966's
Canon – re-tasted 1981
   Same as above
Canon – tasted 1982
   Quite dark
   Lovely chocolate/caramel nose
   Superb claret, a beautiful wine now at its
   peak. Stylish, refined Merlot wine, dry finish
Canon-la Gaffelière – tasted 1976
   Good, deep colour, orange rim
   Soft, sweet, Merlot
   Good fruit, good chocolate finish, nice
   balance
Canon-la Gaffelière – tasted 1977
   Nice orangy mature colour
   Sweetish nose
   Full-bodied, big wine, rather immature,
   sweetish, fair style, will keep
Canon-la Gaffelière – tasted 1979
   Dark, mature edge
   Plummy nose
   Fairly rich, heavy wine, still immature, quite
   sweet in style like a big young burgundy
Chapelle de la Trinité – tasted 1978
   Not very exciting wine

Cheval Blanc – tasted 1980
   Strong red some browning
   Beautiful cedarwood perfume
   Rich and full of fruit
   Excellent, rounds off well, still some tannin
Cheval Blanc – tasted 1980
   Deep colour, brown rim
   Superb, violet, oaky nose
   Huge depth of fruit, superb balance, long
   alcoholic finish
Cheval Blanc – retasted 1981
   Same as above
Clos l'Église (LB Justerini & Brooks) – tasted
1975
   Orangy/dark red colour
   American blackcurrant nose, which also
   predominates in the taste, i.e. Bouchet. Very
   good, drinking well and will continue to do
   so for a long while. Full-bodied yet quite
   delicate
Clos l'Église (LB Justerini & Brooks) – tasted
1981
   Very deep, brown rim
   Enormous fruit, ripe Merlot
   Very rich, long finish
Clos René (LB Brown & Pank) – tasted 1975
   Showing well
   Not ready
Corbin – tasted 1972
   Good deep colour
   Light-weight nose
   Thin, dry, lacks body
Figeac – tasted 1980
   Very deep, browning at edge
   Very rich, deep, oaky, soft, chocolate nose
   Superb balance, a lot of fruit, excellent finish
Figeac – re-tasted 1982
   Same as above
Figeac – tasted 1980
   Very deep colour
   Huge, creamy nose, wonderfully rich and
   oaky
   Creamy and powerful taste. Very long finish
   A very fine wine
Figeac – re-tasted 1981
   Fully mature, slightly light centre
la Fleur Pétrus – tasted 1979
   Deep colour, orange rim
   Good, tight, rich nose
   Well-balanced, slightly closed, tannic finish
la Gaffelière – tasted 1974
   Thin, poor nose
   Very thin in flavour and watery. Overall dull
la Gaffelière – tasted 1978
   Very deep red
   Fine, grapey, velvety style, full of fruit,

slightly coarse compared with Cheval Blanc

la Gaffelière – tasted 1980
Quite deep colour, orange rim
Soft, sweet, quite light
Sweet, smooth, light finish

la Gaffelière – tasted 1980
Medium red, brown rim
Muted nose
Quite good balance, but not outstanding

Gazin (LB Berry Bros) – tasted 1976
Very full wine, still a lot of tannin and immature but tasting very well now
Has the flat earthy flavour

Gazin – tasted 1978
Medium colour, brown rim
Slightly *musty* but nice sweet Merlot nose
Chocolate taste, good firm finish

Grand-Barrail-Lamarzelle-Figeac – tasted 1973
First bottle
Quite deep colour, orange edge
Light fruit, slightly dusty bouquet
Thin, slightly acidic, musty finish

Second bottle
Brown
Good, full, blackcurrant, soft, velvety nose
Good fruit and some tannin

Laroque – tasted 1975
Palish colour
Immature, medium-weight, fairly pleasant

Lyonnat – tasted 1977
Quite dark colour
Poor nose
Rather deficient of fruit, rather Médocain style, nice style and possibly drying out

Lyonnat – tasted 1978
Rather anonymous colour, not purple nor orange
Creamy nose
Pleasant classic claret, not much to suggest its origin, but good-style Pomerol would seem a better guess than Saint-Émilion

Lyonnat – tasted 1977
Good deep colour, orange rim
Chocolate, delicate, sweet nose
Light of fruit, thin finish

Lyonnat – tasted 1980
Medium depth of colour, brown rim
Deep chocolate, Merlot and tough Cabernet background
Good body, soft, smooth, good finish

Magdelaine – tasted 1974
Lovely clarety nose
Rather Médocain in style, soft wine with strong fruit flavour

Magdelaine – tasted 1979
Good deep colour, brown edge
Tight, rich, toffee nose
Tight with tannin, lacks fruit in centre

Magdelaine – tasted 1981
Deep colour
Good deep fruity Merlot nose
Disappointing palate, quite high acidity
Fruit drying out on finish

Moulin du Cadet – tasted 1978
Medium colour, brown rim
Soft, sweet, Merlot nose
Light-weight, lacks fruit, slightly unbalanced, acidity quite high on finish

Nenin (LB Army & Navy) – tasted 1977
Very dull, flat and flabby

Pavie – tasted 1980
Very deep colour, brown rim
Very rich, deep concentration of violets and fruit
Long, chocolate, fruity with tannin. Long way to go.

Pavie – re-tasted 1981
Same as above

Pétrus – tasted 1980
Very deep red
Great intensity of bouquet and flavour
Very thick, rich texture, dark taste. Lots of tannin, still fairly closed, a long way to go, will be a great wine.

Pétrus – tasted 1980
Slight tawny edge
Lovely nose, very perfumed cedar
Superb, but finishes in two parts and a bit hollow. Still tannic

Pipeau – tasted 1981
Deep colour, orange rim
Big, ripe, developed Merlot
Soft, fruity, well-balanced, fully-developed

la Pointe – tasted 1975
Good colour, fairly mature
Soft, fruity, violet nose
Full, sweet and soft, good balance

la Pointe – tasted 1977
True clarety nose, not quite Pauillac but trace of softness, vaguely violety, earthy, woody
Good wine, mature, fruity, more Saint-Émilionish
Resembles a young burgundy in some respects

la Pointe – tasted 1980
Nose not so good as above, becomes toffee-ish. Wine is more delicate, fragrant liquid. Fragments rather quickly and is a trace cardboardy

Régent – tasted 1981
  Medium colour, brown rim
  Nice fruit, but slight volatile acidity
  Quite rich fruit, good chocolate finish
Roudier – tasted 1982
  Medium colour, brown rim
  Lovely rich Merlot
  Good, deep, fruity palate with firm finish
la Tour-Figeac – tasted 1978
  Really plummy, meaty wine, great depth
  Tremendous mouthful
  Excellent
Trotanoy – tasted 1976
  Very good, rich, mature colour
  Lovely nose
  Full-bodied, softer than some 1966's and very
  well-made
Trotanoy – tasted 1976
  Good red colour, brown rim
  Pleasing, classy nose
  Good fruit, and tannin, will improve
Trotanoy – tasted 1980
  Good, deep colour, brown rim
  Quite hard, closed, fruity nose
  Good fruit, well-balanced, tannic finish
Trottevieille – tasted 1973
  Deep colour
  Good depth of soft fruit, similar nose to Pinot
  Noir
  Full, fruity, soft, round finish with some
  tannin

1967 Mild spring followed by a hot summer
      which was better in Saint-
      Émilion/Pomerol than the Médoc as the
      vintage was picked earlier and missed
      the rain. Excellent vintage.
Ausone – tasted 1976
  Good, refined or delicate wine with lot of
  finesse and grace
  Better than the Cheval Blanc. Resembles a
  mature 1970 in some respects
Ausone – tasted 1982
  Pale in colour, brown rim
  Light, sweet, caramel nose
  Light, sweet, short finish
Beauregard – tasted 1980
  Very deep colour, brown rim
  Soft, sweet, violet nose
  Very well-balanced, lovely round, smooth
  finish
Bergat – tasted 1974
  Good colour, pink rim
  Full, soft, violet nose
  Light, but fruity, nice finish with tannin

Bourgneuf (LB Robert James) – tasted 1971
  Good colour
  Attractive but rather slight nose
  Well-integrated flavour and texture, plenty of
  tannin but forward
Canon – tasted 1981
  Good, deep colour, brown rim
  Soft, rich, toffee nose
  Rich, sweet, well-balanced with tannic finish
Canon-la Gaffelière – tasted 1976
  Good mature colour
  Classic example of the woody-style of Saint-
  Émilion
  Very true
  In very good shape at present
Cheval Blanc – tasted 1975
  Deep red
  Very full nose
  Great fat wine
Cheval Blanc – tasted 1975
  Deep colour, brown rim
  Round, rich smell and hint of Merlot rot
  Velvety texture, good fruity, fair finish
Cheval Blanc – tasted 1975
  Dark colour
  Rather flabby nose
  Soft, rather characterless wine with the
  slightly metallic aspect
Cheval Blanc – tasted 1975
  Pale wine showing maturity
  Smells of scent
  Tasting quite well, trace of sweetness with
  fair fruit and tannin
Cheval Blanc – tasted 1976
  Full, soft, good
Cheval Blanc – tasted 1979
  Great colour
  Rich, oaky nose
  Very meaty, full and fruity
Cheval Blanc – tasted 1980
  Mature colour, brown rim
  Good, soft, fruity nose, quite tough
  Good depth and extract, still quite closed,
  long tight finish
Cheval Blanc – re-tasted 1981
  Opening out slightly
Cheval Blanc – tasted 1982
  Good deep and brown
  Sweet rich nose
  Lovely balance, good depth of fruit
  Fine finish
Clos l'Église (LB) – tasted 1975
  Rather harsh, very clarety
la Clotte – tasted 1972
  Deep, red
  Round, rich, sweet, luscious nose

Attractive, creamy finish, delicious, a very easy wine to enjoy

Croque-Michotte – tasted 1981
Medium depth of colour, brown rim
Light-weight with acidity
Drying out, past its prime

Domaine de l'Eglise (LB Berry Bros) – tasted 1976
Lovely colour, trace pale
Very good nose
Very nice wine, big for 1967, almost mature, possesses the earthy flavour

Feytit-Guillot – tasted 1982
Deep in colour, brown rim
Good extract, rich, truffle nose
Good but drying on finish

Figeac – tasted 1982
Medium depth, brown rim
Good, rich, violet, Merlot
At its peak, good, soft, fruity flavour

la Fleur Pétrus – tasted 1980
Good deep colour, brown rim
Light-weight nose but fruity
Quite light and thin, lacks body

la Gaffelière – tasted 1980
Medium depth of colour, browning on rim
Light, pleasant nose, good Merlot rot
Good fruit and balance and finesse
Nice finish

Haut-Sarpe – tasted 1982
Medium/pale colour, brown rim
Very sweet, rich, ripe Merlot, violets
Good balance, still time to go, tannic finish

Lyonnat – tasted 1980
Medium depth of colour, brown rim
Lovely, soft Merlot
Sweet, round, well-balanced, qyite light centre, but good finish

Magdelaine – tasted 1979
Medium depth, brown rim
Light-weight nose, quite thin
Unbalanced, watery, light finish, possibly poor bottle

Magdelaine – tasted 1981
Medium depth of colour, brown rim
Nice, light, fruity nose
Lacking centre, weak finish

Magdelaine – re-tasted 1982
Deep colour, brown rim
Quite rich with acidity
Light fruit, dry finish

Monbousquet – tasted 1980
Deep colour, brown rim
Lovely, rich, truffle nose
Good, rich, fruit, great length and finish

Monbousquet – tasted 1981
Same as above

Nenin (LB Grants) – tasted 1976
Markedly full in colour
Slighly sharp or coarse wine, yet certain amount of delicacy
Quite a lot of tannin
Quite good

Nouvelle Église – tasted 1974
Lovely, rather pale
Slightly perfumed, woody nose
Rather individual taste, very clarety, tasting quite well

Pavie – tasted 1981
Good, rich, deep colour, brown rim
Lovely rotting vegetable nose, truffles
Soft, full round, complete, fully mature, long fruity finish

Petit-Faurie-de-Soutard – tasted 1980
Deep colour, brown rim
Good, rich, violet nose
Good balance, slightly light centre, tannic finish

Pétrus – tasted 1980
Huge colour
Nose muted
Very good balance, still tannic, good fruit

la Pointe – tasted 1980
Good deep and brown colour
Rich, truffle nose
Lots of fruit, well-balanced

Soutard – tasted 1982
Deep colour, brown rim
Light, delicate, Merlot, violet nose
Sweet, delicate, beautiful balance

Trotanoy – tasted 1976
Good red colour, brown rim
Slightly earthy nose
Attractive, maturity, a lot of fruit, sweet, rich finish

Trottevieille – tasted 1973
Light with watery rim
Light on fruit and acidity on nose
Light, fruity finish with some tannin

Trottevieille – tasted 1975
Quite full colour, trace of brown, rather non-descript red
True Merlot nose, suggestive of Pinot Noir
Pepperminty, woody, perfectly balanced, relatively light-weight mixture, typical Saint-Émilion

1968 A poor vintage. A cold spring, and a cold and wet summer, producing light, thin wine.

All the Premier Grand Cru Classé Châteaux, except Figeac, declassified their wine to AC Saint Émilion, but still

under their Château name:
For example, Chateau Cheval Blanc
AC Saint-Émilion
Chateau Figeac
AC Saint-Émilion Premier Grand Cru
Classé
Cheval Blanc – tasted 1980
   Medium red, brown colour
   Quite full, fruity nose
   Quite high acidity, lacks centre, short finish
Figeac – tasted 1974
   Medium red, brown rim
   Some richness on nose like an old burgundy
   Slight rich taste, slightly burnt, sweet finish

1969   Cold spring, followed by a warm sum-
mer but a lot of rain. This produced a
small crop of indifferent wine with the
odd exception.
Beau-séjour (Bécot) – tasted 1980
   Medium depth of colour, brown rim
   Soft, elegant
   Good fruit, well-balanced, nice fruity finish
   A good 1969
Beau-séjour (Bécot) – re-tasted 1982
   Same as above but slightly dryer on the nose
Carvin – tasted 1979
   Medium red colour, brown rim
   Neutral nose
   Quite good texture, sound but losing fruit
Cheval Blanc – tasted 1977
   Pale colour
   Soft nose, trace perfumed, very gracious,
   which opens up and sweetens
   Lovely wine to drink, quite light, not much
   depth of fruit, softish
   Very clarety initially but becomes much more
   burgundian and sweet
Cheval Blanc – tasted 1976
   Not very good, suffering from the 1969
   disease
Cheval Blanc – tasted 1979
   Quite deep colour, orange edge
   Good, fruity, oaky, deep nose
   Soft, chocolate, good fruit and balance, nice
   long finish
Cheval Blanc – tasted 1980
   Deep colour, brown tinge
   Tight, and quite high acidity
   Good fruit, but slightly drying finish
Cheval Blanc – tasted 1982
   Mid and brown
   Odd medicinal nose
   Lost a lot of fruit, dry finish
Clos-des-Jacobins (LB half-bottle) – tasted 1976
   Pale colour

Light-scented nose
Light style of wine, no tannin, has acidity.
Quite pleasant and drinks quite well, not too
bad for the year
Clos-des-Jacobins (LB half-bottle) – tasted 1979
   Fairly light colour, orange rim
   Soft, smooth, sweet, quite burgundian
   Tight with acidity, lacks centre, firm finish
Figeac – tasted 1982
   Medium depth of colour, orange rim
   Good Merlot rot
   Fully mature, drying on finish
la Fleur Pétrus – tasted 1979
   Light colour, brown rim
   Light, thin, acidic nose
   Lacks fruit and body, thin finish
la Fleur Pétrus – tasted 1981
   Pale colour, orange rim
   Light, sweet
   Light centre, watery finish
la Gaffelière – tasted 1981
   Very deep colour, tawny rim
   Very delicate, light, Merlot
   Quite well-balanced but just drying on finish
Magdelaine – tasted 1980
   Medium depth of colour, brown rim
   Nice, fruity, violet, Merlot nose
   Quite well-balanced for a 1969 but beginning
   to dry on finish
Pavie — tasted 1979
   Medium depth of colour, brown rim
   Light, chocolate nose
   Light-weight, lacks body and finish
Pavie – re-tasted 1981
   Medium depth of colour, brown rim
   Deeper, sweet, chocolate nose
   Light-weight but opening up
Pétrus – tasted 1978
   Scented Merlot nose
   Soft, good fruit, many similarities to Cheval
   Blanc 1969
   Reasonable wine and quite pleasant to drink
Pétrus – tasted 1980
   Light red colour
   Sweetish, perfumed nose
   Fine with fruit but acidity, tannin over-
   powers
Pétrus – tasted 1981
   Very deep colour with brown rim
   Enormous concentration of fruit, superb
   Lovely long, sweet, fruity finish
de Sales (Magnum) – tasted 1974
   Pale colour
   Dull nose
   Fairly distinct flavour, slightly thin but
   woody

Acidity still present

de Sales – tasted 1977
Slightly pale, translucent, some depth
Good nose, Cabernetish
Good, pleasant, semi-mature, good quality claret, classic

de Sales – tasted 1977
Very nice, mature, light-weight claret, sort of cross between light-weight delicacy of Margaux and Saint-Émilion

Soutard – tasted 1981
Deep colour, brown rim
Sweet, light, violet
Sweet and farmyard, slightly drying out

la Tour Bélair (LB) – tasted 1972
Light red, brown rim
Soft, round, sweet nose
Full-bodied, good fruit, nicely-balanced finish

1970 Good, late spring followed by hot, dry summer, with rain later in August. This resulted in a large crop of excellent wine.

Ausone – tasted in 1976
Soft, light in tannin
Refined, delicate sort of claret. Showing well, very good i.e. an early maturing wine

Ausone – tasted 1980
Deep colour, orange rim
Strong oak, lovely rich, deep but still quite closed
Tight, closed, good depth, a long way to go

Ausone – tasted 1982
Same as above but slightly opened up now.
Lovely rich wine

l'Angélus – tasted 1980
Deep in colour, pinkish rim
Good, chocolate Merlot
Tannin and soft fruit
Hard centre, and finish

l'Angélus – tasted 1980
Good deep red
Good rich flavour, fruit, structure and length
Plenty of tannin

l'Angélus – re-tasted 1982
Medium depth of colour, tawny rim
Soft, Merlot, sweet, rich nose
Rich, sweet, well-developed, long ripe finish

Balestard-la-Tonnelle – tasted 1982
Deep in colour, brown rim
Good, deep Merlot
Good, tight, closed, tannic finish, not ready yet

Barbe Blanche – tasted 1980
Good, deep, tawny colour
Concentrated rich, sweet nose

Well-balanced, good fruit and extract, rich finish

Belair (Lussac) – tasted 1974
Dark in colour
Very immature wine
Good body
Needs long time

Bertin (Montagne) (LB Corney & Barrow) – tasted 1977
Quite big wine, very well-made
Good substance and fine balance
Tasting very well and true

Bertin (Montagne) (LB) – tasted 1978
Deep with pink edge
Big fruity nose, soft but tight
Still closed, good depth, tannic finish

Bourseau – tasted 1980
Good medium depth of colour, brown rim
Good, rich Merlot, violet nose
Very good balance, good, fruity finish

Canon – tasted 1978
Medium-weight, still rather astringent and immature, not particularly Merlotish

Canon – tasted 1982
Mid/deep brown
Good ripe rich delicate Merlot
Well-balanced with finesse, long finish

Canon-la Gaffelière – tasted 1975
Medium red colour
Good, Merlot rot
Quite light, but pleasing, very forward

Canon-la Gaffelière – tasted 1978
Good, deep colour, mature
Fruity, sweet
Chocolate, sweet, Merlot finish

Canon-la Gaffelière – tasted 1979
Rich, creamy nose
Rich and creamy in the mouth, but slight imbalance
Some tannin, not quite together

Canon-la Gaffelière – tasted 1981
Medium depth of colour, brown rim
Nice, ripe, violet nose
Slightly medicinal, tannic and oaky finish

Canon-la Gaffelière – tasted 1982
Pale/mid and orange
Light sweet sugared nose
Lacks fruit in centre
Commercial wine

Cap de Mourlin (LB Jacksons) – tasted 1975
Slightly sugary nose
Rich, big, soft wine, fairly advanced with good tannin and good balance

Cap de Mourlin – tasted 1975
Medium red
Soft, rich, slight hint of Merlot rot

Very charming and pleasing

Capdemourlin – tasted 1980
Medium red
Elegant fruity nose
Good balance, fruity, deep wine with good long finish and tannin

Capdemourlin – re-tasted 1982
Medium colour, brown rim
Rich, excellent balance, full finish

Cheval Blanc – tasted 1977
Medium colour
Warm, round, welcoming nose
Good, full, firm taste, plenty of tannin
Needs time to open up

Cheval Blanc (half-bottle) – tasted 1981
Good, full, red colur
Big, warm, slightly earthy nose
Rich and round in the mouth combining characteristics of a top Pomerol with some of the flowery elegance of a top-class Côte Saint-Émilion, very firm on the finish

Cheval Blanc – tasted 1980
Deep colour, brown rim
Lovely deep, rich, violet, chocolate nose
Good, rich, high alcohol, long finish
Very good balance and tannin. Still slightly closed. Very good future.

Cheval Blanc – re-tasted 1981 and 1982
Same as above

Cheval Blanc – tasted 1982
Deep and orange
Immense depth of fruit and concentration
Very big, still closed, great future

Chêne Vieux – tasted 1980
Good, deep colour, brown rim
Soft, Merlot with slight volatile acidity
Lacks centre, slightly acidic finish

Clos Fourtet (LB Berry Bros) – tasted 1982
Quite dark in colour
Closed Merlot nose
Quite a big wine, typical of Saint-Émilion which dries in the glass (no decanting)
Rather clumsy, lacking definition and breeding

Clos René – tasted 1978
Good colour, with pink rim
Good fruit on nose
Sweet, good balance, firm finish

Clos René – re-tasted 1981
Beginning to fade after two hours

Clos des Cloches – tasted 1979
Fairly dark colour
Stalky, clarety nose
Good finesse, nice delicate balance but a big wine all the same, rather Médoc in style

Clos Fourtet (LB Berry Bros) – tasted 1982
Pale in colour, orange rim
Thin, fruitless nose
Lacks fruit and centre, thin finesse

la Clotte – tasted 1975
Good, showing well, needs time

la Conseillante – tasted 1980
Very deep colour
Rich, sweet nose, a lot of depth
Superbly rich, good fruit, long finish, great finesse

la Croix St Georges (LB Grants) – tasted 1974
Pale in colour
Poor, unrevealing nose
Showing signs of opening up. Rather dull wine without much charm at present

Curé Bon la Madeleine – tasted 1980
Good, deep red
Rich, ripe nose
Good texture, fair balance, lacking fruit. Firm tannic finish with slight sourness

Curé Bon la Madeleine – tasted 1982
Deep red
Quite rich and sweet
Still closed with tannin
Good balance

Figeac – tasted 1980
Deep red colour
Flowery elegance
Full fruity with intensity of flavour, lots of tannin, not fully ready yet

Figeac – re-tasted 1981
Still superb

Figeac – re-tasted 1982
Medium colour, brown rim
Rich, excellent balance, full finish

la Fleur Pétrus – tasted 1977
Good colour
Very distinctive, rather exaggerated passion-fruit nose
A lot of fruit in the mouth, promising, very full and rich, a lot of tannin

la Fleur Pétrus – tasted 1980
Good medium depth, brown rim
Good, fruity, tough nose
Well-made and balanced, slightly light for a 1970

Fombrauge – tasted 1975
Deep colour, orange rim
Soft, sweet nose
Soft centre, sweet, chocolate finish

Fombrauge – tasted 1976
Big wine, fruity, will last but drinks well now

Fombrauge – tasted 1978
Dark wine
Quite nice, plummy Merlot nose

Lovely wine, just mature. Heavy, slightly sweet, lots of character with plenty of fruit. Not the usual insipid Merlot but very powerful rich style

la Gaffelière – tasted 1977
Full, orangy, mature, lovely colour
Find fruity rich nose
Drinking very well as a young semi-mature good wine, typical of its style

la Gaffelière – tasted 1982
Medium depth of colour, brown rim
Soft, sweet, well-balanced
Forward, chocolate finish

Grandes Murrailles – tasted 1982
Very deep and brown
Lovely rich sweet Merlot
Very rich, superb balance
Long fruity finish

Haut Manoir (LB Berry Bros) – tasted 1980
Dark colour
Good big nose – quite rich
Lovely wine to drink now, lot of fruit, mature, very weighty, trace earthy

Larmande (LB) – tasted 1978
Deep colour, browning
Good, rotting Merlot
Fat, slightly thin centre, quite high acidity on finish

Lassègue – tasted 1974
Good colour
Firm agreable now but will develop well. Pleasant.

Lassègue (LB) – tasted 1979
Good, deep colour, browning
Soft, sweet, good Merlot rot
Nice soft fruit, but lacks centre, nice finish

Lestage (Parsac) – tasted 1977
Nice clarety nose, still not very mature
Still rather difficult to define qualities through immaturity
Quite big, fairly woody

le Loup – tasted 1975
Typical soft wine, quite nice but nothing special

Lyonnat – tasted 1980
Medium depth of colour, orange rim
Slightly woody, but good fruity nose
Leafy, stalky, tough with light centre, strong finish

Magdelaine – tasted 1979
Good, deep colour, browning on rim
Lovely Merlot, rotting vegetables, toffee
Good balance and depth, still a lot of tannin

Magdelaine – tasted 1980
Big, deep red, pink rim
Big, rich, velvety nose

Lovely fruit, fine complex character, soft with tannin, lovely finish

Magdelaine – tasted 1982
Mid/deep and brown
Lovely rich ripe violet Merlot
Lots of fruit deep rich finish and tannin

Magnan la Gaffelière – tasted 1975
Average-style wine, quite big and acidity present
Not ready yet

Mazeyres (Magnum) – tasted 1982
Very deep in colour, orange rim
Good, deep rich, truffle nose
Good fruit and balance, tannic finish

Monbousquet – tasted 1980
Deep colour, brown rim
Elegant, spicey nose
Lovely fruit, fine mature wine

Moulinet (half-bottle) – tasted 1978
Still a bit immature. Typical young austere Pomerol, rather earthy sweet and heavy, vaguely like some St Ésteph's.

Moulin St Georges – tasted 1982
Deep colour, tawny rim
Deep, ripe, well-balanced nose
Good fruit and finish

Montlabert – tasted 1975
Good colour
Odd taste, not showing very well

Pavie – tasted 1980
Very deep colour, brown rim
Rich, ripe Merlot, violet nose
Good depth of extract, superb, rich, full-bodied, excellent balance and finish

Pavie – re-tasted 1981 and 1982
Still the same as above

Pavie-Macquin – tasted 1975
Tough and very big

Petit-Faurie-de-Soutard – tasted 1981
Deep in colour, orange rim
Good, tight, sweet, violet nose
Good length, fruity centre and finish

Pétrus – tasted 1980
Very deep, black red
More fragrant than younger wines
Very deep, lot of tannin with meat, needs years
Slightly tight at finish

Pétrus – tasted 1982
Deep colour, tawny rim
Enormous, rich, sweet, chocolate Merlot nose
Superbly rich, lots of fruit and tannin, lovely full finish, long way to go

Pipeau – tasted 1980
Lovely deep colour, orangey tones. Very little

nose, vague touch of spearmint
Soft, rather big and clumsy wine. Not very
appealing

Plaisance (LB half-bottle) – tasted 1976
Good colour, slight orange rim
Soft, smooth, slightly musty and acidity
Good body and weight, soft fruity finish

Plaisance (LB half-bottle) – tasted 1977
Good, full colour
Soft perfumed nose
Mature, not very heavy sort of wine but very
well-made. Medium-style of Saint-Émilion
wine, nice fruit, not woody. Still bit closed
but opens up on opening. Good wine

Plaisance – tasted 1982
Mid/deep and brown
Quite old nose, fading
Thin, light-weight and high acidity on finish

la Pointe – tasted 1980
Deep red, brown rim
Big, round nose, marked blackcurrant smell
Very big, a lot of fruit and tannin, rich,
almost thick texture

la Pointe – tasted 1979
Very deep colour, brown rim
Huge depth of fruit on the nose
Well-balanced, fruity wine, rich with long
finish and tannin

la Pointe – re-tasted 1982
Same as above

la Pointe – tasted 1982
Deep
Huge rich nose
Very full of flavour, chocolate finish

le Pont de Pierre – tasted 1980
Medium depth of colour, orange rim
Soft, sweet Merlot nose
Quite good centre, acidity on finish too high

Rocher Bellevue Figeac – tasted 1974
Average colour
Soft wine, good fruit, drinking now, will
improve

la Rochette – tasted 1973
Deep with pink rim
Soft, tight and closed nose
Round, full-bodied, well made

Roudier – tasted 1982
Medium depth of colour, brown rim
Deep, rich, chocolate nose
Good fruit, balance and finish

Saint Brice – tasted 1973
Medium depth of colour, pink edge
Soft, smooth, silky nose, closed up
A lot of tannin and particularly high acidity

de Sales – tasted 1980
Deep colour, brown rim

Rich extract of violets/truffles
Lots of body, rich full finish

de Sales – re-tasted 1982
Deep colour, brown rim
Ripe, sweet Merlot
Rich centre, slightly light on finish

Siaurac (Lalande de Pomerol) – tasted 1974
Deep colour, pink rim
Slightly burnt, light on fruit
Light-weight with high acidity on finish

Siaurac – tasted 1978
Good, deep colour, mature
Light, but good Merlot rot
Nice balance, slightly light centre, good
fruity finish

Taillefeur – tasted 1980
Very deep red
Deep chocolate/velvet nose
Noble wine, still a long way to go, plenty of
tannin

la Tour Capet – tasted 1972
Deep colour with pink edge
Big fruity nose, soft but tight
Still close, good depth, tannic finish

la Tour Figeac – tasted 1976
Good colour
Big classy nose with Merlot richness
Good and full in mouth, velvety texture, deep
long flavour

la Tour Figeac – re-tasted 1980
Still the same

la Tour Mont d'Or (Montagne) – tasted 1975
Good colour
Slight nose
Very good fruit

la Tour Mont d'Or – re-tasted 1974
Immature. Will develop well in a few years.
Pleasant
Similar to above

la Tour-du-Pin-Figeac – tasted 1976
Good, deep colour, pink edge
Soft, full, round fruit, good Merlot rot
Fruity, slightly closed, nice balance

Trotanoy – tasted 1976
Good, deep red
Rather shy closed nose
Quite attractive, characterful in the mouth
Not ready yet, still a lot of tannin

Trotanoy – tasted 1980
Good depth of colour, brown rim
Lovely, soft, sweet violets
Good depth, well-balanced, rich finish

Trottevielle – tasted 1973
Very pink
Big, soft, fruity nose
Full-bodied with a lot of tannin

Trottevieille – tasted 1977
 Lovely deep, orange colour
 Soft nose
 Typical semi-mature good quality Saint-Émilion. Lot of fruit, early woodiness, good
Trottevieille – tasted 1980
 Deep colour, orange rim
 Good, soft, violet, Merlot nose
 Good balance, slightly light centre, but good fruity finish
 Drinking now, forward
Vieux Château Calon (Montagne) – tasted 1975
 Good, fruity wine, typical of its vintage, but showing very well and with much life left
Vieux-Château-Certan – tasted 1976
 Rich, full colour
 Lovely fruity nose
 Big well-made wine, lot of fruit, semi-mature and showing extremely well
Vieux-Château-Certan – tasted 1976
 Early maturation
 Quite big wine, very good indeed now with excellent fruit, relatively soft
Vieux Château-Certan – tasted 1980
 Very deep colour with pink rim
 Excellent bouquet
 Good fruit and finish
Vieux Chevrol – tasted 1981
 Medium depth of colour, brown rim
 Light, leafy, delicate nose
 Slightly drying out, acidity showing through
Vieux Château Tropchaud – tasted 1982
 Brown colour
 Oxidized, chocolate nose
 Drying out, slightly pétillant on the finish
Yon-Figeac – tasted 1974
 Deep with pink edge
 Fruity with good depth of extract
 Firm, fruity finish, a lot of tannin
Yon-Figeac – tasted 1975
 Good red colour
 Rich, attractive, hint of Merlot rot
 Big mouthful, a lot of character, plenty of tannin
Yon la-Tour-Figeac – tasted 1975
 Soft, well-finished wine, not nearly ready

1971 A superb vintage in Saint-Émilion and Pomerol. A good early spring. There was a poor June which produced a lot of *coulure* in the Merlot grape. A good summer and the vintaging conditions were very good. The weather was rather better in Saint-Émilion and Pomerol than in the Médoc.
 A relatively small harvest was pro-

duced; for example, Château Pavie produced only 95 tonneaux.
Ausone – tasted 1980
 Deep red colour
 Rich, elegant, velvety nose
 Big and sweet, yet elegant taste, very fragrant, a lot of character still some tannin but good drinking now
Ausone – re-tasted 1982
 Medium colour, tawny rim, otherwise same as above
Balestard-la-Tonnelle – tasted 1982
 Deep colour, brown rim
 Lovely, ripe Merlot nose
 Good, sweet, rich Merlot, long finish
Beauregard – tasted 1977
 Good red colour
 Distinctive nose
 Touch of pleasing rottness and spice on nose
 Good, fleshy texture, enjoyable to drink now but should improve
Beau-séjour (Bécot) – tasted 1980
 Deep red with brown rim
 Quite fragrant with maturity on the nose
 Lots of flavour, enjoyable fruit, not a lot of tannin, good finish
Beau-séjour (Bécot) – tasted 1980
 Deep colour, brown rim
 Lovely sweet Merlot, soft, violet, vanillary
 Soft, well-balanced, at its peak
Beau-séjour (Bécot) – re-tasted 1982
 Same as above
Belair – tasted 1980
 Good mid-red colour
 Lightish elegant nose, rather withdrawn
 Some fruit, but less rich and full than Ausone.
 Still closed with tannin
Canon – tasted 1980
 Very deep colour, orange rim
 Deep, rich extract, great finesse
 Superbly rich, fully-developed
Canon – re-tasted 1981
 Slightly light finish
Canon-la Gaffelière – tasted 1982
 Medium colour, brown rim
 Soft, light Merlot
 Well-balanced, light centre, but good fruity finish
Cheval Blanc – tasted 1976
 Very big. No faults at all. Good fruit, semi-mature, hint of sweetness
Cheval Blanc – tasted 1980
 Strong Merlot nose. Deep garnet red. Very full, perfect balance and yet delicate. Will continue very gracefully

Cheval Blanc – tasted 1981
  Quite deep colour, brown rim
  Tight, quite leafy, but sweet and rich, immense concentration
  Full, tight, dry tannin, long way to go
Cheval Blanc – tasted 1982
  Good deep colour, browning
  Good rich Merlot nose
  Still a rich full, well-balanced wine
Clos-des-Jacobins – tasted 1976
  Good medium colour, pink rim
  Soft, sweet, Merlot nose, slightly metallic
  Light, fruity, fairly closed, soft chocolate finish
Clos-des-Jacobins – tasted 1977
  Woody nose
  Very big fruity wine, nice balance, good style, trace immature
Clos René – tasted 1980
  Deep red colour
  Beautiful deep nose
  Lovely long deep flavour, well-made
Clos René – re-tasted 1982
  Deep colour, brown rim
  Rich, truffle nose
  Lots of fruit and flavour
la Clotte – tasted 1980
  Medium colour, brown rim
  Soft, fruity, toffee nose
  Sweet, smooth, long, rich finish
  Tastes of dark chocolate
la Clotte – tasted 1980
  Medium colour, orange rim
  Good, sweet, Merlot nose
  Good fruit but slightly thin centre, nice firm finish
la Clotte – tasted 1982
  Mid and brown
  Sweet raspberry nose
  Quite sweet but drying on finish
la Conseillante – tasted 1980
  Medium depth of colour, brown rim
  Lovely, sweet, rich nose
  Attractive, soft, pleasant but lacks complexity and structure
la Croix – tasted 1982
  Medium colour, brown rim
  Lovely, rich, ripe truffle
  Good, rich, ripe fruit, good balance, slightly light finish
la Croix de Bertinat (Bow Wine Vaults Bottling) – tasted 1976
  Very soft agreeable example of a Saint Émilion. Very forward
Croix de Laborde – tasted 1980
  Pale/medium depth of colour, orange rim

Good, soft, Merlot, well-balanced nose
Good balance, nice fruit, well-made, soft finish
la Croix St Georges – tasted 1976
  Good, slightly earthy nose
  Semi-mature, nice wine, typical weight of 1971
Domaine de l'Église – tasted 1977
  Good, deep, red colour, brown rim
  Rich, almost burgundian nose
  Good fruit, voluptuous rather than elegant, a big mouthful
Domaine de la Vieille Église – tasted 1981
  Medium colour, brown rim
  Rich, ripe, sweet, oaky Merlot nose
  Disappointing, light, lost fruit
Domaine de l'Église (LB Berry Bros) – tasted 1982
  Mid and orange
  Warm Merlot nose
  Attractive, slightly woody. Light finish
l'Église Clinet – tasted 1982
  Medium depth of colour, tawny rim
  Sweet, jammy nose
  Rich, with sweet centre, light finish
Figeac – tasted 1978
  Very big, deep colour, browning on rim
  Superb, soft, fruity Merlot nose
  Full, great depth of extract, long chocolate finish
Figeac – tasted 1980
  Very deep colour, orange rim
  Rich, sweet, very good depth, toffee smell
  Very full-bodied, a lot of extract, excellent balance, long finish, top quality
Figeac – re-tasted 1982
  Superb as above. At its peak, but will remain superb for years
la Fleur Pétrus – tasted 1980
  Medium depth of colour, orange rim
  Lovely, sweet, truffle nose
  Good fruit and balance
la Fleur Pétrus – tasted 1981
  Pale/medium depth of colour, orange rim
  Stalky and woody nose
  Light, dry, lacks depth
Fombrauge – tasted 1976
  Good nose
  Nice style, mature, light, early maturing, drinking well
Fombrauge – re-tasted 1977
  As above
Fombrauge – tasted 1981
  Deep colour, tawny edge
  Soft, tight, Merlot nose
  Well-balanced, tannin, not ready yet

Grand-Pey-Lescours – tasted 1981
  Pale colour, brown rim
  Slightly leafy, sour nose
  Lacks fruit and centre
Larcis Ducasse – tasted 1977
  Medium colour red
  Mild, pleasant fruit gum nose
  Attractive flavour, fleshy, round, quite forward
Larmande – tasted 1981
  Medium colour, brown rim
  Nice, rich, delicate, sweet nose
  Delicate, well-balanced, slightly light centre, but good finish
Magdelaine – tasted 1978
  Medium depth of colour, orange rim
  Rich Merlot rot, soft caramel nose
  Soft, chocolate, sweet, good balance and finish
Magdelaine – tasted 1979
  Pale to medium depth of colour
  Leafy, light, re-tasted Merlot nose
  Light-weight, lacks depth, sweet finish
Magdelaine – tasted 1980
  Medium red colour, slightly orange rim
  Attractive, fruity nose, strawberry
  Light centre, feminine wine, delightful to drink now
Magdelaine – tasted 1982
  Rather too pale for year and Château
  Very attractive Merlot nose
  Not a big wine, probably at its peak now. Bit deficient in fruit, possibly poorly stored or a 'dud' bottle
Monbousquet – tasted 1980
  Good red colour
  Round, smooth, elegant nose
  Rich, firm with good structure
Pavie – tasted 1980
  Good colour
  Smooth, round, ripe nose
  Gracious, smooth and round in mouth. Rich, sweet, fragrant, well-balanced, near its peak
Pavie – re-tasted 1981
  Same as above
Pavie – re-tasted 1982
  At its peak now
Pavie-Decesse – tasted 1980
  Medium red, brown rim
  Full, strawberry nose
  Elegant, slightly high acidity
Pétrus – tasted 1980
  Deep dark red
  Very chewy huge flavour but even more power hidden
  More elegant than 1970

Plince (BB Saccone & Speed) – tasted 1974
  Purplish edge
  Fairly fruity nose
  Fruity wine, still poorly-balanced. Not acidic or tannic
Plince – tasted 1976
  Good colour
  Rich, soft nose, hint of Merlot rot
  Very good in mouth, good intensity, tough finish
Plince – tasted 1980
  Intense colour
  Nose closed
  Very rich but rather souped up. Short finish
la Pointe – tasted 1979
  Deep red colour
  Note very marked nose, hint of spice
  Good character, fruity with spice, good extract, lots of tannin
la Pointe – re-tasted 1982
  Deep colour with brown rim
  Full, developed, rich truffle, bouquet full-blown
  Lovely, rich, truffle finish
Roudier – tasted 1982
  Medium depth of colour, brown rim
  Nice, sweet Merlot nose
  Good balance and centre, slightly light finish
Rouget – tasted 1980
  Medium depth of colour, brown rim
  Lovely, rotting, vegetable, Merlot nose
  Disappointing, thin centre, lacks fruit, soft finish
de Sales – tasted 1980
  Medium colour, orange rim
  Slightly green, leafy nose
  Lacks centre, medicinal finish
Siaurac (Lalande) – tasted 1978
  Good depth of colour, browning on rim
  Caramel, tight, closed nose
  Musty, sweet, lacks centre and fruit, thin finish
la Tour-du-Pin-Figeac – tasted 1982
  Deep colour, brown rim
  Stalky, medicinal nose
  Lacks fruit, could be a problem bottle
des Tours – tasted 1980
  Quite deep colour, tawny rim
  Tight, slightly cooked nose
  Sweet, fruity, slightly stalky but good finish
Trotanoy – tasted 1977
  Deep colour, pink rim
  Good, rich, tight, sweet nose
  Nice fruit and balance, tight finish
Trotanoy – tasted 1980
  Deep red colour

Very big nose, huge character
Deep, flowery, lovely rich, soft texture
Very big extract, soft, but still tannin, a long way to go
Trotanoy – re-tasted 1980
Good deep colour, slight browning on rim
Superb rich violets and chocolate
A lot of depth and extract, good rich finish
Trottevieille (LB Berry Bros) – tasted 1982
Mid and brown
Nice light Merlot nose
Lacks centre, drying on finish with high acidity
Vieux-Château-Certan – tasted 1980
Deep colour, brown rim
Lovely, rich, sweet, Merlot violets
Good, rich, soft fruity nose
Good firm finish
Yon-Figeac (LB Berry Bros half-bottle) – tasted 1981
Very pale with even paler mature rim
Sweet nose
A light style of wine, fully mature, trace tart on finish. Has some tannin showing with sweetness and reasonable fruit

1972   Cold spring with very late flowering. A poor summer with some sun but quite a lot of rain, resulting in a reasonable crop of indifferent wines, some are now softening down and losing their harsh acidity. The harvest was late. The Médoc was generally better than Saint-Émilion and Pomerol.
Canon – tasted 1981
Medium depth of colour, brown rim
Light and sweet nose
High acidity on finish, generally light
Cheval Blanc – tasted 1981
Medium depth, brown rim
Quite thin, with acidity on nose
Green, medicinal, light-weight, chaptalised finish
Cheval Blanc – tasted 1982
Mid and brown
Quite deep fruity nose
Well-balanced, sweet finish
Figeac – tasted 1980
Medium colour, brown rim
Oaky, sweet, slightly minty nose
Quite light, but nice balance of fruit, light finish
Fonroque – tasted 1977
Good wine, pepperminty, ready and quite full

Gazin – tasted 1982
Mid and brown
Minty, sweet nose
Lacks centre dry finish
Matras – tasted 1980
Light colour, medium red
Soft, fruity nose
Light-weight, lacks centre and finish
Pavie – tasted 1981
Medium colour, brown rim
Soft, sweet nose
Good fruit, but high acidity
Well-made 1972 with good finish
Pétrus – tasted 1980
Pale red
Lovely, slight leafy nose with oaky creaminess
Very good fruit, slight acid background
Troplong-Mondot – tasted 1981
Medium depth of colour, orange rim
Soft and acidity, thin nose
Fairly soft and sweet, good balance for a 1972
Trotanoy – tasted 1980
Pale/medium colour, brown rim
Nice, soft, fruity, sweet nose
Nice balance, soft fruity finish
Trottevieille – tasted 1982
Mid and orange
Light sweet nose
Lacked fruit and depth. Weak finish
Vieux-Château-Certan – tasted 1980
Fairly successful. Merlot-type nose. Light in fruit, not too stalky or acidic. Typical light Merlot wine, fully mature, short life. Quite good
Vieux-Château-Certan – tasted 1981
Medium depth of colour, brown rim
Light but good fruit and balance
Nice, sweet, light-weight but good balance
Vieux Sarpe (Saint-Christophe) – tasted 1976
Rather pale, semi-mature colour
Merlot nose
Tastes bit young but more like a 1967. Not firm but acceptable

1973   A fine spring, wet summer, but sunny later in August, resulting in a large crop of early drinking wines.
Beau-séjour (Bécot) – tasted 1980
Medium/deep in colour, tawny rim
Good violet Merlot nose
Soft, chocolate taste, light-weight throughout
Beauséjour (Duffau-Lagarrosse) – tasted 1982
Medium depth of colour, orange rim
Light, sweet Merlot

Quite light-weight in the mouth, forward sweet wine

Canon – tasted 1981
Medium colour, brown rim
Light, fruity, sweet nose
Good balance, but slightly light finish

Cheval Blanc – tasted 1981
Medium colour, orange rim
Sweet, concentrated violets on nose
Light-weight, lacks centre, nose better than palate

Cheval Blanc – tasted 1982
Mid and brown
Good fruity, concentrated raspberry nose
Lots of fruit, well-balanced, good finish

Clos Fourtet – tasted 1980
Light in colour, orange rim
Light, fresh, fragrant, sweet nose
Charming, light-weight, but a nice 1973

la Dominique – tasted 1981
Medium/deep colour, orange rim
Soft, sweet, violet nose
Quite nice balance, slightly lacking centre, but firm good finish

Figeac – tasted 1980
Deep colour, orange rim
Superb Merlot rot, mature, like ripe Pinot
Charming, light-weight with good character
Mature Merlot showing through to the finish

la Fleur Pétrus – tasted 1980
Medium/pale colour
Soft, sweet, toffee nose
Quite light, easy to drink, short finish

la Fleur Pétrus – tasted 1981
Medium colour, orange rim
Nice, sweet, soft nose
Quite light, with sweet short finish

Fonplégade – tasted 1981
Deep colour, tawny rim
Good, rich, Merlot violet nose
Full, sweet, well-balanced finish

la Grave (Lussac) (bottled by G. Renaud in Cavignon) – tasted 1977
Nicely mature wine. Good Saint-Émilion style, lightish

Pavie – tasted 1980
Deep colour, orange rim
Nice rich, deep, fruity, sweet nose
Quite rich, lightish centre, but good length on the finish, nicely-balanced

Pétrus – tasted 1973
Light purple red colour
Lovely light oaky nose
Creamy, very full of grape flavour, slightly medicinal. Great follow-on

Peyreau – tasted 1981
Light in colour, orange rim
Nice, soft, light, violet nose
Light on fruit, but good firm finish

la Rochette (Puisseguin) (LB Christopher's) – tasted 1977
Quite a pleasant wine but nothing special. Typical fairly young, yet reasonable mature, wine.

Roudier – tasted 1982
Medium colour, orange rim
Sweet, light nose
Very light-weight, lacks depth, short finish

Siaurac (Lalande) – tasted 1978
Light colour, pink rim
Light, soft, sweet, caramel nose
Light-weight, lacks depth, but good firm finish

la Tour-à-Pomerol – tasted 1975
Deep, young red
Nose rather under-developed but a hint of class
Unmistakably good Pomerol flavour and quality in mouth, creamy, nutty, very long finish and tannin

Troplong-Mondot – tasted 1980
Lightish, medium red
Pleasant attractive nose
Light, pleasing, velvety finish

Trotanoy – tasted 1980
Medium colour, brown rim
Good, soft, violet nose
Nice balance, soft, sweet finish

Vieux-Château-Certan – tasted 1980
Relative pallor compared to other *Vieux-Château-Certan* wines but darker than many 1973's
Well-developed nose – rather refined for Château
Light wine, bit austere for weight, not a great example of year
Sort of plumminess

Vieux-Château-Certan – tasted 1980
Light colour, orange rim
Light, sweet violets nose
Light-weight, lacks centre and fruit on finish

Vieux Rivallon – tasted 1981
Deep colour, tawny rim
Good, well-balanced nose
Quite light-weight, lacks centre, short finish

1974 Good spring, hot summer, but rained at vintage time producing a large quantity of indifferent wine.

Balestard-la-Tonnelle – tasted 1981
Quite deep colour, orange rim

Good, sweet, violet nose
Good, sweet, balance, slightly light finish,
but a good 1974
Balestard-la-Tonnelle – re-tasted 1982
As above
Barbe-Blanche – tasted 1980
Pale in colour, orange rim
Nice fruit and balance, good concentration
for a 1974
Well-balanced, fruity, good finish
Beauregard – tasted 1980
Medium/pale colour, brown rim
Sweet but stalky
Thin, light, acidity on finish
Canon – tasted 1981
Medium depth of colour, orange rim
Light, sweet nose
Light-weight throughout
Canon – tasted 1981
Medium colour, pink rim
Good balanced nose
Quite light but good balance for a 1974
Cap de Mourlin – tasted 1982
Pale colour, orange rim
Woody, chocolate nose
Sweet, stalky, light finish
Cheval Blanc – tasted 1982
Good colour
Fruity nose
Light-weight, sweet finish
la Conseillante – tasted 1980
Medium depth of colour, brown edge
Soft, stalky nose
Good balance, slightly high acidity
A nice 1974
la Dominique – tasted 1981
Pale in colour, brown rim
Light, sweet, lacks charm
Light-weight, lacks fruit and centre
Figeac – tasted 1980
Medium depth of colour
Some burgundian richness, but a little thin
Similar in mouth, charming with some
richness, light and attractive
Figeac – tasted 1981
Deep in colour, pink rim
Tight, tough, sweet underneath
Tough, stalky, slightly green centre
A well-made 1974
Figeac – re-tasted 1982
Medium depth, tawny rim
The same as when tasted in 1980
la Fleur Pétrus – tasted 1978
Pale colour
Weak, fruity nose, quite sweet
Quite fruity, light-weight but nice finish

la Fleur Pétrus – tasted 1981
Medium colour, orange rim
Sweet and fruity nose
Nice body, chaptalised, light, pleasant finish
la Fleur Pétrus – tasted 1980
Medium/pale colour, brown rim
Soft, sweet, slightly woody nose
Dry, austere, lacks fruit
Larcis Ducasse – tasted 1981
Deep colour, tawny rim
Fairly tight, deep, stalky nose
Quite well-balanced, good fruity finish
Magdelaine – tasted 1981
Good colour, brown rim
Nice, sweet, scented nose
Quite sweet and light, pleasant finish
Monbousquet – tasted 1980
Red colour, brown rim
Faint but elegant nose
Pleasant tasted, light finish
Pavie – tasted 1980
Medium depth of colour, orange rim
Slightly sweet, chaptalised, Ribena nose
Light, sweet, lacks centre, short finish with
acidity
Pavie – re-tasted 1981
Same as above
Petit Village – tasted 1980
Medium-red colour
Light-weight nose
Quite hard and thin, lacks fruit
de Rol – tasted 1977
Strong Merlot, stalky, woody nose
Quite pleasant wine which opens up well
de Tabuteau (Lussac) – tasted 1981
Light colour
Sweet, chaptalised nose
Light-weight, commercial wine, weak finish
Trotanoy – tasted 1980
Medium depth of colour, brown rim
Light rim and acidity
Light centre, but well-made and sweet finish
Trotanoy – re-tasted 1982
Deep colour, pink rim
Good truffle nose
A well-made 1974, sweet finish
Vieux-Château-Certan – tasted 1980
Young appearance, pink hue
Elegant fragrant light nose
Charming, light-weight wine

1975 Superb vintage. A warm spring with
some early frost damage. A good summer with well-balanced weather resulting in a smallish crop of excellent
quality.

Balestard-la-Tonnelle – tasted 1981
  Very deep colour, browning on rim
  Deep, oaky nose
  Good, deep, well-balanced, long finish
Balestard-la-Tonnelle – re-tasted 1982
  Same as above
Barbe Blanche – tasted 1980
  Medium depth of colour, orange rim
  Deep, sweet, violet nose
  Good concentration of fruit, sweet finish, well-made
Beauregard – tasted 1980
  Deep colour, orange rim
  Violet nose, good extract
  Very good depth and balance
  Needs more time
Beau-séjour (Bécot) (Double magnum) – tasted 1980
  Deep colour, pink rim
  Sweet, tight, closed nose
  Good fruit, slightly light centre, good fruity finish
Bellevue (Lussac) – tasted 1980
  Medium depth of colour, orange rim
  Closed, slightly leafy and medicinal
  Lacks centre, quite high acidity, sweet finish
Canon – tasted 1980
  Quite deep young red
  Subdued nose with character and depth
  Rich fruit, finesse and tannin, a long way to go
Canon – re-tasted 1981
  Same as above
Cap de Mourlin – tasted 1982
  Medium depth of colour, orange rim
  Lovely, rich, sweet Merlot
  Good, chocolate palate, long fruity finish
Cheval Blanc – tasted 1980
  Very deep colour, slight tawny rim
  Slight SO_2, high oak, enormous depth of fruit and concentration
  Outstanding depth, huge fruity long finish, superb 1975
Cheval Blanc – re-tasted 1981
  Same as above
Cheval Blanc – tasted 1982
  Very deep and pink
  Full rich ripe Merlot nose
  Lots of fruit and depth superb finish
Clos l'Église – tasted 1982
  Medium depth of colour, orange rim
  Lovely, sweet, rich, well-balanced Merlot nose
  Superb fruit and balance and plenty of tannin
  Will last a long time

Clos Fourtet – tasted 1980
  Good, deep colour, pink rim
  Good balance of fruit, closed nose
  Tight, light centre, thin finish
Clos Fourtet – tasted 1980
  Russet red
  Ageing nose
  Good fruit but dryness creeping in
la Conseillante – tasted 1980
  Medium colour, orange rim
  Deep, closed, rich concentrated Merlot
  Tight, and closed, good balance and finish
Dassault – tasted 1980
  Deep, red colour
  Closed, subdued, fruity nose
  Big, rich, closed, elegant, superb depth
la Dominique – tasted 1981
  Good, deep colour, orange rim
  Tight, rich and sweet
  Closed, but a lot of fruit and tannin
l'Évangile – tasted 1981
  Deep colour, browning rim
  Soft, sweet, Merlot, truffles and iron, black cherry
  Very full, a lot of extract and centre, full-bodied, rich, long, tight finish and tannin
Figeac – tasted 1980
  Very deep colour, pink rim
  A lot of depth of fruit, superb rich, oaky nose
  Great extract, rich, superb, lots of fruit, long, well-balanced tannic finish, a super 1975, will last for years
Figeac – re-tasted 1982
  Very deep colour, tawny rim
  Nose and palate the same as tasted in 1980
la Fleur Pétrus – tasted 1980
  Deep colour
  Good, deep, rich, violet nose
  Good fruit and body, long tough finish
la Fleur Pétrus – tasted 1981
  Deep colour
  Rich, superb, full, truffle nose
  Great depth and centre, long tannic finish
la Fleur Nardon – tasted 1982
  Medium depth of colour, orange rim
  Sweet, light, Merlot nose
  Soft, fruity, light finish
Fonplégade – tasted 1982
  Medium depth of colour, orange rim
  Light, ripe, sweet, Merlot nose
  Light-weight, with firm finish
Haut Bonneau – tasted 1982
  Medium depth of colour, orange rim
  Nice, ripe, violet nose
  Good balance, firm finish

Lyonnat – tasted 1980
  Good, deep colour, orange rim
  Nice, soft, sweet Merlot nose
  Good balance, well-made, long finish
Magdelaine – tasted 1979
  Good, deep colour
  Lovely chocolate Merlot nose
  Good balance, a lot of tannin there
Magdelaine – tasted 1980
  Very deep, young red
  Deep, classic nose with richness
  Closed, but a lot of hidden fruit, tannic finish
Matras – tasted 1980
  Fairly deep red colour
  Attractive fruity nose
  Quite closed but with good depth and future
Monbousquet – tasted 1980
  Very deep red, almost opaque
  Huge, fruity bouquet
  A very big wine, lots of flavour and tannin
Monbousquet – tasted 1981
  Very deep colour, orange rim
  Forward, violet nose
  Tough, tight, a lot of fruit, good balance and finish
Monbousquet – tasted 1982
  Deep and orange
  Lovely rich violet nose
  Lots of fruit, soft, well-balanced
  Fine firm finish
Monlot-Capet – tasted 1978
  Medium depth of colour, orange rim
  Soft, sweet, slightly light nose
  Fairly sweet, slightly burnt, chocolate, and tannin and acidity
Moulinet – tasted 1981
  Deep colour, tawny rim
  Closed, deep, truffle nose
  Tight, food fruit and balance, firm finish
Moulinet – re-tasted 1982
  Same as above
Pavie – tasted 1978
  Very deep, colour, pink rim
  Good, deep, fruity, sweet nose
  Good balance, chocolate finish
Pavie – tasted 1980
  Deep colour, orange rim
  Tight, good depth of concentration
  Closed with tannin, long tight, fruity finish, a long way to go
Pavie – re-tasted 1981
  As above
Pavie-Decesse – tasted 1980
  Very deep, young red
  Rather closed nose
  Good extract, closed, a lot of depth

Petit Village – tasted 1978
  Good, deep colour, purple edge
  Tight, closed nose with acidity
  Light-weight centre, tannic finish
la Pointe – tasted 1980
  Deep, rich colour
  Lovely truffle nose
  Superb, rich, fruity flavour, long finish
la Pointe – tasted 1982
  Deep colour, tawny rim
  Lovely, deep, rich, closed, truffle Merlot nose
  Rich, deep, good fruit, long, well-balanced finish
Plince – tasted 1982
  Quite deep colour, orange rim
  Nice, rich, truffle nose
  Good, rich, sweet, slightly light finish
Roudier – tasted 1982
  Quite deep colour, orange rim
  Good deep, Merlot nose
  Tight, fruity, slightly stalky finish
St Georges – tasted 1980
  Medium depth of colour, tawny rim
  Slightly stalky nose but fruity
  Quite a green, stalky taste, and acidity
de Sales (half-bottle) – tasted 1980
  Deep red colour
  Very deep, full, fruity nose
  Great character, and extract, with tannin
la Serre – tasted 1980
  Deep, rich colour
  Lovely Merlot, violet nose
  Lots of rich fruit, good, deep finish
la Serre – tasted 1982
  Deep colour, pink rim
  Soft, sweet, tight, just opening
  Round, soft, well-structured, tannin, good finish
Soleil – tasted 1981
  Good, deep colour, orange rim
  Nice, deep extract of fruit
  Sweet, good fruit, well-made, good, long finish
la Tour de Grenet (Lussac) – tasted 1978
  Deep colour, slight browning on rim
  Soft, spicy, sweet, nose
  Soft, creamy palate, tannin and acidity
des Tours (Magnum) – tasted 1980
  Deep colour, purple rim
  Fruity, full-bodied nose
  Good balance, fruity, tannic finish
Vieux-Château-Certan – tasted 1979
  Good colour, paler than some 1975's
  Subtle, closed nose, oaky Merlot
  Wine is slightly less heavy than some. Very good balance, tannin, Merlot-style, very

oaky, will become fine in future, typical good 1975
Vieux-Château-Certan – tasted 1980
  Very deep colour, brown rim
  Tight, closed, rich, a lot of extract, oaky nose
  Very rich fruit, excellent balance, long rich finish, a long way to go
Yon-Figeac – tasted 1982
  Very pale colour
  Rather medicinal Merlot nose
  Odd wine, tasting very dubious as though something was wrong with the wine

1976 A mild spring, followed by a very hot, dry summer but it rained during the vintage. This resulted in a reasonable quantity of varying quality wine. Saint-Émilion/Pomerol wines were less successful than the Médoc.

l'Angélus – tasted 1980
  Medium depth of colour, pink rim
  Light-weight, sweet nose
  Lacks centre and finish
Ausone – tasted 1980
  Deep colour, pink rim
  Lovely, rich, sweet, violet nose
  Tight, good balance and tannin
Ausone – tasted 1981
  Deep colour, pink rim
  Good fruity, soft, sweet, Merlot nose
  Good fruit, slightly light centre and finish
Ausone – re-tasted 1982
  Deep colour, tawny rim
  Nose and palate the same as tasted in 1981
Balestard-la-Tonnelle – tasted 1982
  Medium depth of colour, orange rim
  Good, sweet, Merlot nose
  Slightly light-weight, but good fruity finish
Beauregard – tasted 1980
  Deep young red colour
  Intense, violet bouquet
  Long, deep flavour, good finish
Beau-séjour (Bécot) – tasted 1980
  Medium depth of colour, pink rim
  Leafy, medicinal nose
  Green, leafy tasted, light-weight, short finish
Beau-séjour (Bécot) – tasted 1980
  Young, medium red colour
  Quite full, fruity, flowery nose
  Big, attractive, rather obvious fruity flavour in first half of taste, quite firm finish
Beauséjour (Duffau-Lagarrosse) – tasted 1980
  Medium red, slightly orange rim
  Tight, closed, almost raspberry concentrate nose

Very tight with tannin, a lot of depth, well-made with good extract
Bélair – tasted 1980
  Very deep colour, pink rim
  Tight, closed nose
  Tight palate, tannin, very closed, not yet opened up
Bélair – tasted 1980
  Medium depth of colour, orange rim
  Nice, sweet, well-balanced nose
  Very sweet, forward, drinking now
Belles-Graves – tasted 1980
  Medium depth of colour, orange rim
  Delicate, soft, sweet nose
  Light-weight, sweet, forward, drinking now
Bellevue (Lussac) – tasted 1979
  Good, deep colour, purple rim
  Soft, Merlot sweetness on nose
  Well-balanced, good, firm finish
Bellevue – tasted 1981
  Light colour, orange rim
  Light, sweet, sugary nose
  Light-weight, thin centre, lacks fruit and depth
Beychet – tasted 1981
  Deep colour, pink rim
  Soft, sweet, Merlot nose
  Nice fragrant, good balance, well-made
Bourgneuf Vayron – tasted 1981
  Medium depth of colour, orange rim
  Violet nose
  Quite leafy, light finish
Canon – tasted 1981
  Medium depth of colour, orange rim
  Soft, sweet, light nose
  Attractive but light-weight
Canon la Gaffelière – tasted 1982
  Mid and brown
  Light-weight, sweetish nose
  Stalky, bitter finish
Cap de Mourlin – tasted 1980
  Light, young red
  Fresh, fruity nose
  Good balance, slightly light centre, good finish
Cap de Mourlin – re-tasted 1982
  As above
la Carte – tasted 1980
  Medium depth of colour, pink rim
  Nice Merlot, but leafy nose
  Soft, quite good weight, light finish
Cadet Piola – tasted 1981
  Deep colour, tawny rim
  Sweet, not rich, medicinal nose
  Light-weight, lacks centre, watery finish, tannin and alcohol

Cheval Blanc – tasted 1980
　Medium depth of colour
　Lovely, soft, violet nose
　Full-bodied, rich and deep, good firm finish
Cheval Blanc – tasted 1981
　Same as above
Cheval Blanc – tasted 1982
　Good deep rich colour
　Light sweet fruity nose
　Quite light in character but good firm finish
Clos Fourtet – tasted 1978
　Pale, garnet red
　Very fruity but ageing
Clos Fourtet – tasted 1980
　Medium depth of colour, pink rim
　Very sweet, light-weight
　Lacks centre, light-weight finish
Clos Fourtet – tasted 1982
　Mid and orange
　Slightly woody nose
　Soft quite sweet forward
Clos des Moines – tasted 1979
　Good deep colour, pink rim
　Soft, earthy, Merlot sweetness
　Light-weight, lacks centre, earthy finish with tannin
Clos du Rocher – tasted 1981
　Deep colour, orange rim
　Lovely, soft, rich, truffle nose
　Very good depth of fruit, very good future
Clos René – tasted 1982
　Deep colour, brown rim
　Good, rich, truffle nose
　Lovely balance of fruit and tannin
la Clotte – tasted 1982
　Deep colour, orange rim
　Sweet, Merlot nose
　Fruity, sweet wine with short finish
la Conseillante – tasted 1980
　Medium depth of colour, orange rim
　Very soft, creamy, sweet nose
　Smooth, light on fruit, forward
la Croix – tasted 1982
　Medium depth of colour, brown rim
　Nice ripe, rich, truffle nose
　Ripe sweet, light-weight, but nice, fruity balance
Curé-bon la Madeleine – tasted 1980
　Medium depth of colour, brown rim
　Light, Merlot nose
　Light-weight, thin, leafy finish
Dassault – tasted 1980
　Deep red colour, pink rim
　Big, rich, fruity nose
　Very fruity, and elegant, long finish, quite forward

Domaine de l'Église – tasted 1980
　Medium depth of colour, orange rim
　Light, sweet nose
　Lacks body and finish
Domaine de Lamarzelle Cormey – tasted 1982
　Medium colour, tawny rim
　Chocolate, Merlot nose
　Soft, sweet, light finish
la Dominique – tasted 1981
　Medium pale colour, orange rim
　Nice, soft, violet nose
　Sweet, smooth, nice balance and finish
Durand Laplaigne – tasted 1980
　Medium colour, orange rim
　Nice, sweet-scented violets
　Good body and centre, long, well-balanced finish
l'Église Clinet – tasted 1982
　Deep colour, brown rim
　Sweet, Merlot, truffle nose
　Slightly tough, light finish
l'Évangile – tasted 1981
　Medium depth of colour, orange rim
　Tight, complex, soft Merlot, iron nose
　Very well-balanced, nice fruit, slightly light centre but good soft finish
l'Évangile – tasted 1982
　Mid and orange
　Rich caramel nose
　Creamy, plenty of fruit, forward and ready now
Figeac – tasted 1981
　Very deep colour, pink rim
　Deep, rich, concentrate fruit nose
　Very soft, rich. A very good 1976
Figeac – re-tasted 1982
　Deep colour, tawny rim
　Rich, truffle, chocolate nose
　Full of rich, soft fruit and tannin. Good future
la Fleur Pétrus – tasted 1980
　Medium depth of colour
　Light-weight, sweet nose
　Nice light, pleasant, wine, good finish
la Fleur Pétrus – tasted 1981
　Deep colour, gradulated
　Sweet, chocolate nose
　Light-weight, but good balance and finish
la Gaffelière – tasted 1980
　Good medium red colour
　Charming fragrant nose
　Good fruit and balance, tough finish, will develop well
la Gaffelière – re-tasted 1982
　Medium colour, orange rim
　Light-weight dry nose

Sweet, light finish
Gazin – tasted 1981
  Good depth of colour, orange rim
  Good, rich concentrated fruit
  Full, tannin, good firm finish
Grand Corbin d'Espagne – tasted 1981
  Medium colour, pink rim
  Full, truffle nose
  Rich fruit, good centre, slightly light finish
le Grave Trigant de Boisset – tasted 1981
  Already very forward and fully mature. A lovely wine, ripe, sweet and showing the character of Pomerol. Not a heavy-weight
Guadet Franc Grace Dieu – tasted 1981
  Medium colour, pink rim
  Hot, burnt raw, sweet Merlot
  Light-weight, lacks centre, alcoholic finish
Gurbot la Fourveille – tasted 1980
  Good colour, orange rim
  Sweet, scented nose
  Slightly high acidity, thin centre and finish
Haut-Sarpe – tasted 1982
  Medium colour, tawny rim
  Nice, soft, fruity, sweet, violet nose
  Good soft, fruity, well-balanced finish
Magdelaine – tasted 1980
  Medium depth of colour, orange rim
  Soft, full, sweet nose
  Nice, full, rich wine, a lot of character
  A good 1976
Matras (half-bottle) – tasted 1980
  Medium red
  Light, fruity nose
  Strawberry taste, light-weight, acidity and tannin on finish
Maurens – tasted 1982
  Mid and orange
  Medicinal nose
  Flat, stalky, thin finish
Monbousquet – tasted 1980
  Good colour
  Good depth, closed
  Big, tannic wine, good structure, very closed
Monbousquet (Jeroboam) – tasted 1981
  Very deep colour, pink rim
  Deep, truffle nose
  Slightly pétillant, chocolate taste, good finish
Moulinet – tasted 1982
  Medium colour, orange rim
  Nice, sweet Merlot nose
  Good balance, light finish
Nenin – tasted 1980
  Good red colour
  Subdued quality nose
  Well-made, soft, fruity wine with tannin

Patris (Magnum) – tasted 1982
  Deep colour, pink rim
  Rich, sweet, violet nose
  Well-balanced, slightly light finish
Pavie – tasted 1980
  Quite deep colour, pink rim
  Still quite closed, sweet, quite fruity
  Slightly light centre, but nice chocolate, fruity finish
Pavie – re-tasted 1981
  Same as above
Pavie – tasted 1982
  Deep and pink
  Still very immature, closed up and tannin
Petit Village – tasted 1980
  Deep red colour
  Deep, fragrant nose
  Well-balanced with long tannic finish
Pétrus – tasted 1981
  Very deep colour, pink rim
  Full concentrated rich Merlot nose
  Very full, tannin, good long firm finish
la Pointe – tasted 1980
  Medium red colour
  Attractive, sweet, fruity nose
  Quite light centre but well-made
la Pointe – tasted 1982
  Quite deep colour, orange rim
  Soft, sweet, iron nose
  Tough light centre, firm, slightly hard finish
St Georges – tasted 1980
  Deep colour, pink edge
  Nice, soft, sweet, Merlot nose
  Well-balanced, good long finish
de Sales – tasted 1981
  Good, medium colour, brown rim
  Sweet, Merlot nose
  Quite good fruit, slightly light finish
de Sales – re-tasted 1982
  Medium depth of colour, brown rim
  Good, sweet Merlot nose
  Lovely, rich, ripe, opened up
de Sales – tasted 1982
  Deep colour, but already showing mature rim
  Well-developed Pomerol nose
  Strange wine, ready to drink in some respects and moderately pleasant, yet in others rather woody, medicinal and unbalanced. Not a wine for keeping but will suffice for a few years
la Serre – tasted 1981
  Purple colour
  Rich, deep, fruity, Merlot nose
  Good depth, fruity finish
la Serre – tasted 1982
  Medium depth of colour, tawny rim

Ripe, rich, violet nose
Good balance, light centre and firm finish
Soutard – tasted 1980
Medium red
Elegant fruity nose
Good fruit and extract, light-weight balance,
forward
Teillac – tasted 1980
Medium/pale colour, orange rim
Good, soft, Merlot nose
Good balance, nice, fruity finish
Latour à Pomerol – tasted 1980
Big, rich colour, pink rim
Soft, chocolate nose
Rich, full-bodied, firm, fruity finish
la Tour-du-Pin-Figeac – tasted 1982
Medium depth of colour, tawny rim
Sweet, fruity nose
Lacks finesse, short finish
Troplong-Mondot – tasted 1980
Medium red colour
Fragrant, violet small
Tannic, closed but fruity finish
Troplong-Mondot – tasted 1981
Medium depth of colour, brown rim
Good, firm, Merlot, violet nose
Soft, sweet, light finish
Trotanoy – tasted 1980
Deep red colour
Very big nose
Huge character, deep with a hint of flowers.
Lovely rich, soft texture, very big extract,
soft in the middle and plenty of tannin. A long
way to go
Trotanoy – re-tasted 1982
Same as above but softening up and becom-
ing lighter in the centre
Vieux-Château-Certan – tasted 1981
Good, deep colour, pink rim
Soft, fruity, truffle nose
Nice full, fruity wine, slightly light centre
Vieux-Croix-de-Gay – tasted 1981
Medium depth of colour, orange rim
Sweet, truffle nose
Quite nice fruit, dry firm finish

1977 Cold, frosty spring. A variable summer
with quite a lot of rain. A very late
harvest resulting in a small crop of
indifferent wines.
des Arnauds – tasted 1980
Pale colour, pink rim
Green, stalky nose
Thin with high acidity, lacks fruit
Ausone – tasted 1982
Pale/medium depth of colour, brown rim

Smells of pine kernels
Light, quite sweet, short finish
Balestard-la-Tonnelle – tasted 1982
Medium colour, orange rim
Nice, sweet, fruity nose
Well-made, nice fruity finish
Cap de Mourlin – tasted 1980
Medium depth of colour, purple rim
Good, fruity nose, slightly harsh
Light with acidity, fruity finish
Cap de Mourlin – tasted 1982
Medium colour, tawny rim
Tough, stalky nose
Green, stalky, firm finish
Cheval Blanc – tasted 1982
Pale and brown
Old rubbery nose
Quite fruity, burnt finish
Fombrauge – tasted 1982
Light tawny
False sweet nose
Quite fruity and acidity on finish
Figeac – tasted 1980
Medium depth of colour, pink rim
Light-weight, sweet violets
Light centre, tannin, and acidity on finish
Fideac – re-tasted 1982
Medium depth of colour, tawny rim
Slightly stalky, medicinal nose
Green, vegetable, stalky finish
la Fleur Pétrus – tasted 1980
Pale colour, orange rim
Quite soft, sweet but high acidity on the nose
Light, quite thin, chaptalised finish
la Fleur Pétrus – tasted 1981
Pale colour, pink rim
False sweetness on nose
Light-weight, lacks character
Fonplégade – tasted 1982
Medium depth of colour, orange rim
Tough, stalky and sweetness on nose
Light-weight, quite thin finish
la Gaffelière – tasted 1980
Light red in colour
Warm, elegant bouquet
Attractive and fruity but slightly light, with
stalky finish
Laroze – tasted 1982
Pale colour, orange rim
Sweet, light-weight nose
Light on fruit, easy drinking
Magdelaine – tasted 1980
Medium depth of colour, pink rim
Good, Merlot, sweet nose
Good balance but light finish

Matras (half-bottle) – tasted 1980
Vivid purple colour
Slightly unbalanced, acidity and tannin

Monbousquet – tasted 1980
Young red colour
Fresh raspberry nose
Light, thin, fruity finish

Moulinet – tasted 1982
Quite deep colour, orange rim
Light, thin nose
Quite good fruit, sweet finish

Pavie – tasted 1980
Medium colour, pink rim
Tight, sweet, violet, slightly green nose
Light, slightly leafy taste and finish

Petit-Faurie-de-Soutard – tasted 1982
Pale colour, orange rim
Soft, sweet, pleasant nose
Nice, sweet, easy to drink

Petit Village – tasted 1980
Medium/light in colour
Light-weight pleasant nose
Light, easy to drink, short finish

Roudier – tasted 1982
Medium/pale colour, tawny rim
Light-weight, sweet, Merlot nose
Light on palate, short finish

de Sales – tasted 1980
Pale in colour, pink rim
Soft, sweet, truffle nose
Light-weight, forward wine

Sansonnet – tasted 1982
Medium depth of colour, orange rim
Soft, sweet Merlot nose
Light-weight throughout

Trottevieile – tasted 1980
Medium depth of colour, orange rim
Nice, deep, sweet truffle nose
Well-made 1977, light centre but good fruity finish

Trottevieille – tasted 1980
Quite deep in colour, pink rim
Leafy, medicinal nose
Light, lacks fruit and centre, green finish

la Tour-du-Pin-Figeac – tasted 1982
Medium depth of colour, tawny rim
Quite soft, sweet nose
Good balance of fruit, firm finish

Vieux-Château-Certan – tasted 1982
Mid and pink
Soft sweet Merlot nose
Light, sweet, weak finish

1978 A late spring, poor summer at first but then fine conditions. There were also fine conditions throughout the vintage as well. This resulted in a fairly short crop of good quality wines.

l'Angélus – tasted 1980
Medium depth of colour, pink rim
Light-weight nose but good fruit
Nice, soft, fruity wine with good balance and finish

Ausone – tasted 1980
Very deep, superb depth of colour
Good, raw, Merlot nose
Lots of tannin and fruit, will be a good wine

Ausone – re-tasted 1982
Deep colour, pink rim
Nose and palate same as above

Balestard-la-Tonnelle – tasted 1981
Quite deep colour, pink rim
Raw, woody, chocolate nose
Well-made, tannin and acidity, good finish

Balestard-la-Tonnelle – tasted 1982
Medium depth of colour, orange rim
Good, rich, deep Merlot
A fruity, well-balanced wine

Barbe-Blanche – tasted 1981
Light colour, pink rim
Light, sweet, tinned-fruit nose
Light-weight, lacks centre, but nice finish

Beauregard – tasted 1980
Medium depth of colour, pink rim
Soft, sweet, slightly stalky nose
Tough, tight, good balance, firm finish

Beau-séjour (Bécot) – tasted 1980
Deep colour, purple rim
Leafy, medicinal, new oak predominant on nose
Tight, tough, oaky taste

Beau-séjour (Bécot) – re-tasted 1982
Deep colour, pink rim
Deep, tight, tough nose
Good balance, and tannin

Beauséjour (Duffau-Lagarrosse) – tasted 1980
Deep in colour, purple rim
Leafy, tough, slightly medicinal nose
Well-balanced, but leafy and tough

Belair – tasted 1980
Good colour
Lovely depth of violets on the nose
Superb richness of fruit, well-balanced, good finish

Belair (Puisseguin) tasted 1980
Medium depth of colour, pink rim
Sweet, fragrant Merlot nose
Light, nice balance and finish

de Bellevue – tasted 1980
Light in colour, pink rim
Light, sweet, commercial nose
Light-weight, lacks fruit and centre, light finish

Bourgneuf – tasted 1980
   Medium depth of colour, pink rim
   Good truffle nose
   Light on fruit but pleasant finish
Canon (half-bottle) – tasted 1980
   Medium depth of colour, pink rim
   Fruity, nice depth, quite closed
   Fragrant, lighter than 1979, with less extract,
   but good length and well-made
Canon la Gaffelière – 1982
   Medium depth of colour, orange rim
   Nice, sweet, fragrant nose
   Well-made, good fruit and balance, light
   finish and tannin
Cap de Mourlin – tasted 1982
   Medium depth of colour, orange rim
   Sweet, fruity nose
   Light centre, but good fruity finish
Certan de May – tasted 1981
   Medium depth of colour, pink rim
   Woody nose
   Slightly stalky wine, light centre and finish
Cheval Blanc – tasted 1980
   Very deep colour, pink rim
   Huge Merlot, truffle nose
   Enormous, rich, concentrations of fruit
   Lovely full finish, not ready yet
Cheval Blanc – tasted 1982
   Deep and pink
   Full, fruity, sweet rich nose
   Lots of fruit, long firm finish
Chevrol Bélair – tasted 1980
   Deep colour, purple rim
   Nice, soft, violet Merlot nose
   Good depth of fruit, chocolate finish, quite
   forward
Clos de Clocher – tasted 1981
   Good colour
   Nice soft nose
   Good fruit and balance, long finish
Clos l'Église – tasted 1981
   Good, rich colour
   Attractive, sweet, truffle nose
   Good fruit, and finish
Clos l'Église – tasted 1982
   Deep and pink
   Deep rich truffle, lots of concentration
   Very rich deep fruit and tannin
   Long finish
Clos Fourtet – tasted 1980
   Deep red colour
   Wet dog smell
   Very fruity, delicious
Clos Fourtet – tasted 1981
   Good, deep colour, pink rim
   Lovely, rich, soft, sweet nose

Good fruit and tannin, a long way to go
Clos Fourtet – re-tasted 1982
   Deep colour, orange rim
   Sweet, violet nose
   Rich, well-balanced
Clos de l'Oratoire – tasted 1982
   Quite deep in colour, orange rim
   Lovely, deep, rich, violet, Merlot nose
   Soft, full, good finish with tannin
Clos René – tasted 1980
   Very deep colour, purple rim
   Very closed, great depth
   Tough, tight, well-made, tannic finish
la Conseillante – tasted 1980
   Good, deep colour, pink rim
   Good depth of fruit on nose
   Slightly light centre and finish
Croix de Gay – tasted 1980
   Medium colour, pink rim
   Sweet, pleasant, cooked fruit nose
   Quite forward, nice finish and centre
Croque Michotte – tasted 1980
   Medium colour, pink rim
   Lightweight, lacks depth and centre
Curé Bon la Madeleine – tasted 1980
   Good, deep colour
   Rich Merlot, violet nose
   Good fruit, balance and finish
l'Église-Clinet – tasted 1980
   Young, pink red
   Clean, rather hard, fruity nose
   Good fruit, long finish with a hint of burnt
   brown sugar
l'Église-Clinet – tasted 1981
   Medium depth of colour, pink rim
   Nice, sweet, truffle nose
   Good fruit and balance, firm finish
l'Église-Clinet – tasted 1982
   Medium depth of colour
   Nice, sweet, Merlot nose
   Good fruit and balance, tannic finish
Feytit-Clinet – tasted 1980
   Medium depth of colour, pink rim
   Sweet cooked nose
   Lacks depth of fruit and finish
Figeac (100% Merlot) – tasted 1980
   Very deep colour, purple rim
   Soft, sweet, smooth, violet/cherry, almost
   like tinned fruit
   Smooth, soft, slight tannin
Figeac (50% Bouchet, 50% Cabernet Sauvig-
nan, no Merlot) – tasted 1980
   Big, deep colour, purple rim
   Blackcurrant, dry nose
   Tough, tight, austere, tannic finish

Figeac – tasted 1980
  Very deep colour, purple rim
  Soft, sweet, violet nose
  Good balance, full-bodied, long finish with tannin
Figeac – re-tasted 1982
  Deep colour, pink rim
  Same as above with richer finish
la Fleur Gazin – tasted 1980
  Medium depth of colour, pink rim
  Pleasant, sweet nose
  Lacks fruit and balance, light finish
la Fleur Pétrus – tasted 1980
  Good deep colour
  Fine, delicate, rich, truffle nose
  Lots of fruit and depth
  Long tannic finish
Fombrauge – tasted 1980
  Good, rich colour
  Quite forward, light-weight nose
  Good balance but light finish
Fonplégade – tasted 1980
  Very deep purple colour
  Good, deep bouquet
  Good, depth of fruit, well-balanced
Fonplégade – re-tasted 1982
  Deep colour, orange rim
  Tight, tough, short, acidity
  Light centre, firm finish with acidity
Fonroque – tasted 1980
  Good, deep colour
  Ripe Merlot, violet nose
  Good balance, and fruity finish
Franc-Mayne – tasted 1980
  Medium depth of colour, pink rim
  Nice, sweet, violet nose
  Good fruit and balance, quite forward
la Gaffelière – tasted 1980
  Medium colour, pink rim
  Sweet, soft, light delicate nose
  Quite forward, lighter than the 1979, nice finish
la Gaffelière – re-tasted 1982
  Medium colour, tawny rim
  Light and delicate nose
  Soft, fruity finish
Gazin – tasted 1980
  Good colour
  Nice, rich, truffle nose
  Good balance, but slightly weak finish
Grandes Murailles – tasted 1980
  Medium depth of colour, pink rim
  Good Merlot sweetness on nose but lacks centre and finish
la Haute Claymore (Lussac) – tasted 1980
  Light colour, pink rim

  Thin, medicinal nose
  Light-weight, thin,
  lacks centre and finish
  High acidity on finish
Haut Quercus (Saint Émilion Co-operative) – tasted 1981
  Very deep colour, purple rim
  Raw, Merlot and oak nose
  Tight but lightish centre, tannin but lightish finish
Haut Plantey – tasted 1982
  Medium depth of colour, tawny edge
  Nice, deep, tough Merlot nose
  Tight, good balance, light finish
Lagrange – tasted 1981
  Good deep colour, pink rim
  Tough, dry, tannic nose
  Good depth of fruit and flavour, firm finish
Larcis Ducasse – tasted 1980
  Medium colour, pink rim
  Light-weight, sweet nose
  Quite good depth, but light finish
Laroze – tasted 1982
  Medium colour, brown rim
  Nice tight Merlot nose
  Good fruit and balance
Magdelaine – tasted 1980
  Very deep colour
  Strong raspberry-jam nose
  Good extract, a lot of flavour, not a lot of tannin on finish
Matras – tasted 1980
  Deep young red colour
  Full, fruity nose
  Light, fruity, forward
Monbousquet – tasted 1980
  Deep young red
  Subdued pleasant nose
  Well-formed, lots of tannin
Moulinet – tasted 1980
  Deep in colour, pink rim
  Fresh fruit nose, slightly spicy
  Well-made, good, soft balance and finish
Moulinet – re-tasted 1982
  Medium depth of colour, orange rim
  Fresh, sweet, fruity raspberry nose
  Full, fruity, lightish finish
Moulin du Cadet – tasted 1980
  Medium colour, pink rim
  Nice soft Merlot nose
  Well-balanced, good finish
Nenin – tasted 1980
  Good, deep colour
  Solid, concentrated truffle nose
  Lovely, rich fruit, good balance and finish
Nenin – tasted 1980
  Youthful red colour

Elegant, spicy nose
Good fruit, oaky taste, light on tannin

Pavie – tasted 1980
Medium depth of colour, pink rim
Sweet, soft Merlot nose
Well-balanced, good fruit, long tight finish

Pavie-Decesse – tasted 1980
Deep, young red colour, purple rim
Attractive young, fruity nose
Good fruit, extract and balance

Petit-Faurie-de-Soutard – tasted 1982
Medium depth of colour, orange rim
Light, sweet nose
Forward, sweet, light finish

Petit Village – tasted 1980
Deep colour, purple rim
Developed, sweet nose
Well-balanced with firm finish

Pétrus – tasted 1980
Good deep colour, pink rim
Very rich full-blown, truffle nose
Excellent balance of fruit and tannin, very long finish, a long way to go

Peyreau – tasted 1982
Very deep colour, brown rim
Tight, tough, raw Merlot nose
Very attractive, soft, light-weight finish

Plince – tasted 1982
Deep and orange
Rich deep chocolate nose
Lovely fruity wine good finish

la Pointe – tasted 1980
Medium depth of colour, pink rim
Light-weight nose, but quite fruity
Nice light balance, lacks finish

la Pointe – tasted 1982
Medium depth of colour, orange rim
Quite tough young Merlot and iron nose
Light and sweet

Ripeau – tasted 1981
Deep colour, pink rim
Good, soft, chocolate nose
Well-balanced, good depth and finish

Roc de Puisseguin (Co-op) – tasted 1980
Medium depth of colour, pink rim
Soft, sweet Merlot nose
Well-made, good balance and finish

la Rose Figeac – tasted 1980
Medium depth of colour, pink rim
Light-weight nose
Lacks fruit and depth, light finish

Roudier – tasted 1982
Medium depth of colour, orange rim
Tough, Merlot, dry nose
Slightly stalky, and sweet finish

St Georges – tasted 1981
Pale colour, pink rim
Leafy, stalky, medicinal nose
Light-weight, green stalky finish

St Georges – tasted 1980
Deep colour, purple rim
Woody, leafy, raw, Merlot nose
Lacks centre, green stalky finish

de Sales – tasted 1980
Good colour, pink rim
Soft, quite forward, truffle nose
Good balance, but light finish, lacks tannin

Sansonnet – tasted 1982
Quite deep colour, pink rim
Tough, stalky nose
Light centre, fruity finish

Sansonnet – tasted 1982
Mid and orange
Light sweet violet
Nice light fruity sweet
Well-balanced

la Serre – tasted 1980
Good colour
Nice, soft, forward nose
Good fruit and balance, slightly light finish

Soutard (Magnum) – tasted 1981
Very deep, slight browning
Deep, raw Merlot nose
Very soft, well-balanced, good fruit, quite forward

Soutard – re-tasted in bottle 1982
Deep colour, orange rim
Tight, tough, raw Merlot
Good balance, soft finish

de Tabuteau (Lussac) – tasted 1980
Medium depth of colour, Merlot nose
Well-balanced, good fruity finish

Taillefer – tasted 1980
Deep colour, pink rim
Subdued nose, quite light
Fruity, full and tannin

Tertre Daugay – tasted 1980
Deep colour, pink rim
Nice depth, oaky, soft, closed nose
Lovely depth, tough, Cabernet Franc showing through, good long finish

Tertre Daugay – re-tasted 1982
Medium colour, tawny edge
Sweet, ripe, Merlot nose
Ripe, opened, full finish

des Tours – tasted 1981
Deep colour, pink edge
Light, sweet, slightly cooked nose
Light, thin, lacks fruit and centre

la Tour Figeac – tasted 1980
Very deep purple

Slightly spicy, fruity nose
Closed, a lot of depth and extract, will develop into a wine of character
la Tour Figeac – re-tasted 1982
    Deep colour, tawny rim
    Rich, violet nose
    Opened up into a rich well-balanced wine
Troplong-Mondot – tasted 1980
    Good colour, pink rim
    Nice forward violet nose
    Good fruit, well-balanced
    Forward finish
Trotanoy – tasted 1980
    Very deep, young red
    Good fruit, raspberry/blackcurrant
    Big fruity wine, ready now
Trotanoy – tasted 1980
    Deep rich colour
    Lovely depth of truffle and fruit on nose
    Superb length of flavour, good balance and finish
Trotanoy – re-tasted 1982
    Deep colour, pink rim
    Nose and palate same as above
Trottevieille – tasted 1980
    Medium depth of colour, pink rim
    Light-weight, sweet, jammy nose
    Light centre, lacks body, very light finish
Vieux-Château-Certan – tasted 1980
    Lovely deep colour
    Full, rich, oaky, iron nose
    Lovely full rich wine, fine finish
Vieux-Château-Certan – tasted 1982
    Deep and pink
    Rich ripe truffle
    Well-balanced, lovely fruit and finish
Villemaurine – tasted 1980
    Deep purple
    Elegant, fragrant nose
    Good fruit, closed, will develop well

1979 A wet spring, a dry summer and good vintaging conditions which resulted in a large crop of good quality wine. The conditions were better in Saint-Émilion than in the Médoc, the reverse of 1978.
l' Angélus – tasted 1982
    Deep/medium depth of colour, brown rim
    Ripe, mature Bouchet, dusty, almost vegetable nose
    Nice depth of fruit, good balance and finish
Ausone – tasted in cask at the Château in 1980
    Very deep and purple
    Tight, deep, sweet with finesse, complex, oaky leather nose

Good depth and extract, well-balanced, long finish
Ausone – tasted in cast at Château in 1981
    Very deep colour, pink rim
    Raw Merlot, violets, closed nose
    Good concentration of fruit, tight, closed, long finish
Ausone – re-tasted in 1982 in bottle
    Deep colour, pink rim
    Lovely, rich concentration on nose
    Very big wine, good fruit and finish, a good 1979
Balestard-la-Tonnelle – tasted 1981
    Deep colour, pink rim
    Forward, soft, chocolate nose
    Well-made, light, quite forward
Balestard-la-Tonnelle – tasted 1982
    Medium depth of colour, orange rim
    Good, deep Merlot nose
    Good fruit, good firm finish
Barbe-Blanche – tasted 1981
    Medium depth of colour, purple rim
    Very sweet, tinned-fruit nose
    Sweet, good balance, good long finish
Beauregard – tasted 1980
    Big, deep purple colour
    Soft, deep, smooth, violet nose
    Well-made, quite forward, fruity finish
Beau-séjour (Bécot) – tasted in cask at the Château 1980
    Very deep colour, purple rim
    Nice, deep violet, Merlot, nose with oak
    Tight, light-weight centre, lacks acidity
Beau-séjour (Duffau-Lagarrosse) – tasted 1980
    Medium depth of colour, pink rim
    Light, dry, violet nose
    Light on fruit in the centre and finish
le Caillou – tasted 1982
    Deep colour, orange rim
    Nice, sweet, toffee nose
    Good balance, light finish
Canon – tasted in cask at the Château in 1980
    Medium depth of colour, purple rim
    Good Merlot, well-balanced nose with lots of finesse
    Good fruit and balance, tough with tannic finish
Cap de Mourlin – tasted 1981
    Medium depth of colour, pink rim
    Good, soft, forward, Merlot nose
    Nice, sweet, fruity wine
Cap de Mourlin – tasted 1982
    Medium depth of colour, orange rim
    Good deep, violet Merlot
    Good fruit, nice sweet finish

Cheval Blanc – tasted 1980
  Very deep colour, purple rim
  Lovely rich, violet nose
  A lot of fruit and tannin, will develop into a
  superb wine
Cheval Blanc – re-tasted 1981
  Same as above
Cheval Blanc – tasted 1982
  Deep and pink
  Quite rich sweet nose
  Lacks body a little, but long finish
Clos Fourtet – tasted in cask at the Château 1980
  Very deep colour, purple rim
  Nice, rich, nose, good extract
  Good fruit, tannin and extract
Clos Fourtet – tasted 1981
  Very purple
  Rather malic bouquet
  Good, meaty, fruity, acidity on finish
Clos Fourtet – re-tasted in bottle 1982
  Medium depth of colour, orange rim
  Tight Merlot nose, good depth
  Well-balanced, good fruit and finish. A good
  1979
Clos René – tasted 1980
  Deep colour, purple rim
  Good, young, fruity nose
  Good fruit, tough tannic finish
Clos René – re-tasted 1982
  Deep colour, tawny rim
  Good, deep, rich Merlot nose
  Good balance and fruit, slightly light finish
Clos Toulifaut – tasted 1981
  Deep colour, pink rim
  Good, deep, soft truffle nose
  A lot of fruit, good balance and finish
la Conseillante – tasted 1980
  Deep colour, purple rim
  Light-weight, Merlot, violets on nose
  High oaky taste, firm but light finish
la Croix – tasted 1982
  Medium depth of colour, orange rim
  Nice, rich, iron, truffle nose
  Light, tight, good, fruity finish
l'Église-Clinet – tasted 1980 (new oak cask)
  Deep colour, purple rim
  Big, fruity, jammy nose
  Amazingly full, fruity flavour, long finish
l'Église-Clinet – tasted 1980 (6 year old cask)
  Deep colour, purple rim
  Nose has less depth than above
  Good fruit but tighter and more tannic
l'Évangile – tasted 1981
  Very deep colour, purple rim
  Deep, rich extract, soft, Merlot violets on
  nose

Great depth of fruit, very good balance, long
finish
Figeac – tasted 1982 (January)
  Good deep colour
  Nice, light, fruity, violet nose
  Quite forward, light centre, but good firm
  finish
Figeac – tasted 1982 (March)
  Same as above
Fonplégade – tasted 1980
  Deep purple colour
  Good texture, weight and fruit
Fonplégade – tasted 1981
  Good colour, pink rim
  Delicate, raw, Merlot nose
  Well-made, light-weight style
Fonplégade – re-tasted 1982
  Deep colour, pink rim
  Same on nose and palate as above
Franc Bigaroux – tasted 1981
  Good deep colour, pink rim
  Tough, raw, Merlot nose
  Good fruit, well-balanced
la Gaffelière – tasted in cask at the Château in
1980
  Medium depth of colour, purple rim
  Good, Merlot, well-balanced nose with lots
  of finesse
  Good fruit and balance, tough with tannic
  finish
Haut-Sarpe – tasted 1982
  Medium depth of colour, orange rim
  Soft, sweet, earthy nose
  Light, sweet, forward, nice fruity finish
Larmande – tasted 1981
  Medium depth of colour, pink rim
  Good tight, raw, Merlot nose
  Well-balanced but light
Laroque – tasted 1980
  Deep colour, pink rim
  Light, sweet, Merlot nose
  Lacks centre, light-weight, sweet finish
Laroze – tasted 1982
  Medium depth of colour, pink rim
  Nice, sweet, light, fruity nose
  Well-balanced, with tannic finish
Magdelaine – tasted in cask at the Château in 1980
  Very deep colour, purple rim
  Young, fruity, raspberry-jam nose
  Tannin, extract, a lot of depth
Matras – tasted 1980
  Purple in colour
  Fruit closed
  A lot of tannin, good balance
Mazeyres (Magnum) – tasted 1982
  Very deep and purple

Deep tight truffle nose
Good tight, well-balanced finish
Moulinet – tasted 1980
Deep colour, purple rim
Big, heavy, oaky nose
Good fruit and tannin
Moulinet – tasted 1981
Deep colour, pink rim
Tight, raw, truffle nose
Well-balanced, good fruit and tannin
Moulinet – re-tasted 1982
Same as above
Nenin – tasted 1980
Very deep colour, purple rim
Big, fruity nose
Good balance and finish
Pavie – tasted in cask at the Château 1980
Very deep colour, purple rim
Deep, rich, violet nose
Full-bodied, very well-balanced, long full finish
Petit-Faurie-de-Soutard – tasted 1982
Medium depth of colour, orange rim
Light, sweet, violet nose
Nice, sweet, forward wine
Petit Village – tasted 1980
Deep colour, purple rim
Full, young, fruity nose
Good depth of fruit, tannic finish
Pétrus – tasted 1980
Very deep colour, pink rim
Deep, rich, Merlot, oaky nose
Very tannic, oaky, rich, a lot of depth, very long finish
la Pointe – tasted 1982
Medium colour, orange rim
Quite tough and tight, sweet nose
Tough, closed, slightly light centre, firm finish
Roudier – tasted 1982
Medium depth of colour, orange rim
Quite sweet, Merlot nose
Forward, sweet, light finish
St Georges – tasted 1981
Very deep colour, purple rim
Deep, rich, well-balanced, Merlot nose
Well-balanced, full, good extract
de Sales – tasted 1980 (90% Merlot) (12.3° in cask)
Deep colour, purple rim
Pleasant, young, fruity nose
Light-weight but well-balanced
Sansonnet – tasted 1982
Deep colour, pink rim
Tight, raw Merlot nose

la Serre – tasted 1982
Medium depth of colour, pink rim
Tight, hard, Bouchet showing through
Tough, tight, closed, but slightly light centre
Soutard – tasted 1980
Good deep colour, pink rim
Lovely tight, raw, Merlot nose
Tight, tough, good balance and finish
Soutard – re-tasted 1982
Same as above
Taillefer – tasted 1981
Medium depth of colour, pink rim
Well-balanced, closed nose
Good fruit and tannin, closed
Taillefer – tasted 1980
Very deep colour, purple rim
Good raspberry/elderberry nose
Very good fruit and tannin
Taillefer – re-tasted 1982
Deep colour, purple rim
Tight, tough, closed nose
Good fruit and tannin
Tertre Daugay – tasted in cask at the Château in 1980
Very deep colour, purple rim
Lovely, concentrated, soft nose
Good depth, well-made, tight finish
la Tour-Figeac – tasted 1980
Very deep purple
Big, deep, fruity nose
Good structure, tannic finish
la Tour-du-pin-Figeac – tasted 1982
Very deep colour, tawny/pink rim
Good, deep, tight violet nose
Lovely, rich, fruity, Merlot finish
la Tour-du-Pin-Figeac (Giraud) – tasted 1982
Deep colour, tawny rim
Tight, tough, raw, Merlot
Nice, sweet, well-balanced, wine with firm finish
des Tours – tasted 1981
Medium depth of colour, purple rim
High SO_2, medicinal, leafy nose
Thin, lacks centre and finish
Troplong-Mondot – tasted 1980
Very deep purple
Big jammy nose, hint of elderberry
Lots of fruit and dark, stern flavour
Trotanoy – tasted 1980
Very deep colour, purple rim
Fresh, raspberry smell
Deep, fruity taste, acidity and tannin evident, still closed
Trotanoy – re-stated in 1982
Deep colour, pink rim
Still closed, raw Merlot nose

Good concentration of fruit, still time to go
Trottevieille – tasted in cask at the Château 1980
  Very deep colour, purple rim
  Big, tough, cabernet influence
  Good, deep, lots of fruit, a good finish
Vieux-Château-Certan – tasted in cask at the Château in 1980
  Dark purple
  Lot of depth on nose
  Very good wine in balance of fruit, depth, etc.
  Good prospects
  A good 1979 and better-keeping prospects
Vieux-Château-Certan – re-tasted 1982
  Deep and pink
  Good fruity sweet nose
  Well-made but light finish
Villemaurine – tasted 1980
  Full purple colour, red rim
  Good, fresh fruit nose
  Good depth, closed, needs time

1980 A late spring with a lot of *coulure* in the Merlot grapes. This was followed by a poor summer but a little sun later on in August and September. It rained during the harvest.

l' Angélus – tasted 1982
  Very deep colour, purple rim
  Quite deep, rich, violet Merlot nose
  Light, tight, good balance and finish
Ausone – tasted in cask at the Château on 1981
  Very deep colour, purple rim
  Huge concentrated, raisin-juice nose, almost like vintage port
  Good concentration of fruit, young raw Merlot, good firm finish
Ausone – tasted 1982
  Medium depth of colour, purple rim
  Delicate, closed nose
  Good fruit and extract, slightly light-weight
Balestard-la-Tonnelle – tasted in cask at the Château in 1981
  Deep colour, purple rim
  Big, raw, oaky Merlot nose
  Quite forward, light centre, fruity finish
Balestard-la-Tonnelle – tasted 1982
  Medium depth of colour, pink rim
  Nice, rich, Merlot nose
  Well-balanced fruit and finish
Beau-séjour (Bécot) – tasted 1982
  Medium depth of colour, purple rim
  Delicate, oaky, quite raw nose
  Light, tight, blousey finish
Beauséjour (Duffau-Lagarrosse) – tasted 1982
  Big, deep colour, purple rim
  Tough, tannic nose

  Well-balanced, good depth, big finish
Beauséjour (Duffau-Lagarrosse) – tasted 1982
  Deep colour, purple rim
  Closed, delicate, fruity nose
  Fruity, light centre, forward finish
Belair – tasted 1982
  Medium depth of colour, purple rim
  Closed, delicate nose
  Light-weight, tight finish
Canon – tasted 1982
  Medium deep colour, purple rim
  Tough, oaky extract on nose
  Well-balanced, delicate with good extract, long
Canon la-Gaffelière – tasted 1982
  Medium colour, orange rim
  Rich, sweet, light-weight nose
  Nice balance, light finish
Cap de Mourlin – tasted 1982
  Medium depth of colour, purple rim
  Fairly full, Merlot nose
  Good balance, light finish
Cheval Blanc – tasted in cask at the Château in 1981
  Opaque colour, purple rim
  Very deep concentration of raw fruit and truffles on nose
  Good balance, lightish centre, well-made
Cheval Blanc – tasted 1982
  Deep colour, purple rim
  Rich, ripe, closed nose
  Good extract and centre, tight finish, slightly light-weight on finish
Clos l'Église – tasted 1982
  Medium colour, pink rim
  Ripe Merlot, slightly over-sweet nose
  Very toffee taste
Clos Fourtet – tasted 1982 (60% Merlot, 20% Bouchet, 20% Cabernet Sauvignon)
  Very deep colour, purple rim
  Good, tough, deep extract on nose
  Raw, light centre, tough, blousey finish
Clos René – tasted 1982
  Deep colour, pink rim
  Lovely, deep, rich, truffle, Merlot nose
  Good fruit and extract, sweet, forward finish
Clos St Martin – tasted 1982
  Medium depth of colour, pink rim
  Light, sweet, forward nose
  Pleasant balance of fruit, a forward wine
Côte Baleau – tasted 1982
  Medium depth of colour, pink rim
  Light, sweet, forward nose
  Pleasant balance of fruit, a forward wine
la Croix Bellevue – tasted 1982
  Deep colour, pink rim

Soft, light, Merlot nose
Forward, light, thin finish
Doumayne – tasted 1982
Medium depth of colour, pink rim
Light, sweet, Merlot, violets
Very light, lacks depth
l'Église-Clinet – tasted 1982
Deep and forward colour
Soft, sweet, forward Merlot nose
Light, forward, light finish
Figeac – tasted 1982
Deep colour, purple rim
Sweet, rich, lots of extract on nose
Rich, round, sweet, very good extract and fruit
Figeac – tasted 1982 (three days later)
As above but because of correct temperature, the fruit was fuller
la Gaffelière – tasted 1982
Medium depth of colour, purple rim
Light, sweet, delicate
Quite light-weight, delicate finish
Grandes Murailles – tasted 1982
Deep colour, pink rim
Good, rich, Merlot, violets
Lovely and sweet, good firm balance and finish
Laroze – tasted 1982
Pale in colour, pink rim
Light, thin, sweet nose
Lacks fruit and finish
Magdelaine – tasted 1982
Quite deep colour, purple rim
Good, deep, rich, raw extract
Rich, deep, lots of fruit
Pavie – tasted in cask at the Château in 1981
Quite deep in colour, purple rim
Raw, tight, sweet, violets
Good firm balance, lightish centre, well-made
Pavie – tasted 1982
Very deep colour, purple rim
Very closed, deep, rich extract on nose
Tough, tight, good fruit and extract
Petit-Faurie-de-Soutard – tasted 1982
Medium/pale in colour, pink rim
Light, sweet nose
Forward and light finish
Pétrus – tasted 1982
Medium depth of colour, pink rim
Closed, very deep, oaky, Merlot nose
Great depth of concentration, long tannic finish, lots of extract, will be a very good wine
Roudier – tasted 1982
Medium depth of colour, pink rim
Light, sweet, Merlot nose
Light-weight, sweet finish

de Sales – tasted 1982
Medium depth of colour, pink rim
Soft, sweet, Merlot nose
Forward, soft, smooth, ripe finish
Sansonnet – tasted 1982
Medium depth of colour, pink rim
Light, sweet, smooth, violet nose
Fairly light and forward, sweet finish
Soutard – tasted in cask at Château in 1981 (55% Merlot, 47% Bouchet, 3% Cabernet Sauvignon)
Deep colour, purple rim
Soft, concentrated, raisin juice
Forward, light centre, well-made
Soutard – re-tasted 1982 (in bottle)
Same as above
Trotanoy – tasted 1982
Medium depth of colour, purple edge
Sweet, tight, rich, Merlot nose
Lots of fruit, slightly light centre, good balanced finish
Trottevieille – tasted 1982
Medium depth of colour, purple rim
Tight, rich, delicate, sweet nose
Sweet, tight, light finish

1981 Indifferent weather in the spring followed by a cool July and a very hot and dry August. It rained during the harvest which was late but produced good quality grapes. Picking started on 28th September and finished on 10th October. Average out-put: 29,000,000 bottles.

l'Angélus – tasted 1982 (two weeks in cask)
Very deep colour, purple rim
Good, tight, tough Bouchet nose
Good fruit, well-balanced, good future
Ausone – tasted 1982 (one week in cask)
Very deep colour, purple rim
Deep, rich, Merlot nose
Good depth, fruit and finish
Balestard-la-Tonnelle – tasted 1982
Deep colour, purple rim
Lovely ripe Merlot nose
Quite forward, but rich, long finish
Beau-séjour (Bécot) – tasted 1982
Very deep colour, purple rim
Rich, deep, Merlot, violets
Quite forward, but good depth of fruit, well-balanced finish
Canon – tasted 1982 (two months in cask)
Deep colour, purple rim
Soft, sweet, iron/truffle nose
Sweet, forward, good balance and firm finish
Canon la Gaffelière – tasted 1982
Medium depth of colour, purple rim

Quite deep, rich, Merlot nose
Good fruit and balance, light finish
Cap de Mourlin – tasted 1982
Quite deep colour, purple rim
Nice, rich, Merlot nose
Good rich, well-made, tight finish
Clos l'Église – tasted 1982
Medium colour, pink rim
Good, tight, closed Merlot nose
Lots of sweet fruit and tannin, well-made
Clos St Martin – tasted 1982
Deep colour, purple rim
Light, forward, Merlot nose
Light-weight, lacks body
Côte Baleau – tasted 1982
Deep colour, purple rim
Light, forward, Merlot nose
Light-weight, lacks body
la Croix – tasted 1982 (in vat, pre cask)
Big, deep colour, purple rim
Nice, rich, deep, forward nose
Light-weight, forward, sweet finish
Figeac – tasted 1982 (one month in cask)
Deep colour, purple rim
Deep, very closed, tight, raspberry nose
Tight, rich, deep, sweet, quite forward
la Gaffelière – tasted 1982 (vat sample)
Medium depth of colour, purple rim
Tight, closed
Light with tannin
Grandes Murailles – tasted 1982
Deep colour, purple rim
Good depth of raw Merlot
Good balance, well-made
Petit-Faurie-de-Soutard – tasted 1982
Medium colour, purple rim
Light, tight, Merlot nose
Light-weight, tannic finish
Pétrus – tasted 1982 (vat sample)
Very deep colour, purple rim
Immense concentration of fruit, still very closed
Great depth, sweet, rich, lots of tannin, a great future
Plince – tasted 1982
Very deep colour, purple rim
Nice, rich, concentrated Merlot nose
Good concentration of fruit, quite forward

la Pointe – tasted 1982
Deep colour, purple rim
Soft, sweet iron/truffle nose
Sweet, forward, good balance, firm finish
Roudier – tasted 1982
Medium depth of colour, purple rim
Tight, Merlot, forward nose
Light, sweet, forward
Sansonnet – tasted 1982
Very deep, purple rim
Deep, rich, vegetable nose
Quite rich, sweet, quite forward
la Serre – tasted 1982 (three weeks in cask)
Medium depth of colour, purple rim
Soft, sweet nose
Forward, soft, sweet
Soutard – tasted 1982
Very deep colour, purple rim
Rich, raspberry nose
Deep, rich, excellent balance
Tertre Daugay – tasted 1982 (vat sample)
Very deep colour, purple rim
Deep, rich, earthy/sweet Merlot nose
Quite forward, but good balance
Trotanoy – tasted 1982
Very deep colour, purple rim
Very rich, closed, truffle nose
Rich, deep, a lot of extract and fruit

1982 The spring was late and it rained at first with sunshine later. The flowering took place in May, three weeks early, with no frost. May and June were extremely hot: July being the hottest for twenty years. August, after the first week of sunshine, had much rain. The grapes at this stage were in an advanced stage of maturity. September was sunny and hot until the 26th/27th when it started to rain. The picking was completed, on average, between the 18th and 21st of the month. The resultant wines have a very deep colour, good alcohol; they are very full-bodied and are of extremely high quality.

List of Members of the Union des Producteurs de Saint-Émilion

(Adhésion au Syndicat Viticole et Agricole de Saint-Émilion)

Note: The following list includes only the heads of the families belonging to the Union. Ownership may be shared, thus several members of the family may be members of the Union.

AMBLEVERT Hérvé   SAINTE FLORENCE
ARAOZ Felix   Grangey SAINT CHRISTOPHE DES BARDES
ARBOUET Henri   SAINT MAGNE DE CASTILLON
ARNAUD   Bernard   Cap Blanc MOULON
ARNAUD Guy   Darthus VIGNONET
ARNAUD Jean Pierre   Merlande SAINTE TERRE
ARTEAU Roger   Rue de Madame Bouquey
ASSO Patrick   Carré
AUDIGAY Michel   Bellerive SAINT SULPICE DE FALEYRENS
AUGRAND Eloi   Arnaud Bicot SAINT SULPICE DE FALEYRENS
BABEAU Georges   Rue de Pressenssé
BALLUE Robert   La Grave VIGNONET
BARBIER Odette   Malus BOULIAC
BARTCHIES Françoise   VIGNONET
DE LA BARTHE (A.E.C.)   La Grave VIGNONET
BAUGIER Jacques Antoine   Chantegrive
BAYLAN Michel   Labrie VIGNONET
BEAUBATIT Jean   Place de Marché
BELY Lydie   64 Avenue de la République
BENEYTOUT Josette   Darthus VIGNONET
BENTHENAT Thérèse   Le Bourg SAINT PEY D'ARMENS
BERTHON Yveline   SAINT PEY D'ARMENS
BERGERIE Yvon   Le Bidon SAINT SULPICE DE FALEYRENS
BERNARD Alain   Port de Branne ST SULPICE DE FALEYRENS
BERTHOUMEYROUX Christian   SAINTE COLOMBE
BERTIN Pierre   Darthus VIGNONET
BIRET Jean   La Coste de Papey SAINTE TERRE
BLANC Jean Pierre   101 rue de Lalande
BOISSERIE Louis   Guérin SAINT PEY D'ARMENS
BONNEFON Marie   Pierrefitte SAINT SULPICE DE FALEYRENS
BONNEFON Abel   SAINT SULPICE DE FALEYRENS
BONNEMAISON Marie Claude   SAINT SULPICE DE FALEYRENS
BONNET Jeanne   Au Gros SAINT PEY D'ARMENS
BONNIN Jean Claude   Pichon
BORDAS Clémence   La Glaye SAINT PEY D'ARMENS
BORDAS Onésime (Succession)   SAINT HIPPOLYTE
BORDE Denise   Le Bourg SAINTE TERRE
BORDE Michel   Le Bourg SAINTE TERRE
BORDIER Pierre   Route de Branne SAINT SULPICE DE FALEYRENS
BORDRON Pierre   Petit Bouquey SAINT HIPPOLYTE
BOST Henri   Monturon SAINT LAURENT DES COMBES

BORTOLUSSI Jeanne   au Panet
BOULADOU Michel VIGNONET
BOUTHE Marc   Mède
BOUYER André   Haut Piney SAINT HIPPOLYTE
BOUQUEY Guy   Rue de la Petite Fontaine
BRUGEILLE André   SAINT SULPICE DE FALEYRENS
CANTE (Héritiers)   SAINT JEAN DE BLAIGNAC
CANTIN Yvan   Lavergne SAINT PEY D'ARMENS
CANTIN Elia   Lavergne SAINT PEY D'ARMENS
CARCAUD Ondina   Le Rivalon
CARREAU Jean   Pey du Prat GREZILAS
CARRIERE Annie   6 rue Victoire Américaine
CASTAING Charles   SAINTE TERRE
CASTAING Pierre   Lavagnac SAINTE TERRE
CASTANET Jean   Le Bourg SAINT PEY D'ARMENS
CASTANET Michel   Le Bourg SAINT PEY D'ARMENS
CASTEL Jean   Biquet SAINT HIPPOLYTE
CASTEL Gilbert   Biquet SAINT HIPPOLYTE
CATUSSEAU Jean   Piney SAINT HIPPOLYTE
CAZENAVE Alain   Destieux SAINT SULPICE DE FALEYRENS
CHAFFAUD Edmond   116 Avenue Foch
CHAMPAGNE Maxime   Clos Cazenave VIGNONET
CHANTUREAU Guy   Pey du Prat GREZILLAC
CHARRIER Albert   Arnaud Bicot SAINT SULPICE DE FALEYRENS
CHARRIER Patrick   SAINT PEY D'ARMENS
CHARRON Andrée   Résidence Pierre 1er 20 Avenue Victor Hugo
CHAUMET Guy   19 Route des Castors LE BARP
CHAUMET Pierre   Bord
CHEMINADE Maurice   Peyrouquet   SAINT PEY D'ARMENS
CHEVAL Raymond   Monturon SAINT LAURENT DES COMBES
CHEVALIER Renée   Bord
CHIGNAC Fernande   Joliet SAINTE TERRE
CHOLET DE ROQUEMAUREL 198 bis Avenue Charles de Gaulle
CLAMENS Raymond   VIGNONET
COCETTA Terzo   Micouleau VIGNONET
COIFFARD Pierre   La Pierre du Maréchal ST CHRISTOPHE DES BARDES
CROIZET Jean   LES BILLAUX
COURCELAS Marcelle   VIGNONET
COURCELAS René   Pinson ST SULPICE DE FALEYRENS
COURRECHE Jean Christian   Les Moureaux ST ETIENNE DE LISSE
COUSTILLAS Charles   SAINT HIPPOLYTE
CRAMAIL Pierre   SAINTE TERRE
DANGLADE Georges   Clos Lardit
DATTAS   35 Chemin de Roudet
DELAHAUT Pierre   La Grave VIGNONET
DELPECH Charles   Les 4 Chemins VIGNONET
DELPECH Simon   Les 4 Chemins VIGNONET
DEMARY René   Mitrotte ST LAURENT DES COMBES
DESCOMBES Jeanne   Bellefond ST LAURENT DES COMBES
DESCUBES Pierre   Ferrandat
DOUMESCHE Josette   Boulevard Anatole France
DUBUC Serge   Le Bourg SAINT PEY D'ARMENS
DUCAS Yves   121 Ter Avenue G. Clémenceau
DUCHAMP Jacques   La Glaye SAINT PEY D'ARMENS
DUGOS (Indivision)   Guérin SAINT PEY D'ARMENS
DUMIGRON Pierre   La Roseraie

DUMIGRON Yvette   SAINT LAURENT DES COMBES
DUMON Pierrette   Le Bourg SAINT ETIENNE DE LISSE
DUPOY (Héritiers)   Badon
DUTASTA Gérard   VIGNONET
DUVERGE Robert   SAINT VINCENT DE PERTIGNAS
DUVERGER Michel   Pailhas SAINT HIPPOLYTE
DUVERGT Régina   Pailhas SAINT HIPPOLYTE
ELLIES Jean Jacques   SAINTE TERRE
ESCAICHE Claude   SAINTE TERRE
FABERES Jeanne   La Glaye   SAINT PEY D'ARMENS
FAURE Henri   Arnaud Bicot SAINT SULPICE DE FALEYRENS
FAURE Paule   6 rue Berthelot
FAURE Robert   La Croix SAINTE TERRE
FAURIE Christian   SAINT CHRISTOPHE DES BARDES
FAURIE Jacques
FAURIE Pierre   SAINT PEY D'ARMENS
FENOUILLAT Louis   Les 4 Chemins VIGNONET
FORT Pierre   Le Sourd SAINT SULPICE DE FALEYRENS
FORTIN Maurice   Labrie VIGNONET
FOURCADE Serge   Pailhas SAINT HIPPOLYTE
FOURNIE Alban   La Fayolle SAINT PEY D'ARMENS
FRITEGOTTO Mario   Cazenave VIGNONET
GADRAT Simon   Le Bourg SAINT SULPICE DE FALEYRENS
GARDRAT Jean   Les Pintey
GARRIGUE Georges   Le Thibeaud SAINT ETIENNE DE LISSE
GARRIGUE Jean   Le Loup SAINT CHRISTOPHE DES BARDES
GELLIE (Héritiers)   Bel Air Ouy SAINT ETIENNE DE LISSE
GEMON Jean Georges   La Nauve SAINT LAURENT DES COMBES
GILLOD Gabriel   Darthus VIGNONET
GINTRAC Jean Claude   Micouleau VIGNONET
GOINEAU René   Le Bourg SAINT CHRISTOPHE DES BARDES
GOUDICHEAU Marie Louise   Rue Guadet
GOUIDON Micheline   Bigaroux SAINT SULPICE DE FALEYRENS
GOUREAU René
GRANDET Henri   Peyrouquet SAINT PEY D'ARMENS
GUERIN Daniel   Mézières ST MAGNE DE CASTILLON
HAAG André   SAINT SULPICE DE FALEYRENS
ITEY Charlotte   Le Platin VIGNONET
ITEY François   LUGAIGNAC
JACQUIER Céraphine   Labrie VIGNONET
JAMET Lucien   SAINT PEY D'ARMENS
JARJANETTE Paul   Pierrefitte SAINT SULPICE DE FALEYRENS
JOLLE Jeanne   Les Maurins SAINT SULPICE DE FALEYRENS
JOURDAIN Marthe   17240 ST FORT SUR GIRONDE
LABONNE Henri   La Croix SAINT PEY D'ARMENS
LABRUGERE René   SAINT PEY D'ARMENS
LACOSTE Pierre et Jean Pierre   Pierrefitte SAINT SULPICE DE FALEYRENS
LAFAGE Simone   Matras
LAFARGE Jacques   SAINT LAURENT DES COMBES
LAFOURCADE Charles et Madame LAFOURCADE Marcelle SAINT SULPICE DE
   FALEYRENS
LAFAYE Elie   Le Basque SAINT PEY D'ARMENS
LAGUILLON Robert   Le Bourg SAINT PEY D'ARMENS
LANAU Fernande   Lartigue
LANDRODIE Maurice   Juguet SAINT PEY D'ARMENS
LAPELLETRIE Claude   La Rouchonne VIGNONET

LAPELLETRIE Jacques   La Rouchonne VIGNONET
LARCIS JAUMA (F.A.)   SAINTE RADEGONDE
LASSUS Marthe   Labrie VIGNONET
LASTOUILLAT Jacques SAINT PEY D'ARMENS
LAUTRETE Arséne   Villemaurine
LAVAL Jean   Bardoulet SAINT ETIENNE DE LISSE
LAVIGNAC Michel   SAINT SULPICE DE FALEYRENS
LEDOUX Bernard   18 rue de la Charmille
LEDOUX Giséle   Larredya CHAPELLE DE ROUSSE
LE MENN Raymond   SAINT LAURENT DES COMBES
LESPINE Jacques   Place du Marché
DE LESQUEN Patrick   159 Boulevard Bineau
LINQUETTE Yvette
LOISEAU Renée   13 rue F. Dalat
MACAUD Yves   Merlande SAINTE TERRE
MAGADOR Jean   Darthus VIGNONET
MAGADOR Jérôme   Darthus VIGNONET
MAGONTIER Jean   Pierrelongue ST LAURENT DES COMBES
MALLO Christian   SAINT HIPPOLYTE
MARGOUTY Madeleine
MARTY Elie   1 rue de l'Hermitage
MARTY Irène   Le Bourg SAINT CHRISTOPHE DES BARDES
MARTY MARTIN   Ferrachat SAINT PEY D'ARMENS
MAUVINON (G.F.A.)   Mauvinon SAINT SULPICE DE FALEYRENS
MAYE Raymond   MERIGNAS
MAZOLENNI Noël   SAINT PEY D'ARMENS
MEYNIER Henri   DOULEZON
MICHELET Gilbert   SAINT HIPPOLYTE
MIE André   Merlande SAINTE TERRE
MIE Jean Claude   SAINT PEY D'ARMENS
MODET Huguette   Rue Guadet
MONSALUT Elisée   La Garelle
MOYRAND Jean Yves   LAMOTHE MONTRAVEL
MOULINIE Antoinette   ST GEORGES
MOURGUET Jean   Micouleau VIGNONET
MOUREAU Armand   Le Peilhan SAINT LAURENT DES COMBES
NEBOUT Germaine   Le Bourg SAINT ETIENNE DE LISSE
NICOT René   Le Bourg ST GENES DE CASTILLON
NICOT Gisèle   Chadouet ST MAGNE DE CASTILLON
NIOTEAU Maurice   Gontey
NOUVEL Françoise   Porte Bouqueyre
NOUVEL Josette   Porte Bouqueyre
OUVRET Jean   Chemin de la Bordette
PAGE Marcel et Michel   ST LAURENT DES COMBES
PAGES Robert   La Chapelle Lescours ST SULPICE DE FALEYRENS
PAGNAC Jean   SAINT PEY D'ARMENS
PAGNAC Léopold   SAINT PEY D'ARMENS
PAGNAC René   Bellevue Figeac
PALARD Lucienne   Mondou ST SULPICE DE FALEYRENS
PALLARO Denis   Justice ST ETIENNE DE LISSE
PALLARO Jean   PARSAC
PALMERI Charles   ST SULPICE DE FALEYRENS
PALMERI Gérard   Jean Marie
PAPILLAUD Simone   ST QUENTIN DE CHALAIS
PAUILLAC Raymonde   ST LAURENT DES COMBES
PAVAGEAU Henriette   Thillet ST CHRISTOPHE DES BARDES

PAVAGEAU Loic   Thillet ST CHRISTOPHE DES BARDES
PENARD Suzanne   Rue de la Fontaine
PENCHAUD Guy   Bigaroux ST SULPICE DE FALEYRENS
PERRIER Joëlle   ST CHRISTOPHE DES BARDES
PEYRAT Michel   Lartigue
PICCOLO Santé   Gombaud ST PEY D'ARMENS
PICCOLO Bernard   SAINT HIPPOLYTE
PIERRE Jean   203 rue de Lossegrand
PINAUD Yvan   Brisson VIGNONET
POUILLET Eugène   SAINT MAGNE DE CASTILLON
PUISSANT Marcelle
QUENOUILLE Jean   Yon SAINT CHRISTOPHE DES BARDES
QUENOUILLE René   Yon SAINT CHRISTOPHE DES BARDES
QUINSAC Jean   Brisson VIGNONET
QUINTANA Micoulea VIGNONET
REDON Daniel   Cuzor VIGNONET
REDON Denis   Cuzor VIGNONET
REYNIER Raymond   La Nauve ST LAURENT DES COMBES
REYREAU Jean Michel   Les Maurins ST SULPICE DE FALEYRENS
RIPES René   Le Garrouilh ST SULPICE DE FALEYRENS
RIVIERE René   Port du Mas ABZAC
ROBLES Joseph   Petit Bouquey SAINT HIPPOLYTE
ROBERT Paulette   COURPIAC
ROBIN Alain   Billerond ST HIPPOLYTE
ROBIN Joëlle   Darthus VIGNONET
ROCHE Jean   Le Grand Sable SAINT HIPPOLYTE
ROCHEREAU Roger   Le Peilhan SAINT LAURENT DES COMBES
RODRIGUEZ René   Micouleau VIGNONET
ROLAIT Serge   COURPIAC
ROUSSELOT Daniel   Micouleau VIGNONET
ROUX Jean André   Darthus VIGNONET
ROUX Gilles   Darthus VIGNONET
ROY Jean   SAINTE TERRE
SABY Roger   Rue Pline Parmentier
SAHUNET Jean Claude   Grande Rue
SAUJON Yvonne   Le Bourg SAINT SULPICE DE FALEYRENS
SAUJON Jeanne   Le Bourg SAINT SULPICE DE FALEYRENS
SEGONZAC Michel   6 impasse François Mauriac
SERRE Jean   Caperot SAINT SULPICE DE FALEYRENS
SERRE Jean Jacques   Bord
SERRE Pierre   SAINT SULPICE DE FALEYRENS
SERVANT Elisée et Patrick   Pierrefitte ST SULPICE DE FALEYRENS
SIMON Guy   Le Gueyrot ST LAURENT DES COMBES
SINSUI André   Lavallade ST CHRISTOPHE DES BARDES
SOULAS Jean Pierre
SOULET Henri   Le Bourg SAINT SULPICE DE FALEYRENS
SOUPRE Pierre   La Glaye SAINT PEY D'ARMENS
SOUPRE Roger   SAINT PEY D'ARMENS
SULZER François   La Bonnelle SAINT PEY D'ARMENS
SUSZKA Conrad   Le Bourg SAINT SULPICE DE FALEYRENS
TABBACCHIERA François, Michel, Joseph   Bourret SAINT PEY D'ARMENS
TARIS LOIRY Michel   Les Alizes
THILLET Gabriel   SAINTE TERRE
TOULON Pierre   Jaugue Blanc
TOULOU Pierre   Gontey
VALADE Maurice   Le Bourg SAINT SULPICE DE FALEYRENS

VALADIER Michel   SAINT HIPPOLYTE
VALADIER Pierre et Michel et Madame   DUFAGET Fonrazade SAINT PEY D'ARMENS
VALLIER Geneviève et Monsieur VALLIER   Dominique Lavignère SAINT PEY D'ARMENS
VEJUX Lucien   SAINT PEY D'ARMENS
VERGNE Michel   1980o ROUFFIAT de SARRAN
VIALARD Claude et Madame VIALARD   Colette   25 rue Brochant
VIMENEY André   Le Bourg SAINT SULPICE DE FALEYRENS
VIROL Simone   Cazenave VIGNONET
XANS Roger   Le Jonc SAINT SULPICE DE FALEYRENS

Glossary

ASSEMBLAGE	Blending of vats of wine made from the various grape varieties.
BARRIQUE	Barrel holding 225 litres.
BOUCHET	Local name for Cabernet Franc grape.
CEPAGE	Grape variety.
CHAI	Building used for storing wine, usually above ground.
CHEF DE CULTURE	Vineyard-manager.
COURTIER	Broker.
CUVAISON	The contact of juice and skins during fermentation and after.
EGALISAGE	A further blending of the wine from different vats.
EGRAPPOIR	Machine to detach grape stalks.
EPOXY	Plastic lining of vats.
FINING	Clearing wine of suspended particles.
FOULOIR	Machine for crushing (not pressing) grapes.
GUYOT DOUBLE GUYOT MIXTE GUYOT SIMPLE	Methods of training the vine.
HECTARE	2.4 acres.
HECTOLITRES	22 gallons.
LACUSTRINE	A geological term meaning 'formed from lakes'.
LIMON	A kind of loam – a deposit consisting of wind-blown material subsequently re-sorted by water.
MAITRE DE CHAI	Cellar-master.
MOLASSE	Mixture of soft limestones, marls and clays.
MUST	Unfermented or fermenting grape juice.
NEGOCIANT	Wine merchant or shipper.
OIDIUM	Powdery mildew.
PHYLLOXERA	Louse whose larval form attacks the roots of vines.
PRESSAC	Local name for Merlot grape.
RACKING	Transferring the wine to a fresh vat or barrel.
REGISSEUR	Cellar-manager.
REMONTAGE	Pumping the wine round in a vat during fermentation.
TONNEAU	900 litres.

Bibliography

ALLEN, H. Warner, *The Wines of France,* 1954

AMERINE, M. A., *The Technology of Wine Making*, AVI Publishing Co., 1972

DE CASSAGNAC, Paul, *French Wines*, Chatto and Windus, 1930

COCKS ET FERET, *Bordeaux and its Wines,*Various editions 1883–1969

DENMAN, J. L., *The Vine and its Fruits*, Longman, Green & Co., 1875

DUSSAUT, *Les Grands Vins de Bordeaux*, 1979

FRUMKIN, Lionel, *The Science and Technology of Wine*, H. C. Lea & Co., 1965

GOLD, Alec (Editor), *Wines and Spirits of the World*, Virtue Publishing Co., 1968

GOUABET, Jean, *Les Grands Vins de Bordeaux*, La Société de l'Annuaire de la Gironde, 1856

GOUNOUILHOU, *Bordeaux et la Gironde*, 1895

HEALY, Maurice, *Claret and the White Wines of Bordeaux*, Michael Joseph

JOHNSON, Hugh, *The World Atlas of Wine*, Mitchell Beazley, 1971

JOHNSON, Hugh, *Wine*, Nelson, 1966, and Sphere Books

LARMAT, Louis, *Atlas de la France Vinicole*, Larmat, 1949

LICHINE, Alexis, *Encyclopedia of Wines and Spirits*, Cassell, 1967

MASSEL, Anton, *Basic Oenology*, Heidelberg Press, 1971

MASSEL, Anton, *Basic Viticulture*, Heidelberg Press, 1971

MORTON SHAND, P., *A Book of Wine*, Guy Chapman, 1926

DES OMBIAUX, Maurice, *Le Gotha des Vins de France*, Payot, 1925

PASTEUR, *Studies on Fermentation*, McMillan & Co., 1879

PATTON, Rev. W., *Laws on Fermentation*, National Temperance Society, 1871

PENNING-ROWSELL, Edmund, *The Wines of Bordeaux*, Penguin Books Ltd., 1969

PONSOT, M., *Complete Yearbook of French Quality Wines*, 1945

ROGER, J. R., *Les Vins de Bordeaux*, André Deutsch, 1955

ROUDIE, Phillippe, *Les Vignoble Bordelais*, Privately published, 1973

SICHEL, Allan, *A Book of French Wines*, 1965

SIMON, André, *In Vino Veritas*, Grant Richards, 1912

TENNENT, Emerson, *Wine*, James Madden, 1852

VILLEPIGUE, Robert and André, *'L'aire de production des Vins de Saint-Émilion'*, 1934

VIZETELLY, *Wines of the World*, Ward, Lock & Tyler, 1875

WARDER, *Vineyard Culture*, R. Clarke & Co., 1867

Wine and Spirit Trade Record, Clarets and Sauternes, 1920

WINKLER, A. J., *General Viticulture*, California Press, 1974

Index

Compiled by Valerie Lewis Chandler, BA, ALAA

General Index

Index to Individual Properties of Saint-Émilion and Pomerol

Italics indicate initials or words ignored in the alphabetical arrangement.

SAINT-ÉMILION

Premiers Grands Crus Classés

Grands Crus Classés

CHÂTEAU CONT'D
  Croque-Michotte 74
  Curé-Bon 74
  Dassault 74–5
  la Dominique 75
  Faurie-de-Souchard 75–6
  Fonplégade 76
  Fonroque 77
  Franc-Mayne 77
  Grand-Barrail-Lamarzelle-Figeac 78
  Grand-Corbin 78
  Grand-Corbin-Despagne 78–9
  Grand Mayne 79
  Grand-Pontet 79
  Grandes Murailles 79
  Guadet-St Julien 80
  Haut Corbin 80
  Haut-Sarpe 80–1
  Jean Faure 81–2
  Laniote 82
  Larcis-Ducasse 82
  Larmande 82–3
  Laroze 83
  Matras 83–4
  Mauvezin 84–5

  Moulin du Cadet 85
  Pavie-Decesse 85–6
  Pavie-Macquin 86
  Pavillion-Cadet 86
  Petit-Faurie-de-Soutard 86–7
  le Prieuré 87
  Ripeau 87
  St Georges-Côte-Pavie 88
  Sansonnet 88–9
  la Serre 89
  Soutard 89–90
  Tertre Daugay 90
  la Tour-du-Pin Figeac (Giraud) 91
  la Tour-du-Pin Figeac (Moueix) 91
  la Tour-Figeac 90
  Trimoulet 91–2
  les Trois Moulins 92
  Troplong-Mondot 92
  Villemaurine 92–3
  Yon-Figeac 93
Clos *la* Madeleine 83
Clos *de l'*Oratoire 85
Clos St Martin 88
Couvent des Jacobins 73

All Other Properties

André Bouye 95
André Chatonnet 96
André Sarrazin 108
Bernard Oizeau 105
Castel-Sartron 96
Cave Co-opérative de Gardegan 96
Cave Co-opérative de Montagne 96
Château
  *l'*Ancien Moulin 94
  *l'*Annoucialiou 94
  Arnault de Jacquemeau 94
  *d'*Arthus 97
  Austerlitz 94
  Badette 94
  Barberousse 94
  Barreau 94
  la Bassonnière 94
  Beau Mayne 94
  Beaurang 94
  Beauregard Figeac 94
  Bellevue-Figeac 94
  Berliquet 94–5
  Bézineau 95
  Bois Redon 95
  la Boucharde 95

la Bouygue 95
Cadet-Pontet 95
Calendream 95
Canon Pourret 95
Cantenac 95
de la Capelle 95
Cardinal-Villemaurine 95
Cardoneyre 95
Carteau Bas Daugay 95
Carteau Côte Daugay 96
Carteau Matras 96
Carteau Pindefleurs 96
Cassevert 96
la Cateau 130–1
Chante-Alouette (Barbary) 96
Chante-Alouette (Berjal) 96
Cheval Brun 96
Cheval-Noir 96
du Clocher (Michel Merias) 96
du Clocher (Robert Merias) 96
Clos Carré 95
Clos Fortin 99
Clos Haut Plante 96
Clos Jean Voisin 102
Clos Saint-Émilion Magnan 96

Communes

Please note that the following abbreviations for the communes appear after each property as cross-references:

St C-d-B = St Christophe-des-Bardes; St S-d-F = St Sulpice-de-Faleyrens; St H = St Hippolyte; St L-d-C = St Laurent-des-Combes; St Pey-d'A = St Pey-d'Armens; V = Vignonet; St E-d-L = St Étienne-de-Lisse

Satellites

Please note that the following abbreviations for the satellites appear after each property as cross-references;

L-StE = Lussac-St Émilion; P-StE = Puissequin-St Émilion; M-StE = Montagne-St Émilion; StG-StE = St Georges-St Émilion; P-StE = Parsac-St Émilion

POMEROL

LALANDE-DE-POMEROL

Albert Blanchet 190
Albert Dubos 193
André Roger Niarfeix 196
André Tridat 198
Andrée Sabourin 197
Annie Largeteau 195
Antoine Fabris 193
Arnaud Byais 191
Aubert Frères 190
Bernard Londin 195
J-C Berrouet 190
J *Émile* Blanc 190
E J Brochet 191
Charles Pommier 197
Château
   Alainjo 190
   *l'*Alouette 190
   des Annereaux 190
   des Arnauds 190
   les Baraillots 190
   Bechereau 190
   de Bel-Air 190
   Belle Graves 190
   la Belle Rose 190
   de Bertineau 190
   Bois de Laborde 190
   le Bon Pasteur 190
   la Borderie Mondésir 191
   Bouquet de Violette 191
   du Bourg 191
   Bourseau 191
   Brouard 191
   Canon-Chaigneau 191
   Cardinal Viaud 191
   du Castel 191
   Castel Viaud 192
   du Centre
   des Cerfs 192
   Chaigneau 192
   Changrolle 192
   Chatain 192
   Chatain-Pinaud 192
   les Chaumes 192
   Chevrol-Belair 192
   de la Commanderie 192
   la Croix 192
   la Croix Bellevue 192
   la Croix Blanche 192
   la Croix Chaigneau 192
   Croix Chenevelle 192
   Croix de Bourseau 192
   Croix des Moines 192

la Croix des Moines 192
la Croix-Perron 192
la Croix Saint André 192–3
la Croix St Jean 193
la Croix St Louis 193
Croix de Viaud 193
les Cruzelles 193
Dallau 193
*l'*Étoile de Salles 193
*de l'*Évéché 193
la Fleur 193
la Fleur Châtain 193
la Fleur Galvesse 193
la Fleur Lambarret 193
la Fleur St Georges 193
la Fleur Vauzelle 193
la Forêt 193
Fougailles 193
Franc Vauzelle 193
Gachet 193
des Galvesses-Grand-Maine 193
des Garaudières 193
Garraud 194
les Gazelles 194
du Grand Bossuet 194
le Grand Cardinal 194
Grand Cormier 194
du Grand Moine 194
Grand Ormeau 194
le Grande Taillis 194
des Grands Moines 194
Grandes Nauves 194
Graves de Brouard 194
Graves des Annereaux 194
les Graves de Goujon 194
les Graved de Lavergne 194
Graves Lavergne 194
la Gravière 194
Gromel Bel Áir 194–5
Guimberteau 195
Haut-Caillou 195
Haut Chaigneau 195
Haut-Châtain 195
Haut Gallvesses 195
Haut Goujon 195
Haut Graves Marchesseau 195
Haut-Laborde 195
Haut-Surget 195
les Hautes Conseillants 195
les Hautes Tuileries 195
du Jard 195
Laborde 195

Michel Monteil 195
Morbert Egreteau 193
Paul Gauthier 194
Pierre Aurier 190
Pierre Delteil 193
Pierre Dubois 193
Pierre Gricolat 194
Pierre J Quet 197
Pierre Melin 196
Pierre Peyronneau 197
Pierre Thibeaud 198
Pierrett Forton 193
Regis Bosc 191
Reine Casenoube 191
Remy Dussort 193
Robert Château 192

Robert Leney 195
Roland Bel 190
V Sartran 197
J G Sautreau 197
J P Tarendean 197
A Vedelago 198
B Vergnol 198
Viaud Grand Chambellan 198
Vieux Château Châtain 198
Vieux Château Gachet 199
Vieux Domaine de Bertineau 199
Yves Giraud 194
Yves Lamarche 195
Yvette Barraud 190
Yvon Dubos 193